MIAMI BABYLON

CRIME, WEALTH, AND POWER—
A DISPATCH FROM THE BEACH

Gerald Posner

Simon & Schuster

NEW YORK · LONDON · TORONTO · SYDNEY

Simon & Schuster
1230 Avenue of the Americas
New York, NY 10020

First Simon & Schuster hardcover edition October 2009

SIMON & SCHUSTER and colophon are registered trademarks
of Simon & Schuster, Inc.

Photography credits are on page 455.

For information about special discounts for bulk purchases, please contact
Simon & Schuster Special Sales at 1-866-506-1949 or
business@simonandschuster.com

The Simon & Schuster Speakers Bureau can bring authors to your live event.
For more information or to book an event contact the Simon & Schuster
Speakers Bureau at 1-866-248-3049 or visit our website at www.simonspeakers.com.

Designed by Paul Dippolito

Manufactured in the United States of America

1   3   5   7   9   10   8   6   4   2

Library of Congress Cataloging-in-Publication Data
Posner, Gerald L.
Miami Babylon : crime, wealth, and power—a dispatch from
the beach / Gerald Posner.—
    p.   cm.
Includes bibliographical references and index.
1. Miami (Fla.)—History.   2. Miami (Fla.)—Social life
and customs.   I. Title.
F319.M6P685   2009
975.9'38106—dc22   2009020474

ISBN 978-1-4165-7656-3
ISBN 978-1-4391-0985-4 (ebook)

For Trisha, my eternal muse

Contents

CHAPTER 1

"Gasoline on a Fire"

APRIL 1, 1980, in Havana was oppressively hot and humid; Miamians would have called it a "steamer." That afternoon a speeding bus manned by five Cuban hijackers smashed through the gate of the Peruvian Embassy. The guards sprayed the bus with machine-gun fire; one guard was killed in the crossfire. Once inside, the Cubans received political asylum. Fidel Castro demanded that the men be turned over to federal authorities so they could be charged in the guard's death. Peru refused.

If the Peruvians were willing to accept five Cubans, Castro decided he would test their resolve with many more. Word spread via *chismoso*, the Havana "bush telegraph," that the guards at the embassy had abandoned their posts, and by Easter Sunday, April 4, some 10,000 Cubans jammed into the embassy's grounds. Then the Cuban soldiers returned and blocked all access.

Conditions quickly deteriorated. There was little food, water, and few adequate bathrooms. But Castro rebuffed the Red Cross's requests to provide assistance.

"Our hearts go out to the nearly 10,000 freedom-loving Cubans who entered a temporarily opened gate at the Peruvian Embassy just within the week," said President Jimmy Carter. He called on Castro to let the people leave the island. Two weeks later, he issued a Presidential Memorandum granting asylum to 3,500 Cuban refugees. Political prisoners had priority; second were relatives of Cubans already in the United States; and third, refugees seeking political asylum. Castro saw this offer as an opportunity to purge his country of many undesirables including political dissidents, hard-core criminals, and the mentally ill.

1

"They want them," he is reported to have told his brother, Raúl, "then they can have them. I will flush my toilets."

Castro announced to Florida's Cuban Americans that they could claim their friends and relatives for transport to the United States at Mariel Harbor in western Cuba; no announcement was made to the Cuban public. In Miami and Key West, exiles hired everything from fishing trawlers to dinghies to old wooden skiffs. Hundreds of make-shift "freedom boats" sailed to Mariel, and on April 21, far more than 3,500 refugees started arriving on Florida's shores. Some boats capsized. "We'll never know exactly how many people we lost during the entire boatlift," says former Coast Guard captain Jim Decker. There were steady reports of bodies and parts of boats floating all over the Florida straits.

As the days wore on, the so-called freedom flotilla burgeoned. By April 29, another 1,700 vessels crammed into Mariel Harbor awaiting the processing of thousands of refugees.

"This was a very erroneous policy of the Carter administration, to consider everyone who wanted to leave Cuba for the United States as a heroic dissident," said Cuban vice president Carlos Rafael Rodriguez. "The United States is now paying the consequences."

By May, Immigration and Naturalization Service (INS) officials pleaded in vain for more workers to process the new arrivals. When a tugboat arrived in Key West on May 7, packed with six hundred refugees, there was life-saving equipment for only a third of the passengers. No U.S. official complained about the numbers arriving or expressed concern about the capability of local communities to absorb them.

In mid-May, Carter announced that no further arrivals from Mariel would be accepted, but Castro ignored him. At gunpoint, Cuban officials ordered one vessel's crew to take on 354 refugees with only 80 life-jackets aboard. Carter called up 600 Coast Guard reservists, but instead of intercepting boats and turning them back, they spent their time saving people at sea and towing dangerously overcrowded boats to safe Florida ports. When Castro finally closed Mariel on September 26, more than 125,000 Cubans had flooded into South Florida.

Two sprawling tent cities served as the first stop for the refugees, one in the parking lot of Miami's Orange Bowl stadium, and the other under the shadow of an elevated stretch of Interstate 95. To avoid generous resettlement financing, the INS denied the Marielitos "refugee status" and instead created a special category for them. INS officials photographed and fingerprinted every arriving Cuban and issued them flimsy IDs with no picture. Counterfeit Mariel IDs were soon on sale in Little Havana, and as the refugees were processed and released, almost 20,000 chose Miami Beach as their new home. The word was out: the cheapest housing in all of Florida was the dilapidated waterfront property south of Sixth Street, a neighborhood that Miami Beach's government had set aside to be razed and redeveloped. The federal government rented blocks of dirt-cheap, run-down apartments for the newcomers. Almost none of them spoke English. In a town of 85,000 residents, two-thirds Jewish and less than 10 percent Hispanic, the Marielitos changed the demographics overnight.

Joining them were thousands of Haitians. Correctly gambling that with the U.S. Coast Guard overstretched they could avoid being intercepted at sea, an estimated 35,000 made the grueling 600-mile journey to Miami, packed aboard hundreds of barely seaworthy vessels in what locals dubbed "the poor man's Mariel." Scores of Haitians drowned off South Florida's shores, often in view of tourists. U.S. Customs established a special unit to retrieve bodies that washed ashore. But the risks were worth it to escape a country with one of the world's lowest per capita incomes ($260) and an oppressive dictator, Jean-Claude "Baby Doc" Duvalier. A popular exile saying was, "The teeth of the sharks are sweeter than Duvalier's hell." In Miami's Little Haiti, there was a sharp increase in fires attributed to all-night Voodoo services, complete with candles and burnt sacrifices meant to help the newcomers arrive safely.

Florida's Governor Bob Graham pleaded in vain with the federal government to resettle or deport the Haitians. Over 1,000 were crammed into Dade County's Krome Avenue North Detention Center, designed for no more than 530 people.

The flood of illegal immigrants pushed up the county's unemployment from 5.7 percent to 13 percent, taxed social services to the breaking point, and exacerbated racial tensions. Whites resented an influx of poor immigrants they suspected would soon be on welfare. A local newspaper report about how some of the Marielitos had quickly mastered food stamp fraud fed those worries. Blacks, stuck on the bottom of South Florida's economic ladder, feared losing low-paying, non-skilled jobs to the newcomers. And even Cubans who had arrived twenty years earlier in the great exodus after Castro's revolution were concerned that the Marielitos could tarnish the reputation they had so carefully cultivated.

That same May, in 1980, adding to the tension, Miami suffered its worst race riots after an all-white jury acquitted several white police officers in the beating death of a black Marine Corps veteran. Black neighborhoods like Overtown and Liberty City erupted. A curfew was imposed, but after three days, 18 were dead, more than 400 injured, and over 1,000 arrested. The city suffered $100 million in damage.

EARLY INS PROCESSING revealed that while most of the Marielitos were decent immigrants who had been politically bothersome to Castro, a sizable number were either career criminals or mentally ill. Some arrived still wearing hospital wristbands. About 24,000 had criminal records; 5,000 were "hardened criminals" and more than 100 had murder convictions. A Miami Detention Center was set ablaze when authorities tried to deport some career criminals back to Cuba. *The New York Times* estimated that "only 30 percent of the refugees on each boat are relatives. The remaining 70 percent included not only criminals [but] prostitutes, delinquents, and mildly retarded people that the Cuban government has sought to get rid of."

During the first year of resettlement, fifty-three Cuban refugees were arrested for murder; many more were jailed for rapes and robberies. Within twelve months, a quarter of Miami-Dade's jails were filled with Marielitos. As some resettled in other parts of the country, trouble followed. In Las Vegas, where 3,000 Marielitos had moved, they would account for about 25 percent of the narcotics trade four years later, and 23 out of 100 homicides. In Los Angeles, several hundred criminal Marielitos boosted the city's crime numbers, especially in robberies and drug busts.

"That first year was like a war zone," says Charlie Seraydar, then a

Miami Beach homicide detective. The Beach had been slowly declining for more than a decade and crime had been rising. Cheap air travel and package tours to Europe, Hawaii, and new lush Mexican and Caribbean resorts had siphoned off hordes of tourists. With legal gambling and newer hotels, Las Vegas had supplanted the Beach for travelers who wanted topflight entertainment. There was little political leadership and the city's tourism promoters were stumped as to how to revive the town's fortunes.

"We went from being a seasonal tourist town to suddenly dealing with seasoned criminals who had nothing to lose," says Seraydar. "No matter how badly we treated them, no matter how low they lived, it was better than the jails they called home in Cuba. That first year, our crime rate went up 600 percent. Our entire police force was smaller than a single New York City precinct. It felt like we had been invaded and were losing the battle."

Alex Daoud was only five months into his first year as a Miami Beach commissioner when the boatlift began. He watched as the Beach buckled under the influx of the Marielitos.

"Mariel was like pouring gasoline on a fire," he says. "Murder, rape, burglary, kidnapping, assault and battery, muggings, home invasions, we were reeling out of control. Our police force was overwhelmed. The city's services were besieged. Narcotics were being dealt openly in the park, on street corners and in the backs of stores. We ranked among the top ten cities in the nation for murder and violent crime. And South Beach's elderly residents were easy victims. The city where I was born was not the one I knew and loved. Miami Beach was a mess."

ALEX DAOUD WAS born to Lebanese Catholic parents in Miami Beach on May 19, 1943. His mother, the youngest person to pass the New York bar exam in the early 1920s, and his father, an antiques dealer, moved from New York to Miami Beach during World War II. His father's eclectic furniture and bric-à-brac collection on Lincoln Road included diverse customers such as mobsters Al Capone and Bugsy Siegel and Hollywood stars Clark Gable and Joan Crawford.

When Daoud was six, he developed polio. At first the prognosis was grim—a priest administered last rites. He was confined to a wheelchair for six months and then a spent year on crutches and in a heavy leg brace. His classmates were brutal. "It was horrible," he recalls. "I lost count of how many times I was tossed out of my wheelchair or knocked off my crutches. Kids used to dance around me when I was on the floor."

After graduating from the University of Illinois law school in 1979, Daoud returned to the Beach. He developed a passion for boxing and hung out at the Fifth Street Gym, where he met Sugar Ray Robinson, Muhammad Ali, and Ali's trainer Angelo Dundee.

A year after earning his law degree, he ran for one of seven city commission seats. South Beach had become one of America's poorest neighborhoods. Daoud became a relentless cheerleader for what he promised would be a renaissance. His political career was launched without focus groups, fund-raising dinners, or glad-handing with lobbyists, things he could barely tolerate. Instead, he walked the city, knocking on doors: the Scher Pawnshop, Goldenstein Clothiers ("A Stitch to Make a Gentleman"), the Modern Drug Store boasting that its standing penny scale was the state's largest, Sonny's Pizza Parlor ("A Taste of New York"), Wolfie's Deli with its flashing 24/7 sign, and the Deuce, a dive bar with a few dozen stools and neon lights tracing the ceiling's edge. Daoud heard how seniors barely survived from one government check to the next and enthusiastically addressed everything from grinding poverty to rampant crime. He visited synagogues, hung out at kosher butchers, danced with elderly widows at Club Seven for senior citizens, and was a regular at feisty Hadassah and B'nai Brith gatherings.

Before long, crowds flocked to pool halls, diners, and the Tenth Street Auditorium to hear him. He gave out free ice cream to children, served hot meals to Jewish seniors, and bought Cuban coffee for local workers. He could not walk down the street without people yelling, "Hey, Alex. How ya doing? Keep it up, Alex!"

"For me, campaigning wasn't work. Many of the elderly residents were politically and culturally active. It was a vibrant community. There were a lot of great thinkers, musicians would play in Flamingo Park, and there were animated debates at the beach between radical Socialists and anti-Zionists. They had a great dignity and character. And their stories were interesting and intriguing, and as I got to know them, they were almost like my extended family."

He ran as—and many people felt he was—one of them, an average guy looking out for their best interests. And his naïveté, mixed with a healthy dose of idealism, made politics seem virtuous. Daoud understood that there were two Miami Beaches. In one, a flood of new cocaine money fueled parties at iconic Beach restaurants like Joe's Stone Crab and the Forge and a building boom in waterfront mansions. In the other were mid-Beach condo towers for middle-class snowbirds and the decaying, poverty-stricken retirement village that was South Beach.

Daoud ran against Joe Malek, a popular commissioner and a successful attorney. Malek was an Orthodox Jewish cantor, and his Israeli wife, Rochelle, was active in social and civic organizations. That was an advantage in a town that was two-thirds Jewish. Gerald Schwartz, a political strategist, warned Daoud: "Your Arab ancestry could cause you a lot of problems if you go against Malek. The campaign will be brutal."

"Schwartz was right," Daoud recalls. "It was a nasty fight. They called me 'Dow-ood' and reminded people I was Catholic, hoping to turn Jewish voters against me. They circulated rumors that my family was anti-Israeli. No lie was too big. It did not take me very long to realize that in Miami Beach, local politics is a blood sport. It's a sewer in which you do anything to win."

But Malek underestimated how much a populist campaign could spark enthusiasm and overcome aspersions and innuendo. In November 1980, Daoud won 75 percent of the vote, the biggest landslide in Miami Beach politics in twenty years.

THE FOLLOWING SEPTEMBER, the last wave of Marielitos arrived in South Florida. Daoud met with the police chief, who described how young male prostitutes now controlled Lummus Park, where elderly Jewish men had once read aloud from the Talmud. Some kosher restaurants had been forcibly taken over for late night cockfights. Robberies of the elderly had increased. "He told me there were two towns," Daoud says. "South Beach, during the day, was a quiet neighborhood filled with retirees. At night, it became a place gripped by fear, where residents would not venture outdoors."

Daoud wanted to see for himself and asked the police chief if he could go on an overnight patrol with a squad car.

On September 26, Daoud went for a ride-along with Detective Seraydar. Their shift kicked off with a high-speed car chase. They went after two heavily armed suspects in a stolen Cadillac who were killed when they smashed into a streetlight. Next were five domestic dispute calls. Then someone threw a cinder block off a building roof and just missed the patrol car's windshield. On another call, an elderly Cuban woman had been beaten by a Marielito nicknamed *El Loco* ("the Crazy One"), a homeless deaf-mute who had been terrorizing the neighborhood.

"Halfway through the shift, I was completely exhausted," recalls Daoud. "I had seen a night population I didn't know existed. There were groups of rough, tattooed young men, shirtless, hanging around run-down bars and small sandwich stands. They were looking for victims."

At dawn, Seraydar took a call about a "bleeding body in the alley" next to the Betsy Ross Apartments at 1440 Ocean Drive.

"Murder?" Daoud asked.

"Could be, but more likely a jumper."

"A jumper?"

"Yeah, it happens all the time, a couple of times a week, especially with the elderly. They get sick and are in pain, their kids don't want them, and they don't see any hope. They have little money. So they kill themselves."

The squad car pulled into one of South Beach's narrow alleys. The streetlights were broken and the surrounding buildings mostly boarded up.

"When we drove into the alley," says Daoud, "I could see a crumpled body on the ground, dressed in a T-shirt and pajamas, and drenched in blood."

At an open third-floor window directly above the body, an elderly woman was staring out blankly. Her eighty-five-year-old husband had jumped to his death.

Daoud couldn't take his eyes off the corpse. "There's got to be a lot of pain to make you do that," he murmured, almost as much to himself as to Seraydar.

"Yeah, Alex. Suicide is one of the worst sins of South Beach."

It was 7 a.m. by the time they left the scene. Daoud recalled the words of the medic as they drove away: "I should've been a cop. They've got a better job. All they have to do is write a few reports. No blood, no shit, and no smell."

At 17th Street, near the Theater of the Performing Arts, Seraydar slammed on the brakes to avoid hitting somebody lying in the gutter. Groceries were scattered around. He and Daoud sprinted over.

Daoud knew the person. It was his friend Elsie Cohen.

"At first, I almost didn't recognize her. She had been beaten. Her face was covered in blood. There were welts near her eyes and around her nose. She was moaning, 'Help me. Please help me.'"

Her clothes were tattered. "It didn't take me very long to realize she had been raped," recalls Seraydar.

Daoud had met Elsie in 1978 while he was studying for the bar exam and volunteering at the Tenants' Association, a non-profit outfit that helped residents with housing problems. The petite Cohen had come to the association because her landlord of ten years was threatening to double her rent. As she had reached into her purse to retrieve her lease, Daoud noticed the number tattooed on her right forearm. When he stared a moment too long, she quickly withdrew her arm under a knitted shawl. Daoud promised that he would not let her become homeless. She was so ecstatic that she returned later with homemade babka. It was the start of a friendship with the elderly concentration camp survivor. When Elsie was eventually evicted, Daoud arranged for her to move into one of several apartments his family owned. It was next door to his mother, and the two became good friends. Daoud regularly checked on Elsie and she would drop off baked goods at the Tenants' Association and keep an eye out for prospective girlfriends for him.

Finding her barely conscious, Daoud remembers, "I didn't know what to do. I kept staring at her tattoo. I kept thinking that she had survived the Nazis only to end up beaten and raped and then tossed aside like a piece of garbage in South Beach."

Seraydar remembers that Alex was "just standing there frozen, staring at her. I screamed at him, 'Go get the blanket from the trunk of the car and bring it to me.'

" 'Oh my God, I know this woman, Charlie. Her name is Elsie Cohen.'

" 'She's in shock, Alex. We've got to get her help right now. I need you, and so does she. Don't go south on me now. Get moving.' "

An ambulance arrived. While the paramedics worked on Elsie, Charlie questioned some people who had slowly come out of their apartments.

"They were elderly and they surrounded Charlie and me like a flock of frightened sheep," says Daoud. "All of them were speaking at once."

Three men had attacked Elsie and run west. When another squad car arrived, Charlie and Daoud sped off to look for the suspects.

They spotted three men walking briskly near the Sun Trust building at the corner of deserted Lincoln Road. They were all tall, over 200 pounds, and muscular. Charlie flipped on the car's flashing red lights and stopped in the middle of the street. The men kept walking.

Charlie called for backup and then stepped out of the car. "Stay put, Alex. Let me handle this."

He yelled at them to stop. They ignored him. He yelled again. The tallest one turned around and said with a heavy accent, "No English."

"While he was talking to Charlie," Daoud recalls, "I suddenly spotted Elsie's antique platinum watch that I knew so well, sticking out of the pocket of his pants. The light from the streetlamp reflected off it and it just jumped out."

Before he could do anything, the tallest man sucker-punched Charlie. The other two joined in and tried to wrestle away his revolver. Daoud jumped out of the car and ran straight into the fracas.

"I grabbed the tallest one by the shoulder," says Daoud, "and turned him around and threw my right fist into his nose. I was running on pure adrenaline. Everything I learned in my boxing days at the Fifth Street Gym came rushing back."

Daoud pummeled the ringleader unconscious, knocking out several teeth. Charlie wrestled the second man to the ground while Daoud tackled the third 20 feet from the squad car.

"I drove him into the sidewalk," recalls Daoud. "The more he struggled, the harder I pressed against his neck. I was completely consumed with vengeance."

"I screamed at him, 'Alex, let go! You're killing him,'" recalls Seraydar. Two backup cars had arrived and it took three cops to pull Daoud off the unconscious suspect. Then, without a word, one of the policemen kicked the guy in the face.

"His head bounced back like a smashed watermelon," recalls Daoud. "There was blood everywhere. No one else moved, and then, all of a sudden, without saying a word to each other, we all began to beat them. It was a desperate act, by desperate and angry men. The justice system in South Beach had failed. The criminals were winning. At that moment, I hated these men. I hated Castro for releasing these sadistic animals in our town. I wanted only raw revenge."

Daoud and the police threw the almost comatose bodies into the back of the squad cars and took the suspects to the trauma unit at mainland Miami's Jackson Memorial. All three Marielitos survived. (Later, they pled guilty to rape and got ten-year sentences.) Then Daoud and Seraydar drove to Miami Beach's Mount Sinai, where Elsie was in surgery.

They sat silently in a private waiting area reserved for police behind the emergency room. Twice, a passing nurse asked Daoud if he needed help. His shirt was torn and spotted with blood. His right hand was swollen and his knuckles were bleeding. His pants were soaked with blood. He waved her away.

At 8 a.m., the surgeon emerged and told them Elsie was in critical condition. She had suffered permanent brain damage.

"The events of that night," says Daoud, "did not scare me. They empowered me."

ON NOVEMBER 24, 1980, a *Time* magazine article titled "Absolute War in Our Streets" reported what Alex Daoud knew firsthand: that handgun sales had doubled in Miami-Dade during the previous year; a $25, three-hour course at a local rifle range on how to protect yourself had a two-month waiting list. The bestselling novelist and *Miami*

Herald crime reporter Edna Buchanan told *Time*, "If everyone in Dade County took this course, it would certainly be a safer place to live." The most popular Miami bumper sticker was HELP FIGHT CRIME: BUY GUNS; to attract new depositors, Lincoln Savings & Loan offered pocket cans of mace instead of free toasters or radios. *Time* reported that in the first eleven months of 1980, thirty-two suspected criminals were shot to death by gun-toting citizens. "No woman or man should venture alone in this city," said Robin Gibb, one of the three brothers known as the Bee Gees, who lived in a wealthy Miami Beach enclave.

The *Time* story included a quote from Daoud: "An absolute war is being fought in our streets at night."

"People in Miami Beach hated that I said that to national reporters," he recalls. "Everyone knew the problem was out of control, but they wanted it as our own dirty little secret. All the businesses were afraid that if the word got out that we were the Wild West, the city would die. Well, it was dying anyway. Our only real industries were smuggling and tourism. And I wasn't going to sugarcoat it for anyone, no matter how many enemies I made."

A story in London's *Daily Express* typified the press coverage: "Florida's holiday paradise has become the holiday murder capital of the world." The Beach considered emergency measures to stem the crisis, including an 11 p.m. curfew. The commission rejected that after intense debate but adopted a temporary ordinance that allowed police to stop and frisk anyone suspected of intending to commit a crime. They approved an interim ban on congregating "in a manner that blocks sidewalks or threatens the safety of property or persons," and they closed the city's beaches and parks between 10 p.m. and sunrise.

A year later, on November 23, 1981, *Time* followed up with a devastating nine-page cover investigation entitled "Trouble in Paradise." *Time* concluded that South Florida was "in trouble" because of an "epidemic of violent crime, a plague of illicit drugs and a tidal wave of refugees" that had hit the region with "the destructive power of a hurricane." Its problems, said *Time*, threatened to turn one of the nation's most prosperous, congenial, and naturally gorgeous regions into a paradise lost.

That year, Mother Teresa came from Calcutta to help feed the Miami homeless. She established a hostel for the bagwomen who slept in parks and under freeway overpasses, her only missionary outlet in America.

Even Governor Bob Graham admitted, "If you want sustained stability, don't come to Miami."

"It was hard then to imagine," says Daoud, "that Miami Beach would stop its slide and overcome its problems. It took years, but it did."

CHAPTER 2

"No Sane Man . . ."

UNTIL THE TWENTIETH century, it was unthinkable that anyone would consider either Miami or Miami Beach "America's Riviera." The Spanish conquistador Ponce de León dubbed the Florida peninsula *Pasqua de Florida,* "Feast of Flowers," but the territory's Spanish masters settled only the temperate northern half. It was a throwaway chip in the European powers' Monopoly game. Florida was traded to England in 1763 when the Spanish had the bad fortune to lose the Seven Years' War, and England swapped it back to Spain in 1783 in exchange for the Bahamas. America got Florida in 1819, after the First Seminole War, and it became the twenty-seventh state in 1845.

Through the nineteenth century, the southern half of the peninsula was written off as inhospitable swampland. Miami Beach—then called Ocean Beach—was an uninhabitable seven square miles of swamp and scrub. Mainland Miami, still called Fort Dallas after the U.S. barracks built for the Seminole Wars, consisted only of some native Indians, a few European gold prospectors, and the ever-present Catholic missionaries. The region was so desolate that the Florida Armed Occupation Act of 1842 offered 160 acres to anyone who moved to the state and bore arms to defend it for five years. Not many applied.

Greedy state politicians used the act's failure to declare that the land's best use lay with private developers. By the late 1880s, Florida had completed America's largest shift ever of public resources into the pockets of private entrepreneurs. A succession of governors gave away 23 million of Florida's 35 million acres, to newly incorporated railway companies, snake-oil salesmen, carpetbaggers, and virtually anyone who promised to drain and develop the state's swampy southern half. Sixty percent of Florida was owned by five railroad companies, a drainage firm, and one northern developer, Hamilton Disston, who had paid a few cents an acre to buy a tract of land larger than Connecticut.

Even hucksters who promised to build cities from the swamps would have considered ludicrous the idea that frontier Miami would one day boast some of the world's most expensive real estate. A *New York Herald* journalist who visited the state in 1864 described Miami as a place that "no sane man . . . no decent man would think of living in."

The 1870s marked the first influx of adventurous investors and developers, mostly midwestern. Among them was Julia Tuttle, a wealthy Cleveland widow turned prosperous citrus farmer, who saw Miami's potential as a getaway resort. Miami Beach caught its first break in 1870, when a former California gold rush pioneer, Henry Lum, sailing home from Havana, explored the wilderness along Biscayne Bay's eastern shores. Lum thought Miami Beach was ideal for a plantation of coconut, a fruit whose shredded meat had become a staple in European pastries. Lum, backed by several New Jersey farmers, bought 165 acres for $58.

Many of Lum's workers were quickly driven away by mosquitoes, scorpions, rattlesnakes, giant palmetto beetles, and occasional crocodiles. The heat was stifling. And the dense, deeply rooted red and black mangroves made farming difficult. But Lum was determined. He brought in 300,000 coconut plants from Cuba, Nicaragua, and Trinidad, and his son, Charles, built Miami Beach's first house right on the beach (site of the present Tides Hotel, at Ocean Drive and 12th Street). Their closest neighbors were six miles north. The long stretches of sand were broken only by a few fishermen's shacks and a so-called House of Refuge, stocked with provisions for shipwrecked sailors. For years Lum tried in vain to make a success of his coconut plantation, never accepting that the marsh rats and rabbits ate most of the young plants. Once, for a break from the relentless grind of their farm, he and his wife sailed across Biscayne Bay and stayed at a Miami rooming house. When they checked out, the bill was $80. Lum asked the owner if he would take 10 acres of land instead of cash.

"Land sakes," he replied, "what in the world would I do with all that swampland?"

Lum threw in the towel in 1894 and sold his land to a New Jersey Quaker farmer, John Collins, who bought it sight unseen. Collins had already invested $5,000 in sixty-five miles of South Florida oceanfront land, purchased at about a dollar an acre.

Eighteen ninety-four was also the year of the Great Freeze. The state's citrus production dropped from 5.5 million boxes to a measly 150,000, but Miami's citrus crop was not destroyed. This presented an opportunity for Julia Tuttle. She had already pleaded in vain with John D. Rockefeller's Standard Oil partner, Henry Flagler, to extend his Florida East Coast Railroad to Miami. The train went only as far as Palm Beach, a town Flagler had created. But Flagler was not interested, not even when Tuttle offered him half her 640 Miami acres. Miami was only a squatters' outpost and he saw no reason to bring his train there. Yet Flagler now realized that losing the citrus crop, even for a season, could hurt his promotion of Florida as a getaway destination. He agreed to build the 66-mile rail extension after Tuttle sent him a giant bouquet of fragrant orange blossoms and added the gift of some of her property.

Two years after the Great Freeze, mainland Miami dumped the Fort Dallas moniker and was finally incorporated. The town council considered naming the town "Flagler," but the tycoon was not interested, fearful that if it was named for him, he would have to spend part of his fortune building it. For Flagler, Miami was just another stop on his railway line—a glorified railroad terminal, he once told a friend. With a population of just over 300, it wasn't even the largest "Miami" in America. An Arizona silver-mining town with the same name had more people. More than 250 years after the Pilgrims had landed, and at a time when New York teemed with 3.5 million residents and Chicago boasted 1.7 million, Miami played no role in the nation's development.

If the potential in Miami was dismissed by northerners, neighboring Miami Beach, still deserted, wasn't even on people's radar. When John Collins inspected the land he had bought from Lum, he realized that most of it was still swampland, with rats more numerous than crops. But as a horticulturalist, he thought he could succeed where Lum had failed. He hired dozens of laborers to tame the marsh. Coconuts and mangoes again failed. The seventy-year-old Collins then bought an additional strip between 14th and 67th Streets. He planted a windbreak of imported Australian "whispering" pines and acres of bananas, mangoes, corn peppers, tomatoes, Irish new potatoes, avocados, and so-called alligator pears.

Over the next few years, a wave of epidemics struck the mainland. Troops returning from the Spanish-American War brought measles and typhoid fever, and in 1899, yellow fever broke out, spread by infected ticks from a Cuban cattle barge. There was no hospital in Miami, and only four doctors for 1,700 residents. Despite a strict quarantine, hundreds fell ill and fourteen died.

The good news for Miami Beach was that the diseases never crossed the bay. The biggest problem was Collins's crop management. But before it was clear that his venture would be successful (it became the world's largest mango and avocado plantation), Collins's son Arthur and son-in-law Thomas Pancoast arrived from New Jersey, concerned that Collins was throwing away the conservative Quaker family's money in a quixotic quest. However, they immediately saw the area's potential. They urged Collins to buy more land, not for crops but to sell as waterfront lots, contending Miami Beach could be transformed into an affordable resort for middle-class northern families looking for a warm winter getaway. John Collins was a farmer at heart, but eventually his family wore him down and he agreed. "Yes," he told his son. "It might make another Atlantic City at that."

Collins formed the Miami Beach Improvement Company on June 3, 1912. Two days later, John Newton Lummus and James Edward Lummus, brothers who ran two local banks, opened Ocean Beach Realty Company. By the fall, the two competing companies had subdivided 580 acres at the southern tip of Miami Beach and offered lots for sale.

There were no takers. Miami had only 5,500 residents, half of them black descendants of freed slaves who had passed through after the Civil War, but even so it was South Florida's only city. Collins and others who wanted to develop Miami Beach realized they could not do so successfully without a link to the mainland. Construction began on a bridge connecting the Beach's 15th Street to Miami's Dade Boulevard.

Locals described the bridge as "Collins's Folly." Despite spending $100,000, and getting a $25,000 loan from the Lummus brothers, Collins ran short of cash halfway through the job. Salvation came from an Indianapolis auto parts magnate, Carl Fisher, who had his own vision for Miami Beach.

CHAPTER 3

Selling Swampland

C ARL FISHER WAS a thirty-eight-year-old Indianapolis entrepreneur born into poverty. As a child, he suffered from a severe undiagnosed astigmatism—his vision was only 50 percent— that made it impossible for him to read the blackboard. His teachers branded him a dunce. And since he frequently stumbled and fell, he was teased mercilessly by classmates as "crip." Carl left school at twelve to work as a railway newsboy after his alcoholic father abandoned the family. His sales zoomed when he offered candy and tobacco in addition to the papers and flashed a photo of a naked woman under his working apron.

He squirreled away $600 in savings while working in a bank and opened a bicycle repair shop. It was 1891, the height of the bicycle craze. Despite his bad eyesight, Carl raced high-wheeler bicycles and formed the Zig-Zag Cycling Club. While his brothers ran the shop, he toured neighboring states with Barney Oldfield and other cycling champions and won a string of races at small-town carnivals and state fairs. Then nineteen, Fisher was almost pudgy at five foot eight, prematurely bald, with a short neck and broad shoulders. He looked more butcher than daredevil. But when he returned to Indianapolis, he convinced one of the country's largest bicycle manufacturers to give him an exclusive dealership, and to stock it with $50,000 worth of their best bikes.

Fisher was a master of promotion, innately understanding that outlandish publicity turned into sales. He celebrated the opening of his expanded shop by riding a bicycle across a tightrope strung between the city's two tallest buildings; another time he spent half the day doing backwards sprints around town. Once, he threw a bicycle from the city's tallest building and offered a free racing bike to the lucky person who retrieved the crumpled frame. He released thousands of helium balloons; one hundred of them had cards attached that could be redeemed at his shop for a bicycle.

It is not surprising that Fisher, fascinated with speed and new technology, embraced the automobile. He bought the first registered car in Indianapolis, a three-wheeled French De Dion Bouton. He opened the city's only auto garage in the rear of his bicycle shop. And with his buddy Barney Oldfield, he toured the same state fairgrounds he had a year earlier, this time giving hair-raising dirt track exhibitions (he set the world record for a two-mile race at Chicago's Harlem track).

Fisher opened Indiana's first automobile showroom. To celebrate, he substituted a 4-cylinder Stoddard-Dayton for the gondola in a giant vermillion balloon and floated around the city. Other days he raced cars against horses on city streets, and once he had a seven-passenger Stoddard-Dayton pushed off a building. Metal and glass flew for blocks, but no one was hurt.

He was only thirty when, in 1904, he bought the patent to Prest-O-Lite, a compressed gas lantern technology that he adapted as the first durable headlight for the fledgling auto industry. It earned him his first fortune.

Fisher had some wild ideas about how to spend the money. He persuaded three partners to join him in building the world's greatest race track. The Indianapolis Motor Speedway opened in August 1909, with hot-air balloons, large bands, the fastest cars, and a crowd of 12,000. But as the three-day, 300-mile race got under way, the tar and gravel track began crumbling from the heat.

"The glorious day he had planned turned into a carnival of death," wrote his fiancée, Jane. "Cars skidded off the track and burst into flame. I watched Carl's face grow white from my box in the stands." By the time Fisher halted the race, five drivers were dead. Fisher spent $100,000 searching for a better surface and finally repaved the course with 3.5 million recessed bricks. On Memorial Day 1911, the "brickyard" was ready for a new Fisher extravaganza—a one-day, 500-mile event, with $25,100 in prizes. Eighty-seven thousand people paid a dollar each to watch the first Indianapolis 500. This time the track surface held.

The hard-drinking, profane Fisher, now thirty-five, shocked Indianapolis society that October by marrying the fifteen-year-old Jane Watts. Soon after, he and a partner sold Prest-O-Lite to Union Carbide and split the $9 million. He was racing cars, speedboats, and balloons, and though he loved his summers on Lake Michigan, the season was short. Searching for warm water in winter, the Fishers visited Miami twice, and in 1912 he bought a house on Miami's Brickell Avenue, sight unseen.

By this time, Fisher had launched yet another ambitious project, raising $10 million from his auto industry friends to build the Lincoln Highway, a hard-surfaced road spanning 3,400 miles from San Francisco to New York. With that under way, the Fishers boarded their 45-foot yacht and sailed south. Carl promised Jane he would stop working once he got to Florida.

Biscayne Bay was the perfect place for speedboat racing and Fisher loved the unobstructed views of the ocean and mainland from the virtually deserted stretch of beach. One day he stopped next to a half-finished wooden bridge across the bay. When he later asked people what it was, they told him it was "John Collins's Folly."

The next morning, Fisher visited Collins, and that afternoon he wrote a $50,000 check to Collins to finish his bridge. "Get it done now, not tomorrow," Fisher instructed. In return, Collins gave him 200 acres, an 1,800-foot-wide, mile-long strip of palmetto scrub running from the bay to the ocean. Within a few weeks, Fisher had bought 150 prime oceanfront acres from the Lummus brothers.

When Fisher visited his property with Jane, she recalled, "The mosquitoes were biting every exposed inch of me. What could Carl see in such a place?" She soon found out when he drew figures in the damp sand. "Look, honey, I'm going to build a city here. A city like magic, like romantic places you read and dream about but never see." Collins and the Lummuses wanted an oceanfront resort that was an adjunct to

Miami, consisting of modest single-family residences. But Fisher, a virulent anti-Semite and racist, dreamt of a wealthy WASP enclave that would be a successful city independent of Miami. He cleverly cloaked his anti-Semitism in the anti-immigration fervor that swept the country after the 1917 Bolshevik Revolution.

Whatever their visions for the Beach, Fisher, Collins, and the Lummuses agreed it was first and foremost a moneymaking opportunity. It was not a colonial trading post or a town where religiously persecuted immigrants sought safety; it was a man-made creation to be sold to the highest bidders.

By the time Collins finished his two-lane, two-and-a-half-mile wooden bridge—called "the longest wagon bridge in the world" by the *New York Herald*—Fisher had bought another 210 acres from the Lummuses. He brought in some of the steamrollers, dredging equipment, and sump pumps used on the Lincoln Highway. With a fleet of tractors equipped with enormous machete-like blades, his crews chopped away broad swaths of mangroves and erected large bulkheads along Biscayne Bay. Fisher's plan was to raise Miami Beach five feet above sea level to lessen the island's vulnerability to instant flooding from tropical downpours. So he began dredging 6 million cubic yards of mudstone and white sand along a two-mile stretch of the bay.

The state was so pleased to find an interested developer that they let Fisher have unrestricted, no-cost access to the submerged shoreline. Fisher tried to figure out how to minimize the sandfly infestation and pulled out palmetto roots with his bare hands. He had a sharp temper and little patience with inept workers.

Eighty-three-year-old Henry Flagler died the day after Fisher's first dredgers arrived in Miami Beach. Fisher's Prest-O-Lite millions were no match for Flagler's Standard Oil fortune, but Carl believed he was just as capable of building a resort empire. His detractors called him "Crazy Carl" and questioned spending a fortune to create new acreage when hundreds of miles of surrounding land could be had for a pittance. But he boasted his creation would be "America's greatest winter resort."

In expectation of a land rush, Fisher opened a real estate office, Alton Beach Realty—picking the name Alton, today one of Miami Beach's main thoroughfares, from a passing freight car marked "Chicago & Alton R.R." In June 1913, his dredging operation still unfinished, he sponsored the first in a series of sales extravaganzas. He hired a flamboyant pitchman—a future mayor of Coral Gables, Edward "Doc" Dammers—to hold a real estate auction. THE ENTRANCE TO FAIRY LAND, proclaimed the sign to those arriving over the Collins Bridge. Dammers offered elephant rides (Fisher owned two pet elephants, Rosie and Nero, that he used as part of his promotional bag of tricks), hot-air balloons, parachute drops, and gifts of china, silver, and Oriental rugs; the P. T. Barnum atmosphere helped sell $66,000 worth of lots ($1.5 million today) over three days. But they remained undeveloped. The Lummus brothers offered free parcels to anyone who promised to build homes on their land. They had six takers, but eventually reclaimed the property when the buyers never built anything.

By 1915, the original 1,600-acre sandbar of Miami Beach had almost tripled, with 2,760 new acres. Collins, Lummus, and Fisher incorporated the town. John Lummus rallied the town's thirty-three registered voters—all but three lived on his development—and became mayor. The Beach's first hotel, Browns, opened for business. (Today, it is a restored two-room hotel whose wildly popular steakhouse, Prime One Twelve, consistently ranks high in annual listings of America's biggest-grossing restaurants.)

Fisher developed an ambitious five-year plan to remake the island into a resort city, with hotels and attractions for tourists: he hired a Japanese gardening pioneer, Shige Tashiro (who had been brought to America to work on the Vanderbilt estates), at $115 per month, and directed him to create a floral paradise. Tashiro started with virtually a blank canvas. The dredging operation had wiped out the island's natural vegetation and wildlife. The ground was as flat and denuded as a midwestern prairie. Fisher had tons of quartz-rich Everglades soil floated in by barge and Tashiro planted grass from Bermuda (which Fisher thought was the greenest), Mexican flame vines, Hong Kong orchids, Rangoon creeper, Canary Island date palms, Surinam cherries, Arabian jasmine, Brazilian peppers, and Chinese holly. An exotic locale needed exotic animal life, so Fisher crated in Canadian geese, Australian pheasants, Indian green peacocks, Chilean parrots, and his personal favorites,

African and Bimini flamingos (his dredging had wiped out the indigenous varieties). Dozens of swans were imported for a tiny artificial lake
Fisher constructed in mid-Beach, but they slowly disappeared. No one
figured out until it was too late that laborers were taking the birds to
their mainland kitchens.

While Tashiro performed his magic with an unlimited budget,
Fisher concentrated on building the infrastructure required to turn the
Beach into a real city. He lobbied close friends at City Hall for public
money, but besides an occasional bond, the funding came from his own
fortune.

Fisher had his Prest-O-Lite millions, but the slow progress was a
heavy financial strain for Collins and the Lummus brothers. When the
Lummuses fell deep into debt, John Newton Lummus sold twenty
oceanfront acres to the city for only $40,000 (today, it is Lummus Park,
one of Miami Beach's few public parks), and the brothers sold all their
holdings west of Washington Avenue to a small consortium of Fisher's
Indianapolis friends. But even after unloading so much property, the
Lummus brothers still owned nearly half of South Beach, from 15th
Street to the island's southern tip.

By 1920, the end of Fisher's five-year plan, he had spent well over
$1 million. At its peak, the dredging operation alone ran to $52,000
daily. Nearly $100,000 went to buy a 200-acre private island adjacent to
the Beach. Now Fisher Island, it was owned by a prominent South Florida black businessman, Dana A. Dorsey. Fisher feared that Dorsey
would turn the island into a resort for blacks, so he bought it to make a
deepwater dock for his wealthy friends.

What did Fisher have to show for all his time and money? There
were only 644 Miami Beach residents and its 80 phones were listed
on one page on the Miami directory. But there were tremendous
changes. The first electric company opened, as did a Puritan house of
worship, and the city launched an automatic phone system, eliminating
the need to use a crank box to get an outside line. So children would not
have to commute to Miami, Fisher built a school and named it after his
mother, Ida.

A tiny two-story building doubled as both the town's fire station and

City Hall. A Western Union Telegraph office opened, and a post office, after Miami Beach earned its own addresses instead of being a rural route of Miami. The city launched an electric trolley service, with thirteen stops and an all-important connection to Miami. And Fisher used his friendship with Governor Sidney "Cracker Messiah" Catts to have state prisoners pave the streets. Under Florida's 1917 Convict Lease Act, so long as a prison doctor gave an okay, prisoners could be leased to private developers. They could work no more than sixty hours weekly, or eleven hours in any one day, but the rules were often ignored and treatment of prisoners was abysmal. Fisher's prison crew finished five streets to service the town's twenty registered cars (one of which was Fisher's custom-built white Packard convertible).

A new link to South Beach, the MacArthur Causeway, completed in 1920, could handle triple the traffic of Collins's wooden bridge. It was the mainland link that Fisher long wanted, and today is still the main artery into Miami Beach. Over a thousand people drove or walked across the new roadway on its opening day.

Fisher next turned his attention to attractions that would define Miami Beach as a world-class resort. He spent $350,000 on the plush, onion-domed pavilion called the Roman Pools and Casino at 22nd Street and the ocean. (Miami Beach "casinos" had no gambling; only dining, dancing, and swimming.) Dubbed "Fisher's Folly," the membership club boasted two pools, an imported Dutch windmill to pump in seawater, a grand restaurant, a ballroom, a performance stage, and even a shopping arcade. Fisher then bought the adjacent Miami Beach Casino for a more pedestrian clientele.

He also funded the Art Center and donated most of the start-up money for the town's first theater, the 1,000-seat Altonia. One day, he decided on a whim that Miami Beach ought to have its own lake, and before nightfall a construction crew was digging the two-block-long Lake Surprise.

Expecting his wealthy clientele often to arrive by private boat, Fisher dredged up enough Biscayne Bay sand to build Star Island. From his yacht club there, he shuttled wealthy prospective buyers on his yachts and speedboats between Miami Beach and Cocolobo, his members-only deep-sea fishing club thirty miles to the south. A day of dolphin and marlin fishing in the breathtaking beauty of the Keys would soften up potential buyers.

Fisher had begun construction on five out of twelve planned luxury hotels: the grand Flamingo, the multistoried Lincoln, the sixty-room King Cole (now the Miami Heart Institute), the Bolivar, and the Spanish Baroque–style Nautilus (now Mount Sinai Hospital). The projects swelled Fisher's payroll to 1,850 workers, making him the town's largest employer. He financed four miles of landscaped horse-back-riding paths; a polo field; seaplane tours and deep-sea fishing expeditions; two trap-shooting perches complete with waiters and cocktails; and an annual Mid-Winter Regatta that attracted yachtsmen from the entire eastern seaboard. He built indoor tennis courts and hired fabled tennis pro Charles Haggert as the manager. Haggert's salary was more than he could earn in two to three years of tournament play.

Fisher planned to finance the massive construction boom with 7.5 percent bonds issued by a friend's Indiana bank. To his surprise, the bonds didn't sell well, forcing him to borrow against his other holdings to raise the money. He even put up his share of the Indianapolis Motor Speedway as collateral.

A few weeks before the Flamingo opened, Fisher wrote to his friend John Oliver La Gorce, an Antarctica explorer and *National Geographic*'s publisher, to inform him that he had placed a rush order for six gondolas. He hoped La Gorce would write an article about Miami Beach's transformation.

"I have some of the most wonderful Bahama Negroes you ever saw to push these gondolas around," he boasted. "They are all going to be stripped to the waist and wear big brass ear rings. And possibly necklaces of live crabs and crawfish." (*National Geographic* eventually published an illustrated brochure, which read as if Fisher had written it. To express his thanks, Fisher gave La Gorce a car.)

The $2.5 million, eleven-story pale pink Flamingo opened with a black-tie party on New Year's Eve 1920. "It probably cost more money for the number of rooms [200] than any other hotel in the United

States," Fisher wrote to an Indianapolis friend. The hotel was set at the edge of Biscayne Bay, and the dome was so brightly lit that ships used the glow as a night beacon. Some guests arrived at the rear dock by gondola. Italian tenors in billowy velvet pants strolled the lawn singing Rossini arias. The grounds were planted with groves of two-decade-old palm, grapefruit, orange, and mandarin trees. There were enormous waterfront rooms and private bungalows, clay tennis courts, a golf putting course, and it abutted South Florida's only polo field. The Beach still had no water mains, but a barn with forty Wisconsin Guernsey cows supplied guests with America's most expensive fresh cream and milk.

An additional $1 million ensured that the polo ground met professional standards. The deep green Bermuda grass was bordered with thick hedges. He brought in English grooms and blacksmiths at $15,000 each. Fisher hired the best breeders and players, hoping to entice the New York banker Averell Harriman and his Palm Beach–based polo-playing colleagues to head south. He partially succeeded. The U.S.-Cuba game that christened the new field was the first international polo match played in Florida. Eventually teams from England, Canada, Australia, and the Bahamas would play during the short mid-January to mid-March season. But to Fisher's dismay, Harriman and his friends joined the rarefied polo community in Aiken, South Carolina. They saw no reason to add another seasonal Florida residence. Fisher had to make do with two English peers, the Marquis of Waterford and Lord Cromwell, both of whom he seduced with gifts of land.

Johnny Weissmuller, Hollywood's Tarzan, could not make the Flamingo opening, but Fisher later paid him to take a much publicized swim in the hotel pool. He paid "appearance fees" to other celebs, from boxing champion Gene Tunney to flying ace Eddie Rickenbacker to golf star Bobby Jones. Fisher's friend Will Rogers visited his projects free. Gene Tunney got the grand tour with a local press crew in tow. (He got a lucrative deal to become the sales manager for Hollywood Pines Estates.) When President Warren Harding visited Miami, Fisher virtually shanghaied him in a speedboat and took him to Miami Beach for a round of golf. Rosie, one of Fisher's two elephants, was rigged up as

Harding's caddy. Fisher's photographers followed only a few steps behind the Secret Service, and photos of Harding's visit were printed
worldwide.

Fisher next spent several hundred thousand dollars on transforming
narrow Lincoln Road, which ran from the ocean to the bay, into a
knockoff of Paris's grand rue de la Paix (of which Fisher had only seen
pictures). By 1920, it was 100 feet wide, its sidewalks separated by a lush
median landscaping, and it was lined with deluxe stores (Cadillac and
Packard car dealerships soon moved in).

Fisher broke ground in the center of Lincoln on the eight-story,
Tudor-style Carl Fisher Building, the Beach's tallest. He built his pala-
tial home, "The Shadows," on the ocean at Lincoln's east end. It failed to
match Henry Flagler's $2.5 million, fifty-five-room, Beaux Arts Palm
Beach mansion, but Fisher did make Lincoln Road and its environs a
much sought-after address. One Fisher neighbor was Goodyear Tire
president F. A. Seiberling, who used his waterfront home—a mock
Spanish castle—only a few weeks each winter. Another Fisher friend,
John Hanan, the shoe king, built an imposing residence across the
street.

Early Miami Beach was one of the most openly anti-Semitic cities in
America. The Miami Beach Golf and Country Club, built partially with
public funding from Fisher's City Hall friends, was accessible to anyone
with a set of clubs and 50 cents. So Fisher built a restricted country club
he named La Gorce. He added restrictive deed covenants into his property sales to prohibit "Hebrew" ownership. The boilerplate language
read: "Said property shall not be sold, leased or rented in any form or
manner, by a title, either legal or equitable, to any person or persons
other than of the Caucasian Race, or to any firm or corporations of
which any persons other than of the Caucasian Race shall be a part or
stockholder." Exceptions were carved out for "Negroes" in "servants'
quarters." Fisher did not consider Jews to be Caucasians. (The last restrictive covenant was ruled illegal in a 1959 court decision.) Businesses, hotels, country clubs, and apartment buildings had GENTILE
OWNED AND OPERATED or NO JEWS ALLOWED signs. One sported the blunt
GENTILE OWNED. NO DOGS.

A few top-tier restaurants and clubs preferred the subtler "Restricted Patronage." One hotel, a favorite watering hole for Fisher and his buddies, advertised: "Always a view, never a Jew." In one instance, Fisher advised a fellow hotelier not to print "Hebrew patronage is not solicited" on his brochure, since Fisher assured him that "You can usually tell by the names of the people . . . whether they are desirable or not." Fisher and his friends would often privately let each other know whether a prominent new visitor was "OK"—our kind—not "TK"— their kind.

Overtly racist signs and ads were not banned by a local ordinance until 1949. Leo Carillo, a popular entertainer, wrote and repeatedly performed for Fisher a ditty (to the tune of Irving Berlin's "What'll I Do?"):

> *What'll I do?*
> *It can't be true my second payment's due*
> *What'll I do?*
> *I know a guy*
> *That I could sell it to,*
> *But he's a Jew*
> *What'll I do?*

The few Jews that Fisher counted as friends were so assimilated that their backgrounds were invisible. Even they, however, were held to his restrictions on the Beach. Julius Fleischmann, a millionaire yeast manufacturer and former Cincinnati mayor, who was Fisher's polo partner, was not allowed inside the restricted clubhouse. Julian Mack, president of both the Zionist Organization of America and the American Jewish Congress, and chairman of the Comité des Délégations Juives at the Versailles Peace Conference, was not allowed to stay at the Flamingo. "I would not have a problem," Fisher assured him, "but some of the other guests might be troubled."

John Collins, instead of embracing the brotherly love of his Quaker faith, followed Fisher's lead and sold his properties with restrictive deeds. But the Lummus brothers, who owned the narrow tip of Miami Beach south of Fifth Street, often heatedly argued with Fisher over

whether Jews should be allowed on the Beach. To Fisher's dismay, two
Jewish families, Rose Weiss and her son, Eugene, of New York, and Joe
and Jennie Weiss (no relation), from Philadelphia, became permanent
residents in the Lummuses' neighborhood. Rose Weiss caused a local
ruckus when she went to the hotel with the sign banning dogs and Jews,
and loudly asked, "What would you do if Jesus wanted to rent an apartment?"

A New York waiter, Joe Weiss, and his wife, Jennie, opened a sandwich counter at Smith's Casino. By 1920, they had saved enough money
to open Joe's Restaurant. Fisher predicted that it would close in a season. Today, Joe's Stone Crab is a Miami Beach institution.

The Lummuses were sons of a Georgia farmer, and their worry was
blacks. But since Miami Beach already embraced the South's Jim Crow
laws, they only had to enforce the status quo. Their advertisements proclaimed Miami Beach "The People's Playground." They were willing to
sell inexpensive summer homes to anyone who was white, law-abiding,
and had enough cash for a small down payment.

During the Roaring Twenties, black entertainers, including Duke El-
lington, Louis Armstrong, Count Basie, and Cab Calloway, became regular Miami Beach acts. But they could not spend the night at any of the
Beach's "whites-only" hotels. They had to cross the causeway back to
Miami, on the "colored" side of the trolley (the bus discrimination did
not end until a 1956 NAACP lawsuit). They usually stayed in Overtown, the city's largest black ghetto. (From 1940 to 1960, Miami had the
greatest racial segregation of America's largest 100 cities; 40,000 blacks
were crammed into less than a quarter square mile of the city's 16
square miles.)

In the thirties, the Lummuses encouraged the city to cite health and
security concerns and to pass an ordinance requiring all hospitality industry employees to carry an identification card. Random ID checks
were mostly used only against blacks, and no ID card meant either a
day in jail or a police escort off the beach and a drop-off in Miami. The
unwritten rules enforced by the police included no blacks on the beach
during the day without a pass from an employer, none allowed after
sunset, and none ever permitted to swim in the ocean. In 1934, Beach
police turned back several cars full of black Episcopal clergymen, who

were attending a Miami convention and had driven across the cause-way to sightsee.

Fisher warned authorities that foreigners might enter the United States by ship via Cuba or the Caribbean and then head north by train. He lobbied to get a small federal immigration task force dispatched to Miami. Soon after their arrival, six illegal Romanian Jews were arrested on a departing northbound train. Fisher threw a grand dinner party for the arresting officers.

Fisher's fear of anything that fell outside his narrow WASP world-view sometimes led him to make decisions that ran counter to what was best for a growing city. When a local resident suggested that some mid-Beach land be set aside for a cemetery, Fisher would hear none of it. He feared that it would only be a matter of time until the Beach's small Jewish population grew and wanted their own. So he decreed cemeteries verboten, citing Henry Flagler's argument that "the gates of death are farther removed here than in any other state."

Fisher was smart enough to know that he could not launch his long-planned land rush if he targeted only his wealthy society friends. With his identity now thoroughly wrapped into the success or failure of Miami Beach, he launched an aggressive national sales campaign. He ran a series of splashy ads in northern newspapers touting Miami Beach as an undiscovered, affordable Riviera. In the middle of the winter of 1920, he purchased a huge illuminated sign set up in New York on Fifth Avenue and 42nd Street proclaiming: IT'S JUNE IN MIAMI, complete with a giant thermometer. In Miami Beach, he planned to build another giant thermometer and publicize the daily temps nationally. Another idea was bathing beauties. "We'll get the prettiest girls and put them in the goddamnedest tightest and shortest bathing suits," he told a business colleague, "and no stockings or swim shoes either. We'll have their pic-tures taken and send them all over the goddamn country."

Billboards emblazoned with bathing beauties enjoying the white beaches—one-piece bathing suits, considered risqué, were banned in Atlantic City—sprouted up throughout the Northeast and Midwest. The campaign succeeded. Working-class families, so-called tin can tourists, piled into train coaches or their $290 Model Ts and headed south, eager to buy a piece of Florida real estate. That the town's several hundred full-time residents had to travel across the causeway for basics like clothes, food, and furniture did not discourage them.

"The Florida boom was the first indication of the mood of the twenties and the conviction that God intended the American middle class to be rich," concluded the economist John Kenneth Galbraith in his seminal history, *The Great Crash*.

Much to Fisher's delight, middle-class northerners weren't the only ones who headed south to buy a piece of Florida. World War I had forced most of America's moneyed elite to forgo their annual European expeditions. That same year, millionaires like Harvey Firestone, Louis Comfort Tiffany, J. C. Penney, the Goulds, the Maytags, rent-a-car king John Hertz, vacuum cleaner maker William Hoover, carmaker Harvey Stutz, spark plug king Albert Champion, dime-store-chain owner Sebastian Kresge, Life Saver co-founder Edward Noble, and oil magnate James Snowden kicked off a mini-construction boom. A three-mile stretch of Collins Avenue became known as "Millionaire's Row."

The newcomers built grandiose homes, designed mostly in Spanish Baroque, Mediterranean Revival, and Venetian Gothic style, with exotic gardens that ran to the water's edge. The Ludens, of the cough-drop fortune, emblazoned their trophy home with their name in flashing neon lights, and the senior Luden marked his seasonal arrival to the Beach with a brass band playing "Hail to the Chief" while several servants carried him on velvet carpets from his yacht to his front porch.

These newly arrived northerners weren't the society families of Flagler's Palm Beach. They were first-generation blue-collar industrial, whom the Palm Beach crowd considered nouveau riche. Not all of them bought property, but they all sailed into town on Fisher's gondolas along the Collins Canal to see what their unpredictable friend had concocted. Fisher ran the photographs of their arrivals in out-of-state newspaper ads to enhance the Beach's reputation as exotic and exciting.

In neighboring Coral Gables, developer George Merrick copied Fisher's gondolas and waterways to promote his Chinese- and French-style villages. That irritated Fisher, but he was angriest when the Mizner brothers, Addison and Wilson, installed electric gondolas to give their development to the north, Boca Raton, a European feel. "The gondoliers in Boca just pretend to row," Fisher complained. The Mizners, who Fisher incorrectly suspected were Jewish, "will sell to anyone," he said. Still, Fisher was jealous that the Mizners' whole-cloth creation attracted some of the very people he wanted in Miami Beach—the Vanderbilts, DuPonts, and sewing machine heir Paris Singer. He was in a funk for days when flour magnate John Pillsbury and the exiled King George of Greece both bought outside the Beach. John Deering, a northern industrialist, also built his stunning Venetian-style palazzo, Vizcaya, on the mainland where Deering brought the entire Ziegfeld Follies chorus down to entertain his guests at rowdy stag dinners.

THE FLORIDA GOLD rush was officially under way. It soon spread beyond Miami Beach. Florida had no laws regulating real estate brokers. The Roaring Twenties in South Florida were consumed by real estate speculation. Enormous swaths of the Everglades soon became "tropical paradises" and "cities of the future," complete with easy credit. Pro-moters and flimflam men moved in to sell bargain basement–priced swampland to northerners who had never visited the state.

Widespread tales of wild price increases and instant fortunes added to the frenzy. Overflow crowds slept in Miami's parks and pored through the voluminous ads in the Sunday papers. Caravans of buses from the upper Midwest brought thousands of prospects to tour new developments. Subdivisions often sold out their first day on the market. One real estate office sold $34 million worth of property in a single morning.

Developer Richard Bolles sold 500,000 swampland acres for ten dollars down, and ten dollars monthly, all of it marketed to northerners as "Florida farmland." The sales pitch was seductive: "One good investment beats a lifetime of toil." Bolles and some other Everglades developers were later indicted in Kansas for their unethical swamp selling. It seems a lot of Sunflower State residents were suckers for a sales pitch that offered them a way out of hard-luck lives: buy two Florida properties, one for their own home and the other to sell and retire on the profits. Bolles died before Kansas could extradite him.

Miami was the site of the mother lode of Ponzi schemes.* For a small down payment, binder boys—unlicensed real estate operators—bought "binders" on empty parcels and flipped them for fast profits. At the market's zenith, for $100 down anyone could get in on the action, buying and selling land without ever setting foot on it. Binder boys would set up card tables in hotel lobbies for a few hours. The more successful ones rented hotel rooms by the day. They employed their own parasites, so-called bird dogs, who hung out at railroad stations and the docks, searching for prospects. Some operators flipped the same properties seven or eight times daily.

One local story described a binder boy who resold a lot for a $10,000 profit during a one-hour stroll along Flagler Street. A property might pass through twenty people, all taking a cut before someone, almost always from out of state who had never seen the land, took legal title.

Carl Fisher didn't like binder boys—he incorrectly told friends they were mostly northern Jews—and he realized early on their speculation could destabilize the market. "Some of the property now being sold in Florida will not bring as much money in thirty years as it is selling for now," he wrote in 1925 to the publisher of the *Miami Daily News*.

Acres that had cost 10 cents only a few decades earlier were fetching unmatched prices. A World War I veteran who had swapped an overcoat five years earlier for 10 acres of beachfront property sold his land for $25,000. In January and February 1922, small Miami Beach lots went for a record $16,000 ($205,000 in 2009 dollars). Five months later, in July, the same empty lots were flipping at $150,000 ($2 million in 2009 dollars). In 1923, one-acre lots were selling for more than the value of the entire city in 1917. Theodore Dreiser wrote in *Vanity Fair* of the "positively insane prices."

The *Miami Herald*'s advertisements, 95 percent of them about real estate, set publishing records. One 504-page edition, with 491 ad pages, weighed in at 10 pounds. The *Herald* routinely published unedited real

---

* Charles Ponzi himself, the most infamous swindler of the era, went to Jacksonville after serving his jail sentence for fraud. There, under a new name, he offered a new pyramid scheme: one that promised investors 300 percent return in two months.

estate press releases as if they were news coverage. More than half of the *Herald*'s journalists doubled in real estate publicity. *The New York Times* devoted a special section to Florida's boom, concluding that "Hardly anybody talks of anything but real estate, and . . . nobody in Florida thinks of anything else these days."

Buyers were lured in part by luminaries who should have known better. William Jennings Bryan, just retired as secretary of state, accepted $100,000, half in cash, half in land—double Babe Ruth's annual salary—to pitch South Florida real estate. (Calling Miami Beach "the child of Miami," Bryan noted that the "child is the only rival a parent can welcome.") Seventy-five hundred real estate licenses were issued in Miami in 1925 alone; almost one out of every four Miamians was selling land. The area's hotels stayed open for the first time through the stifling summer, packed with tourist/speculators. The demand for land was so great that some owners put NOT FOR SALE signs on their parcels just to avoid the constant assault of brokers and binder boys.

New banks opened weekly to service the frenzy. With tales of great profits as bait, working-class families from the American heartland increasingly threw their savings at a slew of developments that promised "next to the new railway," "the new Miami Beach," or "a twenty-million-dollar city." Nebraska farmers and Ohio store clerks packed tents into their cars and headed south to cash in. Some of the opportunities were real. A sprawling pineapple plantation north of the Beach became too valuable to grow fruit. It became Miami Shores. The promoters hired police to keep order among the hundreds of potential buyers, but when they opened their doors for sales, there was a near riot. In less than three hours, the project had sold out for $33 million, double what the developers expected; some people threw checks at the agents to "bind" a parcel. Two days after Ohio's former governor, the 1920 Democratic presidential candidate James Cox, bought $3 million worth of empty oceanfront parcels in Golden Beach, a mob converged on his office and in six hours he sold every plot for a total of over $7.5 million. Within a week, resales had brought in another $12 million.

Two other deals, Manhattan Estates and Melbourne Gardens, sold out just as fast, but the former was an abandoned turpentine camp and the latter an inaccessible swamp. "Beachfront" property turned out to be five miles from the coast.

In 1925, Florida abolished income and inheritance taxes, encouraging even more investors to gorge on the inflated real estate. By this time, Fisher's name had such an allure that small-time promoters could move land on rumors that he might start developments outside Miami Beach. But Fisher never strayed from the Beach, making $37 million with the 1,800 percent increase in land values over the boom years. As his friend Will Rogers noted, Fisher took "Florida from the alligators and gave it to the Indianans." He built a second home even grander than The Shadows. On North Bay Road, it was a copy of an Italian Renaissance villa and boasted carved, hand-painted wooden ceilings, walls covered in gold leaf, and a $30,000 pipe organ. He had long coveted one of the world's most opulent yachts, the 250-foot *Eagle* owned by William Kissam Vanderbilt II, great-grandson of "Commodore" Cornelius Vanderbilt. An avid sportsman, Vanderbilt II wanted Fisher Island, the 200 acres that Fisher had bought six years earlier. Fisher invited him to dinner and proposed a swap: "My island for your boat." Vanderbilt promptly accepted.

A few years earlier, Fisher had posted a large sign on one of his prime oceanfront parcels at 23rd Street: *"If anyone will build on this site a modern tourist hotel costing two hundred thousand dollars we will give them this entire block of land."* Locals had joked, "The climate is balmy, and so is Fisher." But in 1925, Fisher did not have to give it away. A New Jersey developer and attorney, Newt Roney, paid $2.5 million for that lot and the neighboring Roman Pools. Roney built a grand seventeen-story hotel with a Florentine belltower, and a 1,500-foot waterfall. He named it the Roney Plaza. Roney promised that his hotel would be "Jew-free." As for the Roman Pools, according to Fisher, Jews had already "ruined" it, prompting him to encourage fellow developers to build the restricted Bath Club.

America's most successful Rolls-Royce dealership opened and boomtime mansions went up on Miami Beach's Star, Palm, and Hibiscus Islands. The European architects dismissed the neoclassical Beaux Arts style of the Firestone mansion and convinced their clients to embrace a style described by Alva Johnson, Addison Mizner's biographer, as "Bastard-Spanish-Moorish-Romanesque-Gothic-Renaissance-Bull-Market-Damn-the-Expense Style."*

Florida's land fever looked unstoppable. No one thought the bubble would burst.

---

*Conspicuous consumption by the superrich was even worse in Palm Beach. J. P. Morgan partner Edward Stotesbury's nearly 100-room El Mirasol had seventy-five servants and a garage for forty cars. Oklahoma oil tycoon Joshua Cosden built Playa Riente, a 112-room palazzo with a $500,000 Oriental carpet leading from the house to the private beach. But the grandest was Mar-A-Lago, boasting 118 rooms, built by E. F. Hutton and his wife, Marjorie Merriweather Post. Harry Thaw, son of the railroad baron William Thaw, who shot and killed the New York architect Stanford White over their joint passion for a chorus girl, moved south after serving seven years in an asylum for the criminally insane. When he saw Mar-A-Lago, he remarked: "My God, I shot the wrong architect."

CHAPTER 4

Rumrunners
and the Bust

COINCIDING WITH THE land frenzy was Prohibition. From 1920 to 1933, federal authorities closed more than 180,000 bars, 1,217 breweries, and 517 distilleries nationwide. But Florida, with less than 1 percent of the nation's residents, became a key liquor lifeline. It flowed into Miami Beach from Bimini, Nassau, and Gun Cay. Organized crime controlled the major smuggling ports of New York, Chicago, and Detroit, but Miami and Miami Beach were ripe for anyone with the courage to run the risk of arrest and jail (as would later be the case with gambling, then marijuana, and finally cocaine).

Most South Florida residents considered liquor sales a "respectable crime," and some realized profits from it that rivaled the real estate bonanza. Clubs, hotels, and restaurants served drinks as if nothing had changed. Two popular bars flourished only blocks from police headquarters. Embarrassed federal officials pressured the police to do something, but hotels, nightclubs, and large restaurants only moved the drinking to "secret rooms," sometimes closed off by nothing more than a curtain divider in the middle of the room. Congressman Fiorello LaGuardia of New York, during a congressional investigation, declared, "There were more prohibition lawbreakers in Florida than any other state." When challenged to prove it, LaGuardia answered, "Oh, I have been down to Miami." It was, he said, the "leakiest spot in the nation."

Some developers, like Glenn Curtiss, the aviation pioneer turned land baron, boosted their profits with liquor sales. Curtiss converted

14,000 acres of Everglades marshland into Hialeah, a veritable gang-ster's paradise that mixed legit attractions such as greyhound racing, thoroughbred tracks, and a jai alai fronton with flourishing speakeasies and casinos.

Smugglers in 34-foot speedboats made the run to Bimini in only two hours. The U.S. Coast Guard had only six cutters for the entire eastern seaboard. The Feds dispatched an interagency squad of forty agents, armed naval aircraft, sub-chasers, and undercover investigators, but privately estimated that due to geography, Prohibition was 75 per-cent less enforceable in Florida than anywhere else. Stills were easy to hide in the Everglades, where sugar cane, indispensable to moonshine, was abundant. The coastline was etched with hundreds of small inlets and sandbars that provided hiding and landing spots for boats crammed with contraband.

The Feds knew that another key factor that favored the rumrunners was the phalanx of bribed bankers, lawyers, police, judges, and corrupt government officials. In South Jacksonville, for instance, the mayor, po-lice chief, city council president, all the city commissioners, and the fire chief were indicted for smuggling. Nineteen city officials in Fort Lau-derdale, including the police chief, were charged with breaking Prohibi-tion laws. Most of Tampa's city administration was charged with crimes. In Miami Beach and Miami, prosecutions were scarce. The level of bribery was ingrained, the wall of silence strong, and the unambiguous threat of violence ever present. The murder rate of the 1920s wouldn't be as high again until the 1980s cocaine wars. (Cocaine was outlawed in 1922, only two years after Prohibition went into effect. But there was no significant underground trade in it.)

Still, the Feds made some progress. They managed to indict the brother of Miami-Dade's top prosecutor, arrest dirty cops by the half dozen, and disbar crooked attorneys. Confiscated boats were stacked like dominoes along stretches of the Miami River. Local cops smashed hundreds of stills in the Everglades, poured thousands of gallons of home brew down Miami manholes for press photographers to trumpet their "war on moonshine," and seized a record $1 million in contra-band from 1926 to 1928. But booze joints continued to flourish. Some real estate developers spread the word that South Florida had repealed the Eighteenth Amendment, making land worth more than in dry America.

In 1928, Al Capone rented several suites at the Ponce de Leon Hotel. He told a friend that Miami Beach was "the sunny Italy of the New World." Capone soon bought a lavish winter home on swanky Palm Island, and for his first party, Enrico Caruso provided the evening's entertainment. He muscled a quarter ownership in the upscale Palm Island Club, got a majority interest in the glitzy Villa Venice nightclub, and took control of the Fleetwood Hotel's Hangar Room, where he installed two Chicago gunmen to advertise the ownership change. The club brought in roulette wheels, crap tables, and wheels of fortune to complement the illegal booze. The Deauville Hotel Casino, which was doing well without Capone, hired local gangsters to let the Chicago boss know he was not welcome.

Capone cultivated local politicians and police. When three of his captains were murdered in Chicago, two of them had Miami Beach police courtesy cards in their wallets.

Not everyone was thrilled by Capone's arrival: there was some concern that his notoriety was bad for real estate values. Like many other wealthy Beach residents, Carl Fisher had his own rumrunner, stored cases of whiskey in his cellar, and made frequent "fishing" trips to the Bahamas. But he pressured the city commissioners to intimidate Capone so he would pack his bags and leave. Two police officers were posted near Capone's house and shadowed him and his entourage, all to no effect.

Miami Beach filed suit against Al Capone, claiming his home was a haven for "gangsters and racketeers." Fisher testified at the one-day trial that Capone's mere presence had dented land sales, and that pillars of society like Harvey Firestone had become afraid since Capone had moved to the Beach. In court, Capone wore a light blue silk suit adorned with an enormous diamond pin. All this must have seemed like child's play compared to the real prosecutions he had faced in Chicago. By noon, it was over. The city's case was dismissed. Every subsequent attempt to force Capone from town failed.

Unlike real estate promoters, the rumrunners and gambling czars did not seem to care about Capone's naked power grab. For everyone who bragged about selling a $10 acre lot for $10,000, someone else boasted of moving a shipload of liquor that had fetched only $8 a quart when legal, and now brought $100 per diluted quart. Bill Mc-Coy's fleets of speedboats delivered his undiluted rum—dubbed the "real McCoy"—all along the eastern seaboard. After his indictment by a federal grand jury, he served nine months in an Atlanta prison. When he got out in late 1925, he opted out of high-risk rumrunning and opened a South Florida real estate office.

Celebrity rumrunners like Havana Kitty, Bootleg Sue, and "Stingray Jake" Burton were supported by an enormous and profitable infrastructure. They relied on repackaging, distribution, sales, armed protection for the large loads heading north, and laundering outlets for the piles of cash. Hundreds of mom-and-pop businesses provided either bookkeeping, transportation, or the conduits for bribes.

The *Miami Herald*'s editorial page railed against the corruption and violence at the core of the rumrunning trade, but drew the line when law enforcement interfered with tourism. When a New York dentist who had invested heavily in Miami Beach was arrested for possessing a bottle of liquor, a *Herald* editorial fretted about how "this might affect the tourist trade next winter." Not surprisingly, Fisher made no attempt to hide his contempt for Prohibition. He even threatened to become a Democrat if the Republicans did not stop supporting the liquor ban. Commerce was priority one, and part of Miami Beach's lure was that it promised escape from northern drudgery and depression. When New York millionaire Harry Black (co-owner of the iconic Flatiron Building) was arrested at the ritzy Royal Palm Hotel for having several dozen cases of liquor aboard his private railroad car, the *Herald* buried the news on page 15. But his acquittal by a six-man jury in less than five minutes made the front page.

One local rumrunner celeb, Red Shannon, supplied most of Miami Beach's hotels, including Fisher's. When a Coast Guard patrol finally intercepted Shannon in Biscayne Bay, in his *Goose*, a customized 30-foot skiff, he tried outrunning them. From the Flamingo's sprawling terrace, dozens of startled spectators watched as Shannon was killed in a volley of machine-gun fire. Fisher was horrified.

A local Miami judge, a close friend of Fisher's, indicted the five Coast

Guard officers for manslaughter. When the Coast Guard crew refused to honor the subpoenas, the state of Florida charged them with second-degree murder. Fisher was a trial witness, but claimed his severe near-sightedness prevented him from seeing whether Shannon and his smugglers had raised their hands to surrender before the Coast Guard fired. The Coast Guard officers were acquitted, but the local and state governments had sent a not so subtle message to the Feds.

After months of fitful starts and some successes, the federal agents threw in the towel. *The New York Times* noted that the squad had returned to Washington "before it was laughed out of the state, but not before the snickers were audible."

Alas, any good party has to end. In a prescient January 1925 cover story, *Forbes* warned that Florida's skyrocketing land prices were based only on the expectation of finding another customer willing to pay more than the last one, not upon any intrinsic value. South Floridians discounted it as sour grapes from northerners who were angry they had missed out on the party. But New York bankers finally got nervous about the dizzying prices, and some of the easy credit flowing to large property investment syndicates and developers dried up. The IRS kicked off criminal probes into large backroom land sales offices that it suspected were slick scams, and speculators suddenly found a dearth of buyers. The market stalled. Soon panic followed. In mid-1925, the bubble finally burst. It was Florida's first real estate debacle. Miami Beach, which during the real estate frenzy had seen a record 15,000 people employed, soon had one of the highest unemployment rates in Florida.

Tens of thousands of small investors lost their life savings. According to a *Chicago Tribune* article, Florida banks were "popping like firecrackers on a Chinese New Year." For years to come, the stark, unfinished remnants of failed mega-residential developments served as visible evidence of how badly the market had crashed. Promised metropolises of the future—Picture City, the new home of the American film industry, and beach resorts such as Fulford-by-the-Sea and Idlewyld—remained barren stretches of land pockmarked with FOR SALE signs. Broken families from the heartland returned home on the Dixie Highway sporting hand-scribbled signs on their windshields: "Don't go to Florida. Don't get robbed." The entire state looked like a giant Ponzi scheme. It was a reputation Florida would not shake for decades.

A YEAR AFTER the bust, 1926, Carl Fisher's net worth reached its zenith, an estimated $100 million. The full realization of his Miami Beach dream had been tempered early in the boom when his personal life fell into disarray. In 1921, his only child, Carl Junior, died twenty-six days after his birth. Fisher, who had sent out telegrams heralding the birth, was devastated. When a business colleague at the Roman Pools passed around cigars celebrating the birth of his own child, Fisher burst into tears. Jane tried to lift him from his deep funk by adopting a two-year-old boy, but Fisher wanted nothing to do with him and refused to join in the adoption. His drinking increased and his womanizing became brazen.

His marriage to Jane ended late in 1926, just as Florida real estate values were imploding. His longtime secretary-mistress, Ann Rossiter, left him and married a Pennsylvania clergyman. Only Fisher's closest friends knew he was under tremendous strain. To everyone else, he seemed to throw himself into his work with renewed vigor. He had a new venture in mind, this one up north. Against almost every friend's advice, he spent $2.5 million for the entire 10,000-acre peninsula of Montauk, Long Island. His plan? To develop a grand resort, Montauk Beach, ten times the size of Miami Beach. "Miami in the Winter, Montauk in Summer" was his new slogan. When friends questioned why he would want to undertake another daunting development venture, Fisher said, "I just like to see the dirt fly."

Nineteen twenty-six was also the year of the Great Miami Hurricane—the Big Blow. It wiped out some of the Beach's recent construction and tore apart Collins's 2.5-mile wooden bridge. Even the Flamingo's dome blew off. More than 100 died in Miami and Miami Beach; nearly 1,000 were hospitalized; and 2,000 homes were destroyed. The storm cost Fisher $1 million in repairs. In Montauk, he received a telegram reading: "Miami Beach Total Loss. Swept Away by Hurricane. Untold damage." That overstated the case, but Fisher calmly told an employee, "We built it out of nothing and we'll build it again." He even wrote Jane that the hurricane would "prove to be the greatest blessing to Miami Beach in the long run. Miami Beach will be more beautiful, bigger and better than before. After we get rid of this shyster boom trash there will be only hurricane-proof structures allowed to be built."

Fisher and other developers tried hard to minimize news of the storm's damage in the hope that it wouldn't scare off a final wave of bargain hunters. John Pennekamp, the *Miami Herald*'s new city editor, was ordered by his publisher to lower his reporting of $100 million in local damages to just $10 million. Miami's mayor refused state or federal aid, saying the city could fend for itself, and hurricanes were once in a lifetime events that paled in comparison to annual midwestern floods or cataclysmic California earthquakes. A brief rebuilding frenzy earned Miami the nickname "the Magic City."

FISHER'S PROBLEMS MULTIPLIED. In 1927, he got married again, to his new secretary, Margaret Collier. But what they seemed most to have in common were heavy drinking and an inability to remain faithful to each other. He was still a stocky bear of a man, but his fitness had long ago given way to fat. A tennis ball had struck his good eye, making his vision worse than ever.

The 1928 Okeechobee Hurricane ravaged Miami and left a deadlier human toll than the Big Blow—1,836 dead and 2,000 injured. This time, Fisher and his publicist, Steve Hannagan, scheduled major sports events to show that not even Mother Nature could stop the fun. The 1928 Regatta was the largest Fisher ever produced and included the country's top racers. He sponsored the biggest golf tournament ever held, at the La Gorce Country Club, which lured big-name players and garnered extra press attention by naming each of the eighteen holes after celebrities.

When the stock market crashed less than a year later, Florida real estate was suddenly Kryptonite. The results in Miami Beach were swift and terrible. With financial survival at stake for millions of families, Florida vacations were the last thing on their minds. Most local banks failed. The East Coast Railroad went bankrupt. Three fourths of Beach residents—the population had swelled from 644 in 1920 to 15,000 in

1925—went on welfare during the Depression, one of the highest percentages in the country. The Lummus brothers were unable to pay their taxes and had to sell off most of their remaining assets at fire sale prices.

Fisher himself was wiped out. He had committed $8 million to his Montauk project, convinced that its success would bail him out. To raise cash, he sold his beloved Indianapolis Motor Speedway to his friend Eddie Rickenbacker. And he borrowed whatever he could from New York bankers by providing his twenty-one companies as collateral. But it was too late. His vast landholdings had lost much of their inflated peak-of-the-market value, and some bankers who had extended huge loans called them due. His grand hotels cut their suites into smaller rooms and slashed rates in an unsuccessful effort to attract bargain-seeking tourists. When America's first theme parks—Winter Haven's Cypress Gardens and Marineland in St. Augustine—opened during the 1930s, Fisher couldn't compete.

He was no longer able to service the debt on his collapsing empire. He was drinking more than ever and his best days were a few fishing trips to Bimini with old auto-racing friends. When Miami Beach's first synagogue, Beth Jacob, opened in the basement of an apartment building south of Fifth Street in 1929, Fisher told a friend, "It's over. It will become a tropical ghetto."

In 1932, his Miami Beach companies went bankrupt. In 1934, the Montauk Beach Development Company went under, $4 million in debt. Creditors seized the Carl G. Fisher Company the following year. In a final humiliation, he filed for personal bankruptcy and was stripped of everything—his remarkable car collection, the yachts and speedboats, his bayfront castle, even his country club memberships. The two pet elephants were sold and sent off in chains to the Atlanta Zoo.

The Collins family, whose Quaker cautiousness had allowed them to emerge from the financial turmoil with some of their holdings intact, offered Fisher a job at an extremely generous $25,000 a year. But by that time his heavy drinking prevented him from even being a good front man. His salary was cut to $10,000.

Fisher now lived in a small cottage off a nondescript block in mid-Beach, numbing himself with a case of beer a day and a nightly bottle of Scotch. As a further insult, his first grand residence, The Shadows, was purchased by Mert Wertheimer, a Jewish member of Detroit's criminal Chesterfield Syndicate, who converted it into a swanky night club.

Fisher ignored his doctors' many orders to stop drinking even after he was diagnosed with cirrhosis of the liver. For three years, he made almost weekly trips to the Beach's St. Francis Hospital to have his swollen body drained of up to 20 pounds of accumulated liquids that pressured his heart. If he refused to follow any medical advice, he did however constantly complain about the costs of his treatment.

"I have your bill," he wrote to Dr. E. B. Maxwell in 1938, "and to say that I got a shock at the size of this bill puts it mildly. It would have been cheaper by far to die."

His net worth was barely $50,000. That was a fortune to most Americans, but it was less than Fisher had once spent on a good party.

"I used to be able to make dreams come true," he told a friend. "I can't do it any more. I'm only a beggar now. The end can't be far away."

"I wish I was the Carl Fisher of yesteryear," he told a Miami colleague as they commiserated over their huge financial losses.

When Fisher died at St. Francis Hospital in 1939, at sixty-five, he was alone and half blind.

His ex-wife Jane, who went through six more marriages, did not consider him a failure. She saw him as somebody who had lived precisely as he had wanted to.

"Living with Carl Fisher was like living in a circus," she recalled; "there was something exciting going on every minute of the day. Sometimes it was very good; sometimes it was very bad. Still, it was living. It was excitement that I never found again."

CHAPTER 5

"Too Much Is
Never Enough"

O N FEBRUARY 19, 1940, Miami Beach's comeback from the bust and the Depression was announced on *Time* magazine's cover. The story, "Pleasure Dome," exclaimed that the Beach was "like no other town in the U.S., or in the world."

Three factors were instrumental in the city's resurgence. First, air-conditioning. Second, low-cost air travel, which had transformed the entire region into what travel agents touted as "Florida Year Round." In 1936, for instance, a coach flight from New York to Miami cost less than the train: $22.48 ($347 in 2009 dollars) versus $41.45. And third, in 1931, the state legislature legalized pari-mutuel betting—on horse and dog racing and jai alai.

ILLEGAL BOOKIE CONCESSIONS on the Beach flourished, as did nightclubs that had private rooms with blackjack tables and roulette wheels. Beach police turned a blind eye to slot machines that popped up in bath clubs, hotel lobbies, corner drugstores, and even gas stations.

The Roney Plaza's beachfront Café de La Paix was the place to be seen. During the season, Walter Winchell broadcast from the Roney's Cabana Club pool deck. Two thirds of America tuned in to his Sunday-night show or read his weekly syndicated column. Winchell told his listeners that he was living at the "Rooney Pleasure" and that Miami Beach was "a branch of heaven." (He got the penthouse suite every winter in exchange for his pitch.)

Largely because of Winchell, such luminaries as Al Jolson, Irving Berlin, Eddie Cantor, George Jessel, and Sophie Tucker were Roney regulars. The lush grounds were packed with affluent tourists, local gigolos hoping to find a wealthy northern widow, and the newest and flashiest money.

Winchell was credited with saving the 1935–36 tourism season. He arrived a month after a November hurricane, and when he assured the country that all was well in Miami Beach, the tourists finally began to pour in.

World War II threatened to interrupt the party. After America declared war in December 1941, the U.S. Army designated Miami Beach as a major training center and more than half a million troops passed through there in the next three years. The Army requisitioned 85 percent of the Beach's hotel rooms, more than one hundred apartment houses and eighteen homes, and converted Fisher's Nautilus Hotel into a hospital. The Municipal Golf Course was leased to the federal government for a dollar annually and became the Officer Candidate School and drill ground. The Army made a public show of closing the brothels, but prostitution flourished. Teenage "Victory Girls" plied the trade in Bayfront Park.

All along Florida's Atlantic coast, grim evidence of the war was unavoidable. To the north, in Jacksonville and Jupiter, German U-boats attacked freighters and tankers within sight of oceanfront sunbathers. In February 1942, when a U-boat torpedoed a tanker carrying 100,000 gallons of gasoline and kerosene, the explosions were heard in Miami Beach, and the flames lit up the skyline. In July 1942, a U.S. Navy blimp was shot down by small-arms fire from a Nazi U-boat just south of the Beach. The crew was rescued, but the incursion prompted the Coast Guard to begin intensive shore patrols in South Florida. German and Italian POWs, detained at a southwest Miami camp, dug ditches and cleaned up construction sites in the Beach. A fortunate few became maintenance personnel at some of the hotels that were used for recuperating American soldiers.

Despite the U-boats, the gas and food rationing, and the intermittent blackouts, Miami Beach tried hard not to let the war intrude. Nightclub impresario Lou Walters (father to Barbara) opened the Latin Quarter in 1940 and three shows a night were packed with wealthy visitors, servicemen, and locals who saw the era's biggest performers: Frank Sinatra, Dean Martin and Jerry Lewis, Jack Benny, and Tony Bennett. The tourist board encouraged celebs to give testimonials to offset any impression that the war might have changed the town for the worse.

"Miami Beach is never better," said Al Jolson. Joan Crawford assured reporters that her few weeks there was a "beautiful and peaceful interlude." A midnight curfew on serving alcohol was mostly ignored and some club promoters exploited the Army's orders for dim-outs and blackouts to offer indoor parties that ran 24/7. The Beach's most popular drink was a potent blend dubbed the B-29. Lucius Beebe, the *New York Herald Tribune*'s society columnist, described Miami Beach at this time as "the last Gomorrah, the ultimate Babylon," while *Time* reported it was "uninhibited paganism."

Look magazine castigated the Beach in 1945 for having "probably the greatest concentration of war-money-to-burn citizenry from every state in the nation." The reporters compared $10 dinner tabs at "chi chi supper clubs" and $40 daily rates at the Roney to $50 monthly salaries for GIs. "Sumptuous gambling casinos operate full blast," wrote *Look*. "Black markets are rampaging. Everyone's having a wonderful time. One GI, who had been awarded a Purple Heart, wondered: 'Is this what I've been fighting for?' "

But after peace was won in May 1945, many veterans who had trained there returned to the Beach. Florida had no income tax, a low unemployment rate, and one of the nation's fastest-growing economies. And the press, having castigated the Beach for its relaxed wartime attitude, now lavished it with praise. In 1947, *Life* magazine did a 12-page feature that gushed: "Each winter [Miami Beach] becomes the mecca for stage stars, songwriters, playboys, labor leaders, big-money executives and big-money gamblers." It concluded that Miami Beach was "America's affordable Riviera." By 1950, the Beach's population had swelled by 80 percent. Dozens of enormous apartment towers were constructed along Collins Avenue. They offered large, modern, and affordable spaces, often with ocean views. The new middle-class residents radically changed the demographics of Fisher's restricted island. It was now nearly half Jewish, most of them transplants from New York, St. Louis, Baltimore, and Pittsburgh. In country clubs like the Bath Club, Indian Creek, Surf, and La Gorce, a prerequisite to membership was still two Christian parents. Only La Gorce allowed a member to bring along a Jew for a meal or a round of golf. Society ladies in the Miami Beach Women's Club complained about Temple Emanu-El's dome. "We are a tiny Arabia surrounded by a very large Israel," said one member. But anti-Semitism was obvious only to those who lived there.

The city's travel bureau successfully sold the revived Beach as fabulous yet affordable. There were no black neighborhoods—blacks worked on the Beach but lived in Miami—and no white slums. Mobile homes were banned. Even train passengers had to go to Miami. Beach leaders did not want a train station that might become a hangout for hustlers and bums.

Edith Piaf, Sophie Tucker, and Joe Lewis packed the hotel ballrooms. Eddie Cantor's show at the Fleetwood Hotel was a favorite, and the next day tourists could read about the visiting celebrities and local gangsters in Damon Runyon's column. (Runyon had made the Beach his winter home and wrote the town's most widely read gossip column.)

Gambling was the consistent thread in the Beach's postwar resurgence. Major hotels had a resident bookie, usually operating at the pool cabanas, but also sometimes at the lobby cigar stand. They were installed by the local S&G syndicate: five local bookmakers—Harold Salvey, Jules Levitt, Eddie Rosenbaum, Charles Friedman, and Sam Cohen—who had joined forces in 1944 to service the enormous Army population. S&G was not only tolerated by the city; thanks to its judicious and generous payoffs it had a Lincoln Road office, the "S&G" initials etched on tinted glass windows. And the over two hundred S&G bookies were the only ones who were never arrested. After a New York hoodlum, Frank Erickson, paid the Roney Plaza $45,000 for a three-month bookie concession, the police closed his operations within two weeks. "We don't want any outsiders here," a detective told Erickson.

By 1950, S&G had bookies in practically every hotel along Collins Avenue, and one did a booming business out of the second-floor office of a local bank. The organization was so successful—it took in an estimated $50 million annually in bets—that the Chicago mob bought a one-sixth share. There was so much money that S&G became a major contributor to the local Boy Scouts and Red Cross.

All of this attracted Washington's attention. That same year the U.S. Senate's Special Committee on Organized Crime in Interstate Commerce brought its hearings to Miami. Chaired by Tennessee senator Estes Kefauver, it laid out a devastating indictment of the links between local officials and mobsters. The evidence showed that the town's illegal trades flourished largely because of police corruption and the local politicians who unofficially sanctioned it, believing the associated vices of gambling and prostitution were good for the tourist trade. In Miami's Dade County, Sheriff James Sullivan's assets had soared from $2,500 to more than $75,000 in his six years in office, and a deputy testified that a fellow policeman had regularly delivered payoffs from gamblers to the sheriff's wife. Said the committee, "there is a gentleman's agreement [among the mobsters] . . . not to infringe on the activities of each other." Kefauver was so outraged at the excesses that he wrote an article for the *Saturday Evening Post* titled "What I Found Out about the Miami Mob."

The Kefauver Hearings ended the gambling party. The U.S. Treasury Department seized S&G's assets. Backroom casinos in supper clubs closed, and although there were still scattered small-time bookies, open gambling was finished. Mob kingpin Meyer Lansky packed up his roulette wheels and shipped them to Havana.

But shutting down S&G did not end the Beach's lure for mobsters. After finishing his federal sentence for tax evasion, Capone had returned to the Beach in 1940. His death in 1947 was a non-event in a town then held spellbound by the latest mansion-buying spree by crime bosses. Mafia captains from Philadelphia and Cleveland bought homes a few blocks apart. Grand waterfront villas went to senior capos in New York's Costello family and Detroit's Purple Gang. The *Miami Herald* ran pictures of the gangland mansions and the coverage made mobsters local celebrities.

When gambling disappeared, the new winter season mobsters

branched out into legitimate enterprises that were part of the Beach's DNA—nightclubs, liquor distribution, the construction business, and container companies at Miami's bustling docks. Miami Beach was an open town—no one crime family controlled it. Al Capone's brother, Ralph "Bottles," stayed in Miami to run the wildly successful Paddock nightclub. New York's Lucky Luciano, Frank Costello, Joe Adonis, and "Dutch" Schultz invested in local racetracks and resorts.

While some of the mobsters flashed their money, just as many kept a low profile. Meyer Lansky, with his tentacles in dozens of hotels, bars, jukebox operations, and waste disposal companies, lived in a modest condo, and his headquarters was a smoky card-playing room at the tourist-class Singapore Hotel on Collins Avenue. A small man, in baggy pants, Lansky was often seen shuffling along with his pet Pomeranian.

The demise of gambling coincided with Delta Airlines' inauguration of package tours. Vacations that included air travel, hotel, and often meals, at remarkably cheap prices, kicked off a new tourist bonanza. Internal memos show that Delta's wildly successful "Millionaire Summer Vacation" was targeted to "shoe salesmen, secretaries, factory workers and teachers." The prices were so low that it was cheaper for a New Yorker to visit the Beach for a weekend than to stay at the Jersey Shore. Seventy-five percent of those who came during the summer were single young women. Those tourists could never have afforded the Beach during the much more expensive winter season. Newly air-conditioned hotels, restaurants, and clubs made significant price concessions during the summers when they would otherwise have been idle. Miami Beach hotels introduced the "American plan." A single package price included breakfast and dinner, poolside cocktails, and even admission to a couple of shows. "It's like the Ford Falcon," noted one publicist; "it isn't classy, but it's what the public wants."

In the 1950s, the city's promoters convinced Arthur Godfrey and his ukulele to relocate his show to Miami Beach. Godfrey, who had the nation's number one television and radio programs, gave the city a mass appeal that couldn't be attained through a hundred ad campaigns. Local government officials named a major mid-Beach thoroughfare (41st Street) for him. (Like Carl Fisher, Godfrey was an unrepentant anti-Semite. Ironically, Arthur Godfrey Road today is the heart of the city's Orthodox Jewish community.)*

New attractions such as nearby Tropical Hobbyland—a one-block Biscayne Boulevard "village" that boasted alligator-wrestling, caged monkeys, macaws, and flamingos—thrived. In 1954, two local restaurateurs, James McLamore and David Edgerton, opened the first Insta Burger King.

That same year, Morris Lapidus's sprawling, extravagant Fontainebleau Hotel opened. Lapidus, a New York designer of store interiors, was hired by developer Ben Novack to design a hotel on the site of Harvey Firestone's former estate. The Firestone heirs had taken the city to court to rezone the residential property for use as a hotel or apartment building. The city offered to buy it for $1 million, but the heirs held out for $1.4 million. At an impasse, the Firestones sued the city and won. They sold the property to Ben Novack, an elegant aging playboy, for $2.3 million in 1952.

"I had been waiting for this opportunity all my professional life," said Lapidus of his first building commission. Firestone's granite mansion served as the construction crew's headquarters. Lapidus recycled its enormous marble maidens and floor-to-ceiling gilt-framed mirrors in the hotel's white marble lobby. In the middle of a four-acre French parterre, Lapidus installed one of three grand pools. One side served as the glass wall of the basement bar—patrons could watch the swimmers underwater. After a single visit, Truman Capote declared it his favorite Miami hangout.

The 554-room, 14-story hotel embodied Lapidus's mantra, "Too much is never enough." He called his style "fantasiste extraordinaire." Novack called it "Miami Beach French." There were tennis courts, yacht docks, Roman-style baths, sundecks and solariums, an ice-skating rink, putting greens, billiard rooms, plus all the requisite restaurants and nightclubs. Novack proudly proclaimed it "the world's most preten-

---

* Eddie Fisher, in his autobiography *Been There, Done That*, wrote that "One of the best-known anti-Semites in show business was Arthur Godfrey. I didn't care that Godfrey wouldn't let me in his hotel [he owned the Kenilworth and barred Jews] as long as he let me sing on his radio show."

tious hotel." In its first season a Texas oilman spent $100,000 for two suites and two cabanas.

No one was quite sure how much of the hotel Novack actually owned. Al Capone's cousin, Joe Fischetti, and a drug dealer, Max Eder, bragged repeatedly about owning some of it, something Novack adamantly denied. When the *Miami Herald* ran a front-page story saying that the Fontainebleau's land was owned by "gamblers and hoodlums" and that the hotel was a shell company owned by Meyer Lansky, Novack sued for libel. The $10 million suit was settled when the *Herald* ran a correction stating that an insurance company owned the land and that Novack was the sole owner of the shell corporation. There were still enough questions about his associates that when he later applied to open a Bahamian casino, the Justice Department supplied the British government with ample information to get Novack's application rejected.

Lapidus, though much maligned by architecture critics, was hired to design the opulent Eden Roc, next door to the Fontainebleau. The Eden Roc's owner, Harry Mufson, had asked Lapidus, "You must have something besides French. How about Italian Renaissance?" Lapidus showed Mufson pictures of rooms in the Vatican, as well as Florence's opulent Pitti Palace and Uffizi Gallery. The 349-room hotel boasted two mosaic tile panels that ran the full height of the building, and black-and-white terrazzo floors, and it was crammed with ornate blue and lavender furniture.

The two Lapidus landmarks initiated yet another building boom and served as anchors for hundreds of smaller hotels. Streamlined Art Deco hotels such as the Penguin, Nemo, Astor, Seymour, and Nash, which looked as if they could cruise anytime at 30 knots, lined Collins Avenue. The smaller prewar hotels stayed competitive by modernizing their lobbies and coffee shops, redecorating the guest rooms, and polishing the murals. In the decade after World War II, Miami Beach built more hotels than all other major American, European, and South American resorts combined.

CHAPTER 6

Lost Mojo

WHILE MIAMI BEACH underwent a middle-class boom that had made it half Jewish, neighboring Miami experienced a very different but just as dramatic postwar demographic shift. At only 35 square miles, the smallest land area of any major U.S. metropolis, Miami is the American city located closest to notoriously unstable Latin and South American tinpot dictatorships, making it a natural Ellis Island for immigrants. Periodic coups throughout the 1950s—primarily in Argentina, Panama, Peru, and Bolivia—led to spectacular flights of capital that flooded Miami, and each successive arrival of the ousted ruling class subtly changed the cityscape. But nothing matched the changes following Castro's rebel army's capture of Havana on January 1, 1959. Cuban dictator Fulgencio Batista packed three planes with 180 people—family, friends, and sycophants—millions in cash crammed into wooden crates, pallets of gold bars, and a massive jewelry collection, and flew into exile to the Dominican Republic.

The Eisenhower administration had refused Batista exile status in Miami, but it did whatever it could to destabilize the upstart Fidel Castro and encourage Cubans to flee to America. They were welcomed as Communist refugees and granted permanent U.S. residency. Ten thousand of the island's wealthiest families and entrepreneurs arrived in Miami within months of Castro's takeover. Another 150,000 came in an almost continuous airlift that ran until the 1962 Cuban missile crisis. A further 245,000 Cubans arrived after the flights were resumed in 1965.

These were not Emma Lazarus's huddled masses or the Mariel boatlift Cubans who would arrive twenty years later. They were educated, white-collar professionals and included most of Cuba's Jews—dubbed "Jewbans" in Miami—who had been captains of the Cuban banking and real estate industries. Unlike earlier immigrants, who came believing that America offered a better future, they counted the days until a counterrevolution would topple Castro and they could return home. But while the years turned to decades, they accepted Miami as their "Exile Capital." They solidly established themselves faster than any immigrants in American history. And in so doing, they fundamentally changed Miami.

In 1960, a year after Castro seized power, only 4 percent of Miami's population of more than 1 million was Hispanic. By the late 1990s, more than two thirds of Miami's citizens were Hispanic, and more than half of those Cuban. Not surprisingly, the dramatically changing demographics led to an exodus of Anglos. For twenty years after the Cubans arrived, 95 percent of election registrations canceled in the county were from whites moving out. A popular bumper sticker asked: "Will the last American to leave Miami please bring the flag." But Miami Beach remained largely unchanged in the aftermath of Castro's revolution. A majority of the Cuban Jews settled there, but their numbers were few compared to the mainland. And many moved to North Beach, away from the tourist zone. Beach vacationers who didn't cross the causeways never saw the changes that the wave of Cuban immigrants made to Miami.

THROUGH THE MID-1960S, the Beach remained the country's most popular tourist spot. But regional changes were pulling some visitors away. Wealthy visitors, who came for the high-end shopping along Lincoln Road, were diverted to a luxurious outdoor mall some 100 blocks north, Bal Harbour, that opened in 1965 and boasted the first Neiman Marcus outside Texas. In the wake of Bal Harbour, Lincoln Road was left with downscale merchants and even some shuttered storefronts. And there was stiff new competition for middle-class tourists. Fort Lauderdale, only half an hour north of Miami Beach, was immortalized in 1960 in the film *Where the Boys Are*, and became the favorite destination for tens of thousands of college students on spring break. Gulf

Coast cities such as Tampa and St. Petersburg launched major success-ful tourism campaigns. Out west, Las Vegas lured away headline per-formers with huge contracts, leaving the Beach only B-grade acts. Ever cheaper airfares and shorter flight times meant that tourists were fre-quently forgoing another Miami Beach vacation for Mexico, the Carib-bean, or Europe. Negril, Jamaica's first popular resort, and the Bahamas' Paradise Island, both opened in 1965. The Mexican government had carved Cancún from a sliver of sand off the Yucatán coast and new highways connected the fledgling getaway to the mainland and an in-ternational airport. Noted Hal Cohen, executive director of Miami Beach's Tourist Development Authority, "What you might call dilapi-dated here is considered quaint and charming in Jamaica."

The biggest blow came in 1967, when the Walt Disney Company bought 27,400 acres near Orlando for $6 million and announced plans for a theme park a hundred times larger than Disneyland.

Miami Beach hotels slashed their prices to a third of what they had commanded at the end of the 1950s. Large blocks of rooms were sold at huge discounts to tour operators and conventions. With the advent of package tourism, locals bemoaned that mass had defeated class, but hotel owners did not care so long as they were filled. They offered free entertainment to guests, and low fixed rates to bus tours, with a free midnight snack tossed in. Headwaiters dissed the newcomers as the "chicken sandwich crowd."

As the packages became more competitive, they also killed off many independent resort venues. The swanky Brook Club went bankrupt and became a supermarket. The popular Park Avenue Club was replaced by a parking lot. The celebrity hangout Hickory House was converted into a garage. Miami's Clover Club was torn down and remained a vacant lot.

The town was still a magnet for popular television and radio shows. Larry King broadcast his radio show from Pumpernik's Deli. Ed Sulli-van did a series of shows from the Beach, including his most famous one introducing the Beatles in 1964. Jackie Gleason moved his number one–rated variety show from New York to the Beach in 1964, saying he wanted to live in a town where he could play golf 365 days a year. The "Miss USA" and "Miss Universe" contests moved there in the mid-1960s. In 1965, on Miami Beach's fiftieth anniversary, Jackie Gleason and Maurice Chevalier, who was older than Miami Beach itself, hosted a pageant. Fifteen bands, dozens of floats, and over a hundred drill teams and marching bands paraded down Ocean Drive, and hundreds of bathing beauties strutted along the boardwalk.

EVEN INTO THE swinging and more politically liberal sixties, the Beach remained as firmly segregated as the Deep South. It wasn't until 1960, six years after the U.S. Supreme Court's landmark *Brown* decision, that Miami Beach High (the only high school) was integrated. Blacks were nonexistent in city government and the police and fire departments until 1971.

The new generation of black performers—Lena Horne, Dorothy Dandridge, Sammy Davis, Jr., Billy Eckstein, and Gregory Hines—still could not stay overnight in the Miami Beach hotels where they performed. When Jackie Robinson and Joe Louis tried to play at the Bayshore golf course, they were told they had to first be registered at a Miami Beach hotel. They called several hotel owners directly, even enlisting the help of the city manager, but were told there wasn't a single room available since it was high season.

Many stayed at Sir John's Hotel, on Miami's Biscayne Boulevard. Owned by a twenty-nine-year-old attorney, Al Malnik, it had opened in 1960. Born to Russian Jewish immigrant parents in St. Louis, Malnik had just opened his law office on Lincoln Road and was well known locally for briefly representing Meyer Lansky; he had met Lansky through Alfred Mones, a major Miami Beach layoff bookmaker. A colleague of Mones shared Malnik's office.*

"We had many of the black entertainers as guests because they still couldn't stay at the Beach hotels," Malnik recalled. "They didn't like

---

* Years later, Malnik, who declined to be interviewed for this book, told *The New York Times* that his Lansky representation was probably from a referral, but he couldn't remember whose. He said he met Lansky only once, and even then only by chance in an elevator in the Imperial House condominium where Lansky lived. "My representation of a man in some civil matters," Malnik told the *Times*, "in the early '60s has been converted by the media into relationships that never existed. It's the most preposterous, ridiculous, indefensible situation to be in."

what was going on—they complained among themselves—but the Beach hotels paid them a lot of money, so they tolerated it." Malnik paid the star black performers $5,000 weekly for two shows a night, six nights a week. At Overtown clubs like Knight Beat, Sam Cooke and James Brown headlined for $3,000 a week. A top Beach hotel paid $25,000 for the same gig.

Even black boxers who fought or trained at the Beach's Fifth Street Gym, with Angelo Dundee, had to sit in the back of a bus to return to Overtown daily. For title contenders, such as Joe Louis, Archie Moore, Sonny Liston, and the young Cassius Clay, who would train there for a month or more, Miami's Mary Elizabeth or Carver Hotels offered discounts.

The rule against blacks staying overnight on the Beach finally cracked—not from public outrage or NAACP lobbying, nor even from Miami Beach's political leadership. It took Frank Sinatra to force the issue on behalf of one of his closest friends, Sammy Davis, Jr. Sinatra asked Ben Novack to let Davis stay at the Fontainebleau.

"Novack knew that Sammy was upset about the race issue," said Malnik, "but he told Frank that he was worried about what his guests would think if he let a black man stay at his hotel. He told Frank that he was afraid to do it."

"You either let Sammy stay here or I quit," Sinatra told Novack.

Novack relented. Sammy could stay but could not hang out in the lobby and had to take the service elevator to his room.

"Of course, Sammy did just the opposite," Malnik added. "He was always in the lobby, being flashy about it, making a statement. It was great. Novack didn't like it, but he wasn't about to do anything about it."

After Sammy Davis broke the Fontainebleau's color barrier, the competing Eden Roc let in Harry Belafonte in 1963. But these continued to be exceptions. The city had more urgent problems than desegregation. As the 1960s came to a close, Miami Beach seemed to have lost its mojo. It had a heavy annual deficit, despite receiving the largest share of the state's resort taxes and huge capital expenditures to host business conventions and to promote the city for tourism. Developers had overbuilt. Five thousand new condos flooded an already sluggish market. Infrastructure projects were stalled. The Beach also waged nasty and protracted court battles with hotels that contended the beachfront was their private property. The city eventually prevailed, but the beach it reclaimed had suffered serious erosion, and it had not addressed the problem of millions of gallons of untreated sewage that poured into the ocean.

"As a kid growing up in the sixties, Miami Beach was like an aging beauty queen with her skirt too tight, her legs too big, and her lipstick a little over the lip line," says Mitch Kaplan, a native who owns South Florida's premier independent bookstores, Books & Books. "The world was remaking itself, and Miami Beach was this odd combo of Borscht Belt and Vegas and had just fallen out of favor with the world."

Many of the children who had grown up on the Beach had moved to Coral Gables or Coconut Grove, places that seemed hipper, offered more space, and weren't as tourist-dependent. South Beach Elementary School closed because there were so few children. Mount Sinai reduced its maternity ward. The hotels had not worn well. Most owners spent little money on upkeep. There was no leadership from City Hall, and the Beach lacked direction on how to land a new generation of visitors. It had been the Beatles' first South Florida stop when they visited in 1964. By the end of the decade, rock acts like Led Zeppelin and The Doors preferred Coconut Grove.

IN 1968, THE Republicans held their presidential convention in Miami Beach. Expecting a possible replay of the violence in Chicago at the Democratic Convention, Florida called out the National Guard. But there were no mass protests and the less than a dozen arrests were for public intoxication and rowdiness. But in Miami's black Liberty City ghetto, an angry crowd beat up a man who had a George Wallace bumper sticker on his car. Police set off tear gas. The next day, officers reacted to possible sniper fire with a hail of bullets, leaving three men dead and a young boy injured. The National Guard moved in. The violence stopped after a couple nights of curfew and rain. Sixteen were dead and four hundred injured. It was Miami's first riot.

In 1972, both political parties chose Miami Beach for their presidential conventions. The city appeared to be on the brink of a revival. Despite the Liberty City violence, Republican Convention organizers remembered that the Beach had been calm in 1968. Nixon's winter White House was in neighboring Key Biscayne, and many of the president's closest friends, such as the financier Bebe Rebozo, were locals.

The Democrats went first, starting on July 10. Flamingo Park, one of the Beach's small green spaces, was designated a "free speech" zone, in the hope of confining all the protesters to a single location. Hippies and demonstrators made it their base for planned protests against the expanded war into Laos and Cambodia and the intensified U.S. bombing of North Vietnam.

"Drugs were everywhere; emotions were running really high against the war," recalls Mitch Kaplan, who was then seventeen. "We hung out watching replays of bootleg copies of the Zapruder film and talking about how we could stop what was happening at the conventions." Yippie leader Abbie Hoffman, who was promoting his own fringe candidacy, was a regular at "Quaalude Alley," the name given by local cops to the Flamingo Park encampment.

The protesters did not target the Democrats—they saved their firepower for Richard Nixon and the Republican Convention. In August, Miami Beach's twenty-five cops were reinforced by hundreds of FBI agents, Secret Service agents, state law enforcement agents, and Army intelligence officers. A massive chain-link fence was hastily installed across the street from the Convention Center in the hope of containing the protesters.

On August 22, Nixon flew into Miami. Demonstrators blocked traffic at the Fontainebleau and burnt the American flag. Near the Convention Center and Lincoln Road, protesters smashed windows, ripped down signs, and threw garbage cans. Only a couple hundred people were arrested. Jane Fonda led a more peaceful march that evening, but a tense standoff continued until the last day of the convention, when Nixon accepted the nomination.

The demonstrations then turned violent. Some protesters wore gas masks (a lesson learned from 1968 and Chicago), shattered store windows, and threw Molotov cocktails. The police, joined by National Guard units, responded with tear gas. In South Beach's confined twenty-five blocks, police chased demonstrators as clouds of tear gas and the sound of sirens filled the air.

Hunter Thompson, who covered the conventions for *Rolling Stone,* wrote that Miami Beach police saw him staggering around searching for water to wash the tear gas out of his eyes, and he was grateful they did not beat him senseless. "That was the difference between Chicago and Miami," he noted. "If the cops in Chicago had found me crawling around in somebody's front yard, wearing a 'press' tag and blind from too much gas, they'd have broken half my ribs and hauled me away in handcuffs for 'resisting arrest.'"

"It was a major fucking embarrassment," says attorney Harold Rosen, who is now eighty-three, and a lawyer and lobbyist for most of the Beach's entertainment industry. In 1972 he was a city commissioner. "All these long-haired freaks running around. One tried to throw a pie at me and I just decked him, knocked his lights out. Miami had all the breaks that year. They had the Dolphins (the Miami football team had an undefeated season), while we had those fucking hippies."

The political conventions were a disaster for the Beach. And the televised scenes of thousands of rampaging protesters pushed the Beach even further off the list of popular destinations. Even the Fontainebleau and the Eden Roc were struggling.

The average citizen was sixty-six, the oldest average of any American town. And half the town's population—more than 40,000—that lived south of Lincoln Road received the highest proportion of pension and Medicare checks monthly of any neighborhood in the nation. A remarkable 80 percent of South Beach's residents were sixty-five or older, and 85 percent were Jewish. If Spanish was Miami's second language, in South Beach it was Yiddish. City Hall's Citizens' Service Bureau posted its name in English, Spanish, and Hebrew. *Newsweek, The Times* of London, Toronto's *Globe and Mail,* and even the *Miami Herald* described South Beach variously as God's Waiting Room, Senile City, Varicose Beach, Mausoleum in the Sun, and the Elephant's Graveyard.

The generation that settled on the Beach was not today's financially secure Jewish seniors who favor gated communities and golf. These fixed-income retirees were the last great wave of Eastern European immigration, the original trade unionists from the 1920s. They had spent their working years in solid blue-collar jobs in New York's garment district, were staunch left-of-center Democrats, and after a lifetime of toil they looked forward to the ease of retirement. Many had spent their lives moving from one Jewish ghetto to another; South Beach was their final stop. They were mostly secular Jews who read books and kept up with the news. As Alex Daoud had discovered firsthand during his first run for the city commission in 1979, the South Beach retirees had the highest voter turnout in the state: 90 percent.

The neighborhood had chess clubs, a string ensemble, debate clubs, and canasta and mahjong groups. At First Street and the ocean was the Miami Beach Kennel Club, a dog track, originally financed for $1 million by Al Capone in the thirties. Fifty cents bought an evening in the grandstands, and retirees pooled their quarters to buy the minimum $2 bet.

Kosher meat and fish markets, delis, newsstands with Yiddish newspapers, and cheap clothing shops dotted the neighborhood. The only supermarket, the grimy Fifth Street Food Fair, sported a giant illuminated billboard with movable letters: "Look What Ten Cents Can Buy."

Every week six hundred retirees would pack into the Tenth Street Auditorium, a simple, square building in Lummus Park, for an evening of dancing to Arthur Murray, the bossa nova, and the tango. The 25-cent admission fee hadn't been raised in three decades. The frailest sat in cushioned metal-frame chairs, under a spinning mirrored ball.

Between the warm weather, the tightly knit Jewish community, and affordable apartments, South Beach had once seemed the idyllic spot for retirement. It resembled northern cities from which they had moved: no fast food restaurants, no suburban shopping malls, and compact enough so there was no need for a car. But through the 1970s, the retirees' fixed incomes and pensions had been decimated by runaway double-digit inflation. Most survived on meager Social Security payments, some as little as $28 a week. A third supplemented their income with state or county welfare.

The police maintained a list of nearly four hundred people who could not find their way home. Every day, at police headquarters, an elderly Eastern European refugee wandered in and asked, "Where am I?" or "How do I get back to the East Side?" As South Beach deteriorated, it became a chaotic mix of Latin immigrants and refugees, but its population of elderly Jews was too poor and too old to go anywhere else.

CHAPTER 7

"The Death of an American City"

I N THE EYES of Miami Beach politicians, solving the problems of the poor and elderly crammed into South Beach was less of a priority that restoring the Beach's fading image as a top vacation destination. By the time Walt Disney World opened in Orlando in 1971, the Beach was yesterday's resort. Disney World boasted 13 million visitors annually. No new hotels had been built in Miami Beach in a decade; indeed, for the first time in thirty years the number of hotel rooms had dropped by 3,000. Hawaii, meanwhile, had added 27,000 extra rooms in a single year, and Las Vegas 15,000.

Nineteen seventy-eight started badly on the Beach. One of Florida's very few unions, the 11,000-member Local 355 of the Hotel, Motel and Restaurant Employees, staged a walkout. Guests were left to make their own beds, carry their own bags, and serve themselves buffet meals. Although the strike was over in a week, it was a public relations nightmare at the height of the winter season. By the end of the year, the Fontainebleau—now sorely in need of refurbishment—was forced into bankruptcy after Ben Novack mortgaged it heavily to finance new projects.

The new buyer was developer Steve Muss, who bought it for $27 million, claiming he did so "out of civic duty." He spent $12.5 million in renovations and hired the Hilton group to run it.

The six-foot-five, 280-pound Muss could be gruff and overbearing, but he was a relentless town booster. A few years before he bought the Fontainebleau, he had convinced the city to create an independent and powerful Miami Beach Redevelopment Agency (RDA). Muss and other city power brokers were convinced that they could privately create their own renewal in run-down South Beach. Muss was appointed RDA's vice chairman. The RDA's jurisdiction covered the 250 acres from the southern tip of the island up to Sixth Street. Originally called South Beach, the city commission changed the name in 1950 to South Shore. This poverty-stricken neighborhood had 6,000 residents, almost all elderly Jews, with a few Italians. This was the land originally owned by the Lummus brothers, and for many years it was the only area in Miami Beach where Jews could live and work, the so-called Jewish Riviera.

In 1973, city government took the first step toward a complete overhaul of the neighborhood when it imposed a building moratorium. In 1975, with the blessing of the state legislature, Miami Beach commissioners declared the area "a special redevelopment district." The idea was to rebuild a resort after allowing the entire neighborhood south of Sixth Street to deteriorate to the point where it would have to be demolished, and then relocating the area's elderly. But to condemn the 372 buildings, the city needed state approval, which could come only if the area was officially declared "blighted." Most of South Shore's buildings were in good condition; twenty new condominiums had been built since 1968, and the city's housing authority had just opened Rebecca Towers North, a rent-subsidized multistory building for senior citizens. Over the objections of many residents and the state attorney general, Janet Reno, the city commission made it official.

"It wasn't that blighted," says Harold Rosen, the mayor at the time. "Some parts of it were bad but other sections were okay. That was just a word we had to use to give us the powers we needed. No one wanted South Shore to become one major retirement home, and that is where it was heading."

WITH BROAD POWERS, Muss and the RDA decided to buy out the landowners after condemning their property, and then to sell to private developers who would bulldoze the buildings and start building a luxury resort.

One of the ten buildings not slated for destruction was the iconic restaurant Joe's Stone Crab, then owned by the RDA's chairman, Irwin

Sawitz. "It was to have been the biggest urban renewal project in America," Steve Muss told me.

The RDA operated under a state authority that required Miami Beach to pay "fair market value" for every property it acquired. But unlike in regular real estate deals, a person whose property was condemned was compelled under the law to sell only to the city. Two city appraisers determined the fair market value, and the commissioners made an offer. The city could sue if the owner rejected it. If a jury determined that the property owner was entitled to significantly more than the city's offer, the city could cancel the deal. If the jury sided with the city, the owner had to accept the original offer and pay all legal costs.

"The cards were stacked in the RDA's favor, no doubt about that," says Rosen.

Since the city had first halted all development in 1973, not a single property owner had spent money on a spare coat of paint, landscaping, building repairs, or upkeep. It was a limbo that spurred an even more pronounced downturn. And since a "fair" price was computed on the comparable sales of nearby properties, whose value had equally deflated, the RDA was in a position to grab the land at distressed prices.

The RDA received competitive projects from fifty-four architects and consulted with ten developers, including Charles Cheezem, one of Florida's most successful luxury builders of thousands of oceanfront condominiums. Like many successful businessmen who create their own empire from the ground up, Muss was not accustomed to the public scrutiny and compromise required by a publicly financed entity like the RDA. During its first year, Muss met privately with Cheezem, business executives, and architects, ignoring the state's "sunshine law" that required advance notice and public meetings. Only after the state's deputy attorney general, James Whiseand, ruled that Muss's meetings violated state law did the RDA become more transparent.

The RDA chose a design that called for a grand $650 million knock-off of Venice, complete with 2.7 miles of canals and dozens of water taxis serving nine grand hotels and outdoor cafés and restaurants. The blueprints and drawings revealed a plan for 4,350 hotel rooms, 3,300 residential units, 470,000 square feet of retail and entertainment space, 62,500 square feet of office space, and a grand marina of 750 wet and dry berths. There were additional plans for several parks with three miles of paths for walking, jogging, and bicycling—and a tram line. In 1977, the U.S. Army Corps of Engineers had completed an $80 million restoration program that added 200 feet of new oceanfront beach. Muss wanted even more landfill to expand the beaches, with facilities for water sports, sailing, and fishing. Stephen Siskind, the RDA's director, told colleagues that the area would be a tropical cross between Copenhagen's Tivoli Gardens and San Francisco's Ghirardelli Square. (The winning architectural firm, Wurster, Bernadi & Emmons, had designed the Ghirardelli redevelopment.) Muss's project was larger than New York's World Trade Center, which had just reshaped lower Manhattan by flattening blocks of flourishing businesses and Civil War–era buildings.

The RDA also promised that in addition to converting the area into an upscale tourist draw, the neighborhood would contain new housing for every current resident who was sixty-five or older, and that new rentals would not exceed 25 percent of pensioners' incomes. But that was nearly double what most of them paid under government subsidies.

"All of South Beach was a dead zone," says Harold Rosen. "No one was willing to invest any money, and then the RDA gave us a plan to make things much better. It involved some public money, but Muss promised to raise most of the dollars privately. It seemed like a no-brainer."

"We had a great idea," says Muss. "It would have revitalized a neighborhood that was dying. We were saving an area no one wanted."

Not everyone agreed. David Dermer, an attorney and the son of a Miami Beach mayor, who would later become commissioner and mayor himself, argues, "The Redevelopment Agency was actually a major cause of the area's decline. These were developers, appointed to an agency with great public money and power at their disposal, and the motivation was greed over the public good. There were enormous abuses and mismanagement in the RDA and that was clear to anyone who did not have money at stake in the project."

The RDA's public meetings were packed with South Shore residents and others who had their own ideas of how to best stop the deterioration. The debate over whether the best way to improve a neighborhood was to bulldoze it sparked Miami Beach's first community activism movement. Morris Katowitz, who paid $24 a month in maintenance fees on a co-op he shared with his wife, challenged the RDA to prove that its relocation and rent subsidies would offset more expensive rent elsewhere. Mel Mendelson, whose family-run wholesale meatpacking business had been in South Shore for thirty years, knew firsthand that the Beach's politicians made their deals in a small backroom of his business, where they met weekly for steaks and beers. Mendelson vowed to spend his last dollar fighting Muss's plan.

Max Silnicki, a Polish immigrant who ran the Washington Avenue Barber Shop, had shaved the heads of Jewish corpses at Auschwitz before they were cremated. His fifteen-year-old, four-chair shop charged $3 for a haircut and $1 for a blood pressure check. He told the commission he would never leave it, even if they came to the door with a bulldozer. "I've survived too much, for so long."

At one city commission meeting, a discussion over where to move the neighborhood's residents became so heated that K-9 police had to restore order. Many of the elderly residents who had retired from New York remembered when Knickerbocker Village was built on the Lower East Side in the 1930s. That state-sponsored slum clearance project raised rents an average of four times and forced the poorer and fixed-income residents into other slums. There were soon signs at RDA meetings declaring: "No Knickerbocker in Miami Beach."

The South Shore activism spread to the neighborhood north of Sixth Street. That area, also crammed with retirees, was out of the RDA's jurisdiction. Extending north eleven blocks to Lincoln Road, it was filled with hundreds of Depression-era Art Deco buildings. Many of them were converted hotels that had been built for brief stays during the winter season, and the tiny residences were ideal for the single elderly who lived from month to month on government pensions.

"The buildings didn't look like buildings that had been wonderful at one time," recalls a Miami photographer, Manny Hernandez. "No one took care of them."

But a handful of people saw something worthwhile in the dilapidated buildings.

In 1975, Denis Russ, a thirty-one-year-old Miami Beach native who had just gotten his law degree, got involved in community development. "The area was at a turning point," he says now. "There was prostitution on the streets, and many parts were dangerous, seedy, and crime-ridden. The parks had deteriorated. There simply was no public investment in keeping up the city."

The federal government had given Miami Beach $2 million in redevelopment funds as part of a national program to help distressed communities. The city authorities weren't sure how to best use the grant—which was separate from any RDA funding—so the mayor appointed a nine-person commission, with Russ as its chair.

The following year, one local community activist, a feisty fifty-six-year-old former style and design magazine editor named Barbara Capitman, founded the Miami Design Preservation League. She and others worried that if Muss's south of Sixth Street development succeeded, it was only a matter of time before the Art Deco district came under the wrecking ball. The stocky Capitman, whose husband had recently died, was looking for a cause in which to immerse herself. Raised in an intellectual, activist New York Jewish family, she had moved to Miami Beach in 1973.

"This neighborhood is irreplaceable," said Capitman. "When I first appeared on the scene, they called it garbage." She drove reporters around the neighborhood in her old Dodge, dragging them into welfare hotels and retirement homes to point out the architectural details, making her case that the Deco district was worth saving. She got articles about what she called "Old Miami Beach" into the *Saturday Review*, *The New York Times*, the *Wall Street Journal*, and *Preservation News*.

In 1974, Lynn Bernstein of Philadelphia visited Miami Beach with friends. While buying some Art Deco prints in the lobby of the Miami Design Preservation League, she met Barbara Capitman, who told her about the incipient preservation crusade on which she and other concerned residents had embarked. Two hours later, Bernstein informed her friends she would not be returning to Philadelphia. She had decided to move to the Beach and become part of the movement to save the district's buildings.

"I was ready just to be a volunteer," recalls Bernstein, "sorting through posters and old clips, filing bills, whatever could help. When I was hired as part of the staff a couple of weeks later, I was over the moon. It really felt as though we were doing something that could have a real impact."

"We were all very early in the formation of government renewal programs," says Russ. "The RDA, headed by Muss, wanted our federal grant. They had all these lawyers and the city backed him. I said, 'No, you really don't need our money.' The powers in the city were not very happy with me."

At one contentious meeting, Barbara Capitman grabbed the mike, and in her high-pitched voice said that while she wasn't sure what could be done with the $2 million, she could use $10,000 to survey the Art Deco buildings in South Beach. She had learned from the state preservation office that a building-by-building survey was required to start the preservation process.

"She was tough and confrontational when she had to be," recalls Nancy Liebman, another local activist who had met Capitman early on during a protest against demolishing a school. "She was a master of smoke and mirrors. She could make people believe Art Deco was the biggest treasure they'd ever seen. Barbara was authentic and really believed in what she was doing, but she was also all theater. She could turn on the tears at a hearing, and she understood, as I did, that if you got a crowd together, you could move the local politicians. They were spineless then."

Denis Russ pushed. Capitman got her $10,000.

Russ, who is now the community development director for the Miami Beach Development Corporation, was as committed to urban renewal as Capitman was to preservation. The two became fast friends. He successfully resisted the efforts of City Hall politicos to take away his federal grant and planned his own redevelopment projects. They included a face-lift for Washington Avenue and an ambitious plan to redo the city's parks.

"By this time I started working closely with Barbara," Russ says. "We knew what we wanted to do, the area we wanted to preserve, but I had to figure out how to work through the bureaucracy to get it done at the state and federal level. There were so many hurdles, and we had constant resistance from the local chamber of commerce, political officials, and the private developers. They all had a 'tear down and build philosophy.' They just needed a reason to rip down the Miami Modern and Art Deco buildings, and they would have stripped the last remaining character out of the Beach."

One developer, Abe Resnick, who owned seventy small buildings scattered around South Beach, was one of Capitman's steadfast foes. Resnick said he was a Holocaust survivor. His name had been shortened from Resnickowitz, and he had deserted the Russian army in 1945 and moved to Cuba with an uncle. He fled to Miami Beach when Castro took power and built up a small real estate empire. Resnick's properties had dropped in value with the neighborhood decline and he wanted to replace them with high-rises. He told a reporter, "I really don't find any beauty in Art Deco. But it might be I'm shortsighted. Maybe I need glasses, rose-colored glasses." He often argued that it was a Miami Beach tradition to tear down so-called landmarks for newer buildings. Since 1950, the city had given the green light to demolish William Taradesh's 1921 Beaux Arts mansion, the J. N. Lummus Building (Lummus himself landed the first sledgehammer blow), Smith's Casino in 1964, and the grand Roney Plaza in 1968. When the Fifth Street Gym came down, fight doctor Ferdie Pacheco saved Muhammad Ali's training table only minutes before the wrecking ball struck the building.

"Capitman and her volunteers were mostly underestimated by the Miami Beach power base," says David Dermer, a former mayor. "They were just viewed as some kooky activists who would never pull anything off. I mean, depending on when you saw her, Barbara Capitman could look like a bag lady in tentlike dresses and old tennis shoes. And at some point, she alienated just about everybody, she was so driven. There was a time in the late eighties when she had had so many feuds with her own volunteers at the Miami Design Preservation League that they didn't even invite her to the annual dance. Sometimes they stopped talking to her for long stretches."

"Barbara Capitman was my friend," says David Wallach, who is now owner of one of South Beach's most outrageous Latin-themed clubs, Mango's. At the time, the building that houses Mango's was a nursing home owned by Wallach's father. "Barbara was bohemian. We connected because my background was not the typical one in South Beach at the time."

Wallach, who has a law degree and has studied Eastern philosophies with Indian gurus, recalls that "Barbara had big problems with City Hall. They didn't take her seriously. I was friendly with the artists and the hippies and my father was good friends with all those politicians. Barbara came to me a few times to help with City Hall. It took me about five minutes to realize that Miami Beach politicians considered Art Deco nothing more than a paint job. It was a fad, they thought, and if they delayed long enough in making any decision, they hoped it would all just disappear."

"New York City had Robert Moses and a city administration that understood the importance of urban planning and preservation," says Denis Russ. "Here, we didn't have anyone of that stature or influence, so it was all citizen participation. And we did not have the little old ladies with white gloves hosting afternoon teas to save a building in which George Washington had slept. This was a neighborhood of common folk. We were trying to do something unprecedented, save the buildings simply for their architecture."

IN 1978, WHILE the grand design for a new South Shore was still in the planning stages, and volunteer preservationists were working to save the Art Deco buildings, Steve Muss spearheaded a statewide referendum to legalize gambling on a sixteen-mile beach strip from Hollywood to the southern tip of Miami Beach. The "Let's Help Florida Committee" waged a $2 million campaign, promising voters that tourist revenues in Miami Beach alone would jump from $3.5 million a year to $10 million. Muss contended that the casinos would create jobs and add property taxes to the state's coffers. Opponents said it would scare away family vacationers and bring back organized crime. Lured by the prospect of legal gambling, Bob Guccione, the founder of *Penthouse* magazine, bid $15.5 million for the Eden Roc Hotel. Thirty-two-year-old Donald Trump offered the city council a $100 million guarantee to fund construction of the Beach's first new hotel in a decade—a sprawling 1,000-room complex adjacent to the city's Convention Center. And

Chicago millionaire A. N. Pritzker, whose family owned Hyatt Hotels, pledged half the financing for a $40 million amusement park for Watson Island, in Biscayne Bay.

Legalized gambling would have doubled the value of Muss's Fontainebleau overnight. And it would likely have been the death knell for South Beach. When casinos were approved in Atlantic City in 1976, real estate speculators bought and shuttered buildings in anticipation of big profits in the "East Coast Vegas." Rents soared and low-income housing became scarce overnight. Some of Atlantic City's grand hotels, including several listed on the National Register of Historic Buildings, were demolished. While the boardwalk became a magnet for tourists, the neighborhood a few blocks inland deteriorated fast and crime increased. Opponents feared a similar bleak fate for South Beach. Voters overwhelmingly rejected the initiative. Guccione, Trump, and Pritzker withdrew their development offers.

Meanwhile, three years of volunteer work paid off on May 14, 1979, when the Miami Beach Architectural Historic District (popularly known as the "Art Deco District") was listed on the National Register of Historic Places. It was the nation's first twentieth-century historic district. To the shock of developers, the designation covered 800 buildings in a 125-block area, the largest preserved zone in America. The buildings were younger than most of the neighborhood's residents.

One of Capitman's friends was Leonard Horowitz, a thirty-four-year-old interior designer who worked as a doorman at one of Steve Muss's luxury condo towers on Collins. A self-described "outrageous faggot," Horowitz had convinced Capitman that the facades were drab and needed a face-lift. He did away with the standard faded white and beige buildings trimmed in dark brown or green, and substituted a pastel color wheel of pink, blue, peach, periwinkle, and violet that became the neighborhood's trademark.

There was widespread press coverage of the new district. Among the magazines Barbara Capitman cold-called was *Interview*.

"This woman with a wavering voice called to invite us to distribute magazines at their first makeshift Art Deco festival," recalls Glenn Albin, who was then *Interview*'s managing editor. "The receptionist, Jane Sarkin [now a *Vanity Fair* editor], joked and said to me, 'It's your grandmother calling from Miami Beach.' I took it and the caller introduced herself as Barbara Capitman. I pitched the invitation to Bob Colacello [a writer], who said, 'Yeah, go do it. Andy [Warhol] loves Miami.' And the next thing I knew Andy and Bob traveled to Miami."

Lynn Bernstein and Diane Camber, the Design League's assistant director, took Warhol and a busload of news reporters and photographers on a tour of the district.

"We were at the cutting edge of the way people began to think about historic preservation," says Russ. "Before our movement, people would fight to get historic preservation status for a single building. Ours was the first attempt to have an entire neighborhood granted that status. We knew this was a historic moment."

Capitman's Miami Design Preservation League used federal and local grants to commission a firm of Boston architects, Anderson, Notter & Finegold, to develop a plan to preserve and renovate existing buildings while encouraging compatible new ones. But with the country mired in a deep recession, the plan got indefinitely stuck at the city's Planning Board. It was up to progressive private developers to take the lead for any change in South Beach. Its historic preservation status provided a 25 percent tax credit on all "qualified rehabilitation expenses" intended to keep the original character and style.

Capitman's son, Andrew, was working on his Ph.D. in economics at the New School for Social Research in New York. He visited his mother in 1979 for the first Art Deco Weekend, a street fair celebrating the district. Barbara knew that even though the district would soon be on the National Register of Historic Places, local laws controlled demolitions. She helped draft an ordinance to require developers to submit their plans to a historic preservation board before tearing anything down. That would delay demolition in most cases for at least six months. But in the meantime, she told Andrew, someone had to show it was possible to make money from the existing buildings. She was convinced that "all the ingredients are here to create one of the most distinctive urban environments in America."

Andrew understood that restoring the buildings for art's sake alone was not enough. If the neighborhood's revival balanced preservation with "sensitive new construction," Capitman thought the area could morph into a tropical French Quarter, attracting "educated, well-employed, and well-traveled people who shun massive, impersonal environments."

The twenty-eight-year-old believed that if he set a personal example, he could convince like-minded developers there was money to be made in the neighborhood. In December 1978, Andrew Capitman signed a contract to buy the classic 1939 Cardozo Hotel for $800,000 as his pilot project. It was a run-down seventy-room residential hotel at 13th and Ocean that had been designed by Henry Hohauser and named for U.S. Supreme Court Justice Benjamin Cardozo. Capitman didn't yet have the money but the Cardozo's owner was so thrilled to have anyone interested in his hotel that he gave the developer six months to find the funds.

Andrew moved to Miami Beach. A month later he met Mark Shantzis. Shantzis, a native of Miami Beach, then twenty-seven, who had worked as a pool boy at the Fontainebleau, specialized in tax-sheltered partnerships and was looking for deals in the Art Deco zone. Together the two men formed Art Deco Hotels Ltd. and decided to buy more hotels.

Shantzis traded on his knowledge of South Beach and his born salesmanship to raise money. He enticed conservative investors like Procter & Gamble heir William Gamble and Wometco's Richard Wolfson. All told, Shantzis and Capitman had more than one hundred investors, only three of whom lived in Miami Beach.

The type-A, numbers-driven Shantzis and the laid-back marketing strategist Capitman were an ideal pair. On June 25, 1979, the duo bought six hotels, all classic examples of Art Deco—the Cardozo, Tides, Carlyle, Victor, Senator, and Leslie—for $4.9 million. They had raised 30 percent of the purchase price (including $40,000 of their own money).

The sellers agreed to take back mortgages at a trifling 8 to 10 percent (virtually half the historically high average of 16 percent for commercial mortgages). Shantzis set up each hotel as a limited partnership so that the investors got tax breaks and earned 70 percent of any future profits. Shantzis and Capitman split the remaining 30 percent and received an annual salary of $75,000 from the partnership for managing the hotels.

Andrew Capitman hoped that City Hall might be pleased to have investors renovating dilapidated buildings in a run-down neighborhood. But instead, he and Shantzis ran into a wall of resistance. "In the early days the city could not have been more difficult," said Capitman. "The city and the chamber of commerce both had opposed the Art Deco District. The people who opposed it had no idea what a resource it would be, and were not aware of the success of other historic districts in other areas."

When he applied for a permit to open a restaurant and outside bar and lounge at the Cardozo, Ocean Drive's first food and beverage operation, the city fought him over zoning technicalities for eighteen months. By the time the restyled Cardozo Café opened, the Marielitos had arrived and South Beach had deteriorated even further. Any excitement about the preservation designation or the early efforts by Capitman to kick off a renovation movement was tempered by the realization that the neighborhood around the saved buildings was gripped by poverty.

The year after the Art Deco District had been created, after Warhol and the architecture magazines had gone home, the federal government released its figures on poverty in America. By 1980, most South Beach residents lived just below the annual $8,000 poverty level. It was the state's poorest neighborhood, and one of the poorest in the country outside of some districts in Appalachia. Ninety-six percent of South Beach's 36,000 apartments had been converted into honeycomb-sized one-bedroom rentals or efficiencies. Many were pullmanettes, a room with only a bed and a hotplate, and more than 1,000 of the rentals did not even have toilets; the buildings often had one shared toilet per floor. The elderly who remained were usually alone. City inspectors called the streamlined Art Deco hotels that had become retirement homes "warehouses."

Ninety-three-year-old Anna Berking, a Hungarian-born refugee, had lived for thirteen years in a $100-a-month studio. Her single bed took up a quarter of the apartment. She had a hotplate, one bare naked light, a dresser, and a sometimes working refrigerator. As was common of many buildings for the elderly, there was no air-conditioning. Nor did she have her own toilet or telephone, and she could not afford to replace the fan that had broken three years earlier. At least 2,000 residents like her needed part-time care, and another 1,500 needed full-time assistance. Every morning, Jewish Vocational Services used the Tenth Street Auditorium to serve 1,200 free meals. At least a hundred people lined up every day by nine thirty for the 11:30 a.m. meal.

When the city threatened to demolish one of the last elementary schools, the Leroy D. Feinberg on Washington Avenue, PTA activists such as Nancy Liebman and Matti Bower led a successful fight to save the school.

"We were trying to stop the death of an American city," recalls Russ, "trying to come up with any idea to revitalize it."

So was Muss, who had become the RDA's chairman and had proceeded with the grand plan just south of the new historic zone. In 1979, the RDA negotiated with a partnership of three developers—Atlanta-based Earl Worsham, the Miami-based Turner Development, and Dade Federal Savings & Loan Association—but the deal soured over financing details. Muss resigned as chairman but stayed on as a board member and the chief negotiator.

"Muss thought all the preservationists were wackos and he had no time for them," says Alex Daoud, who was by then city commissioner. "He didn't have his own money invested in the Art Deco District because he didn't see any future there." Muss summoned Daoud to his sprawling penthouse in Seacoast Towers. (Muss had built all four luxury towers that made up the complex.) He wanted Daoud's vote on an RDA request to be given ownership of a large city-owned waterfront parcel. One new commissioner was the South Shore butcher, Mel Mendelson, who had turned his RDA opposition into a successful political debut. "It was an extremely pressure-filled situation," Daoud told me. "Muss was the largest landowner in Miami Beach, the biggest taxpayer, and one of the wealthiest people around. He had friends in all the right places. He could attack you, finance a campaign against you. No one wanted to needlessly make an enemy of him."

The commission was split over redevelopment and Daoud's vote would decide the matter.

"Muss complained about how badly all of South Shore's elderly residents had treated him," Daoud goes on. "And he said that he and the RDA had been subject to unnecessary abuse from the residents and the

press when they were merely trying their hardest to save the Beach."
Muss told Daoud that the next day's vote was "the most important in
the history of Miami Beach." Daoud voted no. A day later, he changed
his mind. The commissioners decided finally to put the RDA issue up
for a public vote.

In March 1980, after a short, bruising campaign, 23,449 voters approved the redevelopment proposal by a 3 to 2 majority. Even in South
Shore it won support by a vote of 1,339 to 1,234. Many residents said
they had voted for it because they thought it was the only way to stop
the deterioration caused by the 1973 construction moratorium.

After the vote, Muss restarted negotiations with developers. The
Florida Supreme Court approved a mechanism sought by the RDA's
lawyers that enabled the agency to sell $200 million in bonds at 14 per-
cent interest. But by the time they found an underwriter, interest rates
had spiked and equivalent investments were paying 17 percent or more.
Unable to change the bond's terms, the RDA could not sell them. Seven
developers were rejected as too costly, and Muss was having problems
raising the massive funding. Blocked on the bond financing, he went to
private sources. But the recession had dried up credit in the commercial real estate market. South Shore's fate was on hold.

CHAPTER 8

Cocaine Cowboys

THE MIAMI BEACH preservation movement and the battle over the RDA were knocked off the news on a blistering summer day: July 11, 1979. A white Ford Econoline van rolled through the parking lot of Miami's largest mall, Dadeland, in Kendall, a bedroom community ten minutes south of downtown. If anyone had bothered to look carefully, they would have noticed that the crudely stenciled red signs on each side did not match. The right read: "Happy Time Complete Supply Party," the left: "Happy Time Complete Party Supply." There was a telephone number, but the line was disconnected.

The driver drove slowly around the outskirts of the 50-acre mall and pulled up in front of Crown's Liquors, squeezed between a beauty salon and a deli.

A few minutes later, a white Mercedes sedan with black-tinted bulletproof windows parked near the liquor store. The passenger was one of Miami's top cocaine dealers, thirty-seven-year-old Jimenez Panesso, and the driver was Jimenez's twenty-two-year-old bodyguard, Juan Carlos Hernandez. An unwritten code for a drug kingpin is never to have a set schedule, but this was Panesso's weekly visit to Crown's Liquors. His success and power had made him overconfident. When the two men went in to place their usual order for several thousand dollars' worth of Chivas Regal and rare cognacs, Hernandez felt so comfortable that he'd left his 9mm Browning in the car.

They'd been in the store for less than a minute when two men from the Ford van walked in. Without a word, the taller one walked up to Jimenez, whipped out a .380 Beretta handgun with a silencer, and shot the Colombian drug lord four times in the face. Hernandez and the store clerk began running. The other gunman sprayed the store with a .45 caliber MAC-10 machine pistol, emptying the thirty-round clip in a few seconds.

The two gunmen calmly walked back to the idling van and jumped in back. A third accomplice slammed the accelerator. As the Ford careened out of the mall, the two men fired indiscriminately out the van's rear doors, smashing store windows, tearing up cars, and sending shoppers fleeing in terror.

The Ingram Military Armament Corporation-10 was a favorite of Miami's drug dealers, dubbed the "Miami chopper" by local police. A compact weapon, it could fire 1,000 rounds a minute. It made a tremendous noise when fired and the ricochet was so great that the wild spray of bullets proved an effective killing machine.

MAC-10s were the gun of choice in so-called turnpike shootouts. Shortly before the Dadeland attack, two Colombians with MAC-10s exchanged machine-gun fire for nearly a mile along I-95.

In the liquor store, part of Jimenez's head was blown away. It would take several days before he was identified and the Miami police learned they had a major drug dealer in the morgue. Hernandez's corpse was so riddled with bullets that the coroner told reporters: "I started counting the holes, but gave up."

The store clerk was hit in the shoulder and feet but made it outside and hid under a parked car.

By the time the Special Homicide Investigation Team (the police called it the SHIT squad) arrived, the gunmen were gone. The van was found abandoned in the rear of the mall, the driver's door open and the motor still running. They had left behind their weapons, including two sawed-off .30 caliber rifles, a .357 magnum pistol, a 12-gauge pump shotgun, and a 9mm handgun. Every gun had been fired. Hundreds of shell casings covered the van floor. Next to the guns were six bullet-proof vests. The van's side panels were reinforced with quarter-inch steel plates.

Dadeland did not just represent the year's thirty-seventh and thirty-eighth drug homicides. The brazen assassination, at midday, in a mall packed with families and ordinary Miamians, was a worrisome escalation. Miami's police chief told a friend that he feared the Colombians were turning Miami into Medellín. The shootings also introduced "cocaine cowboys" to millions of Americans and almost overnight gave South Florida a Wild West reputation. A prominent Miami executive, Arthur Patten, told *Time*: "I've been through two wars and no combat zone is as dangerous as Dade County."

A recent flood of cocaine into South Florida was at the root of a spike in violence and murders. Colombian drug dealers had been dying in interesting ways: one was delivered DOA in a white convertible Cadillac, its engine left running and the car abandoned in front of a hospital emergency room; another was machine-gunned to death while sitting at a traffic light at noontime in upscale Coral Gables; three bodies that had been subjected to horrific torture were discovered in a car's trunk after children playing nearby noticed a terrible stench; a drug distributor was shot to death in front of his family while on a tour boat on Biscayne Bay; and a killer wearing a motorcycle helmet shot a man waiting for his luggage at Miami International Airport, at point-blank range, then jumped on his motorcycle and sped away. "Shootout at the Cocaine Corral," was a *Miami Herald* headline about a restaurant shooting just weeks before the Dadeland chaos.

The crime wave swept mainland Miami and its bedroom suburbs, but initially Miami Beach was spared. The Colombian dealers crossed the bay to party at a few high-end Beach clubs and restaurants, but they did not live, fight for turf, or sell their coke there. The principal reason for this was the Beach's demographics. Elderly retirees on fixed incomes were hardly an untapped market for kilos of uncut coke worth $30,000 wholesale or street grams at $100 each.

In the early to mid-1970s, marijuana had been South Florida's number one drug, imported from Colombia or grown locally in the isolated countryside near the Everglades. South Florida is closer to Colombia than to Chicago. Fishermen received $10,000 to deliver 500-pound burlap-covered bales to Florida's west coast, where dealers loaded up moving vans and made the four-hour road trip to Miami. Fishermen's shacks in poor outposts like Steinhatcher, Everglades City, and Cortez saw a surge in new money. Men like Junior Guthrie, Bubba Capo, and Totch Brown, among others, became local legends, spreading their largesse to the delight of their neighbors and friends. Porsches, pleasure

boats, and gold jewelry appeared in west Florida towns where the average annual income from shrimping was $10,000.

On the east coast, Fort Lauderdale's Amity Yacht Center was one of
the largest marijuana smuggling centers until federal agents closed it in
a 1981 raid that netted 15 tons of grass hidden on dozens of yachts.
Only one person was arrested.

"But eventually there was so much pot," recalls Bob Palumbo, an
ex-DEA agent, "you couldn't sell it since prices dropped so low. So coke
came in."

"Doing coke was glamorous and cool. Everyone wanted it," said Max
Mermelstein, the Colombian cartel's American financial wizard. "It was
a harmless vice, as far as we were concerned. . . . Lawyers' offices, judges'
chambers, movie stars—you name it. In the upper echelon, cocaine was
the way to go." Robert Sabbag, in *Snowblind* (1976), his book about a
cocaine smuggler, wrote: "As inelegant as snorting anything seems to
be, most people who can afford cocaine are not the kinds of people one
is likely to find in public hospitals or listed on police registers. More
likely they are to be found coming out of the Athletic Club or the rear
door of a Rolls. To snort cocaine is to make a statement. It is like flying
to Paris for breakfast."

In Miami, the South American cocaine dealers discovered a town
filled with its own intrigue; Haitians plotting "Baby Doc" coups, Bay of
Pigs veterans talking of overthrowing Castro, Somozistas issuing death
contracts on Sandinistas, Salvadoran exiles forming death squads, and
Voodoo high priestesses dumping headless roosters into the Miami
River.

The introduction of the cocaine trade and its inherent violence was
the end for the fishermen smugglers. Marijuana stayed a potent source
of illegal money but became an adjunct business for coke dealers. A
saying began circulating: a pot deal was done with a handshake while a
coke deal was done with a gun.

Typical of the new breed was the five-foot-two, 200-pound Griselda
Blanco de Trujillo, known variously as the "Black Widow," the "Godmother of Cocaine," or *Muñeca* ("Dollface"). Born in Cartagena, she
had moved to Jackson Heights, Queens, in the 1960s. In 1975, when a
New York grand jury indicted her and forty others for conspiracy to

smuggle 150 kilos, she fled to Miami. Despite a national fugitive arrest warrant, she did not change her name, yet no one found her. A former prostitute, Blanco was married three times to drug dealers who were killed in shootouts. She smuggled her cocaine inside false-bottom shoes, dog cages, hollowed-out coat hangers, girdles, and bras before advancing to larger amounts hidden inside the false walls and ceilings of shipping containers. Like many successful mid-level traffickers, Blanco favored heavy gold- and diamond-encrusted jewelry, and boasted several garish rings and necklaces that she claimed once belonged to Eva Perón. She had such a romantic vision of the American Mafia that she named the youngest of her four sons Michael Corleone Sepulveda. (Three of her four sons were later killed in Colombia, after being deported from the United States.) Blanco's Miami gang was called *Los Pistoleros* ("The Shooters"). It was run by Jorge "Rivi" Ayala, a Chicagoan who had moved to Miami and become a small-time coke dealer before he met Blanco and she enlisted him as her chief enforcer.

Membership in Los Pistoleros required killing someone and slicing off an ear or finger as proof of the murder. It was a Pistolero who first shot a rival with a machine pistol from the backseat of a racing motorcycle. Another Pistolero was renowned for duct-taping the mouths and eyes of his victims, draining their blood into a bathtub, then folding the corpses into large cardboard boxes and delivering them to rival gang leaders or the dead men's families. The Dadeland Mall shooters were Los Pistoleros.

By 1976, Colombia was producing three fourths of the world's cocaine. The major cartels were content to act as producers and wholesalers to syndicates in the States, mob families in northeastern cities, motorcycle gangs in the West, and Cuban traffickers in South Florida. But that year the business changed dramatically after a summit meeting between four families in Medellín, cocaine's Wall Street. They agreed to eliminate American middlemen and send their own soldiers to the United States to integrate their businesses from production to importation and distribution of coke in the world's biggest consumer market. They calculated—correctly, as it turned out—that if they imported higher-quality coke and flooded the U.S. market to lower the prices, the drug's popularity would soar. It was a decision that laid the groundwork for the epidemic of cocaine, and then crack, that would last throughout the eighties.

In 1977, Jorge Luis Ochoa, one of the nephews of Fabio Ochoa, don of a Medellín ruling family, moved to Miami and settled into Kendall. He was the highest-ranking crime family member in the States. Ochoa's cover was managing an import-export firm, Sea-8 Trading, but his real assignment was to control East Coast cocaine distribution for the Colombian families. While there, he met Carlos Lehder, nicknamed "Crazy Carlos," who two years earlier had been deported to Colombia from the United States after serving a federal sentence for smuggling marijuana. Lehder had illegally reentered Miami and become a cocaine smuggler. In six months, he went from moving a couple of kilos monthly to fifty. The cartel was impressed with the twenty-eight-year-old Lehder, and Ochoa had a business proposal. He wanted to begin importing thousands of kilos but lacked a nearby distribution point.

The Colombians were still relying on the old-fashioned method of hiding a few kilos at a time in luggage or on the bodies of low-level smugglers known as "mules." Small aircraft could carry 1,000 kilos every trip, but because of the distance, they could not return to Colombia without refueling. That presented U.S. law enforcement with a chance to monitor South Florida airports and watch for planes that came in from Colombia low on fuel. As a result, some pilots simply left their planes at makeshift South Florida runways. Ten planes had been abandoned by the time Lehder and Ochoa met, a price the cartel considered unacceptably high. A distribution and refueling center close to the United States would allow the planes to make the round-trip with far fewer risks. Ochoa suggested the Bahamas.

By August 1977, Lehder had settled on Norman's Cay, forty miles southeast of Nassau. He turned it into his private island and the cartel's distribution center for all of South Florida. For $1 million cash he purchased the island's western and eastern tips, as well as the hotel, boating club, and clubhouse—all of which he promptly shuttered. He started construction on a forty-yacht marina, as well as a 3,300-foot airstrip, a communications tower, and navigational aids for nighttime landings. He hired two dozen German security guards who patrolled the island in Range Rovers, guns openly displayed, with a complement of Doberman pinschers. (Lehder was fascinated with Hitler.) If visiting boats got too close, Lehder's helicopter usually buzzed them away. His men shot at small airplanes and blocked runways against stray fliers.

The few residents, many of whom had lived there for several generations, did not know what Lehder was up to, but they did not like seeing their island turned into an armed camp. Those who didn't move were told by Lehder to leave. Charles Kehm did not want to go. "If you are not off this island today," Lehder told him, "your wife and your children will die."

That first Christmas, Walter Cronkite, an avid yachtsman, sailed his 42-foot boat into the empty harbor. A man on the pier shouted, "You can't dock here, and you can't dock out there." Cronkite left; at the next island the locals explained to him that Norman's Cay had been taken over by people who did not want visitors.

With the Bahamian authorities looking the other way and the residents scared off, the island was transformed into a stopover and refueling hub for cocaine flights and a safe haven for debauchery by Lehder and his friends. Carlos Toro, Lehder's liaison to government officials and bankers, remembers, "Norman's Cay was a playground. I have a vivid picture of being picked up in a Land Rover with the top down and naked women come to welcome me from my airplane.... And there we partied. And it was a Sodom and Gomorrah . . . drugs, sex, no police . . . you made the rules . . . and it was fun." There were always two women for every man, and some of the parties lasted three days before everyone crashed.

For the 250-pound Jorge Ochoa, nicknamed *El Gordo* ("the Fat Man"), Lehder's takeover of Norman's Cay meant the cartel could now move up to eighty clandestine payloads a day into South Florida. But Ochoa's uncle's inner circle in Medellín had been infiltrated by an informant, and Ochoa and Lehder were soon on the Drug Enforcement Agency's investigative radar.

On October 12, 1977, two years before the Dadeland mall shootout, the DEA set up a sting for Ochoa at the Dadeland Twin Theatres. As drugs and money were being exchanged, thirty heavily armed DEA agents swept in. They arrested nine Colombians, including Jorge's sister and brother-in-law, but Ochoa raced off on a motorcycle. He got away after a harrowing twenty-minute chase that reached 130 mph and caused three massive car pileups.

Despite a red flag security block on his name at every U.S. port of exit, and his picture distributed to all airlines and Customs authorities, Ochoa somehow managed to escape to Colombia. He killed his uncle for allowing a DEA informant to gain the family's trust and took over as don of the Ochoa clan. Every other ranking cartel family member agreed to take extraordinary precautions when in America. Only trusted crime family captains and lieutenants would handle drug handoffs.

In September 1979, after much prodding by the DEA, the Bahamian police raided Norman's Cay and seized large stashes of coke, marijuana, guns, and cash. They arrested thirty-three people, including Lehder. But Lehder had access to millions in Bahamian banks and he made the necessary telephone calls to have some of it immediately distributed to key officials. Within a day, everyone arrested was released on $2,000 bond. Only one conviction was obtained, against a Bahamian who had an unregistered shotgun. A week after the police raid, operations were up and running.

In New York, the Colombians executed a non-violent takeover of the cocaine trade. Instead of waging war, Italian mobsters worked out an agreement with them on distribution and protection in return for a small cut of the profits. But in Miami, the Colombian invasion ignited the cocaine wars. The few pre-Marielito Cuban traffickers did not want to give up their turf, but the Colombians swiftly and brutally carried the day. They did not subscribe to the unwritten Mafia rule that families were off-limits. Anyone remotely related to a target was fair game. When their wives and parents were killed, the Cubans lost their nerve and the battle over territory was over. The ascent of Colombian rivals, mainly the Cali cartel, soon broke the Medellín monopoly and Colombians began to fight among themselves for control of the dope business. Bolivian drug lords controlled whatever cocaine production was left.

Every year starting in 1979, murders in Miami set a record (349 in 1979; 569 in 1980; 621 in 1981). Fifty percent were drug-related; 25 percent died from machine-gun fire; 15 percent were public executions. The Dade County Medical Examiner's Office rented a refrigerated trailer from Burger King to handle the overflow of corpses. In 1980, in the middle of the Mariel and Haitian influx, *Time* named Miami the nation's "crime capital" and the home of the "largest narcotics network in America."

In the year following Mariel, gun sales nearly doubled. By 1981, there were seven registered guns for every Miami-Dade household. The editor in chief of the French *Le Monde* commented that at least "the television broadcasts practical information—the telephone number to call in case one discovers an unidentified body."

Federal authorities estimated that by 1980, 70 percent of all cocaine and marijuana entering the country passed through South Florida. The DEA said the annual Miami dope trade brought in about $12 billion, outpacing the area's two largest legitimate businesses: $11 billion in real estate and $9 billion in tourism. Although Miami had had a reputation for money laundering since the days of the Batista and Somoza dictatorships, an astonishing volume of narco-cash now passed through the city. Miami's Continental Bank was typical of many small independent banks, 70 percent of them Latin American–owned, that had opened in recent years. It averaged $12 million in annual deposits during the mid-1970s. By 1980, it was flooded with more than $600 million. The Federal Reserve branch that covered Miami and Miami Beach had a $5 billion currency surplus, most in fifty- and hundred-dollar bills, larger than the eleven other Federal Reserve banks combined. Federal Reserve districts elsewhere were running deficits.

One of the few complaints from some banks, such as Miami's Great American, was that the cardboard boxes that arrived daily sometimes contained cash that was wet and smelly from having been buried a few weeks. Counting the money was more time-consuming because the wet bills often jammed electronic money machines. It was not uncommon to see men roll a dolly up to a bank with boxes stuffed with money, a deposit slip between their teeth. Isaac Kattan Kassin, a Miami-based money launderer for the Medellín cartel, parked his car outside one bank and went inside to ask the guard to help him carry several large, rope-handled shopping bags filled with cash. When they got back outside, the car had been stolen.

"The money was rolling in so fast and became such a problem because of its volume and bulk," recalled Max Mermelstein, "that just to make things go faster, we used to weigh it—you know, a quick estimate. We'd separate everything in its own denominations. And one bill, U.S. currency, is approximately a gram. So we'd just package it up, weigh it, get a quick estimate of what we had, and when we had time later we'd count it."

Since 1970, the Bank Secrecy Act had required all banks to report cash transactions greater than $10,000; but the rule was almost never enforced and mostly ignored. Surprisingly, money laundering alone was not a crime. Before making a case, investigators had to find a currency transfer violation or a drug connection. By 1980, the IRS had identified twelve people in Miami who had deposited $250 million to $500 million a year in *non-interest-bearing* bank accounts. At another bank, a Colombian walked in with several aides and opened an account with $13 million in cash from suitcases and shopping bags. Restricted by law, the IRS could not share the information with other federal agencies like the DEA or FBI. Even after 1986, when the federal government finally passed the Money Laundering Control Act, placing tighter controls on cash deposits over $10,000 as well as wire transfers and cashier's checks, change was slow. A decade later, 40 of Miami's 250 banks had still failed to regularly report cash transactions greater than $10,000. They incurred fines, but their profits from handling drug money were obviously a sufficient inducement to ignore the law.

The traffickers adapted fast to any legal changes. Once there was some enforcement of the $10,000 threshold, they resorted to "smurfing": literally hundreds of people were paid $500 daily to visit several dozen banks and make deposits of $9,999.*

Eventually, when the dealers realized that the IRS might move against them, they shifted some of the money to offshore accounts in banking havens like Panama, the Isle of Man, and Lichtenstein. At first,

---

* The government would not catch on to this technique until 1992, when it passed a law requiring banks to report "suspicious financial activity" regardless of the amounts involved. Since "suspicious" activity was subjective, some banks continued to operate as drug stash houses. Remarkably, not until 2002 was this law expanded to cover some drug dealers' favorite methods of washing illegal cash, including security and stock trading houses, travelers check and money order firms, and check-cashing outlets.

they didn't even need sophisticated lawyers and accountants. The dealers knew that American law enforcement concentrated on incoming aircraft. Outgoing aircraft was not checked. So couriers carried millions in suitcases and duffel bags—a million in hundreds weighed only 22 pounds—and ignored the legal requirement to fill out a U.S. Customs Currency Report, required if more than $10,000 was being transported. (Only after the 9/11 attacks did a provision in the USA PATRIOT Act make smuggling cash a felony, punishable by five years in prison.)

Some major foreign banks charged a commission to accept the enormous deposits. "They were charging 2 percent to accept a deposit, with a straight face," said Michael Levene, a former Miami tax attorney who served a federal sentence for laundering money for his coke clients. "I can't imagine anyone making a deposit and paying a bank to take their money unless it was illegal."

If the laws regulating banks to prevent dealers from hiding their enormous profits were weak, there were no laws at all to track the money as it was spent. Real estate agents, car and yacht dealers, and jewelers were not required to report large cash transactions. Prosecutors estimated that nearly $100 million in cash was being spent annually in Miami.

The seemingly unlimited flow of money also meant that even if a dealer was arrested, the worst thing he had to worry about was posting bail and returning to South America. In 1980, after many months, DEA agents cracked one of Bolivia's biggest drug rings. Bail for the U.S.-based ringleader was $1 million. He promptly posted it and skipped the country. Forfeiting bail, sometimes within hours of arrest, was simply part of doing business with the cartel. Joe Martino, a mid-level Miami dealer, used to sit in on some of the Colombian meetings after arrests had been made.

"The Colombians never chose their own attorney," Martino says. "They were told who to go to. There were a handful of attorneys that specialized in these cases. And the attorneys would be paid a small amount in a check, so that if anyone later looked, the lawyers could show how much they earned on the record. But they always got ten times that in cash. And that was because everyone knew what was going to happen next. Bail would be set at $500,000 to $600,000, and then the guy arrested would be freed on bail and just go back to Colombia. So every mid-level arrest might cost the Colombians over a million, between the lawyer and bail, but it was better than running the risk of someone going to trial and helping the Feds. And every Colombian who was arrested, they knew if they talked, the dealers would kill his mother and wife, blow up his house, and kill his children." By 1982, one out of every three fugitives tracked by U.S. Marshals had jumped bail on drug cases in Miami. Defense lawyers called them "Colombian acquittals." (Congress eventually overhauled the bail system, requiring defendants to prove that their bail money was not from illegal sources.)

According to Martino, in the few cases in which the judge set no bail, the cartel focused on how to ensure the defendant walked free. In court, top drug lawyers could make a case go away by getting evidence suppressed or persuading juries that government informants and agents were lying. If that didn't work, there were more extreme measures. "I sat in a room where some local dealers argued for an hour whether the offer to a juror should be $200,000 or $250,000. It was crazy. They talked about who they could bribe as insurance, a witness or an assistant prosecutor. And plenty of witnesses against them got killed."

IN THE DEPTHS of a recession, the drug trade provided demand for an estimated 25,000 legitimate jobs in banking, real estate construction, and the service industries. Dade County brought in $400 million extra a year in sales tax receipts. Ten thousand building permits were issued at a time when national construction was at a standstill. More than twenty skyscrapers were erected. "Cocaine was the currency that built that skyline," Alex Daoud told me, while looking at the dense clusters of mainland high-rises across Biscayne Bay.

In Colombia, the cartel members flashed their coke profits because police and government officials were so corrupt that an extravagant lifestyle did not put them at risk. Many brought that same attitude to America—they were entitled to their big homes, private zoos, and stables of exotic cars.

According to one veteran real estate broker, "it was one of the busiest times ever." A single drug dealer bought $20 million in prime Miami real estate. At a time when national interest rates were high and real estate was in a tailspin, South Florida was the only market where housing prices boomed. About one third of all property transactions were all cash.

One real estate agent, who requested anonymity, says: "I had clients who could barely speak English, but they would go house-hunting packed into two or three Mercedes. They always had bodyguards. These dark suits made them stand out like sore thumbs in the bright colors of Miami. And there was very little effort to hide the guns—usually one under their jackets, and when they'd cross their legs you'd see one strapped to the ankle. One house I showed had a fake wall that opened to a steel-encased room. It sold the first day. The biggest cash deal I did was for $1.7 million in Coconut Grove. I thought the seller's lawyers were going to faint when the buyers showed up and started unloading boxes of cash from a van. The most aggravating sale I did was for just over $300,000, where the buyer paid in twenties. We were there half a day counting."

That slow count was atypical. Banks had electronic counting machines that made deposits simple and coke dealers tried to make their big purchases as straightforward as possible. Most dealers stored some of their cash in stash houses—heavily armed homes in suburban Miami. Those 24/7 stash houses took a protection fee, and dealers withdrew the money in packages of exactly 100 bills of the same denomination, making counting it easy. In any case, many local businesses trusted dealers when they said how much cash was in a bag. So much was pouring in there was no reason to cheat anyone on the count.

"I didn't know what was happening until *Scarface* came out," says Sam Robin, a leading international interior designer who moved from Chicago to Miami Beach in 1979. "People were paying you with hundreds of thousands in suitcases. I was clueless. I never knew what someone did for a living. Until they came to pay. All cash. They would send boxes of it. Other times they asked for something that gave it away. 'I want a panel next to my bed where I hit a button and all-metal shutters come down over the windows.' Some wanted bulletproof crawl holes in attics and video surveillance everywhere. One client was a pilot in Coconut Grove. He wanted two safe rooms. He brought me two Halliburton cases with $500,000 in cash. *Scarface* is so true because everything gets magnified when you do that much coke, and everyone, it seemed, was doing it all the time."

Robin says there was no request "too outlandish" for the right price. "No one ever paid me in kilos, but I know others who got paid that way. I think what saved me was that I was into meditation and wasn't smoking or drinking then."

By 1980, the federal government concluded that local police departments and governments were so riddled with corruption that outside intervention was the only way to put heat on the Colombians. The federal salvo was the first multiagency money-laundering task force ever assembled, the U.S. Customs–IRS Operation Greenback. Its goal was to electronically track large cash transactions. Its first seizure was a plane carrying $1.2 million, about to take off from Miami for Colombia. Two Colombian pilots were arrested. The Medellín cartel held the pilots personally responsible for losing the money; each had family members murdered in Colombia.

During its first six months, the operation made several dozen high-profile busts, from a young Colombian woman at Miami International carrying $1.5 million hidden in Monopoly game boxes to Isaac Kattan Kassin, who was charged with laundering $96 million through Great American Bank. It also raided some of the area's fastest-growing institutions such as Bank of Miami and Landmark Bank. Still, the Feds knew they were picking up only a few of the cartel's currency dealers, not stemming the bulk of the illegal cash. And they hit a wall when it came to seizing the assets of drug dealers. Before a seizure, the government had to prove the asset was derived from the dope trade. A lucrative specialty had developed among dozens of South Florida accountants and lawyers who employed sophisticated strategies that stymied investigators. Yachts, cars, and homes were often owned by Delaware corporations, which in turn were owned by offshore companies whose directors were anonymous. Tying direct ownership of the asset to the drug dealer who was using it became almost impossible.

"The more layers of insulation you place between the investigator and the ultimate asset, the more difficult it is," says Michael Zeldin, chief of the Anti–Money Laundering/Trade Sanctions team at the international accounting firm Deloitte. "A major part of the problem was that there were so many professionals and public officials who benefited from the drug trade and simply did not see themselves as part of the problem. They were blinded by all the money." Cocaine corruption ran deep. Four Miami mayors were indicted and three of them convicted. Most of the police academy class of 1980 would be dead, indicted, in jail, or fired by 1990.

CHAPTER 9

The Players

FOR THE AVERAGE coke dealer, Operation Greenback was a non-event. It did not change the way dealers did business or how they spent their money.

Before his arrest in Miami on a New York murder charge, forty-nine-year-old Jose Antonio Cabrera Sarmiento was typical of mid-level dealers. He swaggered around Miami sporting a solid gold necklace with a six-inch medallion with his nickname "Pepe" emblazoned in diamonds. He said his money came from his family's phantom casino and real estate holdings in Colombia. He bought his $37,000 Mercedes 450SL and his $135,000 Rolls-Royce with attaché cases of cash. He paid cash for his condos and plane and $700,000 in hundreds for his 60-foot Hatteras yacht. When he was arrested in a Miami Beach disco in 1980, he had $8,400 in cash in his pockets, nine emeralds worth $500,000, and so much gold jewelry that a U.S. attorney said it would have kept "him well anchored in a hurricane."

Sarmiento's arrest did not make local news: there were too many like him. Edgar Blanco was the Medellín cartel's point man in Miami. He was a nightlife fixture, with a fleet of cars, half a dozen bodyguards, and many different girlfriends. He could often be seen floating around Biscayne Bay on his yacht, brazenly titled *Captain White*. (He returned to Colombia in late 1981 after jumping bail for having smoked grass and snorted coke in the first-class section of a commercial flight to Los Angeles.)

Jon Roberts was a former nightclub owner who moved to Miami at age twenty-five and ended up distributing $2 billion in cocaine for the Medellín cartel. When he arrived in the early seventies, as he explained,

"Miami back then was the South. It was like Alabama. There was no money here. There were no big buildings. Downtown was pretty barren. Miami Beach, it was a lot of old people sitting around on rocking chairs waiting to die. It was a whole different world down here back then. Like a virgin city. It was wide open." Roberts became friends with Mercury Morris, a star running back for the Miami Dolphins who later went to jail for drug possession. The 1979 Super Bowl between the Dallas Cowboys and the Pittsburgh Steelers was held in Miami.

"Two nights before," recalled Roberts to a reporter, "I've got the whole front line of the Pittsburgh Steelers in my house. They all sat down and: 'Come on, come on. Break the shit out. Break the shit out.' They partied, and they really partied hard. I mean, you have no idea what these guys would go through. I'm saying, 'You guys are going to go out tomorrow and play football?'

" 'Yeah, and we're going to win.' "

The partying Steelers won 35 to 31.

Roberts's partner was Mickey Munday, "a redneck from South Florida," who all told would fly in 38 tons of cocaine from Colombia to Miami. A Ford Agency model whom Roberts was dating had introduced him to Munday, and together they built two runways and hangars that looked like barns. They had their own towing company and hauled cars loaded with cocaine to Colombian wholesalers throughout South Florida. At their height, in the early eighties, the duo made $1 million a week. They were taking in cash so fast they didn't always have time to get the latest payoffs to a bank or stash house, so they left large garbage bags, each holding between $700,000 and $1 million, scattered on their lawns. "I simply had nowhere to put it," says Roberts. "Nobody was questioning anything. My neighbor was getting ten kilos a week; the neighbor across the street was getting twenty. I had three Cigarettes [speedboats], two Cougars, and a helicopter in the backyard. I would fly to the racetrack. I'd land to see my horses run. I had forty to fifty horses at a time. It's $50,000 a month just to feed them. At the Forge you'd spend $20,000 a night. It was like waste. It was nothing, the money."

Max Mermelstein came from a working-class Brooklyn family and moved to Florida in 1978. He married a Colombian girl whose family was in the coke business. For the next seven years he moved 56 tons of coke into South Florida and recycled hundreds of millions in dirty profits back to Colombia and into front businesses across America. Mermelstein was the only non-Latin ever to sit in on the cartel's council meetings in Medellín, and eventually he answered only to Pablo Escobar, who was now so brazen he owned a seasonal home in Miami. (At the time he was in Miami, Escobar, whose motto was "Gold or lead," was mistakenly identified by the FBI as only a mule. Less than a decade later, *Forbes* listed him as the world's seventh-richest person.)

"I made it snow in Florida," boasted Mermelstein.

Many of those in the coke trade ended up in jail, dead, or back in Colombia. Others partied on their stash and burned themselves out. A few who were "players" are today prominent Miami Beach businessmen or real estate tycoons. Their days in the drug business are a hidden part of their past.

"I earned $3,000 a key [kilo] for bringing it in," boasts Julio Bermudez,* a Cuban who arrived in Miami in the mid-1970s and within a few years earned a reputation as the best "low-ride boatman" in Florida. "It meant that I could run a Cigarette in shallower water than anyone else, and no one, not even the best Coast Guard skipper, could touch me."

His pay came in bags and boxes of cash.

"Two hundred and fifty thousand in twenties weighed 76 pounds," says Bermudez. "We knew that. You just had to make certain that if you were picking up money, no one had wet a lot of the bills and then covered them with dry ones. The water made the money heavier and you could lose up to 10 percent off the count. There were stories about guys who got burned that way, but I never did."

Today, Bermudez is retired. He saved enough from his drug-dealing days to buy a dozen million-dollar-plus apartments in South Beach's best buildings. He is still on the party scene—his waterfront town house has a floor-to-ceiling dance pole for strippers—but he has never

---

* The names Julio Bermudez, Bobby Weinstein, and Joe Martino and those of their family members and associates are pseudonyms. The three men have cooperated fully in retelling their stories, and I have corroborated their stories through my own reporting. But they requested that none of them be identified by their real names.

used the drug that made his fortune. "Too many guys went down partying with their own stash," he told me.

The boat on which Bermudez earned his fame was built by his friend
Don Aronow. The six-foot-two, 215-pound Aronow was a former Coney
Island lifeguard who was once invited to take a screen test for Tarzan. A
world champion speedboat racer, he developed four speedboats that redefined the powerboat industry: Formula, Donzi, Magnum, and Cigarette, the last and most popular named after a Prohibition-busting boat
that ruled the New York shoreline in the 1920s. Aronow, who counted
among his clients the kings of Spain, Sweden, and Jordan and the
Kuwaiti Emir, had a lock on the South Florida drug trade.

"Don was a genius when it came to boat design," says Bermudez.
"But one of the reasons I hung out with him was that he also knew
how to party. I love to fuck. But Don made me seem like nothing. He
was unstoppable. When we used to hang out at his office, he had a
false wall inside a closet. And when you pushed on it in the right way,
it opened and led to a room with just a bed, a mirrored ceiling,
and a marble shower. It was his secret fuck room. He'd have four or
five women sometimes a day. He had pictures of himself on the wall
taking the Beatles around Miami in one of his boats. The guy was my
hero."

Aronow's circle wasn't limited to drug runners like Bermudez. He
was also friends with most of Miami Beach's power brokers. One of his
best friends was Al Malnik, whom he'd met back in the early 1960s
when Malnik owned the Sir John Hotel. In 1968, Malnik purchased the
Old Forge restaurant on 41st Street in the heart of Miami Beach. Back
in the Roaring Twenties, the Forge was a real blacksmith shop owned by
artisan Dino Phillips. In the thirties, Phillips turned it into a sophisticated dinner-dancing club and gambling casino whose patrons included Judy Garland, Arthur Godfrey, and Walter Winchell. By the time
Malnik bought it, elegance had given way to disrepair. Only twenty-five
blocks south of the Forge, but a world apart, was poverty-ridden South
Beach and the Art Deco District. Aronow and his friends would never
have contemplated spending any time there. It was off the radar for the
coke trade.

"Who would have wanted to go there?" asks Joey Martino. "It was a dive. The buildings were all run-down and it was filled with Cubans fresh off the boat and old people counting out their days. It was No-wheresville."

Malnik demolished the restaurant and started from scratch. He filled the 30,000 square feet with European antiques, what he dubbed "a bit of Ludwig of Bavaria." It included stained glass from New York's Trinity Church, crystal chandeliers from the White House during the Madison administration, Tiffany lamps, and French paneling. A large oil painting of a reclining nude dominated the main dining room. Malnik bought a 12-foot Victorian fireplace, imposing sconces from Napoleon's Waterloo headquarters, German and Italian tapestries, and artworks by Dalí, Le Douanier, and Rousseau. The new Forge also included an enormous wine cellar—300,000 bottles, some of the rarest vintages. An 1822 Château Lafite Rothschild Pauillac was priced at $10,000 on the menu (today the bottle is worth $150,000).

When the new Forge opened in 1969, one critic pronounced it "bordello meets Louis XVI," but the steakhouse food was good, if expensive. It was a hit and became the town's new hot spot. Malnik then opened a nightclub nearby, the Penthouse, to catch the Forge patrons who wanted to party till dawn. Next there was Club 41, a $5,000-a-year, membership-only restaurant next to the Forge, in a former bank. It was Miami's most expensive restaurant. The hostesses wore Valentino and Dior gowns. When guests approached the steel front door, a slit opened as in speakeasy days, and they had to show their membership card. The ultramodern interior was the opposite of the ornate Forge. The dining room was in the vault, with glass tables, clear china, brushed stainless steel walls, and neon lighting around the ceiling's edge. In this pre–cell phone era, every table had a telephone jack in the floor.

"I had been on the job a few months when the Eagles [the pop group] came in and had dinner," recalls Stephen Hass, a captain at the Forge. "The general manager had to make an exception to let them in since they arrived wearing only T-shirts and jeans. But they drank '59 Margauxs and '61 Lafites and ran up a $14,000 bill. You could spot the cocaine cowboys. Ninety percent were Latinos. They drank champagne all night, and no matter how much food they ordered, they never ate it. When the bill arrived, they always counted out the cash under the table. You'd watch them as they peeled off bills from this enormous wad of money. The average drug table tab would be between $4,000 and $6,000, and they'd leave $1,000 for waiters. I made a ridiculous amount of money when I worked the door. In 1980, $100 meant you had to wait and $500 got you right in. We had to say no to one guy whose money was all moldy; he must have had it buried."

Whenever Aronow visited Florida, he hung out at the Forge or the Eden Roc's Mona Lisa Room. Aronow had landed in the middle of Miami cool. Movie director Brett Ratner (*Rush Hour, X-Men: The Last Stand*) grew up a block from the Forge, was mentored by Malnik, and still calls him Dad. "I remember seeing him [Aronow] at the Cricket Club, which Al owned," recalled Ratner. "It attracted a cross section of Miami—drug dealers and movie stars and racers—you name it. Guys would bet on tennis games and then race their Cigarettes in Biscayne Bay. Every one of them wanted to be Don Aronow. He had style, he was handsome, women adored him, he had money, and he went 100 miles an hour."

Aronow tested high-speed prototypes without any protective gear, twice jumping from burning fiberglass hulls just before the boats exploded. He took racing risks others avoided, jumping waves, running dangerously close to razor-sharp reefs, and challenging racers to risk collisions if they tried passing him. He had won his first world championship before he moved to Miami, and his racing reputation helped market his boats. He sold his Donzis to LBJ, the Secret Service, and the Israeli navy, which used them as high-speed attack boats against the Egyptians in the 1967 Six-Day War.

But it was his 1969 design, the Cigarette, with its combination of sex appeal and speed, that became an international brand. Early buyers included Richard Nixon, the fugitive financier Robert Vesco, Haiti's "Papa Doc," and U.S. Ambassador to the United Nations George H. W. Bush. When King Hussein visited Miami, Aronow set him up with women and sold him fourteen speedboats.

"It was like buying a Ferrari," says Bermudez. "And if you had lots of cash, it was never your only boat. You had a luxury yacht for the family and friends, and then the Cigarette to impress the boys and some women. When I would take a girl out in that boat, she was ready to fuck after a few minutes. It was a turn-on."

A former Aronow employee says that by the late 1970s, half the boats sold were cash deals. The office would sometimes have $1 million in suitcases. Aronow did not ask about his buyers' work. "But there was no doubt," says the employee. "We all knew who the cash boys were, and what those boats were being used for."

Mermelstein had convinced the cartel to make open-water drops after an old marijuana smuggler told him that during the early seventies, pot from Jamaica was often bundled and dropped offshore for pickup. Because of increased radar and surveillance, sea drops were sometimes safer than flying directly into South Florida. Good speedboat operators like Bermudez quickly became an indispensable part of the trade, picking up the dope dropped by freighters in the Gulf of Mexico or by planes in the Caribbean. Nothing could keep up with an 80 mph Cigarette.

Many South Florida racers on the multi-million-dollar powerboat circuit were seduced by drug profits. Hallandale's Joseph "Joey" Ipolito, Jr., the 1977 offshore powerboat rookie of the year, smuggled marijuana. Fort Lauderdale's Bill Elswick carried cocaine; Eddie Trotta laundered money; and Robert Sheer smuggled marijuana. Miami's Guillermo "Willie" Diaz, who won two world titles, was charged with conspiracy to import, but the charges were dismissed because of an illegal wiretap. Over the next few years, champion speedboater George Morales became another cocaine smuggler while winning race after race. "Willy" Falcon and Salvador Magluta were Cuban-born racing champions who ran one of the country's largest coke-smuggling operations, worth $2.1 billion by the time they were eventually arrested in 1991.

"The druggies would land in there nightly," said John Crouse, a former powerboat race organizer. "At one time, two thirds of the people involved in offshore powerboat racing were directly or indirectly involved in drugs. You had guys racing boats without any source of in- come—or at least not any source that was reportable."

"We in the ocean-racing fraternity are flattered that the dope run- ners prefer our kind of boat," Aronow told *Sports Illustrated* in 1979, "but when they get caught we don't like it. We have torn emotions. A kid who works for me was offered $100,000 to run out to sea one night and resupply fuel for a dope boat. He refused, but it must have been a terrible temptation. Heck, lately we've been getting letters from jail- birds, asking for complete specs and prices on our Cigarettes."

"The legit racers were risking their careers," says Bermudez. "But it was so much money. And Don would build the boat just like you wanted it, so it put the odds on your side. The boats were hollowed out, stripped into just a shell that had as much room as possible for cargo. I spent $900,000 on a boat that listed for $100,000. But it earned me mil- lions.

"We were handling hundreds of keys a week, and we'd work in a ring. Four of us would go to a drop point, which was given to us only on the day of the pickup. We'd get some radar help from anti-Castro Cubans who checked the waters off South Florida. They'd give us a heads-up on anything coming our way, just in case the Coast Guard had a tip, or got lucky. And if we ever saw a government ship, we'd split off in different directions. Only one of us would have the dope, so the Feds had to guess which one. The odds weren't in their favor. Most of the time, we picked up near the Bahamas and made the seventy-mile trip in less than an hour. We always arrived at night in Miami. Lookouts with binoculars watched from the high floors of nearby condos. Some- one else monitored the police bands to let us know if there was any problem."

Bermudez says the largest smuggling day every year was Super Bowl Sunday. "That was the one day you knew that every fucking cop and Fed in South Florida was glued to a TV. You could make runs for hours without any problem. Football season in general was good every Sun- day. You knew you had an easier time during any Dolphins game be- cause senior agents set their schedules so they could watch the game. That left rookies, and we liked that." (Bermudez noted that another standout smuggling day was the Pope's 1987 visit to Miami, when law enforcement was diverted en masse for the pontiff's security.)

"Not everything was profit," he adds. "I had four policemen and a judge on a regular retainer. These guys were making $40,000 a year if they were lucky. I could double it with one suitcase. I learned it's true that everyone has a price, especially in Miami. They saw our lifestyle and they wanted it, so bribing them was easy. And why should I run the risk of having to be lucky all the time? They were my insurance in case I ever got in trouble."

One night in 1980, partying at Malnik's Forge, Bermudez recognized a large table of Colombian coke dealers. One was known locally for describing a $3 million payment as "petty cash." There were the requisite flashy girls—dresses too tight, breasts too large, lipstick too bright. The table was stacked with magnums of Dom Pérignon.

But one stranger grabbed his attention. "He could have been forty years old or sixty, you couldn't tell," recalls Bermudez. "And he stood out because instead of the tan everyone else had, he had this almost gray skin color. He didn't look well."

Bermudez later learned that the man was the dealers' guest of honor. Humberto Sanchez Butiago was the Medellín cartel's best "cook," capable of producing powdered cocaine at purity unmatched by rivals. His pallor was the result of years in coke labs, absorbing vapors of the hydrochloric acid, ether, and acetone integral to converting coca leaves to street-level cocaine. But as Bermudez discovered, "he was proud of it. For him, it was the proof that he was the master chemist."

Below the high-risk speedboat pilots and key players from Medellín at the Forge were many more mid-level hustlers who stumbled into the business. Joe Martino owns one of Miami Beach's most successful real estate firms, South Florida's largest selling high-end practice. In the late 1970s, he was the maître d' at several popular hangouts, including Al Malnik's Cricket Club and the popular Jockey Club.

"I used to get people coming into my restaurant," he says, "and they would hand me a shopping bag and ask me to put it in the office until they finished lunch. All you had to do was to look inside and you'd see a kilo wrapped in plastic wrap and duct tape. I'm not kidding.

The first time it happened, around 1978, I just put it on the top shelf of our coatroom. When the guy left, he gave me a $500 tip. I guess the word went out pretty quickly because soon a lot of players felt comfortable enough to come and bring along stuff that they later had to drop off."

The following year, Joe asked one of the dealers if he could get an advance on some coke to sell it himself. "The guy came back a day later and fronted me a kilo worth about $50,000. 'Pay me after you sell it,' he told me."

Joe unloaded it to friends and customers at the restaurant. In a week, he had paid the dealer for the kilo and pocketed an $80,000 profit.

"I never looked back."

Dressed in Fila tracksuits and covered in gold chains and finger rings, the short, stocky Italian from New Jersey used his contacts at the Cricket Club to build up a solid clientele. "I'm a compulsive workaholic," he says, "so when I decided this was my next business, I just worked harder than anyone else." By 1980, he had met Juan Diaz, who was only one notch under Max Mermelstein. Joe's coke deliveries began arriving at his town house in a Publix van (South Florida's largest grocery chain). "Mine were the first American hands on the cocaine," he says.

He handled transfers to mid-level Miami traffickers, pocketing big payoffs for every meeting. And Joe had grown up with some kids who had become gangsters in New Jersey and New York. "Guys like Vincent 'Jimmy Blue Eyes' Alo [a mob captain in the Genovese family] were our heroes. So it wasn't very hard for me to get in touch with the right guys. They knew and trusted me, and soon I was moving kilos to them. My stuff was top quality and it replaced their Miami sources, who were stepping on it first."

Soon his main supplier trusted him to make dozens of runs to Vegas, carrying two large duffel bags of cash every trip. Joe was a heavy gambler, as was Diaz. "I am not kidding you," Joe says. "Sometimes I'd bet another player $5,000 on which girl at a bar would go to the bathroom first. I'd bet on anything.

"And in Vegas, we'd bet $20,000 to $50,000 a hand in poker. There was a closed-off room for big-time players, and it was just a few coke dealers and some Chinese guys who had tons of money and loved gambling."

Diaz would pay Joe when he returned to Miami. "The first time he gave me an envelope to say thanks," he recalls, "it was bursting with hundreds." One time he was given the keys to someone's BMW.

"I was living the life," he says now. "Since you are getting paid in suitcases of cash, you always think there's another one coming along. So I didn't save a penny. My tax returns showed $15,000 a year in income. And I was spending that sometimes in a night." He became known locally as "Joey Double"—the town's most outlandish tipper—because his trademark was to double the bill wherever he went. "And it was real money. I'd go to the Forge and spend $5,000 and I'd leave $10,000."

Six nights a week, two limousines arrived at Joe's town house. He followed a regular routine, and friends knew which clubs he'd be at during the night. "By the time we ended up at the bottle clubs at six or seven in the morning, the limos were filled with girls. And I'd fuck every one of them by the end of the night."

He would take 20 eight-balls (eighth-of-an-ounce packages) with him. "Those were going for $200 each, and we'd go through all of them." In his pocket, he'd carry a ziplock with coke. "Not one of those silly little bags that people had, but I'd have a large one with six or eight ounces. When I had enough champagne, usually by three a.m., it was time to start on the coke.

"Guys used to come out of the bathroom with me and they'd have white shit all over their shoulders, all down the back of their neck. And people used to say, 'What the fuck is he doing, sticking his face in the shit?,' but I used to grab it out of the bag and put it in a mound and pass it in front of everyone's nose. The shit used to go everywhere. I'd go through 1,000 grams for a weekend, it didn't matter. I partied like an animal."

At the Coconut Grove's Mutiny, Joe did lines of coke on the table. No one said anything to him. He convinced the management at Faces, another Coconut Grove club, to put a double lock on the bathroom door so no one could disturb him and his friends. When the restaurants and clubs employed bathroom attendants, Joe gave them $500 to stand guard outside. "These were guys who were living in

$200-a-month apartments," he says. "They would have done anything for me."

Johnny Diaz, a dealer from Tampa (no relation to his supplier), was one of Joe's friends. When Diaz visited Miami, they would go to a club and order four or five jeroboams of champagne. "One night we ended up driving in his limo to one of his Boca safe houses, and we did some serious partying with girls for about eighteen hours." The next day, two Colombians, neither of whom spoke English, drove Joe back to Miami, sandwiched between two 55-gallon drums of acetone. "I thought we'd either be pulled over any minute by the cops or we'd get in a wreck and the car would explode."

One night he pulled up to the Forge, couldn't stop in time, and rear-ended a police car. "A lot of coke does something to your mind," Joe explains. "It makes you feel like no one can touch you. I got out of my car and just threw the cop my keys. 'I'll take care of you when I get out,' I told him. And it was so fucking crazy back then that he just stood there and let me go in."

The cop left a card with his telephone number on Joe's BMW. Joe called him the next day and personally dropped off an envelope with $5,000. "That was not only to make up for hitting his squad car, but I now knew I had another friend on the Miami Beach police."

MOST MIAMIANS IN the cocaine trade were not high-ranking Colombians or self-made mid-level traffickers. They started by partying with cocaine and then became dealers to earn money to support their habit. Although they operated at a lower level than Joe Martino, they were just as deeply caught up in the business.

Bobby Weinstein's story is that of a thousand players, but the difference is that he not only survived but today at sixty is one of the Beach's most prominent advertising and finance executives. Looking fifteen years younger than his years, he has a "killer wardrobe," drives a $100,000 silver two-seater Mercedes, and is a regular fixture on the Beach's social scene.

In the early seventies, at law school in his native Philadelphia, Bobby smoked grass and dealt a little on the side to pay for his own supply. "It was cool and hip," he told me over lunch at Joe's Stone Crab, "and I hung with the hip crowd. We were gambling, fooling around, and grass was part of living that lifestyle. Moving a few ounces gave me more money."

After law school, in 1978, he moved to Miami, following a friend who told him it was the best place to make money and party. Although Bobby was married and had an infant son, the descriptions of a sybaritic town were too much to resist.

Bobby rented an apartment in South Miami. His next-door neighbor was a Cuban. One day at the pool, his neighbor pulled out a salt shaker from a little pouch, screwed off the top, and poured half the bottle onto a plastic plate. "About ten friends around the pool came over," recalls Bobby, "and the next thing I know, we're all passing around the plate doing monster lines of the most unbelievable coke I had ever come across. It took me about a month to figure out that out of six neighbors on my floor, five were dealing coke. One of them was dealing keys, he was the big-time player, one guy specialized in ounces, and the rest were eight-ball traders."

When some Philadelphia friends visited, Bobby asked his Cuban neighbor, Jose, if he could get some coke for partying. The neighbor gave him two ounces. "I was stunned," says Bobby. "But that's how it was. It was a credit business. No cash up front. Either they trusted you or not. Whatever I made over his price was mine to keep."

Bobby did not even have a scale. So the night before his friends arrived, he and his wife, Lisa, snorted coke and stayed up splitting the large bag of coke into eight-balls and grams.

"We took Sweet'N Low packets," he recalls. "They were one gram each. And we emptied them into plastic baggies, and then we'd put the coke into other baggies and hold them in separate hands to see if the weight felt the same. We were such fucking amateurs, it wasn't funny."

But his coke was a big hit with his friends. They stayed up nearly the entire weekend, and when they left, they bought what was left. He paid Jose on Monday and had an $8,000 profit.

"I figured I had just hit the lottery," he says.

Within two months, Bobby was selling several ounces weekly. He did not take the Florida bar exam and instead landed a job as a salesman at a gold and silver dealer. Many of his co-workers became his new customers. "My quality was real good," he says with pride. "I would step on it only two times, and there were dirtbags out there stepping on it thirty or forty times."

His Colombian neighbor showed him how to test the coke's quality. "I always took a penknife and scrapped the inside of the plastic bag that had the coke," Bobby explained. "Pure coke will not stick to plastic. It's the cut used to stretch it that sticks to the bag. If my blade was clean after I scraped the bag, that was a good sign." Larger dealers tested samples in vials of Clorox: impurities dropped to the bottom while a yellowish oil slick that indicated pure coke floated to the top.

After a while, Bobby could tell the quality by tasting it, determining if it was too bitter or sweet, indicating whether the coke had been cooked too long under sunlamps. And he knew that human skin absorbs pure coke. "I'd rub some powder on my hand, and if there was some residue left after thirty seconds, I knew that was the shit that had been used to step on it."

Bobby realized that he was getting coke that was already cut. In 1979 and 1980, Max Mermelstein and a handful of others sold pure dope from Colombia and Bolivia for $30,000 a kilo to mid-level Colombian drug dealers, who then cut it by an average of 20 percent with powdered vitamin B, quinine, or amphetamines. They resold to the next tier of dealers at $30,000, still claiming that the kilos were "pure." Their profit was the 20 percent from the cut, and they moved hundreds of kilos. By the time the coke had passed through several more buyers and reached the street, single grams were cut at least 50 percent and sold at $80 to $100 each. Each original $30,000 kilo had earned more than $500,000.

Some brands, like Peruvian flake, were in high demand. "Some of the Peruvian stuff was like diamonds," says Bobby. "It was beautiful and commanded a higher price because there was a snob value to having it at a party." By this time, he was snorting daily. And Lisa had become a heavy user.

"At that time, none of us thought it was addictive," he says. "Lisa was partying a lot. She was more fucked than I knew, using it not just with me, but most of the time when I wasn't around. I remember taking my eighteen-month-old kid with me to work one day because she wanted to go shopping on her own for a few hours. Later I learned she just stayed in the house doing coke."

But Bobby didn't complain. He was partying as if he were single. "Everyone, I am not overstating this, almost everyone in Miami did coke," he says. "I knew lawyers, restaurant owners, real estate developers, doctors, you name it. It cut across every profession, every social class. And a lot of it was not just the money, really, it was also all about the girls. Coke did something to girls' brains. On Quaaludes they would lose inhibitions. But on coke they would do anything, 'suck me, fuck me,' anything for a hit."

At nightclubs like Manhattan in South Miami, Ménage at the Brickell Bay Club, and Scaramouche at the Omni Hotel, he and his friends brought small brown bottles each holding a gram. Half of the bottles had white caps and half black. "The black ones were for the girls," he recalls. "They were cut with 60 percent baby powder. They'd go through five bottles in the first half hour. The white tops were the good ones, not stepped on. Those were for me and the boys."

In 1979, a year after moving to South Florida, Bobby celebrated in a private room in the back of one of the town's most popular nightclubs: Manouche. Twenty friends split half a pound of pure coke and eight magnums of Dom Pérignon.

"If my traditional Jewish parents had seen my circle of friends then, they would have fainted." It was a mixture of low-level Cuban and Colombian drug dealers and another half dozen Miamians who were party-circuit regulars. Bobby had graduated from selling eight-balls to ounces to kilos. He was not only celebrating his anniversary in Florida but marking his move up in the coke trade. His Cuban neighbor felt so comfortable with him that when Bobby needed more coke, he just left a plastic-wrapped kilo in a shopping bag at his front door.

By this time they had weekend orgies involving up to twenty swingers. Bobby, afraid that his wife would overindulge from his stash, hid it from her. "It was a business, and I wasn't going to let her snort away all our profits."

They argued a lot. In one coke-fueled fight, Lisa threatened to tell the cops everything. The next day, he told his neighbor about Lisa's threat.

" 'If she's going to spill the beans, we will have to put her into a canal,' " Jose responded. "He was deadly fucking serious."

The Dadeland shooting occurred a week after Lisa's threat. "That scared the shit out of her," Bobby says. "I told her we'll get a divorce and I'll have partial custody of the kid. She moved into an apartment a few blocks away. I went to pick up my son a week later, and she was gone and the house was empty."

A neighbor told Bobby she had left an hour earlier with several suitcases. He raced to Miami International and frantically checked the boarding gates for any flight leaving for Philadelphia. He found her just as she was about to board.

"I tried grabbing my kid, and she started screaming. The cops came over. I couldn't make a big scene, I had coke on me and I was high, and I couldn't risk being taken in. I just watched as they got on the plane. It was their last time in Miami."

Losing his wife and son was not enough to stop Bobby from moving deeper into Miami's coke world. He had a two-bedroom luxury condo in a posh bayside neighborhood, Cocoplum, that DEA agents referred to as "Cocaineplum" because so many Colombian dealers lived there. He bought a Jaguar convertible and partied at Mutiny and Faces in the Grove.

"There were probably a thousand guys like me," he says. "We were all caught up with coke and we were carving out small businesses."

Shortly after his wife left, he met Katie, a petite flight attendant. "Katie was gorgeous. And if you were dating me, you had to be into my scene. It took me a couple of days to realize that she could help me expand my business by bringing dope up north on her flights and taking cash back. There was no security for the airline workers, nothing then, so it was a breeze."

What Bobby didn't know was that local prosecutors already suspected pilots and stewardesses for Air Florida and Eastern were ferrying cocaine regularly for dealers. But every attempt to build a case fizzled. Inside the Miami State Prosecutor's office, Air Florida was dubbed "Air Cocaine." Years later, prosecutors proved that pilots like Eastern's Skip Coltin and TWA's Adler Berriman "Berry" Seal spent their off days flying private planes crammed with hundreds of kilos to improvised runways throughout South Florida. Unfinished suburban subdivisions—places like North Port or Cape Coral—with miles of paved streets and half-finished homes, became clandestine airports. The unique buzz of low-flying DC-3s was a common nighttime sound in towns near the Everglades.

Eventually, dozens of Eastern employees were arrested for smuggling more than $1.5 billion in coke. (One pilot, Gerald Loeb, described how a cartel-run freight company at Miami International Airport loaded crates of cash onto his flights, and that upon arrival in Panama the jet was met by armored cars and military officers who took the crates. When Loeb told the FBI, Eastern fired him.)

"I knew I couldn't get bigger because I didn't have a New York connection, and that was the key to becoming a big player," says Bobby. "But I had the Philadelphia connection. In addition to my Florida business, I was moving a key a month, sometimes two keys, up north."

Bobby was selling to northern dealers at a 25 percent premium. Katie would hide it in her luggage. Sometimes, Bobby traveled as a passenger on flights she worked.

"I would break a kilo into six packages of six ounces each," he recalls, "and I would seal the plastic bags and tape it around my legs and chest. People loved rocks, so I'd always try and make sure that each bag had some rocks, not all powder. And I'd wear sweatpants and an Adidas top, sportswear that fit loose so nothing would look lumpy. One time I taped a thousand Quaaludes to me."

His sales book listed dates, amounts, and the customer. It included partners at prestigious law firms, doctors at the city's premier hospitals, and a few politicians who publicly decried the outbreak of drugs in South Florida.

On one return to Florida, his attaché case slipped out of his hand.

It sprung open and $60,000 in hundreds spilled across the terminal's polished floor. Two policemen questioned him for a few minutes, but Bobby said he often carried a lot of cash since he was a gold and silver dealer. The two cops helped him neatly repack the money into the case.

"And they both took my business card," Bobby says. "About a week later, one of them called and asked if I might ever need anything. He said he could supply me with the highest-quality coke, stuff that had been confiscated and was stored in police evidence lockups. It was so fucking tempting to say yes." Some of South Florida's biggest coke dealers had direct lines into the Miami police. Dealers gave tips to cops about their rivals, and the police did the dirty work by busting them. Much of the seized coke would eventually be replaced with baby powder and moved back to the street. "But I wasn't introduced to this cop by anyone I trusted," says Weinstein. "It could have been a setup. So although I really wanted to say yes, I passed."

One time, Bobby was flying back from Philadelphia and had $200,000 in a duffel bag. The money was covered with a few shirts. As he passed through security, the X-ray machine operator pulled him over. A state trooper unzipped the bag and pulled out the clothes.

"There was this moment of silence," Bobby says. "Here I am, about to catch a flight to Miami and with a bag of cash." But again he produced his gold and silver dealer ID and a concealed weapons permit. They held the plane for half an hour before letting him board with his cash.

"They didn't make me fill out a form, sign anything. I expected the IRS or cops to be at the gate when I arrived in Miami, but nobody was there. No one."

Instead, he was met by a Colombian dealer who took the cash and, at his car in the airport garage, gave Bobby his cut.

"Let me tell you," Bobby says, "on every fucking plane coming in and out of Miami to New York, there was someone like me with a bag."

Meanwhile, Katie's co-workers all wanted to become part of his "cocaine express."

"The first time another stewardess asked me if she could carry dope for me, I thought it was a setup. But I knew if they didn't party, then forget about it. But once they got naked with you and took the blow, then I knew it was okay. I was running half a dozen stewardesses in a couple of months. And to make extra sure that Katie and her friends weren't tempted to screw with me, I'd always give her $1,000 a trip as a tip, and an extra half an ounce on top of it for her and her friends."

Bobby's reputation as a reliable dealer grew. One client trusted him to temporarily store a Chagall painting, *Bride and Groom*, worth about $1.5 million. "I didn't know if it was stolen, I didn't want to know." He propped it against a wall in his house. One night, Katie came back from a flight from New York. "She was so excited because her run had gone so easily." She had just earned $10,000. Bobby and some friends were freebasing. When Katie came through the unlocked door, she started to do cartwheels. "And I saw her heading right toward the Chagall, and all I could think was that I was a dead man," recalls Bobby, who managed to tackle her just in time. "And all we could do was laugh. Except for that split second of worry, we were so stoned that almost nothing bothered us."

One of Bobby's neighbors, Mark Fleischmann, owned one of South Florida's Quaalude clinics. "He was living big, like we all were, but he was going through cash real fast." Late one Friday, during August, there was a knock on Bobby's door. It was Fleischmann. Suddenly Bobby was pushed inside and two armed men rushed in behind him. They shoved Katie to the ground, hit Bobby on the head with a pistol, and kicked him when he fell to the floor.

" 'Don't fucking look up!' they screamed. I thought we were going to die," Bobby recalls. "People were killing you for coke."

The gunmen handcuffed Bobby and Katie to the bathroom toilet. One of them pushed his head into the toilet.

" 'If you fucking say a word, I'll come back here and drown you and your girl.'

"They took everything—guns, my money, my ID, my gold coins, anything that was worth anything. I had hidden a couple of kilos for a rainy day. They even found those."

The two men left, dragging Fleischmann with them. Later, Bobby confronted Fleischmann. "He swore to me that they had come to him first and threatened to kill him, and that was the only reason he led them to me. It didn't sound kosher. In this business, you had no real friends. If someone was down on his luck, he could turn on you in a second."

The Colombians were "very cool," says Bobby, and "fronted me some more keys. And they put some people on it and found out it was two scumbags from up north. They did what they had to do. They found them, set them up with the police on a sting, and they ended up doing twenty-five years in state jail in Maryland."

Home invasions were making the news. Only a few weeks earlier, a friend's wife had been killed when some Colombians ripped off the house's coke supply. It was front-page news.

By early 1981, Bobby was sending his ex-wife, Lisa, half an ounce. "I have no idea if she was blowing it all, or making some spending money, but that was my way of paying some alimony." He paid many of his bills with cocaine. "An eight-ball was worth $350, and everyone knew that. My dentist took coke for his work. I got my hair cut for half a gram, rented speedboats for two eight-balls, bought clothes with grams. If you had coke, almost everyone took it as payment."

FREEBASING—SMOKING COKE IN a water bottle, producing a much stronger and more addictive high—became the rage among South Florida users a year before it did in the rest of the country. Lisa's ex-boyfriend, Steve, had a sprawling penthouse at Key Biscayne's Ocean Colony condominium. He was connected, and Bobby liked him. One night he took out a pipe and torch and told Bobby to try it.

"The first time," recalls Bobby, "it was like, 'Whoooa, baby. Why do I need that crust in my running nose from snorting powder?' That first hit was fucking unbelievable. What I didn't know then was that I would be chasing that first hit forever. And it took me no time to realize that whatever girls would do for coke, they do that times ten for freebasing. They would come into my place and ask for a hit. They would be stripping, ready for sex, ready to do anything. I had one girl climb a tree naked, and I had a gun and kept threatening to shoot her in the ass. We were so fucked up. But she was willing to do it for a hit."

In 1981, Steve asked Bobby to help him bring some coke to Texas.

They flew to Dallas, together with one of Steve's girlfriends, with plastic baggies of coke strapped to their bodies.

"And we would go into the plane bathroom with our little pipes," recalls Bobby, "and light the torch and freebase. There were no smoke detectors then. And we weren't even thinking that we could have blown up the entire fucking plane. We must have done it half a dozen times. We were so addicted that we couldn't fly three or four hours without doing it."

When they got to Texas, Steve took him to a house he said belonged to Tanya Tucker. "There were all these pictures of her everywhere. It was beautiful, but no one was around. They had left a key for us under a planter, and we just waited. After a couple of hours, we figured fuck it, no one is coming."

Bobby emptied an amaretto bottle and used his small torch to make a hole near the bottom, converting it into an enormous crack pipe. For the next six hours they freebased most of the kilo they had brought to sell. Bobby strapped the little that was left to his body in baggies. Then they caught the last flight back to Miami.

Bobby, normally 190 muscular pounds at six feet, spent many days in one of his condos, freebasing with friends. He dropped 40 pounds. He became so lazy that he "paid" girls with a hit on the pipe to drop off dry cleaning and to do his grocery shopping. Meanwhile, Steve began making successful drug runs to Texas. But state troopers got a tip about one handoff and chased him along an interstate before running him off the road. He was killed in the ensuing shootout.

"And I'm at the Mutiny in the Grove," says Bobby, "when Steve's brother shows up and he's looking real bad. He tells me his brother is dead and that he needs $10,000 for the funeral. There might be some legal problems, and the family needed some money. 'Get lost,' I told him. He started screaming at me. 'Forget about it,' I screamed back. 'He fucked my wife. It's not going to happen.' "

NEW YEAR'S EVE 1981, Bobby was celebrating at Miami's Ménage. It was packed with his customers and fellow dealers. Julio Bermudez went to Coconut Grove's Mutiny, where it cost $1,000 to get past the door. And Joey Double made the cut at Malnik's Forge. "The place was a goddamn Who's Who of the coke trade," he recalls. "I knew the maître d' and he waved me and my friends in. If the DEA had just picked up that night's crowd, they would have put South Florida's coke business out of commission. But no one there was even thinking about the cops. We felt invincible. We ran Miami."

CHAPTER 10

The Heir Apparent

T HE FORGE WAS not just popular with drug lords, it was the favorite of power brokers. Al Malnik had the best Rolodex in town. Regular patrons included top politicians, bankers, developers, sports stars, and entertainers; mega-developers like Steve Muss and Jerry Robins, politicians like former mayor Harold Rosen, and bankers like Abel Holtz and David Paul. Malnik mixed high and low, New York gangsters and Palm Beach socialites.

He was the ultimate host who remembered everyone's name and what they liked to eat, and he made the Forge a safe zone. What went on inside was never fodder for the next day's gossip columns.

Malnik had also developed a widespread reputation for being "connected" to organized crime through his brief representation of Meyer Lansky twenty years before. Although Malnik adamantly denied it, the story stuck and morphed over time into his being Lansky's "heir apparent," or at least identified as such in a *Reader's Digest* article. Some restaurant and club competitors who were jealous of the Forge's success believed Malnik liked the underworld hype because it gave him a bad-boy swagger. He lived large, built the Cricket Club, then the city's premier building, and drove a bright yellow Rolls-Royce, one of four.

But almost no one knew how Malnik had really earned his money. Instead of the classic American rags-to-riches story he boasted about, Malnik's rise was tailor-made for Miami Beach, a small town that overlooked questionable connections and deals so long as the end result was tremendous money and the right friends.

Malnik declined to be interviewed for this book because he was tired of talking about the "old rumors that never go away." And he is the first to point out that he has never been convicted of any crime. But his early career reveals that at times he did business with questionable characters and was personally involved in complex deals that kicked off investigations by the Justice Department and the IRS.

In 1961, the twenty-eight-year-old attorney was appointed legal counsel to the Bank of World Commerce, newly chartered in the Bahamas. John Pullman, installed as chairman, was a Russian-born ex-bootlegger who was part of Minneapolis–St. Paul's Kid Cann Gang, and also one of Meyer Lansky's primary money launderers. Investors included other Lansky associates, such as Irving "Nig" Devine and Ed Levinson, both members of the Cleveland syndicate, and Clifford Jones, Nevada's former lieutenant governor. The Pennsylvania Crime Commission later concluded that World Commerce was a "laundry" for Mafia money, while *Forbes* said, "Mob money flowed into its secret numbered accounts by the hundreds of millions—Lansky money, most of it—and then out again into Tibor Rosenbaum's International Credit Bank of Switzerland before returning to the U.S. for reinvestment." Investigators later dubbed it "a Laundromat for cash."

Allied Empire Inc. was listed as a $10,000 corporate stockholder of the Bank of World Commerce. Allied would default on nearly $1 million in loans during the next two years. Malnik was a director of both.

For several months in 1961, Malnik lived in California while working for World Commerce and Allied. A group of investors—including Meyer "Mike" Singer, Jimmy Hoffa's West Coast representative—used World Commerce funds to buy savings and loans. Federal authorities suspected that those banks might have been used to launder mob money, but no indictments were produced.

Malnik was paid in World Commerce and Allied stock. John Pullman loaned Malnik $20,000. Malnik opened up bank accounts in Miami's Mercantile Trust Company, Los Angeles's Ahmanson Bank & Trust, Barclays Bank in Nassau, and Pullman's International Credit Bank in Geneva. Money was flowing in. Soon, Malnik bought his first Rolls-Royce and moved into a luxury condominium tower in Miami Beach, his former residence transferred in a quick sale to the mistress of Anthony "Fat Tony" Salerno, the underboss of New York's Genovese crime family.

By this time, Malnik was the subject of several complaints to the Florida State Attorney's office over his mortgage companies and charges of excessive interest rates and onerous contract provisions. Although the state attorney did not think there was enough information for a formal investigation, Malnik's association with known mobsters had piqued the FBI's interest.

Early in 1963, the bureau bugged Malnik's Miami Beach office. Since they had not obtained a court order for a wiretap, the information obtained was useless in court because the prosecution could not use any information developed from those recordings. Some of Malnik's hundreds of conversations were with Jake Kossman, a mob attorney who represented, among others, New York's Frank Costello and Philadelphia don Angelo Bruno. The FBI was interested in Kossman because he was also Jimmy Hoffa's attorney, and Hoffa was then the target of a Justice Department investigation. Malnik and Kossman were recorded discussing the difficulties of representing mob clients. Once he spoke about buying Bahamian property from Canadian wheeler-dealer Lou Chesler. Another time he noted that "Fat Tony" Salerno's mortgage was secured through a loan from John Pullman drawn on a Swiss bank.

One series of conversations concerned the effort to obtain a gambling license on the Bahamas' Paradise Island. Huntington Hartford, grandson of the founder of A&P supermarkets, had developed the island into a resort and wanted the Bahamian government's permission for a casino. Hartford was friendly with Sam Golub, listed in a 1959 internal Metro-Dade Police Department report as one of the top one hundred mobsters in Florida. Golub had a reputation as a fixer and was close to the Bahamas' finance minister, Sir Stafford Sands. Meeting at the Fontainebleau, Golub and Malnik convinced Hartford that they could obtain the license for him. Hartford signed a contract promising to pay them a substantial fee if the gambling was approved.

On August 19, 1963, Ben Siegelbaum, a Lansky lieutenant under FBI surveillance, visited Malnik and showed him a confidential Justice Department report about the Bank of World Commerce. Siegelbaum told Malnik the report came from "somebody, high intelligence, somebody the boys know . . . just like you have your contacts, they have their few friends. This is from Justice." Siegelbaum said he had been ordered to send a copy to the bank's president, John Pullman, and to "tell Al to lock it up."

The report convinced Malnik that there was a leak inside his organization, and on the wiretaps he talked about checking his office for surveillance. The bureau put together a black bag operation to remove the bug before Malnik could sweep the office, then they would again break in and plant a new device. But Malnik returned the night the FBI had chosen to remove the bug. He walked in on the federal agent, who ran out in a panic before Malnik could stop him. The bureau's spy game was up.

Instead of being chastened, Malnik concluded that his discovery gave him leverage against the bureau. Before destroying the bug, he had a telephone conversation with an unidentified man, threatening to disclose the FBI's illegal activity unless he got "immunity" from any prosecutions.

Malnik's work with the Bank of World Commerce and Allied Empire ended over a dispute about how much money he was owed. He decided on a new venture, this one in showbiz. Like many of his later business deals, it was a complicated maze of companies, stock swaps, limited partnerships, and relationships with both legitimate businessmen and investors with organized crime connections. Malnik bought the U.S. and South and Central American rights to a video jukebox technology that was sweeping Europe: Scopitone.

Malnik had ten other partners, including Irving Kaye, who the following year was denied a Nevada gaming license because of possible mob associations, and Abe Green, a New York City slot machine baron with deep mob ties (New Jersey's mob chief, Gerardo Catena, was a principal in Green's company). Others included Alfred Miniaci, a thirty-year veteran of the coin machine business, and Maurice Uchitel, another Malnik-Scopitone investor, was a Lansky friend and former owner of the Eden Roc.

In July 1964, Malnik, who had power of attorney for all the Scopitone investors, transferred 80 percent of their ownership to Tel-A-Sign, a Chicago manufacturer of plastic electric signs, for $3.5 million in stock. Instead of dividing the proceeds equally, Malnik kept 90 percent as well as a 20 percent interest in Scopitone. He got $38 for every juke-box installed in the United States and became a vice president and di-rector of Tel-A-Sign at $39,500 a year. As might be expected, Malnik's fellow investors raised hell.

To address the complaints, a meeting was held at New York's War-wick Hotel in the fall of 1964. Green, Miniaci, and Kaye represented the other partners. Malnik was represented by Vincent "Jimmy Blue Eyes" Alo, the Genovese crime captain and Lansky associate whom Manhat-tan district attorney Robert Morgenthau called "one of the most signif-icant organized crime figures in the United States." Alo contended that Malnik deserved the lion's share of the proceeds since he had worked the hardest; the others demanded a fairer split. No agreement was reached.

Shortly after a second meeting of the partners, the Securities and Exchange Commission received a tip that Alo and New Jersey mob boss Gerardo Catena were the real parties behind Scopitone, and that Mal-nik was only a front man. The SEC began an investigation.

During the dispute between the partners, Tel-A-Sign's stock almost tripled in value. The SEC began a second investigation into whether the thinly traded stock had been manipulated. Malnik's share, after the second Warwick Hotel meeting, was worth $4.7 million. Some Scopi-tone franchisees sued Malnik for "fraudulent misrepresentations . . . material misrepresentations, concealments, and failures to disclose." But the plaintiffs failed to convince a court that there was fraud.

The other Malnik partner who earned big profits in Scopitone was his self-described "best friend," Jay W. Weiss. The two had other ven-tures before Scopitone, including their 1960 purchase of the Sir John's Hotel on Biscayne Boulevard. The thirty-eight-year-old Brooklyn-born Weiss, whose father and uncle both had criminal records in New York, was a founder of the nation's largest liquor distributor, Southern Wine & Spirits.*

In April 1965, Malnik and Weiss signed an agreement "retroactively adjusting" the amount of Tel-A-Sign stock that would go to Green,

---

* He later raised more than $150 million for the University of Miami and was one of Miami Beach's prominent society figures before his death in 2004.

Miniaci, Kaye, and Uchitel and gave them an additional 5 percent ownership of Scopitone. In September, the two men unloaded their remaining ownership in Scopitone. Both resigned their director's positions. They received $1,165,925 for their shares, nearly $2 million less than they were then worth. When a *Wall Street Journal* reporter caught up with Malnik the following year, and asked why he gave away shares and ownership potentially worth millions, Al said it was the "settlement" of a matter he "preferred not to discuss." Weiss had no comment.

In May 1966, the SEC investigated Scopitone and subpoenaed Vincent "Jimmy Blue Eyes" Alo. Alo pleaded a memory lapse 134 times in an hour and a half of testimony. He claimed to remember practically nothing about the New York hotel meetings beyond attending at Malnik's request and that they concerned a dispute over the distribution of Tel-A-Sign stock. He claimed to have no memory of Scopitone or how the Malnik-Uchitel dispute arose. Morgenthau returned indictments against Alo and Malnik, which he sealed until he could "determine the consequences of the bugging [the illegal FBI tap of Malnik's office]."

Nineteen sixty-nine was a significant year for Malnik. In April, a federal grand jury for the Southern District of Florida indicted him for filing false tax returns for 1962 and 1963. The bad news of the tax indictment was tempered when prosecutors decided not to press the indictment over his Scopitone activities. Later, Morgenthau admitted that because the FBI's wiretap was illegal, "we felt we would be getting into endless litigation which we didn't have the resources to pursue."

Vincent "Jimmy Blue Eyes" was not so lucky. He was indicted in October 1969 for obstruction of justice over his evasive answers before the SEC. Alo was convicted and sentenced to five years, the only person to go to prison over Scopitone.

A year after he had opened the Forge, on July 13, 1970, Malnik went to trial in Miami on tax evasion and perjury charges. Ten days later, the jury acquitted him on all counts relating to the tax year 1962, but deadlocked on the charges for 1963. Prosecutors retried him a month later, but three days after the trial began, the judge dismissed the case.

When the criminal proceedings finished, the Justice Department forwarded its Malnik file to the Internal Revenue Service. On January

11, 1971, the IRS notified him it was civilly investigating his tax returns for the years 1959, 1960, 1962, and 1963. IRS officials subpoenaed Malnik to give sworn testimony and to produce his personal and business books. He hired one of Jimmy Hoffa's attorneys, former U.S. Attorney Harvey Silets, who worked out a deal whereby Malnik would not appear or produce any records, but instead submitted a written statement invoking his Fifth Amendment right against self-incrimination if questioned. It was rare for the IRS to accept a taxpayer's blanket refusal to cooperate. However, after seven months, the IRS officials realized they could not make a case unless they obtained access to some of Malnik's business records. On December 7, 1971, the IRS filed a petition to enforce the original subpoena. Malnik opposed it on the grounds that his written agreement precluded him from having to produce any books and records.

The IRS then obtained a court order enforcing the subpoena, but in a rehearing, the same court reversed itself. The IRS appealed to the Fifth Circuit Court of Appeals, which in February 1974 ruled for Malnik. Without subpoena power, the IRS's civil pursuit seemed over. Malnik turned his attention to business.

Malnik and Sam Cohen owned 370 acres in North Miami Beach. Cohen was president of Las Vegas's Flamingo Hotel during the 1960s and was convicted of commodities violations for illegal trading from 1955 to 1965.

The duo had bought the land in February 1971 with no money of their own, assuming a Teamster Pension Fund mortgage of $8.9 million. The property adjoined a 149-acre country club—Sky Lake—that Malnik had bought in 1966. Now, he and Cohen sought out Clifford Perlman, the chairman of Caesars World, and offered him a long-term lease on Sky Lake—a rare opportunity, they told him, to make large profits by selling country club memberships and developing the land for upscale housing. Perlman passed, but Malnik was persistent and hosted a meeting in July 1971 at Sky Lake, with Sam Cohen, Clifford Perlman and his brother Stuart, and several Caesars World executives and advisers.

When Cliff Perlman presented the deal to Caesars' board, he told them of Malnik's tax evasion indictment and acquittal, and about Sam

Cohen's Commodity Exchange Act conviction. He did not disclose inside information he had that a sealed indictment had been returned against Sam Cohen, four months earlier, for skimming $36 million, together with Lansky, from the Flamingo. Caesars' outside counsel, David Bernstein of Rogers & Wells, suggested that given Malnik's reputation, Caesars not do any business with him unless they first consulted with the Justice Department.

Perlman rejected the advice. The board approved the deal and Caesars World signed a twenty-year lease for Sky Lake. The terms called for Malnik and Cohen to receive $40 million in rent and to clear a $32 million profit.

In 1972, Clifford Perlman invested $350,000 and became a partner with Malnik and Sam Cohen's sons, Joel and Alan, in a partially completed 220-unit, luxury high-rise condominium called the Cricket Club. Malnik and the Cohens had bought it at bankruptcy proceedings a few months earlier from Gaynor Corporation, controlled by Dominick Alongi, a mobster who split his time between Miami and Teaneck, New Jersey. Law enforcement authorities suspected that Alongi had forced the property into bankruptcy by skimming loan proceeds.

When the Cricket Club was completed in early 1973, Malnik moved in. The project was a smashing success.

In 1974, Caesars World exercised a buy option on its Sky Lake lease and purchased all the land and improvements for $23.2 million. Malnik and the Cohens cleared a $14.7 million profit in just three years. Some of the sales provisions later raised the interest of gaming authorities. Caesars paid $164,000 to Malnik for the issuance of a sewer bond, even though they were not required to since this was one of the assets for which they had paid $23.2 million. Also, Malnik negotiated the rights to a $375,000 yacht that Caesars paid for and maintained for him. And Caesars allowed Malnik and the Cohens to retain their ownership of the 18-hole golf course and country club, which they leased back to Caesars for $120,000 a month for twenty years.

Another deal between Malnik and the Perlmans, Cove Haven in the Pennsylvania Poconos, was so suspicious that it was later investigated by the Pennsylvania Crime Commission.

As part of their probe, they looked into Malnik's background. Investigators reported that Malnik had held conversations with Genovese crime family members about an upcoming Florida referendum to legalize gambling, and was told how "some $20 million to $25 million was to be invested in the casinos and profits were to be skimmed off the top and channeled back to the investors."

In a sworn statement, Vincent "Fat Vinnie" Teresa, a member of the Boston Patriarca crime family, then in witness protection, told the Crime Commission, "It was a known fact among the criminal underworld that dealing with Al Malnik was the same as dealing with Meyer Lansky. Al Malnik was an employee of Meyer Lansky and the purpose of his association with Meyer Lansky was that Al Malnik would convert illegal cash by laundering it in various real estate ventures."

Pennsylvania investigators believed that the sale leaseback had occured shortly after a meeting at the Forge, attended by Malnik, Lansky, and several others. But despite all the smoke, the investigators could find nothing illegal in the Cove Haven transaction.

Nevada gaming authorities also began a formal probe of the Cove Haven sale and leaseback to determine whether the Perlmans and Caesars World had violated the state's strict ban on any links to unsavory individuals. On December 10, 1975, the Nevada Gaming Control Board directed that Caesars World not expand its association with Malnik and "not further associate with persons of unsavory or notorious repute."

Philip Hannifin, chairman of the Nevada Gaming Control Board, warned Clifford Perlman outside the official record. "I'm going to say to you very clearly, and I'm not really concerned with whether you want to accept it or not. I have sufficient information now that I think is incontrovertible that Mr. Malnik can be described as an associate in the business world of Meyer Lansky. As such to me, he is personally obnoxious because of the nature of the beast we have to work with in Nevada."

Cove Haven also sparked an SEC investigation. Caesars World's outside auditors qualified their annual report on the company's financial health because of uncertainty over the "ultimate realizability" of the

Malnik investments. When Clifford Perlman was asked by an irate shareholder at the firm's 1975 annual meeting whether "we have cause to be concerned," he said, "No, I don't think so."

The SEC probe took three years before a complaint was filed against Caesars World. In the ensuing consent agreement, Caesars agreed not to do further business with Malnik or Sam Cohen.

In 1980, Caesars applied for a gambling license in New Jersey. The Casino Control Commission, as part of their probe of whether Caesars World had mob ties, gathered information on Malnik. Since the Cove Haven deal, Malnik had garnered more bad press in Miami Beach. In June 1977, Richard Schwartz, Meyer Lansky's stepson, and Craig Teriaca, son of Miami gangster Vincent Teriaca, got into a fight over a ten-dollar bill on the bar at the Forge. Schwartz pulled out a revolver and killed Teriaca. In October, a month before he was to go to trial for the murder, Schwartz was gunned down as he drove up to his Bay Harbor restaurant. His murder remains unsolved.

The FBI provided the New Jersey Casino Control Commission with transcripts of some more recent surveillance recordings on Malnik. In a 1979 meeting at Hallandale's Hemisphere Apartments, Malnik met with an FBI agent who pretended to be an Arab sheik who wanted to purchase Las Vegas's Aladdin Hotel. They discussed how the hotel would cost $105 million, plus $10 million extra to "swing the deal." When the agent asked who would get the $10 million, Malnik said, "Nobody's gonna volunteer that they're receiving it, because the people who are going to receive it, uh, will never under any circumstances be identified or acknowledged as having received it." Malnik boasted that he controlled Caesars World. And he warned the "sheik": "Let me tell you something. I'm a persona non grata [sic]. I mean, I can't be licensed. I can't even appear in the deal." No money ever passed hands. Malnik was not charged with any crime.

The New Jersey Commission granted Caesars a limited license, with "substantial restrictions and conditions"—among them, the severance of the company's connections with Malnik as soon as possible. It concluded that because of his association with someone of such an "unsavory reputation" as Malnik, Clifford Perlman did not "possess the good character, honesty, and integrity demanded by the Casino Control Act."

Only after Perlman left did Caesars eventually obtain an unrestricted gambling license for Atlantic City.*

WHILE THE CASINO wars played out in Nevada and New Jersey, Malnik entered a new business arena, with people whose personal wealth dwarfed that of his gaming and union friends.

In 1978, a Bahamian company, Appolonia Investment Ltd., paid $3.35 million to buy the property just north of Malnik's 34-acre "ranch" near Boca Raton.

Appolonia Investment Ltd., like Malnik, used the same local attorney for its land purchase. But when asked by a local reporter to divulge Appolonia's owners, both Malnik and his lawyer refused. Records from the Register General's Office in the Bahamas reveal that the principal shareholder was Prince Turki bin Abdul Aziz, Saudi Arabia's deputy defense minister, and brother of Crown Prince Fahd.

Prince Turki and his wife Princess Hind al-Fassi Aziz had created a lavish two-story apartment directly below Malnik's at the Cricket Club. Sheika Faisa, the mother of the al-Fassi clan, bought a Cricket Club condo with a great view of Biscayne Bay.

The al-Fassi clan lived extravagantly even by Miami standards. The *Miami Herald* reported that seventeen-year-old Sheik Tarek al-Fassi went on a $25,000 shopping spree at Bal Harbour. Within weeks of his arrival, his home was robbed of $400,000 cash, $80,000 in British sterling, twenty gold and diamond rings, a dozen gold medallions, and fourteen diamond-studded watches. The jewelry was valued at nearly $10 million.

Turki bought the Woolworth estate, a sprawling waterfront mansion, for $3 million in cash. There the prince kept a small herd of goats

---

* In 1993, Malnik visited Caesars and the Taj Mahal in Atlantic City, and the casinos paid all his costs. Malnik's stay was brought to the attention of the New Jersey Casino Control Commission, and Caesars was fined. "He is not welcome here," said James Hurley, the commission's chair. In its published decision, the Casino Control Commission concluded: "The evidence establishes that Mr. Malnik associated with persons engaged in organized criminal activities, and that he himself participated in transactions that were clearly illegitimate and illegal."

and built a giant discotheque, with a machine that simulated thunder. The house-warming party included circus performers, a full orchestra, and an eight-foot cake sporting live flamingos.

Malnik became a financial adviser to Turki. By 1980, according to some of the prince's friends and employees, "it was Al who controlled the cash, who told the Prince to put money in this business or that business." (Twenty-two years later, Malnik became a financial adviser to Michael Jackson, working with the King of Pop from 2000 until 2004.)

By 1981, Malnik's son, Mark, a gregarious twenty-three-year-old law student at the University of Miami, had fallen in love with Princess Hind's twenty-one-year-old sister, Hoda. She too lived in a condo at the Cricket Club. It hardly seemed to matter that Mark was already married. Soon he left his wife and moved into his own Cricket Club condo.

Neither family seemed bothered by their historically antagonistic faiths. The Malniks were secular Jews, and the al-Fassis and Prince Turki were liberal Muslims. The Malniks began studying Arabic and Mark carried around a Koran.

In 1982, after he had earned his law degree and his divorce was finalized, Mark married Princess Hoda in a secret ceremony and changed his name to "Shareef" Malnik. Prince Turki reportedly gave them $2 million as a gift. But 1982 was also the year when things began unraveling for the Saudis.

That January, Princess Hind's older and most outlandish brother, Mohammed, was the subject of national gossip columns. A sixteen-year-old Italian girl he had married in California returned there and retained the celebrity divorce lawyer Marvin Mitchelson. On January 21, Mitchelson announced that Mohammed's wife was suing for divorce and seeking a record $3 billion.

South Florida merchants began complaining that the free-spending Saudis weren't paying their bills. One limo company claimed it was owed $157,000; contractors and architects said the family was thousands of dollars behind in payments. The Diplomat Hotel in Hollywood, Florida, charged that Mohammed owed $1,475,516.34; worse, he had bounced thirty-seven checks. The hotel called the police—most of whom had once worked part-time for al-Fassi—who arrested him for felony fraud. He was in jail for six hours before an aide posted the $1,000 bail. He sued the city for $1 trillion for his "unjust" arrest and the trauma of his six-hour jail stay.

Saud al-Rasheed, Mohammed's spokesman and a former press attaché for the Saudi mission to the United Nations, claimed that the hotel bill and others that were due would be promptly paid. "What is one thousand? One thousand we spend for tip for waiter [*sic*]."

WHEN REPORTS OF the family's outrageous behavior made their way back to Riyadh, Crown Prince Fahd ordered everyone home.

Al and Shareef Malnik decided to join the Saudis.

In a country where Jews were vilified, they were received as honored guests. Rumors reached Miami Beach that Al had grown a beard, taken an Arabic name, and converted to Islam. The *Miami Herald* dubbed him and Shareef the "Malniks of Arabia." But a secretary at Malnik's law office told the *Herald* that any reports that he had moved there permanently were "absolutely ridiculous." He was likely, she said, to return to South Florida "in the near future."

He returned in 1983. Meyer Lansky had died a few months before in Miami Beach after a long battle with lung cancer. *Reader's Digest* swiftly named Malnik as Lansky's "heir apparent."

On March 3, one of Al's canary yellow Rolls-Royces was blown up in the underground parking garage of the Cricket Club. A few weeks later, he traveled with Prince Turki back to the safety of the closed kingdom of Saudi Arabia. When his friend Don Aronow heard about the car bombing, he shook his head and laughed. "Al's gonna get it yet."

CHAPTER 11

Nowheresville

THE ERA'S BIG events, from the cocaine trade to the big money made by Beach players like Malnik, seemed to have left South Beach on the sidelines. The South Beach that was twenty-four blocks from the world of Al Malnik and the cocaine cowboys might as well have been on a different planet. The Art Deco preservation effort had not yet defined any power players. The Capitmans could not have cared less about places like the Forge, and the poor elderly retirees were unaware of it and its larger milieu. But the gentrification that the Capitmans had initiated would soon escalate and, over the next decade, remake the Beach. A group of enlightened developers from New York was about to reinforce the actions of the Miami Design Preservation League in its long battles to preserve the Deco character, against local builders who invariably sought to build new and bigger. In January 1982, a single hotel—the Henry Hohauser–designed New Yorker at 16th and Collins—became a fierce battleground between the preservationists and an old foe of Barbara Capitman, Abe Resnick. This time Resnick was back with a new tactic: demolition.

Resnick and his partner Dov Dunaevsky bought the New Yorker, a seventy-room hotel, which was crowded against Resnick's huge new condominium, the Georgian. Their intent was to demolish the hotel and replace it with something grander. But when wreckers arrived, so did the preservationists, who formed a picket line and notified the press. David Wallach, Andrew Capitman, and Mark Shantzis were there. And at the very front was Barbara Capitman.

"We knew the city commission was considering a new preservation ordinance," says Nancy Liebman, another protester. "This had to be the example to them that the law must change."

"Mrs. Capitman called and pleaded with me," Resnick told a reporter. "She said, 'Abe, you're shortening my life.' I told her it's nothing personal, it's only economics. If we'd known it was so valuable, we would not have bought it. We don't look for extra headaches. She told me, 'It's going to be on your conscience the rest of your life.'"

Resnick went on the offensive, trying to make a case that preserving Art Deco was a financial disaster for Miami Beach, and that the future lay in removing the decrepit buildings and modernizing the neighborhood.

Murray Gold, executive director of the Miami Beach Resort Hotels Association, seemed to have the Resnick team's talking points when he told *The New York Times*: "Miami Beach is 65 years old. George Washington didn't sleep here. Neither did Abe Lincoln come through here. Neither do we have anything that represents history. People coming to Miami Beach aren't coming to see old buildings. They're coming for sand and sun. If you want to see old buildings, you go to an old city. You go to Philadelphia and see the Liberty Bell. You don't make money running a hotel. Money is only made buying and selling. You put this Art Deco scam on Miami Beach, and you're going to lose investors who don't want any more Government regulations than they already have."

When Barbara Capitman suggested Resnick retain an architectural firm to see if there were alternative uses of the land and building that might also be profitable, he agreed to postpone the demolition. He hired the respected Miami firm of Bouterse, Perez & Fabregas and paid $50,000 for a study on alternate uses.

"This is a magnificent, wonderful victory," Capitman said at the time, adding, "I think they'll stop the whole thing."

While the demolition was suspended, the city commissioners voted a zoning change that allowed commercial as well as residential use of the New Yorker, upping the development value for Resnick. Meanwhile, as everyone waited, salvaging contractors removed the hotel's insides, from plumbing to windows to furniture. "People are asking the wrong questions," said Leonard Feldman, one of the salvage representatives, who sold the hotel's large plates of glass etched with swans and birds for $5 each. "Is Art Deco pretty?" he asked a reporter. "For a few blocks, it would be all right, but it's not pretty, and it never was." He pointed across the street at the Berkeley Shore Hotel, which had a pale pink and green spiral on its facade. "It's a monstrosity," he said. "It's like an old woman painted up; she's still old. I feel like I'm in Cuba or Russia— they tell a guy what to do with what's his."

Three months after the suspension, lead architect David Perez submitted an ambitious plan to preserve the old hotel as part of a vertical Deco-style hotel-condominium-shopping complex. Dunaevsky and Resnick did not call Perez to discuss the plans. Instead, they sent a demolition crew to the hotel at 5 a.m. on Thursday, April 23.

"I'm going to make enough damage today so they can't stop me tomorrow," said Jose Juelle, the demolition's chief. In an hour, the wrecking ball had knocked down the pale green cornice, scattering concrete along the sidewalk.

Three weeks later, the Miami Beach commission passed an ordinance making a city board responsible for historic preservation. It would review every future demolition request.

"There was such an outcry when the New Yorker went down," recalls Nancy Liebman, "that the commissioners finally got off their asses and passed something. It wasn't the greatest protection, but it would have been enough to hold up the New Yorker demolition. Just a little too late."

Beyond the bruising battle over the New Yorker, the Capitmans saw early signs of the gentrification that over the next decade would remake the Beach.

Dona Zemo, a free-spirited single mother of three from Connecticut, visited South Beach in 1982. "I had been coming down with my parents since I was a kid," she told me. "And one day I was reading *The Village Voice* and there was this article about Barbara Capitman and the saving of South Beach. I was Art Deco–crazed. I had to get there to see what was happening.

"When we got to Ocean Drive, there was nothing but dilapidated hotels and boarded-up buildings. Not a single restaurant. Only senior citizens on their porches, white plastic nose covers so they wouldn't get burned, and wearing enormous sunglasses. There were weird people, plenty of crazy homeless, and lots of Cubans. There was the feeling that someone might be lurking around who could kill you. I loved it right away."

She booked the best oceanfront room at the Cardozo for $40 a night; she was Andrew Capitman's first guest since the renovation. A colorful and quirky group made up half of the permanent residents, mostly writers, artists, and performers attracted by dirt-cheap oceanfront rents and the freewheeling atmosphere. The thirty-seven-year-old Zemo, with her jet black hair and vintage style, fit right in. Barbara Capitman visited Dona on the day she checked in. "She was almost unkempt," recalls Dona. "But she had this passion and you only had to spend a little while with her to get that loud and clear."

Later that day, Zemo bought a few bottles of inexpensive champagne and invited people to her room for a party. "I knew everyone in one day." Andrew Capitman told her about his dream for the neighborhood.

On her flight home, she remembers, "I'm at 36,000 feet when I said to myself, 'Go back there. You deserve it. Change your life and become part of this vision. Make the Art Deco District happen.' "

She called Andrew before she had unpacked and asked to run the café when it opened. In the meantime, she offered to help with the company's books. She requested room and board and a small salary. He accepted.

Returning to the Beach, Zemo moved to a raw space on the top floor of the seven-story Victor, then a residence hotel at 11th and Ocean where Capitman and Mark Shantzis had their office.

"I was the only person under seventy-five, seriously," she says. "Most of them called me Dolly instead of Dona." Many had been living there for more than twenty years. "It took me only a few weeks to learn that there was no interest by the local government to preserve Art Deco. Sometimes we would say, 'This is an Art Deco building,' and they'd say, 'Really, who is Art?' They didn't even know what we were talking about." One of the hotels, the Carlyle, had been taken over mostly by Marielitos. "I certainly knew they weren't part of any renaissance," says Zemo. "Andrew and Mark were trying to make it better, but no one at City Hall cared."

• • •

"WHEN I FIRST met David Wallach," Zemo recalls, "he was wearing a blue velvet suit, part of the British invasion. He was very good-looking, had this great head of hair, and had pulled together this amazing look. He was the coolest and most alternative attorney I had ever met." The two quickly became friends. When Zemo told him about Andrew's difficulties in getting building permits because of City Hall's massive red tape, Wallach urged his politically connected father to push on their behalf.

"I knew that financially, the five hotels owned by Andrew and Mark were like dominos leaning against each other," he says. "They had financed each against the other, so if one failed, they all might. They had no cash flow and they were burning through what little money they had while City Hall screwed with them."

Some nights, Dona and David would sit on the beach. Most people considered it very unsafe. But Wallach remembered, "I'd look back toward Ocean Drive and the hotels. They were mostly dark, but you could see them in the moonlight. And they were beautiful from far away. At night you couldn't see how blighted it was."

In law school, Wallach had stumbled across a new federal program—Adult Congregated Living Facilities (ACLF)—which gave large tax incentives and government funding to anyone who converted a building into a retirement home. Some were scrupulous and made a decent conversion. But as state and local officials discovered, others like the Grace Hotel on Española and the 13-story, 252-room Blackstone Kosher Retirement Home on Washington (a "Gentiles-only" luxury hotel in the 1930s, best known as the place where George Gershwin composed part of *Porgy and Bess*), were fetid dives where the elderly lived out their lives in misery. At the Blackstone, where 145 of the retirees had been garment center workers, a ten- by seven-foot room cost $600 a month, plus meals. Larger rooms were often shared to reduce expenses.

Alex Daoud was on the Governor's Committee on the Long-Term Care and Housing of the Elderly, and together with its chairman, a Jerry Lewis look-alike, Dr. Irving Vinger, he investigated reports of mental or physical abuse at licensed ACLFs in Miami Beach, and also watched for any small-time operators who had set up retirement homes without meeting state requirements.

When they made a call on the Blackstone, together with firemen, policemen, and representatives from the city's building division and the county's health department, they found "elderly people in dirty pajamas . . . crammed on wooden benches lined up against the wall, staring at us blankly." In the dining room, residents were eating from filthy dishes on roach-infested tables. The stairwell was litter-filled and reeked of urine. The second-floor living quarters, Daoud remembers, "looked like prison cells, with single metal beds and cheap overhead lights." There was a single bathroom for the entire floor. Former suites had been cut in half to increase the number of people the hotel could warehouse.

On the top floor, Daoud was almost overcome by the pungent smell. Behind a locked door, he found an elderly man lying under a filthy sheet. His face was like a "living skeleton" and his body was covered in lesions. The patient was taken to the hospital, completely dehydrated.

Incredibly, even after places like the Blackstone received bad press, were fined, and forced to comply with better standards, they remained open. And compounding the overall problem, individual Beach home-owners took advantage of the ACLF tax incentives by moving in five or six elderly and making a business out of it. There they got a room and meals in exchange for their Social Security or pension checks. There were no registered nurses, medical facilities, physical therapy sessions, or communal sitting rooms with a television.

When state officials acted on complaints in a one-day sweep in 1982, twenty Miami Beach retirement hotels were cited for grotesque conditions like those at the Blackstone. Two thousand seniors were moved to better facilities, most off the Beach.

Property owners started a grassroots movement to limit nursing homes through zoning, banning any ACLFs in designated tourist areas. While Mayor Norman Ciment supported it, Daoud considered the zoning change unconstitutional and discriminatory. After he gave an impassioned speech at a commission meeting, the *Miami Herald* ran a front-page cartoon of the mayor running on Ocean Drive and shoving an elderly man aside. The caption read: "Get out of the way, a tourist is coming."

"They weren't concerned about doing the right thing for the elderly," Daoud told me. "They only wanted to hide the homes so tourists didn't realize there were so many elderly. The tourist boosters wanted to warehouse them far away from Ocean Drive. It was bullshit."

Wallach had other ideas and decided to transform his father's traditional retirement home at Ninth and Ocean into an entirely new concept he called the Eastern Sun. "My motto was, 'If you can afford it, this is your home for life.'" He wanted a place where the standard of care was unmatched and residents could live out their remaining days in dignity.

"The banks had given up on South Beach," he told me. "No one was making loans. They all said it wouldn't work, it was too expensive. I had no money, and my father did not have enough to finance it. So I went to Jefferson Bank and pleaded. I virtually camped out there, and they finally gave me a loan for 50 percent of the building's value."

The Eastern Sun was the first full renovation of a South Beach building, finished even before the Cardozo. Wallach worked with his new residents and took the time to learn about their lives before they ended up at the Eastern Sun. He broke all the rules of a normal retirement home. There were no set menus. "If someone wanted salmon, that's what they got. Someone else wanted pork chops, I'd go out and buy them. And their doctors would always say, 'no sex,' but we would allow them discreetly." He took them on outings to the dog track at First Street and on most summer days, they would sit near the ocean. "And some of them were in wheelchairs," he recalls, "and I'd roll them one by one to the Beach. No one was left out."

He studied Elisabeth Kübler-Ross's work on death and dying. "I never used the word 'hospice,'" he says, "because that would have led to zoning problems at City Hall. But I wanted them to die as peacefully as they lived." After he had watched one of his first residents die in terrible pain from cancer, Wallach vowed never to let that happen again.

"We got Bronfman cocktails from the UK. It was a mixture of morphine, heroin, cherry syrup, and if someone drank enough, it made them unconscious. We found a couple of doctors who were willing to help. No one ever died in pain again. Sometimes, I held them in my arms, and you wouldn't even know they had lost a breath."

Wallach asked Andrew Capitman if he could put an Eastern Sun facility into one of their buildings. But they passed. Although they were grateful that Wallach had renovated his father's buildings and created a quality nursing home, Capitman and Shantzis knew that in their vision of a revitalized South Beach, there would be no place for any more Eastern Suns.

CHAPTER 12

Counterattack

WHILE THE SOUTH Beach preservationists were fighting their first battles, the open drug warfare continued to ravage the Beach's neighbors, especially mainland Miami. During 1981, there was a 180 percent increase for fatal coke overdoses and nearly a 400 percent increase in emergency room admissions. "Remarkably, there was no real community outrage about the drug trade," said one prominent Miami attorney, Dan Paul. "There was no real interest then in preserving or creating a quality of life."

In December 1981, a delegation of Miamians, led by Knight Ridder chairman Alvah Chapman, Jr., and Eastern Airlines' CEO Frank Borman, met with White House officials about the dope epidemic. Business executives and civic leaders formed Miami Citizens Against Crime. "The city was wild," recalls Borman. "We wanted law-abiding and honest citizens to take back control of our streets and we devised a plan of action that would only work if the federal government backed it with a major commitment." In their meeting with President Ronald Reagan, Borman and Chapman pleaded for more police and investigators and stressed the need for federal help for the swamped U.S. Attorney's office, where only seven prosecutors were assigned to major narcotics cases. Their top targets—class one dealers—were anyone moving 100 kilos a month. That meant no one was left to build the far more complex cases against the heads of the Colombian families responsible for smuggling in tons of coke. The Justice Department had used the Racketeer Influenced and Corrupt Organizations Act (RICO) since 1970, with tremendous success against the Mafia, but it had never been utilized against Colombian drug lords.

The small cadre of government prosecutors was overwhelmed by the drug lawyers, the so-called White Powder Bar. Sporting slightly longer hair and gold Rolexes, they packed Miami-Dade courthouses and in some cases became as famous as their notorious clients. It was legal for drug lawyers to accept their fees in drug cash, so long as they reported it to the IRS. (That didn't change until 1987, when grand juries were empowered to break the attorney-client bond and force lawyers to reveal how their clients paid them. If the clients couldn't prove the money was legal, the fees could be seized.)

James Jay Hogan reportedly wouldn't take a case for less than $250,000. "Diamond" Joel Hirschhorn was profiled on the front page of the *Wall Street Journal* and bragged to a colleague that he was once paid in silver bars. Pete "The Count" Baraban owned two Rolls-Royces and two Palm Beach waterfront homes. He was paid in sacks of cash that his associates openly carried into the bank. Hirschhorn boasted just before Borman and Chapman went to the White House, "I don't think I have a single client who got a two-year sentence, or anything near that, for a drug conspiracy in South Florida." Mel Kessler, who had his fees wired to a secret Swiss bank account, made *The Washington Post*. He joked to its reporter about how his clients paid him: "I have more cash than Burger King."

The Miami executives reported crippling rivalries between law enforcement agencies that were compounded by the systemic corruption eviscerating South Florida's crime-fighting efforts. The DEA estimated that the coke trade earned $100 billion annually, the same as Exxon.

President Reagan formed a cabinet-level task force to coordinate the federal offensive against the South Florida drug problem and appointed Vice President George Bush as its chair.

The offensive began in March 1982; it included more than six hundred agents from U.S. Customs, the FBI, DEA, and the Bureau of Alcohol, Tobacco and Firearms. The IRS sent in six forensics criminal tax teams. More than a hundred prosecutors and judges were also temporarily transferred from other jurisdictions. For the first time since the Civil War, the government enlisted the military to fight civilian crime. AWACS and U.S. Navy Hawkeye radar surveillance planes began tracking the drug flights. Army Cobra helicopter gunships, used for field support in Vietnam, chased the smugglers. Navy ships were given blanket authority to stop and board any vessel in American waters suspected of carrying drugs.

One part of the new effort was "Centac 26," an elite central tactical unit consisting of DEA agents, New York City police, and a handful of trusted Metro-Dade detectives. The front-page headline in the *Miami Herald* declared: "U.S. Cavalry Is Coming, and It's About Time."

"Miami was an agent's dream," recalled Frank Chellino, a former undercover agent on the federal task force. "It had everything, cocaine, marijuana, Quaaludes, violence, international cartels, foreign travel. It was you against the world, you against the bad guys." Observed Michael McDonald, a former special IRS agent who co-founded Operation Greenback, "The only thing to compare would be Chicago in the 1920s."

On March 9, 1982, the task force moved on an informant's tip that a two-jet Colombian air cargo company might be a drug pipeline. Customs agents arrived an hour after one of the 707s had landed at Miami International, from Medellín. The agents found pallets of boxes labeled JEANS in the company's small hangar. Inside were 3,096 pounds of pure cocaine, worth $100 million on the street. It was four times bigger than the previous U.S. cocaine record seizure and proved that the Colombians were cooperating at a level far beyond what the DEA and FBI had suspected, since no single trafficker could have arranged for a 2-ton shipment. No one was arrested at the airport or ever charged for the load. The government seized the company's two planes, and the firm's owners and pilots fled to Colombia.

By November 1982, the Feds had enough early success to warrant a photo-op visit from Reagan. Addressing the Miami Citizens Against Crime, he touted the task force's progress. Operation Greenback had brought down its first drug bank, Great American of Dade County. Four bank officials were charged with laundering $96 million in drug proceeds. Trafficker arrests were up 27 percent, drug seizures by more than 50 percent to almost 6,000 pounds, an estimated $3 billion in street value confiscated in a steady series of raids. Almost $200 million in drug-related assets, including cash, cars, boats, planes, and houses, were seized by the DEA, whose entire budget was $330 million. The splashiest arrest came from the DEA's "Operation Swordfish." That bust netted sixty-two arrests, including a local prosecutor, three bank employees, two lawyers, and a plastic surgeon; $800,000 in cash; 250,000 Quaaludes; 107 kilos of cocaine; and evidence that 9 tons had been imported over a few months.

Yet the early optimism was misplaced. The arrests and seizures were records for law enforcement and attracted headlines, but they made only a slight dent in the enormous coke trade. The task force's "powder on the table press conference" mentality rewarded fast, flashy busts rather than extended investigations that might lead to arrests and convictions of drug kingpins. Despite the seizures, so much coke arrived that the wholesale price dropped from $55,000 a kilo to $13,000, a record low. Just five years earlier, only 952 pounds of cocaine had been seized in the entire country. In another five years, the Feds would seize 150,000 pounds in South Florida alone, and the business would still be going strong. A former Centac team leader told me, "We saw the kilos of coke in the police evidence room and knew that we were arresting more dealers in a few months than the Miami police had picked up in a year. But what we didn't know then was how enormous the organization was behind the dope trade. And that we were just scratching the surface."

The cartels responded to the high-profile bust by redoubling the number of flights and saturating the region with even more coke. Peru, Bolivia, and Colombia produced most of the world's 170 tons, and the Medellín cartel controlled 80 percent. The Reagan administration put tremendous pressure on the Bahamian government to crack down on "Crazy Carlos" Lehder's Norman's Cay. Lehder felt it: over several months his bribes to keep his operation running nearly doubled. But the Colombians were bringing in far more than Lehder and his distributors could handle and they made contingencies for the day when those facilities closed. In 1982, Jorge Ochoa flew in 19 tons of coke over several months without any help from Lehder. The big jump in importation and untested entry points meant they lost more planes and coke loads to the Feds, but the cartel wrote it off as the price of doing business. "We hurt them a lot," says a former FBI agent on Centac. "But we were only reducing their profits, not putting them out of business."

"You've got to have a sense of humor or you'd go crazy in this job," said the DEA's Frank Chellino. "We're outmanned and outgunned. You're talking about people who can buy a Learjet and a ranch for $2 million and abandon it as an operating expense on a $30 million deal."

Remarkably, even though law enforcement knew about the Medellín cartel, by the end of 1982, only a few agents knew about the significance of individual dons like Jorge Ochoa, José Gacha, and Pablo Escobar. Escobar was so far off the drug enforcement radar that they were unaware that he owned his Miami Beach mansion and a much grander home in suburban Plantation that he'd bought in 1981 for $8.03 million.

It would be another two years before a U.S. Special Forces raid on a processing plant in Tranquilandia, Colombia, found the paperwork identifying Escobar, Gacha, and Ochoa as Medellín kingpins. They would also find 14 tons of cocaine worth a billion dollars.

CHAPTER 13

"Trash for Cash"

W HILE THE FEDS were trying to make a dent in the area's coke business, Andrew Capitman and Mark Shantzis remained the only investors along Ocean Drive willing to gamble that the neighborhood could revitalize. But the retirement home atmosphere, combined with the grinding poverty and the increase in crime from the Marielitos, kept away all but a few adventurous tourists. The duo had raised some more money, and two of their other hotels—the Tides and the Carlyle—were under renovation.

Capitman knew that Dona Zemo had friends in the theater and asked her to help bring in business. Whenever groups came to town to perform at the Beach's Theater of the Performing Arts, she lobbied them to stay at the Cardozo. "I told them it was avant-garde and cutting edge," she says. "But they would say it was too dangerous to stay south of Lincoln Road. I'd tell them they were wrong, that I was living there. You could almost hear them sigh."

She wrote a letter to Bill Miller, who was a publicist for the road show of the musical comedy *Sugar Babies*. "They were coming into town for three weeks of performances. I sent him a three-page letter about everything he was missing in South Beach. Maybe he felt sorry for me, but in any case he came to visit and loved it."

Miller booked the troupe into the Cardozo, the first time visiting actors stayed south of Lincoln Road. Their rental of thirty-seven rooms allowed Andrew Capitman to pay the handymen and housekeepers. Miller passed the word in New York, and by late 1982, half a dozen other theater groups stayed there. The Cardozo began hosting after-show parties at the café. And Zemo pitched the Cardozo to small cruise lines and cargo ships. One evening, they got a busload of crewmen who stayed for several days while their ship was in drydock.

"It was as if there was this one lightbulb on in the entire neighborhood," recalls David Wallach. "And it was at the Cardozo."

"It was tough going," says Zemo. "We were not yet breaking even, and over the summer, the place was completely dead except for the locals."

Capitman and Shantzis launched a second round of limited partnerships, this time hoping to raise $6 million to completely renovate all five hotels, and maybe buy two more.

Zemo's roommate, Jane Dee, who thought Dona was crazy when she moved to South Beach, had changed her mind a few months later and moved there. Her timing was ideal. Andrew needed someone to oversee the last three months of the Carlyle renovation. A self-described "free spirit who had been radicalized by the 1960s," the striking redhead had gotten tired of being "a hippie in the Connecticut woods." Capitman offered her the job and she moved to South Beach and into a third-floor apartment in the Carlyle in the fall of 1982.

"Dona knew everyone by that time," recalls Jane, "but of course it seemed like there were only twenty people to know."

The refurbished Carlyle opened in January 1983, over Art Deco Weekend.

It was managed by Dona Zemo. She convinced a young piano player to roll the piano onto the veranda and play for hours just for tips. With its neon-lit, swing-era ambience, the café was popular from the start, filled with local Bohemian artists and characters like a fortune-teller and the Scull sisters, Sahara and Haydee, primitive Cuban artists who designed their own outlandish clothes.

"There was also nothing else around," Zemo recalls. "You couldn't go to Lincoln Road, it was too unsafe. You couldn't go west of Washington Avenue [two blocks away]."

"It was supposed to be the showcase," says Jane. "We had these great rooms for tourists, and then I'd be taking a call to make a reservation, and the next call would be from an eighty-five-year-old resident who couldn't remember where his room was. Then ten minutes later I'd be dealing with a Cuban who spoke no English and had just flooded two floors below from an overrun bath. Andrew and Mark had run so much over budget that they used our credit cards to finish the work." Capitman and Shantzis failed to raise the $6 million in additional investments.

The popularity of the café did little to stop the company's financial hemorrhaging. The opening of the partially restored Leslie the following month also did not help. In March, the *Miami Herald* reported that Capitman's company had failed to pay $36,000 in payroll-deduction taxes.

"I didn't even need to see that article," says Zemo. "I'm from a very traditional Sicilian family. I have an eye for Italians in suits. One day at the café, in the late spring, I see these two guys at a table. They were in custom tailor-made suits, crisp starched shirts, real business style, no gold chains. Jane and I used to say that South Beach would only be successful if the Rolling Stones moved in or the Italians came to clean it up. I knew right away something was going on."

Zemo soon learned from Andrew that he and Mark might sell to a group of Philadelphia investors. The two Italians might be among the new owners.

"He [Andrew] was crushed, you could tell," says Wallach. "They were just too early and they couldn't hold out any longer. They weren't mean enough to throw out all the elderly and scare away the Cubans, so they ended up with these hotels that were still half residences. Their non-eviction approach was good public policy, but not great for business. When I ran into Andrew, he half-joked that he now knew why in 1958, the Cardozo was featured in a Frank Capra movie starring Frank Sinatra. The movie was about a hotel owner who had fallen prey to creditors."

Capitman and Shantzis tried their hardest to hold on to the properties. They delayed paying bills, used personal credit cards to buy more time, and even pleaded unsuccessfully with the city for infrastructure improvements they felt might attract other developers. They were especially eager to keep the properties because both men believed that the neighborhood was just beginning to attract some of the attention that would fill hotels with tourists.

In the fall of 1982, a Hollywood studio filmed in Miami Beach for the first time in decades. It was Brian De Palma's remake of the 1932 crime classic, *Scarface*, with Al Pacino as Tony Montana, a Marielito who violently worked his way to the top of the Miami cocaine trade. A *Miami Herald* photographer, Bill Cooke, who had lived in Miami since 1959, went to the set to shoot some pictures. He summarized the problem that confronted Capitman: "I don't ever remember going to Ocean Drive before I went for the *Scarface* photos. There wasn't any reason to go."

The Cuban community was split over the film. Manny Diaz, a Cuban-born board member of the Spanish American League Against Discrimination, lobbied hard for local support, but other prominent Cubans vociferously protested what they considered stereotypical slander. Miami School Board member Demetrio Perez, Jr. (who later pled guilty to five felony counts of defrauding the U.S. government by overcharging low-income Little Havana tenants), tried to ban filming on county property, including any beaches, unless screenwriter Oliver Stone changed the Pacino character into a Communist agent sent by Castro to embarrass Cuban Americans. He denounced the Havana-born co-star Steven Bauer, the son of a Bay of Pigs veteran, for accepting a role as Pacino's criminal sidekick. "It had touched a nerve," says real estate developer Craig Robins, "because *Scarface* was a fully integrated image of Miami."

De Palma was forced to move the production to Los Angeles after just three weeks because of protests and death threats. Only a couple of exterior shots and two scenes were shot in Miami Beach—one, at a run-down hotel at Eighth and Ocean, in which Al Pacino's character takes a chain saw to a Colombian drug dealer handcuffed to the bathtub; the other at the Fontainebleau, where Pacino and Bauer sip tropical drinks by the pool, talking about girls and riches.

Vincent Canby of *The New York Times* was one of the few to give the film a rave review, describing it as "the most stylish and provocative—and maybe the most vicious—serious film about the American underworld since Francis Ford Coppola's 'Godfather' . . . I also suspect that 'Scarface' will be seen as something of an inside joke in Hollywood and other high-flying communities where cocaine is not regarded with the horror it is by this film."

That same week, producer Michael Mann made his first scouting trip to Miami Beach for a series he had just sold to NBC about two wild cops in South Beach. It was called *Miami Vice*. Like De Palma's film, it too did not escape controversy. Although the Beach needed the business that came with a full-time film crew, city officials worried that a show about the very violent South Florida drug scene might not be the best advertisement for a resort trying to rebrand itself. The show's technical adviser, Lieutenant Pete Cuccaro, resigned before the first episode, protesting scripts that were "demeaning" to local police.

In May 1983, on the heels of *Scarface*, the Bulgarian artist Christo and his wife, Jeanne-Claude, completed the installation *Surrounded Islands*, in which they enclosed a dozen tiny islands in Biscayne Bay with 200-foot-wide skirts of neon pink fabric. More than seven hundred volunteers anchored the six miles of polypropylene material. Art critics compared it to a modern version of Monet's *Water Lilies*.

One of the volunteers was seventeen-year-old Carlos Betancourt, a student at Miami's Coral Park School. Betancourt, who is today a conceptual artist with work in the permanent collections of the Metropolitan Museum and the National Portrait Gallery, had learned that Christo was staying at the Leslie Hotel. "I knew little about Miami Beach, except that my parents brought me there for some vacations in the 1970s," he recalls. "Me and some of my other friends who were into design drove to the Leslie. It was my first time ever on Ocean Drive. And I was mesmerized. It was like a jewel." Betancourt had no fear of the run-down streets and the dangerous-looking nocturnal characters. "There were a lot of crack addicts around, but if you left them alone, they didn't hassle you. But what I loved was the daytime, when you could wander around South Beach and look at the buildings. They looked like something out of a Jetson movie or some Buck Rogers comic strip. It took me only a couple of weeks to know this is where I wanted to move, to hang out, to create my art."

Carlos and his friends discovered a fishing pier at the very tip of South Shore, part of Steve Muss's redevelopment zone. "We'd hang out there," he told me. "It was a magnet for surfers because the waves were best there. And there were these Cuban fishermen. The surfers would tie a big piece of meat on the fishermen's lines and paddle out, and they would eventually get large turtles or baby sharks, and by ten p.m. there'd be a bonfire and something roasting. We would all go swimming at night. My first time there I remember eating a giant turtle and seeing this gorgeous black drag queen, probably a prostitute, walking along the beach holding her stilettos. I knew that something was happening here, but I just didn't know what."

HOLLYWOOD'S SUDDEN INTEREST in the Beach did not come in time to save Capitman and Shantzis. In October 1983, they sold all five hotels to Cavanagh Communities Corporation, a real estate development firm headed by Leonard Pelullo, a thirty-three-year-old contractor. It assumed the $5.6 million mortgage and gave the former owners 2 million shares of a new subsidiary, Art Deco Hotels Corporation. "My company didn't have an identity," Pelullo said. "We wanted to create a new image and what better way than with Art Deco?"

The paunchy, fast-talking Pelullo promised to raise $25 million to gut and refurbish the hotels. Mark Shantzis left but Andrew Capitman stayed on as a salaried adviser.

"These guys had zero concern for preservation," says Jane Dee. "They thought they were going to make it into Atlantic City. And Lenny [Pelullo] was all about protecting Lenny. But strange as it seems, they did start to clean the neighborhood up. I joked with Dona at the time that I thought they had taken the crime off the street and put it into their office."

With no other investors on the horizon, locals had little choice but to put their faith in Pelullo, a self-described "workout specialist"—someone who buys troubled companies and turns them around. With his custom-made suits, monogrammed shirts, Rolls-Royce and Cadillac convertibles, and Coconut Grove penthouse, he impressed reporters, residents, politicians, and most important, bankers, who had been petrified of investing a dime in South Beach. Pelullo—who thought it was just a matter of time until gambling was legalized in Miami Beach—boasted that he would single-handedly revitalize the Beach, and his infectious enthusiasm convinced many that he could spearhead its metamorphosis. Capitman and Shantzis had been so anxious to sell that they hadn't checked out Cavanagh, which was a struggling, publicly traded Miami-based holding company for real estate development firms. If they had, they might have reconsidered their faith in Pelullo as South Beach's savior.

Pelullo attended Oklahoma State and Temple University for a while and then worked in his family's construction company. In 1981, his friend John Sgarlat, who owned a major stake in Cavanagh, asked Pelullo to help straighten things out. Pelullo became president. Sgarlat—who went on to convictions in securities and wire fraud and money laundering—was its chairman.

Cavanagh had a checkered past by the time Pelullo came aboard. Founded in 1964, it first sold lots in a Florida fishing lake project named Palm Beach Heights. Its next development was touted in glossy brochures as Rotónda, a dream community near Punta Gorda. Johnny Carson sidekick Ed McMahon was Rotónda's pitchman. Eight thousand northerners mailed in $40 million for land that was mostly uninhabitable, with no access roads or sewage lines. One man had a heart attack when he saw his property. Undeterred, Cavanagh developed Sabalton, another dream community, built on swampland. The FTC repeatedly charged Cavanagh with deceptive sales practices and eventually got consent decrees halting the bad practices.

In 1972, by now a $138 million public company with 46 offices and 1,500 employees, Cavanagh was forced by creditors into chapter 11 bankruptcy and delisted from the New York Stock Exchange. Class-action lawsuits over the Florida projects had pressured the company. When it reemerged a year later, the bankruptcy court ordered it to set aside a $14 million trust for the benefit of Rotónda buyers to bank for necessary infrastructure. The revitalized company bought 17 acres in Atlantic City for $40.3 million in its own stock and announced it would build two $100 million casinos. The *Wall Street Journal* called the deal "an amazing turnaround."

In 1982, a year after Pelullo took control, a Canadian oilman tried selling him a suburban Denver bank that was deeply in debt: Dominion. Before agreeing to a deal, Pelullo asked to be made a board director so he could review otherwise confidential federal reports. He was named co-chairman, moved into the president's office, hired a chauffeured limousine, and tried running the bank without investing any capital. By the time the other directors kicked him out, he had loaned $1 million to his own companies and friends. State and federal banking regulators later concluded the loans were "improper," virtually "uncollectable," and contributed to Dominion's eventual insolvency. Pelullo claimed that there was nothing improper, and that when he discovered the bank wasn't worth buying, he left voluntarily.

A couple of months after Cavanagh took control of the five South Beach hotels, the SEC filed another civil action against the company and three directors, charging they engaged in unregistered distribution of 601,500 shares of common stock to raise money for the Atlantic City casinos. The next day, the Cavanagh subsidiary that owned the New Jersey casino land filed for bankruptcy. The SEC settled the case with another consent order, in which the company and directors admitted no wrongdoing but sold the Atlantic City property at a fire sale to Resorts International.

The Cavanagh that Lenny Pelullo took over was nearly insolvent. Its single most valuable asset was the $14 million trust set aside for the court victims of its marketing scam. In 1979, Florida's Department of Business Regulation filed charges against Cavanagh for illegally diverting $2.4 million of the trust fund, and it was forced to return the money. When he took charge, Pelullo personally directed the trust.

Within a year, he had lost $300,000 of the protected fund on bad investments. He used it as bait with banks by making large deposits and then asking for loans. He put some into Great American, the first bank that Operation Greenback targeted as a drug-laundering center. Great American loaned Cavanagh's new subsidiary, Royale Group Ltd., $1.6 million (and ultimately sued to recover the money). Sunset Commercial Bank made an unsecured and personal loan to him, on which he also defaulted. Pelullo deposited another $1.9 million of the trust fund into the Philadelphia branch of Bank Leumi; the bank then loaned him $325,000 to finance his purchase of an Atlantic City limousine company. He eventually defaulted on that loan as well. Pelullo put his younger brother Arthur in charge of the limo service and the Royale Group financed Arthur's boxing promotion business.

Just before he took over Capitman's hotels, in March 1983, Pelullo put $608,000 of the trust money into a CD at the National Bank of Florida. He agreed to an 8 percent interest rate, even though the national average was 13 percent. Royale used its account there to pull off a check-kiting scheme in which other Pelullo companies wrote checks to one another although it was clear there wasn't enough money in the accounts. The purpose was to give the firms "the appearance of financial stability, when in fact [they] were without substantial financial means," the bank later charged in a lawsuit. Pelullo denied the charges. A bank manager who had approved $277,000 on overdrawn Pelullo checks, and then wrote a loan to cover the missing money, was fired. The bank won a $500,000 judgment, which it never collected.

A few months later, Pelullo secured a $12.5 million loan from Miami's Sunshine State Bank. But by early 1984, he had stopped making payments. That same year, Pelullo persuaded a giant California savings institution, Financial Corporation of America (FCA), to loan Royale $13.5 million to refinance the Sunshine loan and use leftover funds to renovate the South Beach hotels. Royale paid a $500,000 finder's fee, 3 percent of the total loan, to Russell Schweiker, a Philadelphia entrepreneur and a friend of several Royale directors. It also agreed to buy foreclosed town houses that FCA didn't want to carry on its books at a loss. FCA loaned Pelullo the purchase price for the foreclosed properties. In order to repay them, all he had to do was forward the town house rents to the bank. He did not. Nor did he pay off the Sunshine loan. "Trash for cash" is how Pelullo derisively described the FCA deal, after he got the $13.5 million.

In August 1984, he announced that Royale had tentatively agreed to buy a prime oceanfront parcel at 15th Street and would build a 650-room hotel. The deal never closed.

Pelullo won over many people by doing a few renovations on the Leslie and Carlyle with some of the money he had finagled. Cultural activity coalesced at the Carlyle, attracting artists who used to visit the Cardozo Café, as well as politicians and visiting celebrities.

"The Carlyle was definitely the place to go," says Craig Robins, who was just launching his own real estate career in South Beach. "It often looked like the mob of the 1950s but without the gambling."

Sam Robin, the interior designer, witnessed the Royale Group when it hit the town at night. "Lenny, and all those wannabe-hoods from Philadelphia—they were at the Forge and all the clubs. They spent $14 million on big limos, flashy houses, and straight up their noses."

1

Miami Beach was an undeveloped sandbar overgrown with palmetto scrub at the turn of the century. Even into the 1920s, Ocean Drive was deserted except for the Deauville Casino.

2

Indianapolis auto-parts tycoon Carl Fisher spent millions transforming the barren Miami Beach island into a luxury resort.

3

Fisher's Roman Pools and Casino included an imported Dutch windmill that pumped saltwater to its pools. Attendance was by membership only; Jews and blacks were banned.

Floods of immigrants, mostly Cuban and Haitian, have changed South Florida's demographics, especially since the 1980 Mariel boatlift. The bodies of thirty-three drowned Haitians washed ashore at Hillsboro Beach in 1982.

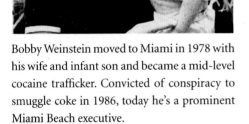

Bobby Weinstein moved to Miami in 1978 with his wife and infant son and became a mid-level cocaine trafficker. Convicted of conspiracy to smuggle coke in 1986, today he's a prominent Miami Beach executive.

Actor Don Johnson (*left*) had a starring role as a stylish detective in *Miami Vice,* the hit TV series that reshaped Miami Beach's image. Alex Daoud (*right*), a cheerleader for the town's renaissance, served three terms as mayor before being tried and convicted of bribery.

Barbara Capitman, a retired New York magazine editor, led a small band of volunteers to save South Beach's 800 Art Deco buildings.

For eighteen months, Capitman fought a developer's demolition of the historic Senator Hotel (*below*), but it was torn down in 1988 and replaced with a parking lot.

Beginning in 1984, nightclubs opened every week and quickly became a driving force in transforming the Beach into a hip resort. Self-described "Queen of the Night" Tara Solomon, party girl, columnist, and photographer, at a club in the late 1980s.

10

An eclectic mix of artists, urban pioneers, and gays guided South Beach's gentrification. Carlos Betancourt (*left*), a renowned conceptual artist, with "King of the Night" Louis Canales.

11

Brooklyn-born hoodlum Chris Paciello with his partner, Ingrid Casares, the daughter of a prominent Cuban family. Paciello was the town's most popular nightclub owner until his 1999 racketeering arrest.

In a rare display of political activism, blacks demonstrated for equal work treatment at the 1972 Republican convention.

Frank Del Vecchio (*left*), a retired HUD official, has been the town's indefatigable activist against overdevelopment since he moved to the Beach in 1995.

Harold Rosen, an ex-mayor, is now the chief proponent for the nightclub and entertainment industry and is often at odds with Del Vecchio.

Jerry Robins built a real estate dynasty in Miami Beach, and his son, Craig, was the only Florida developer to see the potential of the Art Deco District. Jerry (*far left*), with his daughter Stacy (*second from left*), wife Joan, and Craig.

City Commissioner Saul Gross, one of the earliest New York developers in the Art Deco District, with his wife, Jane Dee, at the city's first gay pride parade.

Real estate magnate Don Peebles (*center*), cutting the ribbon in 2002 for the Royal Palm Hotel, after a heavily contested, multiyear battle. Peebles's wife, Katrina, is to his left and Miami Beach mayor David Dermer to his right.

Al Malnik (*at right*) and his son Shareef (who changed his name from Mark when he married a Saudi Princess) own the iconic Forge restaurant.

Mob rumors have long swirled around Al Malnik. One of his Rolls-Royces was blown up in his condo's garage in 1982 (*below*), and the crime remains unsolved.

19

20

Jason Binn (*left*) and Jerry Powers at an Ocean Drive anniversary party.

21

Thomas Kramer, a German playboy and commodities trader, arrived on the scene in the early 1990s and spent $145 million in cash, scooping up most of the waterfront in the Beach's blighted South Pointe neighborhood.

By 1997, despite considerable public protest and financing problems, two residential high-rises were built in South Pointe: South Pointe Tower (*foreground*) and Kramer's own multicolored Portofino Tower.

23

Developer Jorge Perez (*right*) with French designer Philippe Starck, in front of Perez's 1800-unit luxury condo complex, the Icon Brickell, in downtown Miami. The Icon, the largest of dozens of Perez projects in Miami and the Beach, has become the symbol of South Florida's unprecedented real estate boom and bust.

CHAPTER 14

"Building Blocks"

BARBARA CAPITMAN TOLD any developer she met that the Art Deco neighborhood's new status as a historic district meant it was ripe for gentrification. "The architecture, the location, the people, this could be a vibrant community where all kinds of people—elderly retirees, young artists, people from the North and from Latin America, come together to create an exciting, harmonious experience." Her son's failure did not stop others from believing they could revive South Beach. And while Lenny Pelullo might not have been her model developer, it was better than allowing the neighborhood to fall prey to the wrecking ball.

South Beach's ascent was a disjointed affair: sometimes it seemed to be in full revival and at other times a bunch of overhyped dreams. The fitful progress was fueled primarily by out-of-towners. Not a single Florida real estate developer then had the foresight to think that the charming architecture bordering one of the country's best beaches might one day become a tourist draw. They could not see past the crack addicts and the elderly who sat on the terraces lining Ocean Drive. It took developers from other cities, usually New York, to appreciate the potential. The revival of South Beach happened only because Floridians like Andrew Capitman were ready to sell to non-Floridians who had the money and believed they had a better idea about how to revive Carl Fisher's resort town.

Then *Miami Vice* premiered, on September 16, 1984. The show's impact was instantaneous. It delivered a high-gloss, high-octane version of Miami and the Beach into millions of middle-American homes. Not everyone liked it. Police officials mostly criticized it as "too way out," "fanciful," or "just showbiz." A local prosecutor said it "had nothing to do with reality." Only one policeman, a narcotics officer, David Graveline, admitted, "There's no question about it, it's Miami the whole way through." And a prominent defense attorney for many drug defendants, Roy Black, told the *Miami Herald*, "It seems normal to me."

Several members of Miami's Tourism Development Authority were concerned about *Miami Vice*'s impact on tourism. After the premiere episode was a hit, they formed a committee to investigate how it might affect visitors' perceptions of the town. "Sure it makes the city look glamorous, but people are now afraid of it," warned Sigmund Zilber, a tourism official. "If you live in Lincoln, Nebraska, this crime terrifies you."

His was a minority view. The critic for the *Herald* hailed the show. "The cities of Miami and Miami Beach are made to seem a multicultural metropolis of pastel colors, aquatic beauty and vibrant nightlife; they have never looked better." He correctly predicted that Don Johnson's "expensive look of studied casualness was destined to become the *Miami Vice* look." A couple of months later, the *Herald* declared that the show had "redefined Miami's image."

Preservationists were pleased because much of the show focused on South Beach, beaming the forgotten neighborhood into 20 million households weekly. Images of suntanned, good-looking young people, living in a sexy tropical city with a one-of-a-kind architecture, contradicted the stereotypes of criminal Cuban refugees and retired pensioners.

Skeptical Beach promoters changed their minds when they saw *Vice* become part of the cultural milieu. Even its name was mimicked. There was soon a Miami Mice (an exterminator), Miami Spice (a seasonings shop), Miami Twice (a vintage clothing store), Miami Nice (a chiropractor), and Miami Slice (a diner).

Michael Mann thought the city was "the new Casablanca, a city with an edge." Anthony Yerkovich, the show's other executive producer, had been drawn to Miami precisely because of its drug-dealing and money-laundering reputation. "I wanted a city in which the American dream had been distilled into something perverse," he said. "I wanted the city to serve as a protagonist, as a co-star."

The year *Miami Vice* premiered, 1984, South Florida coke seizures topped 25 tons, more than double the previous record. But wholesale prices for kilos dropped 43 percent, from $35,000 each to $20,000, meaning that more coke than ever was still getting into the country. *Newsweek* and *Time* did dueling cover stories the same week about the continuing cocaine epidemic. They featured sidebars about the heads of the Medellín cartel and their estimated net worths, a Who's Who of the narcotics trade. Those cocaine kingpins were the same men— Ochoa, Gacha, and Escobar—who weren't even known to law enforcement a few years earlier.

A few months into 1985, Griselda Blanco de Trujillo, the "Godmother of Cocaine," was arrested by DEA agents while visiting her California distributors. She was busted on a ten-year-old arrest warrant for her conspiracy indictment in New York and held without bail. But her arrest rated only 227 words on a UPI wire service report and wasn't even picked up by the Miami press. A task force of federal agents arrested Max Mermelstein three months later, as he parked his custom Jaguar at his Fort Lauderdale estate. A DEA informer in the John DeLorean sting operation had turned him in. The agents found twenty-seven weapons, $73,000 in a wall safe, and $200,000 in a duffel bag under his bed. He had been indicted by a federal grand jury earlier in the year for smuggling 750 kilos of cocaine. Charged with a "continuing criminal enterprise," and facing life in prison without parole, Mermelstein cooperated with the Feds. Based on his information, Jon Roberts was arrested a year later. Mickey Munday became a fugitive but was eventually caught.

The one case that did get a lot of *Miami Herald* coverage was the so-called River Cops escapade, a series of crimes committed by Miami police who ripped off the criminals they were supposed to apprehend, even murdering some. The gang of dirty cops was run by Armando "Scarface" Garcia. The twenty-three-year-old officer was already a five-year veteran. Along with a fellow cop, Osvaldo Coello, Garcia opened a gym in South Miami called Bodymasters. It became a hangout for the gang. They started by taking drugs from motorists pulled over for traffic violations but soon escalated to stealing money and drugs from their busts.

Next they received a tip that the *Mary C.*, an old boat at Jones Boat Yard on the Miami River, was packed with cocaine. When the cops rushed the boat, the smugglers, who had just finished offloading 400 kilos, jumped into the river. Three drowned. Within weeks, "the River Cops" scandal was plastered across newspapers worldwide.*

But the public reaction was muted. "We were saturated, overloaded with the real cocaine wars," says the Miami Beach detective Charlie Seraydar. "*Scarface* had been deadly serious to those of us who lived in Miami. But *Miami Vice*, even though it was dealing with a problem that was part of everyday life, was a lot more Hollywood entertainment. People wanted to talk more about the latest episode than some story in the *Herald* about another bust." "Sonny" Crockett, the Don Johnson character, drove a Ferrari, wore Versace suits, and lived on a sailboat with his pet alligator, Elvis. "It was hard for real cops to compete with that," says Seraydar.

"I was convinced that *Miami Vice* was a great vehicle for rebuilding South Beach," says Alex Daoud. Many people who would never have otherwise visited Miami now came to see the neighborhood. Michael Caine liked it so much that he opened a restaurant on deserted Lincoln Road. Prince told Sam Robin that Miami was like the nasty streets of his native Minneapolis, but with better weather and a beach. He began scouting for a nightclub.

Miami Vice coincided with the first annual Formula One Grand Prix in mainland Miami, as well as the inaugural Miami Film Festival. Mitch Kaplan, the owner of Books & Books, had launched the Miami Book Fair, introducing readers to Mario Vargas Llosa, Garrison Keillor, Ken Kesey, Richard Ford, and James Baldwin. "They were all small steps," says David Wallach, "but they were building blocks along the road to creating something completely different."

·   ·   ·

---

* It took years, but eventually one hundred cops were arrested, fired, suspended, or reprimanded for their roles in the conspiracy. Garcia fled to Colombia after his trial ended in a hung jury, but he was later extradited and sentenced to twenty-five years in prison.

LOST IN THE *Vice* fanfare were quieter developments in Miami Beach that planted the seeds for the creative growth the moribund community so desperately needed. The Torpedo Factory, an artists' colony in Alexandria, Virginia, persuaded the Beach commissioners to bankroll the South Florida Art Center on Lincoln Road, at the northern edge of the Art Deco District. The $62,500 community block grant that created the center also took leases on fourteen abandoned storefronts, hoping they would become studios for working artists. The grant paid for everything from liability insurance to the tiny salary for the Art Center's director. The center included twenty small exhibit and work "spaces" and attracted fifty artists. One of them was the eighteen-year-old Carlos Betancourt, who made the mostly deserted shopping street a favorite hangout. Carlos later moved into an industrial warehouse on Lincoln, where he tied a hose to his kitchen sink and showered in the alley. "It was very raw," he recalls. A counter at a nearby Woolworth's was the only neighborhood restaurant. "It had the best patty melts. And I'd sit there with friends, surrounded by these old ladies with beehives. It was fantastic."

Betancourt is gay, and over a couple of years, he had noticed a growing gay population. Without a decent school or safe playgrounds, the Beach was not attracting suburban families; but gay men and women, almost always childless, weren't put off by those missing services. In many other cities from San Francisco to Seattle to New York, gay men had pioneered the revival of marginal neighborhoods. There was no organized gay movement to help the Art Deco District, but people came because they were designers, decorators, architects, and urban planners. They found a tolerant neighborhood of displaced minorities that was gay-friendly. (Miami Beach would follow San Francisco as a pioneering city in later passing a gay rights law that afforded full civil rights and equal treatment in employment.) And because South Beach is so small, it was easy to form a network of new friends.

Randall Robinson was typical. He arrived in the mid-1980s with a degree in architectural landscaping. "I planned to move to Los Angeles," he recalls, "but I had done this survey course on the architectural history of Miami and Miami Beach and I was sold on the city." The originator of the Art Deco walking tours, he moved into a tiny apartment at 1245 Meridian, in the heart of the protected district.

"There either were old people or us, young kids," he told me. "It was not gay yet. It was just a wonderful cool place."

Starting in the mid-eighties, there was another draw for gay men. Many from northeastern cities who tested HIV-positive had heard about the new "gay paradise" in South Beach. Some decided that instead of fighting northern winters and high living costs, they would spend their last days at the beach. "I came down after a lot of friends I had known died of AIDS," one local DJ told me. "A lot of people in New York had rented an apartment in South Beach, so I moved. It was another world. The Beach seemed easier on my immune system."

Some of those who arrived were on disability, expecting to survive only a few years. But as AIDS drugs improved, they lived longer. And the wasting disease that left many AIDS patients sickly thin was counteracted with anabolic steroids that translated into muscular gains at the gym. Steroid use, in a town that emphasized the body, meant that many men spent their days at the beach and the gym, looking fitter and healthier than they had before they contracted the disease.

"It never became a gay ghetto like Christopher Street [New York] or Castro [San Francisco]," says Robinson. One of the reasons was that many young Cuban men came from traditional Catholic families in which homosexuality was a mortal sin and the idea of a gay son anathema. Louis Aguirre, now the co-host of South Florida's most successful television entertainment news show, *Deco Drive*, was then a teenager living with his parents on the mainland and trying hard to repress his urges for men. Aguirre, who many TV viewers still believe is straight, told me he steered clear of gay clubs when they finally opened for fear word would get back to his parents. "You have no idea how many of us there were then," he says. "And there were all these gorgeous guys coming in from New York, it was like putting candy in front of a chocoholic."

South Beach's gay paradise moniker made it a place where a lot of gays came to party and overindulge like their straight counterparts. That is why it was almost impossible for the Beach to get out any effective anti-AIDS message in the mid-eighties. Gay men who intended to stay for only a season or two had little interest in community health problems. HIV-prevention messages were precisely what many northern gays wanted to escape. And for those visiting for a wild weekend of circuit parties, they did not want to hear about safe sex. The carefree attitude and the explosion of the drug scene, especially speed, Special K, and coke, prepared the ground for an exponential growth in the local HIV infection rate. A decade after Betancourt noticed that the Beach's gay community was growing, South Beach earned the dubious title of "epicenter of the AIDS epidemic," with an estimated 25 percent of gay men eighteen and older testing positive. *Out*, America's bestselling gay and lesbian magazine, described South Beach as "a palm-lined cliff that mighty water buffalo throw themselves over."

"There was a price for living in paradise," says Robinson.

CHAPTER 15

"The Sultans
of South Beach"*

WHEN LENNY PELULLO purchased Ocean Drive's best Art Deco hotels from Andrew Capitman in 1983, he had no competition from other developers and good support from the local community. But that ended the following March when Andrew Capitman quit his marketing director's job. Barbara Capitman demanded every original worker leave as well. Dona Zemo refused. As far as she was concerned, the Royale Group had "saved the hotels. No one else was going to buy them. They were just going to go into bankruptcy under Andrew and be left to further decay. Royale was hard-core, but they really wanted to shake it up and make it a business." Instead, Zemo became the Royale Group's liaison to the Miami Design Preservation League. And Pelullo, as part of his purchase agreement with Andrew, gave them free office space. "When I stayed, a lot of my preservationist friends thought I was a traitor," she recalls. "Since I was Italian, there was a rumor I was a mobster. Barbara stopped talking to me for six months." Zemo had been an MDPL board director for years, but they took her name off the league's new brochures and Art Deco Weekend preparations.

The community's animosity to Royale and Pelullo opened the door to new developers. In the spring of 1984, a Manhattan law firm that specialized in syndicating properties dispatched a twenty-nine-year-

---

* The chapter title is from Roberta Klein, "The Sultans of South Beach," *Sun-Sentinel* (Fort Lauderdale), January 2, 1992, 12.

old associate, Saul Gross, to South Beach. "Real estate syndications were a booming business, especially in historic restoration projects from Charleston to Boston to Seattle," says Gross. One of the perks of being designated a historic district was that the federal government gave 25 percent tax investment credits to anyone buying and restoring property. Firms like the one Gross worked for raised money from private investors and formed limited syndications, legal entities that passed the tax benefits to the investors and returned profits when the properties increased in value. Historic districts in Boston, Seattle, and Charleston had been largely rebuilt by wealthy investors looking for a tax break through syndication deals.

"It was the middle of winter," recalls Gross. "I saw palm trees and the water and the sun and I thought it was just great. But when I got to the Beach, I saw a lot of drug dealers and a place that looked like time had passed it by. The bones of it were great, but it was a wasteland."

Gross's law firm had set up a syndication company, the Urban Group. Investing in Ocean Drive hotels was too expensive and the local economy too depressed for commercial property; instead, the Group bought and renovated small apartment buildings and hotels away from the Ocean. "Right or wrong, we felt that the people who lived in Miami would sooner live on the Beach than suffer the heavy back-and-forth traffic of the suburbs," Gross explains. "We decided we could redo apartments and have a ready-made market with the locals."

Gross focused on the neighborhood around Flamingo Park. Eight square blocks, it was the historic district's only park. Too far west of the ocean to attract investors, the park had become a hangout for crack dealers and was a no-man's-land after dusk. "There were a lot of people on drugs or living by stealing. A lot of the Beach, especially around the park, was about surviving without working. And most of the landlords seemed to be doing the absolute minimum to maintain their buildings. Some had shut them down when code violations piled up." The police found thirty-five derelicts at a boarded-up warehouse a couple of blocks south of Gross's target area.

Most of the buildings around the Flamingo were built in the 1920s and 1930s, and were two- to four-story structures since converted into short-term rental hotels; the residents were on weekly or month-to-month leases. "These buildings were total gut jobs," says Gross. "At the construction site, you would find crack bottles, needles, everything left over from the night before." The firm's first project, converting the sixty-three-room Hotel Fennimore at 12th and Euclid into a twenty-nine-unit apartment complex, was completed within the year. "When we put the FOR RENT sign outside, we didn't even know if anyone would want to rent there." Gross knew that his asking price, $445 for a renovated one-bedroom, was double the going rate. But all twenty-nine apartments were soon under one-year leases. For syndicators like Gross, Miami Beach offered its own tax incentive if 51 percent or more of the apartments were leased to low- and moderate-income tenants. "That was the easy part. There weren't a lot of people with money living here."

"That was the first time I had overseen a renovation project, and I saw how you can create something wonderful if you are true to the original spirit of the architecture." By early 1985, Gross's syndicators had purchased eight more buildings. They always bought corner lot structures with large central courtyards and plenty of light for the apartments. "Everything we bought was dilapidated. In many other cities, they would have been condemned already."

The work was costly and arduous. Early on, Gross discovered that 1920s contractors had mixed beach sand in their concrete, reducing its durability and strength, and that most of the steel columns and beams had corroded. "We bought the Wilbur for $160,000 and put $600,000 into it. The Henderson at 11th and Euclid, which cost us $25,000, took $550,000 to redo. Another half million went into the Park Vendome." They even sold some as condos, the first new ones in the Art Deco zone in decades. "We didn't make a lot of money. The work was always a lot more extensive than we thought, I was somewhat inexperienced, and the cost overruns were big."

After his first week in Miami Beach, Gross met Lenny Horowitz, the designer responsible for the pastel colors on many of the repainted buildings. Gross hired Lenny for his own renovations. Through Lenny he met Jane Dee and Dona Zemo, and became a regular at Pelullo's Carlyle and Cardozo. Soon, he was dating Jane. A few months later, he gave up his Manhattan apartment and moved permanently to Miami

Beach. "I knew that this was the ground floor, that there were possibilities here to grow with the town." By January 1986, Gross had earned his real estate license and opened his own firm, Streamline Properties, along a run-down section of Washington Avenue.

ANOTHER NEW YORK attorney who turned into an early South Beach developer was thirty-seven-year-old Mel Schlesser, a criminal lawyer who moved to Lighthouse Point, forty miles north of Miami Beach, in 1980. He continued his legal practice but had designed and built several houses—"I was a frustrated architect." One day in 1984, as he was about to leave for federal court, his close friend Arthur Leeds telephoned him. Leeds and his business partner, Bob Gershon, were developers who had successfully rehabbed 30 buildings and owned and operated 1,000 apartments in New York.

"Arthur said he heard it was possible that there was some real estate action in South Beach," recalls Schlesser. "I decided to check it out when I finished my trial that day since I'd just be across the causeway." That evening at the Cardozo Café, Schlesser nursed a glass of wine and studied the area from the terrace. "The street seemed like one long retirement home, but I wondered how such great architecture had been so neglected."

When Schlesser got home he called Leeds. "It could be gold," Schlesser told him. "If you're ready, I'm ready."

Leeds flew down the next week and the two friends walked the neighborhood. "We talked about how no one in Florida seemed to understand the concept of gentrification," says Schlesser. "The real estate mood in Florida was that you tear anything old down and build something new. If it was old, they saw no value in it. In northeast cities like New York, with limited space, rehab developers like Leeds were always going back to neglected neighborhoods, keeping the facades, gutting the interiors, and by increasing the value, bringing the areas back to life."

Schlesser, Leeds, and Gershon formed a partnership and began buying buildings. Rather than syndications, they put a little money down on each property and had the sellers give them mortgages. "No banks would touch the area, at least no one we spoke to," Schlesser recalls.

Their first property was a multifamily building on Meridian. They built a portfolio that eventually included four hotels: Beach Paradise, the Drake, the Ritz Plaza, and the Casa Grande. They paid $3 million for Ocean Drive's Winterhaven, a residential home for the elderly, and the shuttered and condemned 115-room Alamac Hotel on Collins. The Schlesser group had decided to turn the Alamac into apartments, saying, "We'll go after yuppies." That there were none in South Beach didn't dissuade them. They also bought more properties around Flamingo Park. "Something that would have cost $1 million if it were on Ocean Drive," says Schlesser, "cost $125,000 inside the district."

Within a year, Schlesser and Gross were handling two thirds of all the renovations in South Beach's interior. Schlesser's New York friends visited and shook their heads in dismay. "They figured who would be crazy enough to come down here and invest that kind of money when there was nothing but hookers and crack dealers?"

Another pioneering developer was Geraldo "Gerry" Sanchez, a Cuban American restoration expert. He wasn't interested in doing small building renovations; he wanted to replace Lenny Pelullo as "King of Ocean Drive." Sanchez had made news when he bought Nixon's former Key Biscayne home for $400,000 in June 1985, restored it quickly, and sold it for $1.05 million to Latin singing sensation Raphael.

At the height of New York City's financial crisis in 1976, Sanchez, who grew up in New York and studied law and business administration, had founded a realty company: Polonia. Real estate was cheap— Sanchez bought decrepit buildings in run-down areas of upper Manhattan, Brooklyn, and Queens, and hired contractors to restore them. Ultimately unsatisfied with their work, he took a ten-month course to learn the art of historic restoration at RESTORE, a non-profit training program in masonry preservation. He developed an excellent reputation and completed projects at the New York Public Library, Trinity Church, the New York Stock Exchange, and the U.S. Capitol in D.C. He also made a sizable personal fortune when he sold the New York real estate he had bought so cheaply.

Sanchez came to South Beach in 1985 to do a restoration project on the Clay Hotel on Española Way. There he got a fast immersion in the Beach's history when during his work he uncovered a "Gentiles Only" sign under layers of old paint. A month after he arrived, he had three real estate agents checking Ocean Drive's prime real estate. "Locals never see opportunities at the beginning," he said. "Ninety-nine percent of the people doing anything are outsiders." Often referring to himself in the third person, he told the *Miami Herald*, "Gerry saw a gold mine. Everybody else saw a slum. I'm not bragging, but everywhere I sniffed, I smelled money in the breeze of the sea."

Sanchez wore white Gatsby-like suits and drove a silver Rolls-Royce. "At first, people thought he was the Latin mob," says Dona Zemo, "but then we found out he was legit."

His rule of thumb was never to pay more than $22 a foot, which he calculated as less than replacement value. Sanchez found financing in a diverse group of New Yorkers: a Grey Advertising executive vice president, a Rockland County dentist, and a partner in a New York construction firm. Flush with cash, he went on an acquisition binge. He bought six Ocean Drive hotels: the Waldorf Tower, Breakwater, Clevelander, Whitehart, Betsy Ross, and the Edison (where he had the bottom of the pool tiled in the image of his face). He also added two parking lots and most of one side of a block on Española Way. His teams of Polonia workers, in their bright yellow slickers, were soon putting fast face-lifts on the run-down buildings.

The fast-talking Sanchez was every bit as much of a self-promoter as Pelullo. One of the first things he said to anyone he met was that he had sunk $15 million into South Beach.

"I don't know how much he spent," says Mel Schlesser, "but there's no question he came in too fast and heavy. I knew there wasn't anything we had that was making money, so I wasn't sure how he was going to turn a profit."

Sanchez was evidently not burdened by self-doubt. As he revived South Beach, he said, all he asked was that Lummus Park, named after Carl Fisher's contemporaries, be renamed "Gerry Park, with all due respect to Mr. Lummus." Calling himself "the agent provocateur" for transforming South Beach into an American Riviera, he rented what he claimed was Kirk Douglas's former waterfront estate (Kirk Douglas had never owned property in Miami Beach). He donated generously to charities and touted his Riviera concept to local banks and the development community. He courted politicians at Joe's Stone Crab and the Forge. Overnight, he was South Beach's largest landowner. "He is buying up deteriorated property as if Ocean Drive was a board game and he's the only player," said the *Miami Herald*. He pledged not to leave South Beach until the area was revitalized—unless he was called away to restore the Taj Mahal or the Vatican. "If it's not famous or historic, forget it."

Sanchez was the first developer to profit by flipping buildings to eager buyers. Only seven months after buying the Clevelander, Sanchez sold it to a Chicago couple for a $400,000 profit (the new buyers successfully transformed the outdoor glass-block bar into a permanent spring break party central). And three months after that he pocketed another $1.5 million by selling the Waldorf for almost 3.5 times what he paid for it.

"He's the kind of investor we've been dreaming of," said Stuart Rogel, the city's economic development director. Beach commissioner Stanley Arkin remarked, "He's the snow that has started the snowball rolling."

"THE MINUTE I hit Ocean Drive from Fifth Street, I knew my next adventure," says New York developer Tony Goldman, who arrived the same time as Sanchez.

Goldman had gotten to South Beach by chance. He and a Florida partner had invested $2.3 million in several Coconut Grove properties, but on a trip to check on them, he was disappointed in the Grove, which he felt had "lost its sense of soul." Before returning to New York, he took a detour to Ocean Drive to see the sights shown on *Miami Vice*.

"When I got to South Beach, I was not the least intimidated by the crack dealers or the rough street scene. And despite the half-boarded-up buildings, I thought, 'This is the Riviera. Let's go.' I tried to buy everything I could. It was like finding King Solomon's abandoned mines."

Adopted at birth, Goldman had grown up on Manhattan's Upper East Side. After graduating from Emerson College, he stayed away from his father's successful furrier business. "If you take your family's money, you'll always be a slave to it," he said. So, at twenty-four, he opened a one-room real estate office and called it Goldman Properties. His early restorations of New York's Upper West Side brownstones taught him how to make money while preserving a neighborhood's integrity. In 1977, he was the first developer to gamble on SoHo, the lower Manhattan commercial district. He raised enough money from investors to buy eighteen buildings—"I always buy *chai*," the Hebrew word for life, represented by the number 18—converting the industrial spaces to coveted raw residential lofts, and thus leading the district's renaissance.

Goldman moved into a Greene Street building to be part of the neighborhood. He opened a restaurant and jazz club called Greene Street and a hip eatery next door called SoHo Kitchen and Bar. He encouraged wine bars, bookstores, and art dealers to take a chance on the area by offering them retail space at discounted rents.

"SoHo prepared me for Miami Beach," he told me. "In South Beach, the architecture was the right scale and was already in place. But I understood that it was far more than just creating places for people to live. To be successful, you had to create a neighborhood, and for developers that meant controlling the street life and creating the ambience and lifestyle that attracts interesting and adventurous people who want to live there.

"I always like to go into an area five to seven years before it happens. I like the smell of a property, and I like to be able to afford it. Advance real estate is undervalued. Miami Beach was undervalued."

Goldman planned to raise his money through syndications. "I seriously looked past what was there, the block after block of terraces with retired people, the same way I had looked past the empty warehouses in SoHo. I felt that South Beach was tiny enough that if I could make it pedestrian-friendly and create a stretch where people came to hang out, I could help transform it. It's all a matter of whether you're prepared to suffer and endure and sacrifice. I was."

Over the next eighteen months, Goldman bought his eighteen *chai* properties, including some prime Ocean Drive buildings and most of the block from Eighth Street to Collins. The prize was the imposing seven-story Park Central Hotel. It was one of Ocean Drive's finest buildings, designed by Henry Hohauser, but set on the edge of blighted South Shore at Sixth Street. The Carlyle was seven blocks north. "All of Ocean Drive was in distress, but at that time, a few blocks could make a big difference. My purchases were even riskier, and that's why no one else had touched them."

"After Tony bought the Park Central in 1985," Mark Soyka told me, "he said, 'We have to renovate it, I need you and Marlo [Courtney] here.' He might as well have been talking about Buffalo or Detroit." In 1978, Soyka, a stocky Israeli, and Courtney, a slender native New Yorker, opened Metropolis, a 10,000-square-foot Rollerdome on West 55th Street in Manhattan, a block away from Studio 54. "I wanted the New York SoHo feel in Miami Beach," says Goldman, "and I knew the two of them could do that."

"When I flew down to see the place," recalls Soyka, "it was deserted. I wasn't as certain as Tony that it was such a sure thing, but he was the real estate guy and I was the restaurant and hospitality guy. Tony came down every two or three weeks to buy another building and by default I became the director of operations." Marlo helped Soyka and watched the numbers for the growing business.

Soyka's first goal was to convert the Park Central's sixth floor to offices and living space for the team. Everything was a challenge. A water leak caused part of the lobby ceiling to cave in. The electrical system sometimes just gave out, leaving the hotel dark for several hours. "It was strange in the beginning," says Soyka. "People lined up to do a day job and 90 percent of them were crack addicts. I had a Canadian general contractor who didn't know how to do anything more than cosmetic renovations and meanwhile the building needed a gut job. There was no money. Banks just looked at it all as depressed and wanted to tear it down. We had to rent a few rooms to bring in some cash. I never felt unsafe, however. I had walked the worst streets of New York and Amsterdam. I wore a black vintage trench coat, even in the heat, and I never shaved and kept my hair in a wild ponytail. I was born with a face that looks like it's been in fights, so it worked to my benefit in South Beach in those days."

"We lived in these buildings," says Goldman. "We weren't pretend developers who talked the game during the day and then [like Pelullo] went to some luxury apartment across the causeway at night. There was no air-conditioning in the Park Central. But we stayed through the summer, interacted with the residents, and confronted the drugs and street people. Mark and I would stand down the bad ones. We used baseball bats, whatever, but we had to control our own streets. Mark would do a room-by-room check every morning, and whenever he found a crack addict, he personally tossed him into the street. It was not for the faint of heart."

"Tony wanted no architectural changes except to enclose the south-side terrace, in keeping with the original details," says the architect, Les Beilenson, who would go on to oversee more than fifty projects in the historic district. The terrazzo floors were restored and the bouclé carpeting that they discovered under layers of linoleum and industrial carpeting was reproduced and installed in the guest rooms. Twenty-seven layers of paint were scraped from chairs and refinished. Goldman had the original fabrics duplicated by a New York restorer. When additional furniture was needed, it was reproduced locally. He hired Lenny Horowitz, who he dubbed "the Matisse of the district," to come up with the hotel's color scheme.

Goldman says he realized that if change in South Beach was going to happen, Floridians would not lead the way. "I studied a little history and I learned that there was one thing consistent about Miami—it's always been influenced by outsiders. The developers here couldn't see it. They were 'knock this shit down, build them up, big guys'; that's not me. A good developer says if you make it precious and make it one of a kind, and it can't be replicated anywhere—if you stay pure to the vision—you can eventually charge whatever you want per square foot. They didn't get that at all."

Goldman was determined to lead a group of like-minded owners. David Wallach describes meeting him officially. "He told me and several others that we needed a directing vision for the neighborhood, and that if we lost our soul and didn't believe in it, it wouldn't happen. Tony was looking for a passionate group of kindred spirits and wanted to be the custodian of our efforts with City Hall. And he was resolute that if greed got involved, it would ruin it for all of us. I left that meeting thinking that I had just met my first enlightened developer."

Wallach had been the president of his own tiny group, the Ocean Drive Association, trying to get city help in dealing with the street crime. Goldman wanted to give the association teeth. At one point, Wallach surprised Goldman by suggesting that not all the buildings should be saved. "I thought you could knock down half these crummy buildings," he said. "Just leave the good ones. Just because they were built in a certain year doesn't necessarily mean it was good architecture. So I wanted to get a jury to decide which ones to demolish, and then take all the rubble, build a mountain thirty or forty stories tall, and on one side put artificial skiing and on the other a water run. And you could make a volcano that spewed out fireworks. I wanted to call it Magic Mountain." He was then living in South Beach and visiting New Age communes in Coconut Grove. One day while swimming in the ocean, he had a vision of what he was going to do to his Eastern Sun retirement home: convert it into "a place called Mango's, a tropical café filled with parrots and tiki huts and women dressed in teeny leopard-skin spandex outfits. Mango's was going to be a party at my house," he said.

"I liked David a lot," comments Goldman. "He was different, always coming up with something unusual, but when he'd leave, some of the other guys would say, 'What planet is he from?' That's one of the reasons I knew I was the right person to be the team leader. No one had the whole holistic vision, but because of my earlier experience, I brought an unexpected sauce to this South Beach stew. I was confident that I could energize the preservation activist community and the business community into a shared vision either of them could have thought of on their own. The activist group did not have the dollars to make things happen, so they could only protest and stop traffic, and the business side of it, with very few exceptions, didn't have the vision to do the right thing before chasing just the money.

"And slowly the good people came out to help us transform it into a real neighborhood. Insincerity fell by the wayside. We had a common goal although different ideas of how to achieve it. I said we had to speak with one voice. Denis Russ at the Miami Beach Design Committee, Neisen Kasdin [an attorney who would later be a city commissioner and mayor], and the other developers, Saul, Mel, Gerry, and even the Royale Group. They picked me to become the local representative on the Miami Beach Convention and Tourist Board." (Within a year he was chairman, a post he held for twelve years.)

"You were dealing with a lot of guys who had big egos," recalls Mel Schlesser, "but we formed a partnership as colleagues, never as adversaries. We had a shared interest, to get the place going. And you could tell the city establishment was puzzled by us. We were real estate developers who weren't asking for bigger and grander zoning, but were in favor of preservation because we understood the real value was in maintaining the buildings as they were."

"A lot of people thought he [Goldman] was foolish to spend so much time worrying about creating a neighborhood around his properties," says Saul Gross, "but you didn't have to spend much time with him to understand that he was a force of nature."

IN 1985, WHEN Tony Goldman asked his friend Jerry Robins, the major South Florida developer and part owner of the Fontainebleau, to invest in the Park Central, Robins's twenty-one-year-old son Craig showed up as his father's representative. Having just finished studies in Barcelona and then law school, he wasn't sure what he wanted to do. Following in his father's footsteps was uninspiring, but Goldman's ideas about creating a neighborhood intrigued him.

Before meeting with Goldman, Craig had been searching for inexpensive studio space for artists in the district. "I couldn't find a studio until I saw this building with all this great space. I knew I could work with an architect to get some retail stores built there." It was a Goldman-owned property at Fifth and Washington, a block south of the historic district, technically in the RDA's South Shore. When Robins asked Goldman if he could buy an artist's studio there, Goldman suggested he become a junior partner in the building. Robins agreed.

Craig Robins was the only budding South Beach developer who

was a native Floridian. "The business community had concluded that South Beach was a dump," Robins told me, "and they were angry because they just wanted to mow down the Art Deco zone and South Shore, and concentrate on what they considered the real value, mid-Beach condominium towers. There was still a degenerate element that was preying on old people. Tony, Saul, Mel, we all knew it was not going to be easy to alter that mind-set unless we created a buzz, something that couldn't be ignored. When we started, if you wanted to put a café in a building, there were parking impact fees and unbelievable reams of red tape. Most city officials thought if they left us alone, we'd just go away. Instead, South Beach would become the brand that the entire Beach had been looking for, but no one in local government realized that."

Robins convinced his father to purchase Gerry Sanchez's renovated buildings along Española Way. The mostly deserted Española was Craig's chance to foster Goldman's ideas about creating a neighborhood with a brand. Built by Newt Roney in the 1920s as a commercial accompaniment to his Roney Plaza Hotel, Española was a knockoff of a few quaint blocks from a Spanish village. It had been a vibrant club destination until it slid into the same dilapidated state as the rest of the Beach in the 1970s. The street was just around the corner from traditional South Beach outposts such as the Mr. Freddy Food bodega; the Colombian Granada Restaurant with its plastic chandeliers; and the bare-threads Renaissance Café, attached to the Clay Hotel. Osvaldo Bayona, a Cuban exile, was typical of Española's businessmen. After he bought a small restaurant in the middle of Española Way for $60,000 in 1981, he discovered that about half his customers carried guns. Almost every night he had to call the police to stop fights. He had been trying unsuccessfully to sell his restaurant for two years. "I prefer to lose money and just sell and get out of here," he said. "You can't live in a place where you have to carry a revolver."

In March 1985, there was a coming-out party for the conversion of dusty secondhand shops and shuttered storefronts into galleries and artists' spaces. "Everyone knew everyone," recalls Carlos Betancourt. "I had expected a big turnout, and then it was only the same old gang. I figured out that night that it was going to take a little more work than redoing one street to have people put South Beach's artists on their cultural radar."

But Robins was not disappointed by the small turnout. And he learned from Tony Goldman. "Tony taught me that you have to be paying attention if you want to catch them early, to be able to say later: 'I knew it all along.'"

CHAPTER 16

"A Tale of Two Cities"

L ENNY PELULLO'S ROYALE Group still had the keys to the
best hotels, but his carefully constructed mini-empire was
crumbling. By July 1986, five of the South Beach properties
were in temporary receivership. Only the Carlyle and the Leslie were
open. Royale was drowning in expenses and there was no accounting of
millions in loans. In September, Royale and California's FCA struck a
new deal. The bank really wanted its loan repaid, but Pelullo threatened
to default unless FCA loaned him more money so he could complete
his stalled hotel renovations. In vain, FCA argued before a federal judge
that Pelullo had improperly diverted the original funds. Rebuffed, FCA
loaned Pelullo another $12 million, hoping that if his hotels could be
successfully redone and sold, the bank had a chance for repayment.
Pelullo made just two payments on the new loan.

Besides grappling with FCA, Pelullo fended off Sunshine State
Bank's effort to collect on its $12 million loan on which he was sixteen
months behind in payments. And when the Florida Comptroller's office investigated why the money-losing bank had been so slow to collect, it discovered that two former Royale executives had left to work for
Sunshine. Pelullo tried renegotiating the Sunshine loan by pledging
property in Vermont and Atlantic City, but the state comptroller suspected it was property he had pledged to Denver's Dominion Bank,
which had by now been seized by regulators. Six other Miami banks
were chasing Pelullo for $2 million in defaulted loans.

All the litigation was too dense to make the local papers, and Pelullo's
grand lifestyle convinced most people that he was solvent. "To anyone
who spoke to him," says Dona Zemo, "he exuded supreme confidence

that it was only a 'little while longer' until the hotels were finished and South Beach was reborn. He was just a natural salesman, with this great charm." Late that year, the New Jersey State Commission of Investigation issued a report that described Pelullo as a "key organized crime associate," and cited his brother and business partner, Arthur, as having an "unusually close rapport" with key members of Philadelphia's Bruno family, including "Little Nicky" Scarfo, Frankie Flowers D'Alfonso, Sal Testa, and Nicky Piccolo. The New Jersey report received no press attention in Florida. Pelullo dismissed the charges as "ridiculous." He said he would sue the commission were it not for immunity laws shielding public agencies, and he demanded a retraction, which he never received.

"The first warning sign should have been that he was able to get bank loans at all for South Beach properties," says Mel Schlesser. "No bankers were giving money for those properties, not to me, to Tony, or even the Robins family."

While Pelullo was trying hard to keep his business from completely unraveling, the other developers were expanding. In September 1986, the same month that Royale and its largest lender struck a deal to rework the loan, Gerry Sanchez bought the most sought-after building on Ocean Drive, the Spanish Colonial Amsterdam Palace, at 11th and Ocean, from a Swiss banker who had purchased the Amsterdam for $600,000 in 1980. Sanchez had been bidding for a year. He paid double the going rate: $1.2 million, or $85 a square foot. "This is the jewel of Ocean Drive," he said. "Price per square foot is not important. When you select a woman, you don't value her by the pound, do you?"

Built in 1930, the Amsterdam Palace had a fabled history. The three-story stucco building, topped with a Spanish tile roof, was the lavish project of Alden Freeman, John D. Rockefeller's grandson, and his partner, Charles Boulton, a landscape architect. An homage to Santo Domingo's Alcázar de Colón, it was chock-full of quirky architectural details, from elaborate friezes to leaded-crystal sliding doors. Scattered around the building was a collection of busts. One of Lenin had the caption: "Who Will Not Work Shall Not Eat"; Jane Addams: "No More War." A bronze of a kneeling Aphrodite graced the entrance, and a large plaque nearby was dedicated to Florence Maybrick, who had murdered her British society husband in the nineteenth century. It was titled "Prison Reformer."

Dominating the Mediterranean-style courtyard was the Homage Tower, a replica of the structure where Columbus was held prisoner by King Ferdinand. At the end of the courtyard was a mock copper-domed astronomical observatory.

Boulton called the place *Casa Casuarina* ("House of the Australian Pine") after Somerset Maugham's novel *Under the Casuarina Tree*. Jacques "Jac" Amsterdam bought it in 1935 and renamed it the Amsterdam Palace. The name stuck.

The twenty-six month-to-month residents—mostly young sculptors, painters, artists, and other free spirits—paid $325 to $600 to live in what they called their "sanctuary." Peeling paint, cracking plaster, and wobbly staircases were part of the charm. The building manager discounted rents to tenants who made renovations to their apartments. Their units might not have had air-conditioning but they were cooled by ocean breezes through 12-foot French doors.

Jane Dee was still working for the Capitmans when she moved to the Amsterdam in February 1983: "It was like living in an ashram, but the incense smelled like marijuana. It was a very funky, low-rent, bohemian atmosphere. Creative juices were oozing."

Sanchez had invested $22 million in South Beach and said he was too debt-ridden to renovate the building, but he was committed, he said, to turning it into "a national center of homage" to Christopher Columbus. "We will work now to get Columbus's remains moved here. We don't need all of him. Just an elbow, just a fingernail will do." And he unveiled plans for a statue of Columbus on the beach directly across from the Amsterdam. It would be taller than the Statue of Liberty.

Saul Gross, meanwhile, was working closely with the city to sustain the integrity of the district. He sat on several boards and committees and was the liaison for the developers to the Miami Beach Development Corporation. He bought more Flamingo Park properties and added storefronts along Washington. "I didn't miss my legal practice at all. This was far more creative. I was bringing buildings back to life."

Then he added a new business. "I was in the middle of renovating 130 apartments when Arthur Barron [who had worked with Tony Goldman at Greene Street in SoHo] asked if I wanted to open a bar and restaurant. I didn't know much about the business, but as a real estate guy, I knew the lease was great—$1,000 a month for the ground floor of Gerry Sanchez's Edison." The Tropics Bar and Grill opened on New Year's Eve 1986, during a torrential downpour, but the place was packed with locals and friends of the developers who had flown in from New York.

"It was fantastic," says David Wallach. "It was the new wave for the Beach, the anti-Forge way of celebrating New Year's."

As chairman of the Ocean Drive Association, Tony Goldman had converted the group into one that city officials took seriously. He had made a short "must do" list, including convincing the city to widen Ocean Drive's sidewalks so that cafés could create an outdoor promenade, putting more cops on street patrol, and adding extra shifts for beach and street maintenance. "Our Drive, Ocean Drive" was his motto to make everyone in Miami Beach feel as if they had a stake in the street's revitalization.

CRAIG ROBINS HAD formed Dacra, his own real estate company, at 420 Fifth Street, the building in which Craig's $20,000 investment had bought him his first partnership with Goldman. Dacra stood for David (DA) Blum, the son of Bob Blum, a Miami Beach developer, and Craig (CRA). Blum soon sold his share to Craig, who invited his stepbrother, Scott Robins, fresh out of the University of Florida School of Building Construction, to share the office space.

While developers like Robins could spruce up the buildings and look for the right tenants to give an edge to retail shops and restaurants, they knew the Beach's rebirth was not going to happen unless it drew an eclectic and artistic crowd of early pioneers who could move in next to the elderly residents and transform the neighborhood's tone. In 1984, when Goldman and Sanchez were just entering the Beach, a few businessmen gambled that they could draw a nighttime crowd to South

Beach. Club Z, at 1235 Washington, the district's first dance club, opened in March in the Cinema Theatre, one of Miami Beach's great Art Deco vaudeville/movie palaces. Surrounded by tacky souvenir shops, bodegas, and discount drugstores, Club Z was a lavish $5 million renovation that included four bars tended by bare-chested beach boys and scantily dressed women. It had a 3,500-square-foot dance floor, a $500,000 sound system, and laser beams that descended from the ceiling like a colorful spaceship. "It was a knockoff of Studio 54 seven years late," says Mark Soyka.

Z was packed from the beginning. The only other New York–style disco in the area was the upscale Regines in Coconut Grove, but that was a hangout for the cocaine cowboys and visiting Eurotrash. Club Z targeted a different crowd. Don Johnson and the *Miami Vice* cast were regulars. And besides a resident DJ, it attracted solid acts, including Tina Turner, Grace Jones, Chaka Khan, and Kool and the Gang. Divine and John Waters stopped by if they were in town. When Prince— in purple satin and shadowed by a sequined entourage—slipped in through the back door in early 1985 and sat in a second-floor booth watching the floor show of four muscle-bound men with five girls, the visit made the *Herald*'s front page.

Club Z was the first to sell memberships: $600 for silver cards (the member and three guests received free admission for a year), and $40 for black cards (the member and one guest got discounted admissions).

Near midnight on weekends, the line of fashionably dressed club-goers, ready to spend $12 to get inside, stretched two blocks down Washington Avenue. Beach residents dubbed them the "causeway crowd," much as Manhattanites look down on bridge-and-tunnel club-goers.

On Z's first anniversary—March 31, 1985—Grammy Award winner Billy Ocean kicked off five nights of parties. None of the revelers knew that the club was behind on its rent and still owed the final $20,000 for the dance floor. A month after the anniversary bash, the landlords, four brothers—scions of the Brandt movie chain fortune—sued to evict Club Z, demanding $150,000 for seven weeks' back rent. Z countered by claiming the Brandts were secret partners in the club and contended they owed the New York partners $130,000 in federal unemployment taxes. The brothers adamantly denied that they were anything more than landlords. In a Perry Mason moment in the Miami-Dade Circuit Court hearing, Club Z's attorney produced a signed contract in which Gary Brandt had agreed to pay the withholding taxes as part of a partnership arrangement. The Brandts said the signature was a forgery. The Court ruled for the Brandts and closed Club Z. The city sued the Club Z owners for back taxes.

"Z's closing was a real shame," says Alex Daoud, "because it was a great club." He was a regular on the nightclub scene. Several nights a week, always without his wife, he could be found dancing, sweat dripping off his large, overweight frame. He was also in a tough campaign for mayor. People flocked to see him lunch at Wolfie's Deli, dedicate a new bus shelter, or preside at a ribbon-cutting ceremony. They told him of cracked sidewalks, broken streetlights, unsafe playground equipment, and unsightly buildings, and he carefully recorded every complaint in little notebooks.

He worked hard to craft his public persona. "People never realized how much work it took," he told me. He subscribed to a joke service and belonged to Toastmasters, a non-profit outfit that helped people become competent public speakers. He practiced hand gestures in front of a mirror and listened to inspirational tapes in his car. Critics charged he was a buffoon with little substance, but Daoud's cheerleading for Miami Beach was infectious.

The November 1985 mayoral race pitted perfect opposites. Daoud against Malcolm Fromberg, the reserved incumbent. Fromberg accused Daoud of form over substance and claimed that under his own two-year tenure, the moribund city was on the road to recovery. Daoud asked people to look around and judge whether the city looked better. He promised he would be the most accessible mayor in the city's history—even giving out his publicly listed telephone number, while reminding voters that Fromberg's was unlisted.

Daoud told voters that Fromberg judged the city from "his waterfront mansion on Sunset Island Number One, with its private security guard, and from his plush law offices in Coral Gables, far from our city." The statistics were on Daoud's side. Miami Beach crime had increased 16 percent in a year, from already record levels. Murders were up 53

percent and rapes had doubled. And while taxes had gone up 16 percent, for only the second time in the Beach's history the tax base de-
creased. Daoud charged that the highly publicized Theater of the
Performing Arts and South Shore projects were fiascos, and he reminded voters that Lincoln Road had a record high forty-seven empty
stores. Fromberg had voted to close the only public library in South
Beach and to cut 20 percent of the Beach's lifeguards. Daoud had led
the successful opposition to both.

"Miami Beach is definitely a tale of two cities," Daoud said during a
debate before the chamber of commerce. "The one the mayor believes
exists and the one we survive in."

Daoud won by 6 percent. One of his first acts was to polish South
Beach's budding brand image. He gave *Vice*'s Don Johnson and Philip
Michael Thomas special police badges that allowed them to park for
free. The two *Vice* producers were given whatever permits they wanted
and city police provided free security to television crews at night.

"South Beach was being captured on film for all the world to see,"
says Daoud. "Soon, the abandoned buildings that had been backdrops
for so many crimes were being converted into make-believe nightclubs.
Whenever developers, VIPs, or wealthy investors came to the city, I
would take them to the set of *Miami Vice* and personally introduce
them to the stars. Whenever reporters criticized me for being so supportive of a television show that depicted our city overrun by drugs, I
would simply respond, '*Miami Vice* is a television program whose producers spend over one million dollars a week in our community.'
Money talked, especially in South Beach."

Daoud became mayor at a precipitous moment. In the fall of 1985,
new investors were converting South Beach into a nighttime entertainment zone. A late-night brasserie, Café des Arts, opened in the Waldorf
and hosted jazz bands on weekends. And the Brandt brothers opened
Club 1235 in the space they had rented to Club Z. They transformed it
into a throbbing neon nightclub. One Sunday a month, 1235 hosted a
gay night. "More gays were arriving from Key West," says Saul Gross.
"The word had gotten out around South Florida that things were
changing on the Beach."

The classic Warsaw Ballroom at 1450 Collins had survived two demolition attempts before the *Miami Vice* crew spruced it up for an episode. But a few months after Club 1235 opened, the ballroom was rechristened Club Ovo (Latin for "egg"). It was an upscale nightclub owned by George Tamsitt and Ed Sparks. "I saw South Beach on a trip and I went nuts," said Sparks. "George shows me this building. I thought it was fantastic. The area was coming up. I told him it's what the Grove was ten years ago."

The pair plowed $2 million into the forty-six-year-old, 10,000-square-foot Art Deco temple. Ovo was the first club with a separate VIP balcony—Tamsitt and Sparks were optimistic they would use it.

The last of the first wave of new clubs was Club Nu (named after the Egyptian god of night), owned by three Miami Beach brothers, Tom, John, and Tommy Turchin, heirs to the Robert Turchin construction fortune. The brothers bought Embers, a 1948 restaurant that was usually ranked behind the Forge and Joe's Stone Crab as Beach landmarks. They paid $225,000 and then opened up their checkbooks to create a high-end nightclub that featured an enormous curved bar and a second-floor "celebrity" room.

The opening party was impressive even by Miami Beach standards. The Turchins flew in two dozen downtown New York personalities and the waitresses all wore black vinyl sex kitten ensembles.

Louis Canales, a South Beach nightlife pioneer later dubbed "King of the Night," remembered that "the opening was simply amazing. Three nights of parties, something like 10,000 people."

Early on, Nu featured acts by David Bowie, George Michael, and Rod Stewart. Mick Jagger would drop by. Gloria Estefan, who had just had a major hit from the premiere album of her group the Miami Sound Machine, was a regular.

The year 1985 also marked the launch of the Winter Music Conference, seminars and networking for a few days for a couple of hundred kids from the loose universe of dance music. (An annual March event since 1985, the Beach's Winter Music Conference is now the world's largest, attracting more than 200,000 club owners, DJs, and dance fans for 300 events spread out 24/7 over four days.) And Miami Beach's cavernous Cameo, at Española and Washington, reopened in early 1986 as a punk-rock dance haven. With no liquor license or twenty-one-year-old age limit for entry, the Cameo became the weekend hangout for 1,000 slam-dancing teenagers—mainly skinheads and metalheads. "These are suburban kids with middle-class moms and dads," said concert promoter Richard Shelter. "They're the '80s version of the '60s hippies."

Just as Prohibition-era drinking and gambling added an edge to Miami's 1920s clubs, cocaine fueled these new dance clubs. Tom Austin, who wrote a nightlife column for the *Miami New Times*, noted that "dramatic entrances by ponytailed drug dealers surrounded by entourages of henchmen and two or three peroxide blondes, all flashing thighs, cash, and doped decadence—drugs made the clubs overwhelming, sinister, and vaguely threatening, in a fun sort of way."

George Tamsitt said later, "There wasn't any back room for cocaine; it was just everywhere. In the corridors, outside the bathrooms, on the tables in the dining room. It was just there." The Turchins, like other club owners, pointed to a prominently posted sign that threatened to expel and prosecute drug users and dealers. At a few clubs with private rooms, clubgoers could order cocaine by the number of lines and have the charge added to their bill.

"Sure, there were plenty of drugs, but that was a staple of the club business," says Louis Canales. "Miami had more cocaine because it was ground zero for its arrival. Also, there is a certain freedom that comes when partying in a town where no one really gets up to go to the office or a real job the next morning."

The Cuban-born Canales was raised in New York and had worked as an art director in the fashion industry. In 1981, a Midwest fashion client gave him a tight budget for an ad shoot. "Bruce Weber was a good friend and he had just been to Miami Beach. 'Go there,' he said, 'it's cheap, and there's light 360 days a year. You won't need filters.' "

Canales discovered that the Beach didn't even have photo labs capable of doing rushes on film. He had to drop off the day's shots at an overnight courier at Miami International. "That was the downside, but the upside was that since South Beach was empty and hadn't gotten its act together, there was no need for permits, no codes to meet, no forms to file. You just shot whatever and whenever you wanted."

Canales initially considered South Beach so decrepit and dangerous that he stayed in Coconut Grove and drove over daily. By 1984, he had met most of the expatriate New York developers and immersed himself in the local arts community.

"By the time I moved, I had an almost missionary zeal about South Beach. It was edgy in a way that a place can only be once, just on the cusp of being discovered. Cutting edge had not yet been assimilated into the mainstream. There were no A-lists, velvet ropes, VIP lists. The place was friendly, open, with a social structure as flat as the topography. It had not yet become like New York or Los Angeles, where the only way some people could feel like they were in was to keep other people out."

Tony Goldman had told Canales that when "you are in on a good thing, enlighten others." Canales called every magazine editor he knew in New York, and many wrote about the new "American Riviera." He lured New York fashion friends like the runway star Pat Cleveland and Warhol Factory star Edie Beale. Among them was a young designer, Marc Jacobs, who won the Design Student of the Year Award at Parsons in 1984.

Canales left Ovo and went to work for the Turchins at Club Nu. "The rest of the club scene was like Hialeah-by-the-Sea." He promoted several special event parties weekly, mixing them with concerts, fashion shows, and private parties. He worked hard to fill the huge space. "With 500, it looked empty," he says. "In New York, there might have been 10,000 very right, very on-target people—but they didn't go out every night. In South Beach, in the mid-1980s, it was 500 or 600 'right' people."

According to Tommy Turchin, Club Nu was also ahead of its time when it came to pushing sex. The Bone Boyz, a local team of muscled beach boys who were Chippendale knockoffs, started at Nu. So did the performance stripper Lady Hennessy Brown. She would ask someone to pull a ribbon with bells on it out of her ass. "It just went on and on," said Tommy. "Guys at the bar, fifty feet away, were playing with it."

THE NEW NIGHTCLUB action eclipsed the Forge as the Beach's hip spot, but Malnik's place was still packed with old-line moneyed

Miamians and celebs, from Richard Burton to Pia Zadora. There were also occasional tourists and the ever-present cocaine cowboys. "It had actually gotten worse since *Scarface*," says Stephen Hass, the restaurant's chief maître d'. "Now they all thought they were fucking Tony Montana. On any given night, we looked like the set of *Dynasty* or *Dallas*."

On New Year's Eve 1984, the twenty-four-year-old Hass was at the front desk. "I am in a panic, I am 300 people overbooked," he recalls. One Latin guy walks up and says, 'We are seventeen and we don't have a reservation.'" Hass told him he could not accommodate him. The man took out a wad of cash and peeled off seventeen hundred-dollar bills. "That's just to seat us. We'll spend ten times that inside." Hass asked a judge and a congressman, who both had large tables coming up next, if he could put someone ahead of them. They had both seen the very public payoff. "Take the money," the judge told Hass; "we're in no rush."

"I can tell you one thing," says Hass; "that type of action wasn't playing out in South Beach."

Malnik was in the restaurant much less frequently since flying back to Saudi Arabia with the al-Fassis in 1982. It was such big news when he returned to town after eighteen months that the *Miami Herald* reported that "the elusive, jet-setting owner of the Forge . . . who has been hobnobbing with Saudi royalty," was in Miami Beach for "dental surgery." Malnik had already left by the time the story ran.

He quietly fought a last-ditch IRS effort to pursue him for fraud for his 1962 and 1963 taxes. The government claimed he had $950,000 of underreported income and owed $475,000 in taxes. A 1974 appellate court decision seemed to end the IRS's civil pursuit of Malnik, but the government refiled, Malnik appealed, and on September 9, 1985, he won finally his twenty-year battle. A U.S. tax court ruled that the government had failed to prove fraud and therefore was barred by the statute of limitations. "It's nice to close the chapter," said Malnik. "It's a total vindication of any kind of intentional or unintentional civil tax liability."

By the end of the month, Malnik had left for Saudi Arabia and elsewhere. He was not in Miami Beach early the following year when the *Herald* reviewed his restaurant for the first time in over a decade.

The Forge had prospered because no matter what one thought of it, the steaks had always been ranked as the best in South Florida. Now the critic wrote: "Like a Rolls-Royce parked on Lincoln Road, The Forge sits on 41st Street, a remnant of former glory, a legend amid cut-rate pharmacies and banks that serve bagels." Everything at the critic's dinner was disastrous. It had taken forty-five minutes for menus to arrive; another thirty-five for bread. After the critic ordered wine, the sommelier disappeared. There were four birthday dinners that night.

"The crowd is hard to figure: gents in leather jackets, night crawlers encased in lamé, sharpies in Vicewear, ladies in blue hair, and New Yorkers who heard about the meat. The guy at the table next to us was a fella from Brooklyn who asked the steward, 'Hey, you still got that bottle of Lafite for 35 grand?'

" 'Yes, sir,' the steward said.

" 'Hope you never drop it on the floor,' the tourist guffawed.

"As for the food, all I can say is maybe when owner Alvin Malnik jetted off to Saudi Arabia to live with those fun-loving boys, the South Florida sheiks, he took the best recipes with him . . . Not that the evening was a total loss. Free matchbooks."

"The day after that ran," recalls Hass, "we could all hear Al on the phone with [his brother] Irving Malnik. It wasn't a speakerphone. It was just that Al was screaming so loud that it sounded like he was in the room with us."

Malnik was not interested in the South Beach revival and he rejected the few business prospects that crossed his desk. When anybody mentioned *Miami Vice*, Malnik informed them that Don Johnson was a Forge regular and that the swank Ocean Drive nightclubs depicted on the show only existed in Hollywood. "He did not see what was happening only twenty-five blocks away," says Hass. "He missed the chance."

CHAPTER 17

"A Pretty Special Time"

THE EARLY RENOVATIONS of Ocean Drive, Española Way, and the area around Flamingo Park were producing signs of marked improvement. However, Lincoln Road, stretching fourteen blocks from the Atlantic Ocean to Biscayne Bay, was one of the few areas in the Beach where property values were declining. The once grand shopping boulevard had degenerated into a tacky street filled mostly with shoe stores and electronics shops. The former Cadillac dealership became a community mental health center. The Saks store was vacant except for a third-floor Florida Power & Light office. Ellie Schneiderman, at the non-profit Art Center of South Florida, had convinced some landlords to lease storefronts and a cooperative gallery to sixty artists at rock-bottom prices. But the rest of the street was dead, and there was little consensus between the 49 landlords and 195 merchants about what should be done.

One ambitious plan was to reopen the western five blocks to cars and enclose the eastern three blocks with a "giant bubble," creating a suburban-style shopping center. Some landlords wanted to return to luxury and ban discounters. Miami Beach commissioners rejected the giant bubble as too expensive and instead designated the road an "arts district" and financed street improvements, including repaving and landscaping, with a five-year-old $225,000 grant the city had wrangled from the federal government.

Dirt-cheap rents finally began attracting some adventurous retailers, and Lincoln developed a more schizophrenic response to gentrification than Ocean Drive. Nineteen storefronts for art-related businesses and artists independent of the Art Center transformed a two-block stretch into a bohemian strip. Mitchell "Micky" Wolfson, scion of one of the Beach's moneyed families, was meticulously restoring the Sterling Building to its original Moderne style. Edward Villella's Miami City Ballet moved into the abandoned Henri Bendel building, where pedestrians watched the dancers rehearse behind the large windows. The Miami Beach Development Corporation oversaw the restoration of the Art Deco–Mediterranean style Colony Theatre into a 520-seat home for modern dance, music, and theater.

Thirty-year-old Victor Farinas, an artist and furniture designer, opened an ambitious new multimedia gallery, Hyperspace, in December 1985. Since Lincoln was the northern border of the Art Deco District, Farinas correctly gambled that with the city's investment and the incoming mix of artists it could become the popular shopping boulevard it had been decades earlier. Farinas's two-story gallery, sandwiched between the Lincoln Road Mall and the municipal parking lot, was the area's most talked about "happening." It was done in a Pop neo-1950s style with plastic chairs, splattered paint on the walls, and zebra-striped seats. The downstairs House Party Room was for painting, dance, and hanging out, while the upstairs Leisure Room was for fashion, and the Light Gallery in the rear for film and video. Midnight screenings of Japanese Godzilla movies became a regular Saturday-night attraction. South Florida artists such as Betancourt, photographer Joy Moos, and fashion illustrators Sharon Francis, Dena Knapp, Robert Koss, and Carlos Lopez all exhibited their work there. Farinas expanded his film screenings into The Funhouse, an adjacent space. It looked like a wacky small living room, with brightly colored tables and hair dryers for seating. Farinas described it as "a ballroom-auditorium-theater" with "fun foods"—peanut butter and jelly sandwiches, TV dinners, and Kool-Aid.

In the year after Hyperspace opened, Lincoln's vacancy rate plummeted from 40 percent to 10 percent, generating more than $200,000 a year in rents, even at the reduced rates for artists. Farinas's retail neighbors included The Owl and the Unicorn, run by a self-described witch who catered to the occult. It sold rare books as well as mandrake root and graveyard dirt. Utopian Rags, a vintage clothing store, was owned by a short, thin man who designed hats, often wore old wedding gowns, and posed frequently in the window with some of the store's new inventory.

Remembers Betancourt, "We would buy original Deco chairs covered in dust for a dollar each. As people died on the Beach, these things ended up in thrift shops because their children didn't want them. I remember Alvar Aalto–signed glasses, Eames chairs, George Nelson clocks, it was all there." Robert Gottlieb, an avid collector, and editor of *The New Yorker* at the time, loved vintage stores; on his first South Beach visit he bought every clear hard plastic handbag he could find. French film star Catherine Deneuve bought a suitcaseful of Korean War jackets. Anne Rice was a steady customer for everything from thirties candlesticks to rolls of antique fabrics. (Rice bought a condo and set part of her third novel, *Queen of the Damned,* in South Beach.)

Farinas had made a name for himself on one of Saul Gross's renovations. At an apartment complex, Farinas used vivid aqua, bright yellow, and fire engine red as exterior colors for the building and trim. He also splattered paint along the walls. The Florida Bureau of Historic Preservation recommended that the federal tax credits for that building, totaling $129,000, be denied, since "the simplicity that originally characterized the Henderson Apartments has been confused by the heavy, overdramatic and inappropriate use of paint."

"I thought it was cool," says Gross. "We appealed but lost. And when push came to shove, I wasn't going to lose the tax credits, so I painted it over."

Farinas was so furious that he took a picture of his finished building before it was repainted, drove to the *Herald,* and waited until a reporter agreed to see him. The next day's *Herald* ran a picture of Farinas's design under a front-page headline: "The Color of Money."

"The dichotomy of Miami Beach," Betancourt says, "was that there were real people trying to create a new art movement at the same time the artificial clubgoers got the headlines. In New York, artists had many institutions to support and nurture them. In South Beach, we had to invent them."

Betancourt had a work studio in the storage room of a vintage clothing store, Heydays. It was only 20 by 15 feet but had a 20-foot ceiling. There was no air-conditioning. He kept a bottle of vodka for visitors.

Naomi Campbell and Paloma Picasso would rummage through the rattan baskets of clothes, while in the back, separated by a floor-to-ceiling curtain, Betancourt created his first generation of multimedia works. Morris Lapidus discovered him there. Celia Cruz stopped in. "I was twenty years old," Betancourt says. "Even as a kid, I knew this was a pretty special time."

Woody Vondracek, an artist who lived in a $300-a-month apartment at the Cardozo, formed the Deco District Network and persuaded two dozen trendy South Beach businesses to pool their funds so that members could purchase ads in slick publications whose rates were too expensive for the individual businesses. "We don't really need to be together so much to promote ourselves as we need to promote the district and the fact that there are a lot of things to do here," Vondracek explained.

The group's first buy was a full-page ad in the September 1985 issue of *Interview*, which dedicated half its pages to Miami and the Beach (the other half was about Las Vegas). Don Johnson was on the cover. Designed by Vondracek at no cost, the $2,200 ad consisted of the Deco District Network's members' directory. *Interview* put Miami Beach on the radar, running features about Morris Lapidus and the Fontainebleau, Cigarette boats and Deco architecture. It announced: "Miami might be the home of the renaissance, not Los Angeles, Tokyo or Berlin."

The first issue contained Calvin Klein's ad launch of his new perfume, Obsession, with its daring Bruce Weber photos of a tan, muscled young model in briefs leaning against the Breakwater Hotel. The model was Tim Schnellenberger, son of the great University of Miami football coach, Howard Schnellenberger. The influx of models that helped develop the "body beautiful" portion of the South Beach brand was not an accident. Tony Goldman pitched an ambitious marketing gambit to large catalog companies like ATP Productions and the German giant Otto Versan, and convinced photographers and fashion production houses to use the hotels that he and Robins were converting. "The reign of the beautiful people was about to begin on Ocean Drive," says Goldman.

The mix of cultural underbelly and cutting edge worked. Gary Farmer, who had been a popular bartender at New York's chic Odeon, visited South Beach on the recommendation of the artist Philip Smith. He fell in love with the "beautiful beach, the wonderful human scale of architecture and the interesting, eclectic mix of people. I realized right away that Miami needed me. There was no place to go with good food that catered to artists, celebs, and night crawlers. There was no café society." He started The Strand on Washington Avenue, replacing the landmark Famous Restaurant, which had served chopped liver and gefilte fish to elderly Jews for decades. Farmer gave it a dose of Deco and it became as hip as the Forge had been twenty years earlier. In its first couple of months, assorted New York friends visited, including Julian Schnabel, Patricia Fields, Calvin Klein, Lauren Hutton, and Philip Glass.

There was a lot of buzz, but not everyone was making money. Says Craig Robins, "The rents on Española were so low to encourage an artistic crowd that could not have otherwise afforded it; we weren't covering our costs." None of the nightclubs did enough business to be open seven days. Street crime, although down, still scared clubgoers enough that driving the three blocks between clubs was not uncommon. "The area's reputation for bad crime outlasted the actual crime," says Randall Robinson. When Club Ovo closed, it owed $1.1 million to several dozen creditors, $25,000 in payroll taxes to the IRS, $10,000 to the city, and even $30,000 to its law firm.

The Carlyle Café failed. The restaurant staff quit en masse, claiming they hadn't been paid. Three other Art Deco District showpiece hotels, also owned by the Royale Group, were closed.

Royale was under pressure from mounting legal fees and settlements from the Cavanagh years ($4 million had been paid out), and four of its subsidiaries were in Chapter 11 bankruptcy. But Pelullo insisted that all its Art Deco hotels would be open by July 1986. Miami Beach officials knew he was unlikely to reopen any of them. Royale owed the city $213,000 in back taxes. The IRS was demanding $400,000 in federal withholding taxes.

"The biggest reservation of most developers who look at South Beach is that they can't create the critical mass necessary to turn the area around," said chamber of commerce president Ira Giller. "One hotel doesn't do it. A scattering doesn't do it. You need several to create economies of scale."

CHAPTER 18

Where Dreams Die

A DEADLY COMBINATION OF political infighting, government indecision, and record-high interest rates for construction loans killed off Steve Muss's RDA plan for South Shore three times in nine years. Two sets of master developers had come and gone and the city was negotiating with a third. By 1982 the plan's costs had ballooned from $650 million to $1.2 billion, making it the most expensive urban renewal plan ever conceived.

"I thought the whole redevelopment would only take a few years," says former mayor Harold Rosen. "But it was much worse than anyone could have imagined. It's a case where good intentions were lost under the tremendous price the neighborhood, and those who lived there, paid. The saddest thing is I now realize if we had left it alone, it probably would have come back on its own, like the Art Deco District did."

Miami Beach received $2 million annually in federal funds to "prevent or eliminate blight." Under federal guidelines, 90 percent of that money was for permanent public improvements, but the city would not spend any of it in South Shore, since it was slated for demolition. The Beach got another $200,000 federal grant every year for social services, jobs programs, and medicine, but only a small portion was put aside for South Shore. Half of the residents who requested prescription assistance were denied. "Some who asked for medication called me and I told them we did not have any more funding for that area," said assistant city manager Ed Gross.

The once poor but stable neighborhood had been devastated by its own government. The million-dollar fishing pier was now a decaying concrete walkway defaced with graffiti slogans—"Cocaine adds life" and "Teenage Wasteland"—a hangout for young Cubans who peddled dope, and drugged kids and vagrants. The adjacent children's park, handball and basketball courts, and bandshell had all closed from neglect. An estimated thousand feral cats lived in the alleyways. The Beach's homeless, knowing they would not be hassled in the RDA zone, survived in alleyways, abandoned buildings, or along the beachfront. Rebecca Towers, the city's newest public housing project, needed $500,000 in repairs. The police station roof leaked so badly that workers wore rain slickers during heavy downpours.

The neighborhood's three banks, two fruit stands, and two hair salons had gone out of business. Thrifty Supermarket, Florida's largest kosher market, where clerks used to keep an eye out for women who stuck a finger into the sour cream "to see if it's fresh," had closed. The congregation of Temple Beth-Jacob, the city's first synagogue, and the only Miami Beach religious building listed on the National Register of Historic Places, was reduced to 50 members from 500 just a few years earlier, and many of them had trouble paying the annual dues. Rabbi Shmaryahu Swirsky had difficulty getting a *minyan* (the quorum of worshippers needed for services) because the elderly congregants feared venturing out on the Sabbath. Collectively, South Shore was, by 1982, the sickest and poorest neighborhood, with the most old people, in America.

The decaying elderly population—mostly Jews, and some Italians—had watched helplessly as their neighborhood changed after the 1980 arrival of the Marielitos. Since it offered such cheap housing, more Marielitos were resettled into South Shore, per capita, than any other Florida neighborhood—refugees with no family, no ready job, and often with mental health problems or criminal records. Castro exiled a large homosexual community, and many settled into South Shore. Cuban transvestites strolled the streets. The once popular English-style Turf Pub on Ocean Drive and the Tijuana Cat on Washington had become transvestite clubs. The 1935 Spanish-style bathroom at the Third Street Beach became ground zero for cheap street sex. Miami native Bruce Dailey frequented the South Shore clubs. "I'd say 85 percent of the Cuban males down here are gay," he told a reporter. "It's a little world and the only way out is to go back to Cuba or go to the police, so it's a dead end; they stay and hustle. A lot of them tell me it was taboo for them to be gay in Cuba; they had to pretend to be straight. So, now, they really go wild."

South Shore's Marielitos contributed to a doubling of apartment break-ins and muggings. A seventy-eight-year-old caretaker at the Ambassador Hotel was shot and killed when he tried to stop an armed Marielito who was harassing an elderly female resident. When more than $8 million in Social Security checks arrived every week, it was open season on senior citizens as they made their way home from the banks. "There were packs of Marielitos who would take anything that wasn't nailed down," says Charlie Seraydar. "The old people were great victims, and they were scared out of their minds."

But for many Marielitos, South Shore, with its bodegas and Spanish Colonial style, was an improvement over Cuba. A forty-six-year-old former prison inmate, Juan-Antonio Pinel-Carrero, was thankful for his small, roach-infested room. He used an economy-size bottle of Lysol to mask the odor of urine in the hallways. "I am living well here," he told a local reporter as he smoked a 50-cent cigar and made rice and beans on a hotplate. "I am happy I'm not in a jail cell in Cuba." A Jewish man who lived a floor below refused to let the same reporter inside his apartment. "I'm 99 percent dead, so go away."

Jose Rios had spent twenty months in a Fort Chaffee detention center and was released after graduating from a fifteen-hour "Cross Cultural Orientation" class, where he was taught rules for settling into South Shore, such as "Do not throw garbage in the street."

Rosine Smith, who had owned the Ocean Breeze Hotel on First Street since 1962, was almost killed when a Marielito beat her with a hammer in 1980. When she recovered, she tried selling her hotel, but could find no buyers. She wasn't alone. Since the RDA had taken control, property sales had virtually halted. She gave up, taped a NO ROOMS sign to her front door, bought a mobile home, and moved to central Florida. The Ocean Breeze was one of dozens of abandoned buildings in limbo, waiting for the RDA either to buy them or to free the neighborhood from its "no improvements or construction" rule.

Seventy-nine-year-old Bennie Mazor was typical of the residents too poor to move and trapped in a deteriorating neighborhood. At a city commission meeting, he pleaded with politicians "to show the courage to stop this foolishness." A Russian immigrant, a retired furnituremaker from New York, he had lived for fifteen years in a tiny room at the Beachview Apartments at 121 Collins. His rent was only $475 a year, but it did not buy him much. There was no toilet, stove, or airconditioning. Newspapers carpeted the floor. An eight-foot-square hole in the ceiling was covered with tarpaper: Mazor collected the rain that came in in two Savarin coffee cans. The landlord, Howie Bushinsky, like the Miami Beach city commissioners, blamed the unacceptable conditions on the nine-year construction moratorium.

In 1982, Miami Beach's Housing Authority executive director Murray Gilman called for an end to the moratorium. "We cannot wait any longer for redevelopment to come. We have to do something about the living conditions."

In August 1982, a joint partnership of New York's investment bank First Boston and the publicly held shopping mall and community developer, the Rouse Company, submitted the project's only bid. Rouse had built the "new towns" of Columbia, Maryland, and Reston, Virginia, and redesigned Baltimore's inner harbor and Boston's Faneuil Hall Marketplace. South Shore Development wanted to eliminate the 2.7 miles of canals and build far more offices than hotels, so city commissioners liberalized the zoning plan, allowing twice as many condominiums and offices and half as many hotels, as well as agreeing to sell—instead of lease—the land to the developer. Bonds would finance the project, and higher property taxes on the improved land would pay for the bonds. The new developers announced that construction would begin in 1984 at the earliest.

Neighborhood advocates needed a scorecard to keep up with the changes that unfolded over the next few months. The city denied the developers' request for a six-month delay for the final submission of their plans and then objected when they were different from what had been promised. South Shore Development's anticlimactic final draft proposed building six enormous office towers and a $20 million, 400-slip marina on publicly owned bayfront, leaving the rest of the neighborhood untouched. The city had previously required any winning developer to pay $200 million for a 750-unit affordable housing project and to provide relocation benefits for those forced out of the neighborhood. South Shore Development was required to put up only $10 million.

Mayor Norman Ciment, who had negotiated the deal, praised the plan as the only concrete offer on the table. When Muss insisted that South Shore Development post a $100 million bond to ensure the project's completion, they balked.

It seemed less likely than ever that any private company could meet city requirements to redevelop all of South Shore at once. The neighborhood was too far gone and the project too big in a weak national economy for anyone to finance it. No visionaries stepped forward with a plan that excited the residents, RDA, and City Hall. The latest negotiation failed just as the moratorium was set to expire on November 18. In a lead editorial, the *Miami Herald* argued: "Mayor Ciment and the RDA should realize that the South Beach redevelopment dream is dead. They should bury it, move to have the building moratorium lifted, and let private enterprise try to revive South Beach."

A week later, the city commission extended the moratorium for another three months. A South Shore property owner, Terrence Rosenberg, who had been convicted of renting rooms in one of his condemned buildings, sued in federal court to lift the moratorium. A judge dismissed the request but set a December hearing to determine whether the nine-year ban violated the constitutional rights of the neighborhood's property owners.

Late in November, the RDA's chairman, Joe's Stone Crab owner Joe Sawitz, resigned. "I have a lot of things to do and only so much I can do," he said in a statement. Back in May, the *Herald* had reported that Sawitz bought at a fire-sale price a condemned house next to his restaurant. He contended he wanted the land for the restaurant in case the RDA project failed. At the time he resigned, he was negotiating with the property owner on the other side of his restaurant. Sawitz saw no conflict of interest and did not believe that the purchases demonstrated a lack of faith in the RDA. The real estate agent who handled the sale, Sophia Barbarov, admitted the area's decline had enabled Sawitz to buy the properties "at a very cheap price. You can't buy a lot a block from the ocean for $30,000 anywhere in Florida but South Shore."

Sawitz had hired former Miami judge Albert Dubbin to handle the deals. Dubbin was the father of a former state representative who was the RDA's counsel. Sawitz informed city commissioners of the purchase in a May 24 letter, after the deal was finished, asking that it not be made public. When a copy was leaked to the *Herald*, Sawitz was furious.

On December 18, the city commissioners voted 7–0 to lift the construction moratorium. Residents cheered. To buy time, a six-month interim zoning ordinance required the commission to approve new construction on a parcel-by-parcel basis. The city paid $150,000 to zoning experts Frelich & Leitner for advice on what to do next with South Shore.

Given the politicians' history of granting developers whatever they wanted, community activists were skeptical, convinced that the city would somehow find a way to overdevelop the land and force as much new construction into as little space as possible.

"What should really happen at South Beach is low-scale development," wrote Beth Dunlop, the *Herald*'s architecture critic, "with architecture that opens up to both the beach and the city. If scale is a question, the answer is just blocks to the north in the Art Deco District. It basically has two- to four-story buildings, and that is a delightful, harmonious scale for a seaside community." Dunlop expressed the opinion of many urban developers that the neighborhood, "washed by bay and ocean breezes, and bordered on one side by a vast marina, on the other by a beautiful beach . . . should be the most desirable place in South Florida."

But city politicians did not want another restored area of small hotels and apartments; major developments, with multistory hotels leading the way, were the only means of collecting enough real estate taxes to make up for the years the neighborhood had generated little income. The city solicited bids for a parking garage near Third and Ocean. Marriott asked to raze eight city blocks and spend $800 million building two towers containing 3,000 hotel rooms and 2,400 apartments, condos, time-shares, and two retail shopping centers, as well as a 1,000-car garage. Hundreds of local residents and property owners who stood to be evicted formed the South Pointe Association and successfully fought the proposal.

The city instructed Frelich & Leitner to somehow encourage South Shore's small property owners to band together to develop larger projects or to sell their land to established developers. But the architects' final recommendation was for new zoning that encouraged low- to medium-density residential buildings, plus a couple of commercial districts with outdoor cafés, and small shops. It was far less ambitious than the city wanted.

The city did do one thing Frelich & Leitner suggested: it proceeded with plans for a park at the southern tip of South Shore's abandoned pier. The federal government in 1979 had granted Miami Beach 16.87 acres at the site of the former Coast Guard station. It was then valued at $20 million, the most valuable surplus land Washington had ever given to an American city. The government also contributed $1.6 million based on the city's promise to convert the land into a park. But while the construction moratorium was in effect, the city had used it as an illegal dump. In 1982, U.S. Interior Secretary James Watt threatened to take back the land and the grant. City Hall blamed the RDA for the delay, which turned around and blamed the city. Watt gave Miami Beach three months to come up with a workable plan. "We're going to do everything in our power to see that we don't lose the grant or park," Mayor Ciment declared. City crews began clearing away some of the 125,000 cubic yards of junk on the site, an estimated 5,000 trucks' worth.

Like the city, the neighborhood's landlords were in no rush to fix up their properties. Many feared the area would be redlined by investors for years to come. David Klevens, the former RDA member who owned the Biscayne-Collins Hotel, was typical. He refused to spend the tens of thousands required to fix his building's dozens of code violations, and after five months of legal wrangling, the city shut down his residential hotel. The Miami Beach Public Works Department moved the twenty elderly tenants to other area hotels; thirty-five people opted to stay, even though the water was turned off and plywood boards covered the windows. Klevens, like many other owners of condemned properties, refused to pay any relocation costs, charging that the city's nine-year moratorium was responsible for the unsafe, unlivable buildings.

There were some good developments in the midst of the discouraging news. In June 1983, two developers signed a thirty-year lease to develop three city-owned acres fronting Biscayne Bay. The project, a 400-slip marina with a mini shopping center, was the first since the moratorium was lifted.

The city owned 17 adjacent acres along the bay—known as the Marina Uplands—stretching nearly a half mile from Biscayne Street to Fifth Street and affording unobstructed views of the bay. Public officials wanted to lease those acres to a single developer for a project it compared to Baltimore's successful Harborplace. But when South Shore Development had been picked as the neighborhood's master developer, it loaned the RDA $2.5 million. In return, it was promised repayment plus interest and an option to buy 12 of the city-owned waterfront acres. Now that redevelopment was dead, the RDA claimed it did not owe any money. First Boston and Rouse sued the agency and the city for either full repayment or the land itself. The city used the vacant land for parking while the suit was pending.

By December, commissioners had established an Economic Development Council—composed of sixteen local developers and financiers—to advise the city on ways to stimulate the local economy. Jerry Robins, Craig's father, was a member. The chairman was Arthur Courshon, head of Miami Beach–based Jefferson Bancorp, and a close friend of Steve Muss.

In a special election the following March, in 1984, voters approved $9.8 million in improvements for South Pointe, including rebuilding sewer and water lines and street repairs. That June, Charles Cheezem signed an option with the city to buy 20 prime acres at the very tip of the island, the site of the shuttered dog track, the Kennel Club. The property included 1,000 feet of beachfront on the east, the city's planned park and Biscayne Bay on the west, and Government Cut on the south. On the northern side were the clutter of dilapidated thirties-era apartment houses assessed by *Florida Trend* magazine as "Florida's most visible slum," and the adjacent graffiti-ridden Pier Park.

Cheezem told the *Herald*: "I'd have to say it's not the beach you would take your family to on a picnic." He made it clear he wanted the city to remove not only the decrepit pier but also Goodman Terrace, with its $500,000 in code violations, near the site's western boundary.

Miami Beach officials were so desperate for the neighborhood's first major private development that they even agreed to rename the area. Cheezem wanted to call it South Port. "Look what it did for Marina Del Rey," he told the city commissioners. "They could have called it Airport Marina or Los Angeles Marina." The commission finally voted for South Point. "Is that with an 'e' or without?" city manager Rob Parkins asked. "With," the mayor said. The Economic Development Council was renamed the South Pointe Advisory Board.

The city gave Cheezem the right to buy the prime waterfront land at $13 a square foot, the same price an isolated tomato field in nearby Kendall fetched the same year. Property in the Art Deco zone was going for $35 a foot, and on Miami's toney Brickell Avenue it was $185 a foot. Cheezem claimed he had gotten such a great price because "negotiating a cash deal gave us considerable leverage." He was helped in his city dealings by ex-mayor Harold Rosen, now acting as his attorney, and Steve Siskind, the RDA's former master planner, who was his architect.

CHEEZEM'S PLAN WAS called South Pointe Tower, a $355 million development that included four twenty- to thirty-story luxury condo towers with 1,200 units, a 600-room hotel, a private beach, tennis club, restaurants, retail shops, and its own yacht club. The units were priced from $89,000 for one-bedrooms to $199,000 for three-bedrooms. It was intended as a gated community, targeted to young professionals who worked in downtown Miami, five minutes away, and out-of-state second-home buyers looking for an ocean-view apartment at an affordable price.

Not everyone was pleased. When the city moved in July to bulldoze the pier, South Pointe residents protested at a commission meeting. Fewer than twenty showed up, but they represented a broad cross section. Seventy-one-year-old Emanuel Reiss used to dance and watch burlesque theater on the old pier. "This place was once fabulous. I think tearing it down would be so damn stupid," he said. A sixteen-year-old surfer, Pete Paterella, told the commissioners it was South Florida's best surfing spot and could be made into a tourist attraction. "The pier has always been here," he said. "It has to be just as big a part of the Beach as those Art Deco hotels."

Carlos Betancourt did not attend the commission hearing. "I just went to the pier on my own and lit some candles and said a little prayer for all the surfers and Cuban fishermen who used to make those days there so beautiful. The politicians were wiping out memories and starting with a clean slate. None of them understood what a magical place it was for so many of us."

"It was a wonderful old pier," says Beth Dunlop, "and to this day I am convinced that [it] was torn down because the developers wanted an uninterrupted stretch of beach to show in promotional aerial photos."

Further delighting developers, the city passed new zoning regulations that would turn Fifth Street into an office corridor and provide developers incentives such as increased density if they assembled large plots of land. The Economic Development Council had already contacted Hyatt and Hilton about a waterfront hotel. Under the proposed zoning, small lot owners would have to limit renovation to 25 percent of their property's value or be forced to comply with open space and parking rules that favored much bigger projects. Dozens of area residents crammed the third-floor commission chambers to protest.

"You are cheating us. You have been cheating us for ten years," yelled Emanuel Reiss. Said David Lewin, owner of Ocean Drive's Rosemont Hotel, "We won't get what the land is worth. You can outwait us. The businesses are already gone, and now you are taking away our land."

But the politicians felt they needed to jump-start South Pointe. The zoning passed.

Cheezem ran into the same problem that Goldman, Gross, Schlesser, and Robins faced in the Art Deco District: finding banks willing to finance the project. South Florida real estate was just emerging from the early 1980s recession and there was a glut of condos—15,000 vacant units in Dade County alone. But in June 1985, Cheezem convinced David Paul, the president of CenTrust Bank, to loan $13.6 million. Miami Beach agreed to Cheezem's demand to move the beach bulkhead at city cost so his tower would have more beachfront. It also gave him a quit-claim deed to a stretch of Collins Avenue that ran through the 18-acre property. "Promising to close the last block of Collins Avenue," noted Dunlop, "so that any stray member of the general public would not have a logical entrance to the new South Pointe park, was perhaps the most egregious concession of all."

By the time of the last two city indulgences, Cheezem claimed he had presold almost 50 percent of the 208 condos, about 20 percent to lawyers and 10 percent to doctors. And one month after he got the Cen-Trust loan, he assured civic leaders that construction would commence "within a few weeks—there are no ifs ands or buts, we have closed and we will build." A week later, he sold his entire interest in the project for $11.6 million to a Sarasota developer, Rodney Propps, and G. Dale Murray, chairman of Murray Industries Chris-Craft, a Florida pleasure boat maker. Propps and Murray "personally guaranteed" $10 million of the purchase price and obtained another $3.6 million from CenTrust. Cheezem pocketed a $5 million profit. The sale caught the mayor and city commissioners flat-footed, and they lamely tried putting the best spin on Cheezem bailing out for a fast profit.

Three days before the contractors were scheduled to pour the building's foundation, Governor Bob Graham announced that he wanted the state to purchase the site as part of his "Save Our Coasts" program. Blindsided once again, the city realized instantly that if the state bought the property, it would not only abort the long-planned $300 million project but also cast a pall over all neighborhood development. At the time, no one knew that it was Cheezem who had asked the state's Land Acquisition Selection Committee, which recommended land purchases to Governor Graham and his cabinet, if they were interested in buying his Miami Beach property. Cheezem had sold to Propps and Murray before the state bureaucracy had made a decision.

The state had some leverage since South Pointe Tower required environmental permits and the state's Department of Natural Resources contended that the planned construction would encroach 150 feet too far into the beachfront. Although obtaining the permits had been considered pro forma before the state expressed interest in the property, that was now in doubt.

Beth Dunlop, in a typically blunt opinion in a front-page *Herald* editorial, noted: "The proposed South Pointe development has always been an ill-conceived plan with horrible architecture—a self-contained fortress, closed off completely from the city, from the South Beach neighborhood. . . . South Pointe could be the beginning of Miami Beach's long-sought miracle. But this miracle doesn't need magicians or wizards: It needs politicians and planners who have the insight and the vision to know that another oversized monstrosity is just not what the neighborhood needs."

But Dunlop's plea was ignored. "There were no enlightened developers when it came to South Pointe," says Tony Goldman now. The city's desire for extra revenue through property taxes carried the day. City Hall intensely lobbied the state to abandon its interest. It worried that the state takeover might imperil an exclusive concession rights lease the city had entered into in September 1985 with Jack Penrod, for a prime piece of government-owned beachfront property at First and Ocean. Penrod was a tough-talking former Marine from Homestead who parlayed 25-cent Budweisers into a party empire. He had owned sixteen McDonald's from Fort Lauderdale to Homestead, sold them for $9.2 million in 1975, and started his own chain of burger joints called Wuv's, and Penrod's Girls-Gone-Wild bar on the Fort Lauderdale strip. Penrod had read in the *Sun Sentinel* that Miami Beach was offering concession rights for entertainment and food rights for the parcel next door to South Pointe Tower. He and his third wife, Lucia, paid a visit. She thought the area "a little scary," but Jack saw a pristine beach and the chance to get in cheaply on the beginning. He submitted the only offer. Penrod got a twenty-year lease, renewable for another twenty at his discretion, by promising to pay 2.5 percent of the gross, at least $2,500 a month.

Penrod pledged to build a 35,000-square-foot, three-story complex that included two "theme-type restaurants similar to a TGI Friday's or Bennigan's," an enormous sports bar, an outdoor pool, a jacuzzi, gym, volleyball courts, as well as windsurfing, sailing, and scuba diving. He also planned to host jazz concerts, reggae jams, and luaus, and thought he could turn the complex into a Club Med amusement park. He expected to spend $2 million.

No wonder Penrod was privately worried about the state taking control of the adjacent property. He knew a park was not nearly as good for business as luxury high-rises filled with yuppies. He pressed City Hall to fight the state.

In November 1985, the state's Land Acquisition Selection Committee recommended buying only seven acres on the easternmost section, since the entire parcel was too expensive. But Propps and Murray rejected the offer. "The firm certainly can't carry through on its plans on a smaller parcel," said Bob Salem, the developer's attorney. "It would be like us buying a Cadillac, and you keeping the engine."

Mayor Daoud was "overjoyed.... We're going to get moving on South Beach. I'm very confident this project will be built. I'll guarantee it to the people of Miami Beach."

A month later, 10 million pounds of concrete was poured one morning at daybreak as three hundred spectators including city officials, developers, bankers, and Governor Graham sipped champagne and ate stone crabs to mark what Daoud called "the dawning of a new morning." Music from a Paraguayan harp mixed with the din of 240 cement trucks.

The city had condemned and demolished 145 buildings the previous year and moved residents to other homes at city expense. The South Shore Development lawsuit that clouded title to the Marina Uplands was in settlement negotiations. The 400-boat marina was nearly completed. Work on the $3.5 million South Pointe Park was well under way, although City Hall arguments on everything from the number of stalls in the women's bathroom to whether to plant pygmy date palms instead of coconut palms had stalled the project. The city went out of its way to be developer-friendly and even consulted with Propps and Murray about their park plans, including the removal of sea grape trees, strangler figs, and Australian pines so the landscaping would complement their condo tower.

Just days before the foundation pouring, Propps and Murray had begun battling for control of the company. Murray sued Propps, claiming he had breached an agreement to transfer some of his other developments to their partnership. Soon after, the *Miami Herald*, in a long profile titled "Can Rodney Propps Save South Beach?" reported about Propps's nine run-ins with South Carolina tax authorities and quality complaints about some of his construction projects there. The flamboyant Propps—private plane, Ferraris, Cuban cigars—sold his interest to Murray a few weeks after the *Herald* article.

Murray took sole control of a troubled project. There were cost overruns and delays and no condo sales in nine months. Convincing the target audience of mainland yuppies that they should be the pioneers in a run-down neighborhood that did not have a single grocery store or bank or dry cleaner proved a hard sell. Sales to many second home owners, who were seduced by the glossy brochures, were slightly better because many of them—in Florida land sales tradition—bought sight unseen.

"It's been a rough year," Esther Percal, director of sales, admitted to another developer. Early buyers, who put down a 10 percent deposit, were guaranteed a free membership worth several thousand dollars in an exclusive private club. After Murray's takeover, they received letters promising a $5,000 rebate if the club did not open within five years. Murray also sent out a confidential national mailing to an elite group of wealthy real estate investors. He needed money. If he couldn't find an investor, he offered to sell South Pointe, land and building, for $35.5 million. Murray's publicly traded firm, heavily involved in condominium development on both Florida coasts, had lost $5.82 million in a year and its debts approached $70 million.

The following April, he found a new partner, a thirty-nine-year-old North Carolina native, John Hinson—a developer who had made a fortune in Atlanta real estate. Murray and Hinson met on a Sunday at the Carlyle Café. They shared an instant camaraderie. Both men were self-made southerners and loved boating; Hinson had taken a two-year break to sail the Caribbean, a dream Murray had long talked about.

"We went and had lunch, and before we got up I had made this commitment to become a part of it," said Hinson. He loaned Murray $3 million at 12 percent interest and became a junior partner. But Hinson quickly realized that Murray had virtually no real estate experience and had failed to bring in competent people until the project was floundering. "Dale's a wonderful guy," said Hinson after a few weeks, "but he's not by background a real estate developer." In addition to the CenTrust loan, Murray had persuaded Merrill Lynch to give $8.3 million. When

Murray fell behind on his payments, Merrill demanded immediate re-payment. Before Murray could renegotiate with Merrill, CenTrust filed a foreclosure suit in Dade Circuit Court. David Paul told friends that he thought the Beach's political leadership was incompetent and he had lost faith in South Pointe's revival. That lawsuit killed a $15.9 million construction loan from First American Bank & Trust. Murray was stunned.

Hinson had invested an additional $700,000 the Friday before the CenTrust foreclosure suit was filed. He hoped that David Paul might view that as evidence of good faith and change his mind about the law-suit. Paul was unimpressed.

"I could not allow South Pointe just to fail at this late stage," says Daoud now. "It would have scared off every other developer with an in-terest in spending money in the neighborhood. It might have had a rip-ple effect in the Art Deco District. I intervened right away, and very forcefully." Daoud called Abel Holtz, the chairman of Capital Bank, and chief of the South Pointe Advisory Board. Daoud and Holtz worked behind the scenes for two months and got the CenTrust loan repaid ten minutes before the court's deadline. The new financing was a $25.4 million package advanced by a consortium of Holtz's Capital Bank and local trade unions.

A week later, Murray relinquished control of South Pointe Tower to John Hinson, who agreed to loan the project an additional $7 million.

In 1987, the first residents moved into South Pointe Tower. At twenty-four stories, the white skyscraper on the southern tip of the is-land was visible from mainland Miami. The units offered unobstructed views of the ocean, Miami, and North Miami Beach. The new owners also had a clear view of nearby Third Street Park, where an ever-diminishing number of retirees still brought their lawn chairs daily to gather around mandolin players who sang Yiddish folk songs.

There was hope in City Hall that the neighborhood's worst days had passed. *The New York Times* ran a front-page story titled "New Vitality in South Beach." As Club Nu, Club 1235, and Club Ovo battled it out a few blocks north, South Pointe's nightlife finally shook free of the bik-ers and prostitutes. The city kicked off a Friday Night Live series at the still unfinished South Pointe Park, with the Marvelettes and the Drifters. It was so popular, the South Pointe Pops were added for the third Sunday of every month.

And, of course, there was still Joe's Stone Crab. Carl Fisher's prediction that it would close in a season was a laughable reminder of how his anti-Semitism clouded his business judgment. The restaurant that Joe and Jennie Weiss had opened as a sandwich counter was just as much a Beach icon as the Forge. Celebrities, well-known locals, and big-spending drug dealers kept it humming, and they were oblivious to the subsistence-level retirees and Marielitos.

Harold Rosen had his own corner table. "Joe's was the only reason to go down there for years," he says. "If it hadn't been there, no one from Miami Beach would have crossed south of Fifth Street. Even after South Pointe Tower opened, the neighborhood still had a lot of problems. But at last there was some money being spent there and that made some other developers check it out. The pessimism had lifted a little."

ALEX DAOUD HAD scored one of his few substantive achievements as mayor by scrounging up the last-minute financing for South Pointe Tower and parrying the state's interest in buying the property. At the ceremony marking the tower's first residents, he called the project "the living symbol of the rebirth of not only South Beach but all of Miami Beach."

A few days later, he was in his office when he got word that Don Aronow had been murdered on the other side of the causeway. Daoud had a number of connections to Aronow—and didn't like him. Daoud's brother, Jody, had been a throttle man for racer Bobby Rautbord on a custom Donzi built by Aronow. Later, the brothers learned that Aronow had slept with Jody's wife. When he was in college, Daoud had gotten into a fistfight with Aronow. Years afterward he had faced down Aronow at the swanky Palm Bay Club. "He got loud and obnoxious by the pool," Daoud told me, "but when I confronted him, he backed away. It's probably better because I would have hurt him."

But Daoud also knew that despite his personal dislike for Aronow, the boat builder had been an indispensable element in Miami Beach's new international branding. *Miami Vice* was a weekly ad for Aronow's

Cigarette speedboats. Tourists expected to see them tearing around Biscayne Bay. And Aronow's extravagant lifestyle and daredevil antics added to the Miami brand as the last frontier for unbridled risk taking.

Daoud knew that Aronow had been just a few weeks away from a grand Forge party for his sixtieth birthday. He was pulling in millions annually, much of it in cash, and his second wife, Lillian Crawford, a former Wilhelmina model, had recently given birth to the couple's second son. Construction had begun on their twenty-three-room waterfront mansion. The rumor was that at his birthday Aronow intended to confirm a comeback in the annual Miami-Nassau offshore powerboat race in July. It would mark his return to racing after an eighteen-year absence.

At 3:30 p.m. on February 3, 1987, as dozens of marina workers were finishing their shifts, Aronow had stepped into his new $70,000 Mercedes roadster and slowly pulled out of his firm's parking lot, bound for home. He had had several heated phone conversations about 78-footers originally built for the Nigerian government. Aronow had paid $700,000 to get them back, and they were now to be shipped to Panama's Manuel Noriega. General Noriega would have to wait before getting a firm delivery date.

When Aronow stopped at an intersection, a black Lincoln Continental with tinted windows pulled alongside. The driver motioned to him. It was not unusual for strangers to come up to Aronow to talk about boats; some even wanted to take his picture. Aronow rolled down his window. The man in the Lincoln pulled out a .45 caliber semiautomatic. When Aronow saw the gun, a witness recalled, he instinctively put his hand up. The Lincoln driver fired six shots and then calmly made a U-turn and drove toward US 1.

Aronow had been hit five times. The first hit shattered his wrist and his gold Rolex; the other bullets hit him in the throat, chest, abdomen, and groin. He was slumped over his steering wheel, blood spurting from his body. Aronow's foot was still on the accelerator—the engine was racing and the horn blasting. As he lay dying, a worker from Apache rushed to the scene and pocketed his solid-gold Rolex.

Miami-Dade homicide detective Greg Smith arrived while Aronow was still alive. "It was total chaos," Smith recalled. "They had just pulled him out of the car, and one guy was administering first aid." Aronow's bloodstained wallet, with $2,000 cash, had fallen out of his pants and lay on the street. About one hundred workers, many in T-shirts and wind-breakers bearing the names of Aronow's powerboat companies, had formed a circle around the body before the police closed off the street. They watched as the paramedics tried in vain to stem the bleeding.

"Who is the guy?" a paramedic asked one of the workers.

"That's the king. He built the street."

Aronow tried to talk but nothing came out of his mouth.

At 4:28 p.m., thirteen minutes after paramedics helicoptered him to Miami Beach's Mount Sinai Hospital, an emergency room doctor pronounced Aronow dead. A nurse handed Lillian the phone when a call was transferred from the hospital switchboard. "Is that son of a bitch Aronow dead yet?" asked the caller, and hung up.

Spain's King Juan Carlos, Jordan's King Hussein, and Vice President George Bush were among the luminaries who sent his widow condolences.

The police soon discovered that Aronow had had premonitions of dying. He had joked a month before to a few friends about "some nut" blowing him away. He told business associates that he was getting hang-ups at home, up to ten a day. And when someone told him they would soon see him at Miami Beach's large boat show on Valentine's Day, he said: "If I live that long."

The day before his murder, Aronow had dodged a *Miami News* reporter's question about whether drug smugglers bought boats from him. "It's possible," he said, "but my business is with law enforcement." Two years earlier, the Feds had signed a $2.5 million contract with Aronow for thirteen racing catamarans, the 39-foot Blue Thunders. Although each boat had twin 540-horsepower racing engines, and Aronow boasted that U.S. Customs "could catch smugglers with the boats my companies make," the Blue Thunder maxed out at 54 miles an hour versus the 80 mph of his Cigarette. Aronow had ensured his cash-paying customers got the fastest products.

The police had plenty of suspects for Aronow's murder. There were disgruntled smugglers upset that he made boats for the Feds, bookies to whom he might have owed large debts, possibly a jealous husband from his notorious womanizing, a rogue CIA agent connected to Noriega, and even the likelihood of a mob hit because he had defaulted on a loan involving a convicted hitman, Frank Vistero, Jr.

Aronow's secretary told the police that Ben Kramer, a young speedboat racer and builder down the street, had threatened Aronow over a business deal gone bad. Aronow was one of the few people who knew that Meyer Lansky was Kramer's great-uncle. Kramer's street in Hallandale was mob central, and his neighbors included Carmine "the Snake" Persico's brother and Lucchese crime family members "Phil Brother" Moscato and Anthony "Tumac" Accenturo. When the police investigated Kramer, they struck gold. He had been indicted in 1975, at twenty, for smuggling more than a ton of grass. He fled, but was caught after two years on the lam. He pled guilty and was sentenced to four years. While in prison, he had read about Aronow and considered the king of speedboats a "hero." When he was paroled in 1980, he went directly to Aronow and said he wanted to be part of the speedboat world. Kramer bought his first Cigarette, *Mellow Yellow*, and turned out to have natural racing talent. He captured the 1984 world title and a 1986 open-class U.S. championship. And he financed Fort Apache Marina, a few doors away from Aronow, returning to marijuana smuggling, this time on seagoing barges as large as football fields—his biggest load was more than 70 tons—and then moved into cocaine. Some of his partners included an Indianapolis 500 rookie of the year, Randy Lanier, and the Kramer family attorney, prominent Miami drug lawyer Mel Kessler.

In a multicompany deal, Kramer bought Aronow's U.S.A. Racing Team for $2 million in 1985. Part of U.S.A.'s assets was the Blue Thunder line being built for Customs. But when the government discovered that a convicted drug dealer would be manufacturing its boats, it canceled the contract. Aronow gave Kramer half his money back, but he insisted on retaining the other half as a penalty for the failed deal. Kramer threatened violence unless Aronow returned it all.

Aronow complained to Al Malnik, "This prick I sold the company to is really harassing me." Kramer told Kessler, "That cocksucker stole my money and made me look like an ass."

Kramer went to jail for drug smuggling and money laundering in 1988. The following year, he tried to pull off a Hollywood-type escape.

A daredevil track-racing friend landed a helicopter on the prison's athletic field, and as stunned guards and fellow inmates watched, Kramer jumped aboard. He almost made it to freedom, but the copter's tail rotor hit the edge of the last fence and crashed. Kramer had only mild injuries.

Five years after Aronow's death, Kramer, confined to a maximum-security federal prison in Indiana, pled no contest to ordering his idol's murder for $60,000. The hit man was an ex-pimp from St. Louis named Bobby Young, whose cooperation earned him a reduced sentence. (Young died in prison in March 2009.)

Don Aronow wasn't the only player who left the Miami drug scene in 1987. Shortly before Aronow was killed, Bobby Weinstein was arrested in New Jersey and charged with smuggling cocaine. He copped a plea and got forty months in a federal penitentiary.

Jose Bermudez was so shaken by Aronow's death and the arrests of several of his speedboat friends that he slowly pulled out of the trade that had made him so wealthy.

On the day of Aronow's murder, "Crazy Carlos" Lehder, who had been on the run since the Feds finally got the Bahamians to shutter Norman's Cay, was arrested after a two-hour gun battle with Colombian troops at his armed compound outside Medellín. He was extradited, and a year later, a federal judge sentenced him to life without parole plus 135 years.

Aronow wasn't a trafficker, but he was part of the legitimate Miami world that allowed the drug trade to flourish; he gave the smugglers prestige. After his murder, the industry he had built was in shambles. The Cigarette boat company changed hands five times, as customers fled a sport that had once seemed the epitome of excitement and glamour but now seemed sleazy.

"I never shed a tear for him," Daoud told me years later. "He was an abusive guy who picked on weak people. The town was better off without him."

CHAPTER 19

Rebuilding a City

T
HE END OF urban renewal in South Pointe meant that its
future was tied to developers willing to take risks on cheap real
estate in a troubled neighborhood. And investment there was
far from a sure bet. Established real estate magnates like Jerry Robins
and Steve Muss steered clear of the oceanfront land in South Pointe,
because the neighborhood's many problems were so endemic. South
Pointe Tower and Jack Penrod's beachfront property were the only new
projects.

Money continued to flow north of Fifth Street into the Deco District. The most progress was made along Ocean Drive, where Tony
Goldman had finally convinced the city to pass a $3 million bond to
widen the sidewalks to accommodate open-air cafés, improve the landscaping, and renovate Lummus Park.

The neighborhood was also improving west of Ocean Drive. "We
were getting much higher rents in our renovated Flamingo-area properties," recalls Saul Gross. "And the type of renter was changing. I was
signing leases with a much younger group, a lot of gays from New York
or Key West and some artistic types who thought this could be the start
of a shared creative experience."

The developers formed Deco Developers, a union of out-of-towners
that spent $30 million to buy South Beach properties and invested
another $50 million in restorations. Working with Goldman and Rob-
ins, they produced a five-year plan to promote the Deco District, em-
phasizing the need for more restaurants and clubs targeting South
Floridians.

Each of them agreed to loan one employee a week to an Ocean

Drive/Lummus Park cleanup program and successfully lobbied the city for at least two police officers for a nightly foot patrol on Ocean Drive.

They also pressured local banks to loosen their credit standards. Sixty Miami Beach branches had $3.4 billion in local deposits. "It was time for them to give some back to the community," says Goldman. He proposed the banks form a loan consortium with a $25 million pool, allowing each to have a tiny role in every development while sharing the risks. Still, banks were reluctant to lend, and fewer than a dozen South Beach projects had bank financing. "The lenders are always the last ones to recognize what's taking place," says Mel Schlesser.

"I looked at it as a military campaign," Goldman told the *Miami Herald*. "I told my crew, 'We have taken the beach. Our camp is in place. We are ready for the battle.' "

While drug dealers and prostitutes still ruled many alleys at night, crime was no longer a problem that scared away developers. In just a year, twenty-seven South Beach hotels changed hands—a number surpassed only once in two decades. "I'm so sure this area will change that I'd like to buy every building in it," said Gerry Sanchez, still the Beach's most publicized entrepreneur. "When the season of the pioneer ends, the cost of buildings here will be incredible."

The Miami Beach Development Corporation kept track of the burgeoning sales. "We're rebuilding a city," said one spokesman, Woody Graber.

"I always said this was a battle for territory," says Tony Goldman. "As the good people push out the undesirables, the whole area comes back to life."

Daoud used the city's problems to entice the right type of resident. "This isn't the land of milk and honey," he said in a press conference, "but it is a land of opportunity. We are looking for new people who are willing to leave the suburban comfort zone and take a chance on the city. We have some great deals here, deals that wouldn't exist if things were perfect."

Barbara Capitman was uneasy about the gentrification. She wanted to preserve the district as a 1930s time capsule, modeled on Virginia's Colonial Williamsburg. She argued, "Williamsburg is always thronged with people and it doesn't have Florida's beaches and weather. I believe the Art Deco District will thrive on cultural tourism."

Capitman argued that many elderly residents did not like the changes. But only a small minority thought her vision was right. And since her most vocal supporters were the oldest residents, it added to the widespread consensus that her ideas were rooted in the past. "Most of us wanted to create a completely new and bold city," says Craig Robins. "We were trying to build something artistic, a modern urban environment set against the backdrop of those remarkable buildings."

Gary Farmer, owner of The Strand, summed it up: "I'd like to see the area change enough so the drug dealers, pimps and hookers aren't comfortable. But I don't want the neighborhood to lose its character."

The question of the neighborhood's direction once again came to a head in May 1987, around the time the first residents moved into South Pointe. Lenny Pelullo told the Miami Design Preservation League that he wanted to demolish one of his hotels, the forty-two-room Senator, to build a parking lot. The hotel had been designed by L. Murray Dixon in 1939. It was not an upper-crust hotel like the Tides, but it had a unique charm with its veranda and small lobby, etched-glass windows, portholes, and mermaid frescoes. Visitors came back season after season, paying as little as $10 weekly for rooms. But since Pelullo closed it in 1984, ostensibly for renovation, the Senator's paint was peeling, the pool was littered with debris, and the interiors were a moldy mess. Pelullo claimed that his other hotels were not succeeding because they were desperate for parking, so the only way to save them was to demolish the Senator.

The neighborhood's success, especially at night, had indeed made parking difficult, but the idea that the Senator should be replaced by a car park enraged the preservationists. Nancy Liebman, the PTA mom who had been part of the last failed battle to prevent the demolition of the New Yorker, was now a leading figure at the Miami Design Preservation League. She, Capitman, Denis Russ, and Lenny Horowitz, who lived at the Senator for a couple of years in the early eighties, organized the opposition. "The idea that the Senator might come down galvanized all the preservationists," recalls Liebman. "It brought national attention to Miami Beach and brought front and center the question of whether the city respected its historic properties."

City Hall had always been weak when it came to preservation. After the failed 1981 battle over the New Yorker, Capitman tried beefing up city regulations. Beach commissioners approved an ordinance that built in a six-month wait before a developer could demolish an old building, time for the owner to find a buyer who was willing to restore it. But there was a huge loophole—owners who demonstrated hardship could opt out. And although it was supposed to provide incentives for developers to repair buildings, none were offered.

The city's planning director, Jud Kurlancheek, said that the Senator was "not that important" since it was "one of many Art Deco buildings." "We believe in Art Deco," said Leonard "Doc" Baker, the Miami Beach Chamber of Commerce's executive. "But we don't believe one-seventh of the island should be in the district." In fact, the city's own historic zone—where buildings qualified for an additional 20 percent tax credit for restoration projects—was far smaller than the federal zone. Further infuriating the preservationists, Royale Group's executive vice president, Jake der Hagopian, said that "people should remember that the Senator isn't historical because George Washington slept here, it's historical merely because it happens to be part of this district." That was precisely the point. The power of the historic district was that it was made up of eight hundred buildings, and an element of its beauty was its sheer size. Preservationists understood that tearing down a building here and another there would destroy it.

Demonstrators carried handwritten placards: "Save the Senator." At one point, someone sprayed "SAVE ME" over a dozen times in black spray paint on the hotel's columns and walls. The Royale Group immediately covered over the words with white paint. A week later, the graffiti was back. This went on through the summer.

The battle lines were formed. Days Inn won city approval to demolish two fine Art Deco hotels, the Bancroft and the Jefferson, for a 250-unit hotel. Since they were a few blocks north of the district's boundary, there were no demolition restrictions. Still, preservationists tried in vain for several months to convince either the city or Days Inn to work with the existing structures.

Over the same period, preservationists lost a long-running battle over the 242-room Biscaya. Built in 1925, it was a Carl Fisher original, a Florida vacation fantasy come true: red tile roof loggias styled after Mediterranean palazzos and a grand stairway that led to an ornate ballroom. The Biscaya was on West Avenue near Fifth Street, one block outside the historic district. The U.S. Army had converted it into barracks during World War II, and it became a retirement home in the 1970s, before being shuttered as an abandoned wreck in the early eighties. When city officials declared the vacant structure unsafe and ordered that it be torn down, preservationists howled.

"The Biscaya could be to Miami Beach what the Biltmore is to Coral Gables: a glorious monument to civic pride," wrote Beth Dunlop. "Restored, the Biscaya could tell the world that Miami Beach, too, is a place proud of its past, an enlightened seaside city."

"They called themselves preservationists," Daoud says now, "but they were just as often obstructionists. What they said was great in theory, but they weren't dealing with the realities of trying to revive a city and encourage developers to invest here. And every time they came up with an idea, the preservationists would cram the city commission meetings and automatically say no."

"This was the bicycle and shorts crowd, who were against any type of development," says Harold Rosen, who acted as Royale's attorney for the Senator. "You couldn't reason with them. If it was old, they liked it. If you were a developer, you wore a black hat as far as they were concerned."

The war to "Save our Senator" raged on. Liebman proposed a tougher law prohibiting demolitions unless approved by both the Planning and Historic Preservation Boards. But Daoud and the commissioners did not take it up in an election year—too much campaign money came from developers. In August, the Miami Beach Historic Preservation Board voted 10–1 to stall the Senator's destruction for six months and blamed the city for not doing more to provide parking. Several compromises were offered. There was already a municipal parking lot a block away at 13th and Collins. Nancy Liebman suggested Pelullo sell or renovate the Senator in exchange for rights to lease spaces in a multistory garage the city planned to build over the 13th Street lot.

"I can't wait for the city to begin building parking lots," Pelullo objected. "I have too much at stake."

Pelullo's legal problems had become critical in 1987. In May, Flagler Federal foreclosed on his seventeenth-floor Grove Isle penthouse. The next month, he was indicted by an Ohio federal grand jury on forty-six counts of wire fraud and one count of racketeering in misappropriating money from a savings and loan. The government charged Pelullo had paid the bank chairman $145,000 to secure a $1 million loan intended for the renovation of Royale's South Beach hotels, and then used some of it personally. Still pending was a three-year-old Philadelphia grand jury investigation into possible organized crime ties.

Meanwhile, Pelullo fought to keep his Art Deco hotels from going under. While the Historic Preservation Board postponed the Senator's demolition for six months, he lost a key court round in September, when the Financial Corporation of America (FCA) prevailed in its lengthy suit to foreclose on its $28 million loan. A half dozen other banks in Florida alone were trying to collect on defaulted Royale loans. South Florida's Great American Bank was out $1.6 million. National Bank of Florida had sued for $467,000. Miami's Intercontinental Bank was seeking $185,000. Capital Bank wanted $123,000. Sunset Commercial said it was owed $50,000. Elsewhere, Ohio's Home Savings sued for $2.25 million. Three Philadelphia banks—First Pennsylvania, Bank Leumi, and the Marian—were trying to recover $674,000. And Royale's former landlord was suing for $150,000 in back rent.

In September, the SEC announced it was investigating the Royale Group for possible securities violations, and directed Royale to file financial statements dating back to 1985 by the end of the month or be fined $1,000 for every late day. The order also required Royale to name an audit committee made up of independent directors approved by the SEC. It was not Pelullo's first run-in with the federal agency. In 1982, Cavanagh had been charged with failing to file timely financial reports. This pattern of "noncompliance" meant the SEC considered Pelullo's current failures as willful.

Although Royale was collapsing, the month after the SEC action, and with a dozen banks chasing him for millions, Pelullo and his wife, Susan, somehow managed to buy a new home—a sprawling Brickell

Avenue house with seven bedrooms and a pool—for $2.65 million. The seller was a Netherlands Antilles shell company, and the buyer was officially Silver Sands Investment. Susan Pelullo was its president and its sole shareholder.

Barbara Capitman started a daily vigil at the Senator that continued for months. One of the last efforts to save the hotel called for the city to issue a $5 million revenue bond to meet the neighborhood's growing parking needs. But at a contentious commission meeting that degenerated into a shouting match, the city's finance director, Robert Nachlinger, said Miami Beach could not afford the bond. Money was needed for parking, $700,000 to satisfy the code violations on the hotel, and another $2 million for renovation. "The cost to the city to save the Senator is prohibitive," he said. "I couldn't in good conscience move forward with this proposal."

The Senator was demolished eighteen months after Pelullo announced his intention to build a parking lot in its place. Barbara Capitman looked like she was going to faint and was taken to the hospital with chest pains. Nancy Liebman declared they were going to have to bring in the tractors "over our dead bodies." But half a day later, all that was left was the facade along Collins and a portion of the rear alley.

Using the Senator's fate as a rallying cry, Liebman and others defeated a subsequent attempt by Abe Resnick to demolish the St. Moritz and Royal Palm Hotels. And the public outcry finally persuaded the city commission to pass a law that forced developers to get multiple approvals before demolishing any building in the Art Deco District. When Capitman's longtime foe Resnick retired from the commission, he was replaced by Liebman, creating City Hall's first preservationist majority.

"It wasn't that I was happy to see it come down," says Daoud, "it's just that I was relieved it was over. It was a non-stop cycle of demolition ultimatums and last-second reprieves."

Daoud ran for reelection in 1987 as the self-described "people's mayor." He knew that while the preservationists could be vocal, they were a small band who donated little money and constituted a fraction of the city's voters. He avoided addressing the Senator or preservation, instead boasting that he had made more public appearances than any other Beach mayor, appeared in local high school plays, and staged a charity boxing match by sparring with Miami's mayor, Xavier Suarez. He even made two guest appearances on *Miami Vice*. He dismissed as "petty jealousy" his critics' charges that he was grandstanding. He countered that he had taken a city down on its luck and made it feel good again. At every opportunity he pointed out that during his two-year tenure, the city's tax base had stopped declining; there were signs of life in the Art Deco District; and the $67 million expansion and renovation of the Miami Beach Convention Center—which would make it one of the country's largest—had begun. The Fontainebleau had just gotten a multi-million-dollar renovation, showing, said Daoud, that developers still believed the Beach was a great tourist destination.

Daoud raised ten times more money than his three opponents combined and refused to debate, claiming they weren't viable candidates. One was a pharmaceutical salesman, another the editor of a small bilingual monthly newspaper, and the third an eccentric Israeli-born fur merchant who claimed to be a retired Mossad agent, who had run and lost twice before.

On election day, Daoud trounced his challengers with 86 percent of the popular vote. He became the city's first two-term mayor in fourteen years.

After the Senator's demolition, the Royale Group announced almost immediately that it could not afford to build the garage. The Senator parcel became a ground-level parking lot for thirty-four cars.

"We finally had the votes to do something for the Art Deco neighborhood," says Nancy Liebman. "We were just a little late for the Senator."

CHAPTER 20

Club Heaven

FROM 1987 TO 1989, an eclectic group of risk-takers arrived in South Beach and played major roles in the district's nightlife resurgence. Their energy and creative talent were crucial to making South Beach the hip brand Tony Goldman had sought from the start.

One of these pioneers was Barbara Hulanicki, a successful fashion illustrator who covered the Paris shows for *The Times* of London, *Women's Wear Daily*, and *Vogue*. At the urging of her husband, Stephen "Fitz" Fitzsimon, an Irish advertising executive, she designed her own clothing line, and in 1964, they founded a mail-order business in their tiny West London apartment. They called it "Biba," after her sister.

"My friends thought we were mad," she told me. " 'Fashion will never sell by post,' they said, but I thought High Street fashion was overpriced and there was a gap in the market for wonderfully designed clothes at affordable prices."

They had no money for advertising, but when the *Daily Mirror*'s fashion editor, Felicity Green, devoted a page to one of Hulanicki's £3 gingham dresses, the couple received 17,000 orders. That led to the first Biba boutique, in a neglected corner of Kensington. It was soon the center of London's fashion revolution.

"Mick Jagger used to come in to Biba quite a bit," says Hulanicki, in her finely clipped British accent. "Fitz had this tiny desk where he used to count the money we'd take in at the end of the day, and Mick would be there talking about this and that and always keeping an eye on the cash."

Brigitte Bardot shopped there, and her sister, Mouche, modeled for the store, as did Mia Farrow's sister, Stephanie. Cathy McGowan, who was co-host of the BBC's top-rated *Ready, Steady, Go*, a weekly pop va-riety show, had Hulanicki design her on-air outfits. Elton John was an errand runner for the show, and wore only Biba. Soon, so did Rod Stewart, Barbra Streisand, Freddie Mercury, Brian Eno, and the Beatles.

She and Fitz opened a six-story department store, Big Biba, expand-ing the line beyond clothes to furniture, housewares, and cosmetics. There were even Biba baked beans, cereals, and soap flakes, and a 500-seat restaurant, the Rainbow Room, with a stage. Six dollars paid for a dinner and the concert. The Kinks, The Who, Jimmy Cliff, the Pointer Sisters, Faces, the Average White Band, and the New York Dolls all played there. "We had 200,000 people coming through the door every week," she says. "It was the second-most-visited venue in the UK after the Tower of London."

Despite its popularity, the company was only just breaking even, and in 1975, she and Fitz sold it to British Land, a real estate investment firm, which ripped out Biba's individuality, eventually destroying the brand and the business.

"One day Ron Wood [the Rolling Stones guitarist] came to me," she recalls, "and said he wanted to open Woody's, a club in Miami Beach, which he heard was 'happening.' He wanted me to design it. 'It will take six months at the very most,' he promised; 'think of it as a vacation.'"

She and Fitz arrived in January 1987. "I was absolutely dazzled by Miami, the colors everywhere. Oh, don't get me wrong, it was very de-serted, pretty crummy and shabby, but at the same time you had these wonderful old buildings and this beautiful untouched beach and it was still rather grand in an odd way. I found the grittiness and faded glory part of its allure." With her trademark black suits, dark glasses, and im-peccable platinum bob, Barbara stood out from everyone else. Craig Robins relished the dash of style she brought to the Beach. "And the Bee Gees lived in town," she says, "so I wasn't having a complete British withdrawal."

Barbara had designed the interiors for Biba and Big Biba, but Woody's was her first gut job and ground-up restoration. She had never seen anything like the derelict Arlington Hotel at 455 Ocean Drive, on the northern edge of South Pointe. "It was very, very raw. Stray cats had made it their home. Homeless people would try to steal some piece of marble or some fresco. . . . Security guards would collect me to go to work because the back alleys had crack addicts. We needed day laborers, and I didn't know what addicts looked like. I had someone help me pick out the so-so ones from the really dodgy ones. It was a wonderfully unusual experience," says Hulanicki. "We'd be surrounded by buckets of paint and ladders, and Ron would be there drinking a glass of champagne and eating a box of chocolates and listening to Billy Marcus play Gershwin on the piano."

Following the lead of *Miami Vice*, she designed the 750-seat entertainment mecca in minimal black, with glass blocks and lots of pink and purple neon. It included a stage and dance floor, a separate VIP room, and an adjacent space for rotating art displays. There was also a restaurant, and a beach club with a swimming pool and outdoor concerts. (When the guitar-shaped pool opened, mermaids frolicked in the water while Wood and Jerry Lee Lewis played "Great Balls of Fire.")

For the official opening on New Year's Eve 1987, Ron Wood counted down the seconds to midnight for the eight hundred clubgoers, including Bjorn Borg, Vitas Gerulaitis, and the "fifth Beatle," George Martin. Eric Clapton and the Ronnie Wood Orchestra provided the music.

TWENTY-THREE-YEAR-OLD FLORIDA-BORN GARY James Fitzsimmons also moved to South Beach in 1987. He would soon shake up the nightclub scene. "Club Nu was still the cocaine cowboys. There wasn't that much money on the Beach, so the Willy Falcons of the world had their clubs in the Grove, but on weekends they came to the Beach. But there was simply no place I wanted to party." The six-foot, 180-pound James (he dropped his last name) was a star South Florida high school pitcher whose career ended with a rotator cuff injury. He built a successful modeling career in Europe, and when he was in London for his twenty-first birthday on October 20, 1985, he met Mickey Rourke, who was filming *A Prayer for the Dying*. They became best friends.

Before moving back to the States, James spent a month in Ibiza. "That is where I learned about club life. It was the beginning of house and dance music, and ecstasy was everywhere. It taught me how great

DJs mixed the music to have the greatest effect with the drugs that were taken."

James rented an 880-square-foot storefront just off Lincoln for $300 a month and converted it into an illegal nightclub. His partner was Arel Ramos, a party promoter for a local gay club. They called it "Avenue A." The cover charge was $3, enough to cover the liquor and DJ expenses.

"Our first night, I expected a couple of dozen people," James remembers, "and two hundred showed up. It was an artsy crowd, locals, gay and straight, and fashion kids." "It was very underground," recalls Carlos Betancourt, "but it drew the best crowd I'd seen on the Beach."

James held an Avenue A party every Saturday night. The entrance was through the store's rear door. The front plate-glass windows were blacked out. The police soon heard rumors about an illegal club but could not find it. Since no one was living nearby, there were no noise complaints. "You could have rolled a bowling ball down Lincoln at ten p.m.," says Louis Canales, "and you would not have hit anyone."

One night the fire department responded to an electrical fire at a beauty salon around the corner. James heard the sirens and thought it was a bust. He sent everyone out the only exit, carrying speakers and bottles of liquor. When the fire trucks arrived, they found dozens of club kids watching the beauty shop burn. The next day a Code Enforcement team showed up and figured out that the store was not an art gallery. Five weeks later, James moved out.

"It occurred to me," says Canales, "that with so many empty great spaces as well as new and struggling venues, we could turn Avenue A into a weekly traveling party, always at a different location." They picked Friday night. Ramos dropped out, and Canales and James became partners. They made their money from the $5 cover charge, but the places that hosted the parties kept the money from liquor sales. "The idea for the traveling Avenue A parties evolved from raves that friends had taken me to in London," Canales says. "Such-and-such an address would be passed along with a time to meet, a truck would show up, you would pay your ten pounds, get the most amazing tab of X [ecstasy], and be driven to an undisclosed location for this awesome, out-of-this-world party." In South Beach, someone called an unlisted number on the day of the party to find out where it would be held. "That private telephone number turned out to be the worst-kept secret among those in the know in Miami," recalls Canales.

Each week, the party had a different theme. "The first one was at the Eden Roc, and we called it 'Mermaids on Ecstasy,' " says James. Nine hundred showed up. The party was at the bar, with its windows that looked onto the pool. Some of Louis and Gary's friends who were dancers performed the Weekiee-Wachee Underwater Show, dressed as mermaids and mermen.

"By two a.m.," recalls Canales, "they just took all their costumes off and started mooning hundreds of people on the dance floor. By three thirty, I had a mini-Woodstock with over a hundred people skinny-dipping in the pool."

"You would think the Eden Roc would be furious," says James, "but they were thrilled to have us bring almost a thousand people. We had a hip, mobile crowd, and these places weren't ever going to draw them in. So they turned a blind eye to a lot of crazy partying. My crowd never did coke. It was X. A friend from Houston came to one of our parties and asked to score some coke. Louis told him, 'You are at the wrong party.' "

Mickey Rourke came whenever he was in town and brought along Matt Dillon. Calvin Klein soon discovered the parties, and then models like Christy Turlington and Naomi Campbell showed up.

"We started passing out a little flyer with a number on it," says James. "I had this smart kid on a skateboard rolling all over town and he would only give the flyers to the right type of people, those who looked like they would fit in and be cool."

The kid was a long-haired eighteen-year-old surfer, Michael Capponi, whose family had been in the nightclub business in Belgium. "I made $1,000 a week working for Gary," Capponi recalls. "I'd skateboard all over the Beach only handing out the flyers to twenty-something models. No drug dealers. No cheesy guys in limos."

The most memorable Avenue A party, according to James, was the "Cowboys and Indians" held on Monument Island, which Carl Fisher had built in 1920. Fisher deeded the island to Miami Beach in 1939, but it was now in serious disrepair.

"I asked Alex Daoud for permission to have a birthday party there," recalls James. "Alex was always game for a good time, so he said, 'No problem.' Of course, he had no idea I was going to have a thousand people."

Working at night so the Coast Guard wouldn't spot them, James and Canales and friends cut down overgrown grass and weeds and laid down twenty large plywood boards for a dance floor. They snuck in sound equipment and portable generators. "Fifteen dollars bought you all you could drink," says James, "and you had to wear a cowboy or Indian costume." He got friends to donate their boats to transport people to and from the Beach. Even the Turchins loaned their yacht.

Before the first boat left, six cops showed up. About nine hundred partiers were on the dock. "They looked at all these people with warpaint on their faces or cowboy hats and spurs, and they literally got back in their cars and drove off," says James. The party lasted only ten minutes before two Coast Guard trawlers pulled up, at 1 a.m., with lights flashing, and an officer called out over a loudspeaker: "Who is in charge here?"

"It was as if someone had poured cold water over everyone," recalls Gary. "Everyone was on X. People were freaking out."

Six Coast Guard officers with flashlights disembarked. "What the fuck are you doing out here?"

"I'm having a birthday party and I have permission from Mayor Alex Daoud. I have his telephone number, do you want to call him?"

They huddled for a few minutes, then said, "You have to get off the island by 5:00 a.m.," and left.

James became a local celebrity, zipping around in his red convertible Beetle and hanging out with Mickey Rourke. The *Miami Herald* published a profile, "Boxer-Model's Breezy Style Turns Heads on Beach." He began a night at the Cameo that he called "Disco Inferno," which packed in 4,000 partygoers every Friday. "Oh No! Disco the Beast Is Back! Grab the Turntable and Run for Your Lives," warned the headline in the *Miami Herald* over an article by pop music critic Leonard Pitts, Jr. Pitts panned the show, but Disco Inferno was so successful that James opened it at New York's Roxy and later in Boston.

•   •   •

ONE OF THE Avenue A regulars was twenty-nine-year-old Tara Solomon, an aspiring journalist who had moved to South Beach a month
after Barbara Hulanicki. A striking girl, with auburn hair and creamy
white skin protected by "the first 50 spf they ever put on a shelf," Tara
had an original sense of style that for most people was over the top, but
for her was "as natural as getting up in the morning. As a kid, I'd rear-
range my bedrooms by seasons. I went to ballet recitals just so I could
wear a yellow bird and a little kitty cat outfit, with black marabou and
little cat ears. My grandmother was wild about vintage and I used to
race around the house in a vintage ball gown with oversized shoes with
little pompoms on them. I was always in drag."

After Tara got a communications and marketing degree from the
University of Miami, her father, a stockbroker, wanted her to get a responsible job writing ad copy. Instead, she went to work as a personal
shopper at Burdines. "That was ideal," she recalls; "it allowed me to
shop all day and night with an employee discount." She soon left to become the features editor at the *Cape Coral Daily Breeze*. She visited New
York in 1986 and made a cold call on *Vogue*. "I wore a pinstripe suit,
very eighties, with my mother's fox fur, looking like Alexis Carrington's
bad offspring. I failed the typing test twice."

One day, a friend who was the senior vice president for two clothing
chains asked her to meet him in Miami Beach. She had seen *Scarface*
and expected black BMWs and gold chains. The hotels that she had
heard about were so run-down they looked to her like "pastel Butter-
mints with neon signs." She learned that Miss Linda Lou's Cactus Can-
tina Grill had been a crack house a few months earlier.

"It was just amazing," she told me. " 'This is paradise in the making,'
I thought, 'and I want to be here.' I called my dad. I wanted him to buy
a hotel. He thought I had lost my mind."

She picked up a magazine called *Miami Beach*, owned by *Playbill*
and distributed by the chamber of commerce, and immediately walked
the five blocks to its tiny offices and waited until the editor agreed to see
her. "I want to write about the arts," she told him. He gave her a free-
lance assignment. One week later, she handed in her first profile, about
Ellie Schneiderman, founder of the Art Center of South Florida. A day
later, the features editor left on maternity leave and Solomon was hired

full-time. "I was everything from the art director to photo shoot stylist to social reporter," she says. Armed with her Kodak, she met everyone from the old-line Beach crowd to the club kids who saved their money to party every weekend. And she made an instant impression.

"She was like no one else on the Beach," says Carlos Betancourt. "She had this incredible energy, and whenever you saw her, it was such a treat because she was always this vision of some other world. I thought she was like a living piece of art who just changed her look all the time." Betancourt was besotted by her style and machine-gun wit and even briefly dated her.

The first time she went to The Strand, which became her canteen, Gary Farmer did a double take. "She had this foot-high hairdo, tight sheath, pointy high-heeled pumps, and a big smile on her face," he says. " 'This one definitely gets it,' " he thought to himself. "As Holly Golightly captured Truman Capote's New York, Solomon represents the new Miami Beach," wrote the *Miami Herald* in 1989.

"I wanted to document every piece of public art for the magazine," she says. "Carlos and I would look at every bit of art up to 70th Street." They found mosaics and murals on decrepit steakhouses and Chinese restaurants. "We used to walk to each building, jot down notes," says Betancourt, "and then Tara would go off and research the architect."

She worked just as hard every night, chronicling early Beach nightlife with her camera. She was comped wherever she went; having Tara at your club or lounge meant that it was "in."

When Anthony Linzalone, a celebrity hairstylist from New York, first saw her, he says, "I stopped right in my tracks. She was walking into the Havana Club and had this wild black-fringe miniskirt, a black pom-pom-fringed bolero with an antique dachshund pin at her shoulder, a bustier embellished with pink and red roses, some real and some fabric, and a Barbie charm bracelet. She was a wonderful visual overload. And most important for me was the hair. It was like a Dairy Queen dessert, a dark wig, piled high, with bangs hanging down right above her eyes."

"I believe it was my pre-Castro tribute," she says.

Tara had a dozen wigs. "I got into some serious wig action, high 'Queen of the Night' " (which later became the name of her column in the *Miami Herald*) "and I'd use Styrofoam and could wear five wigs at once." Locals got used to seeing Tara zip past in her gold Jetta, her two-foot hairdo sticking through the sunroof. "Coif clearance," she called it.

"People who didn't really know me had a lot of misconceptions. They thought I was wild, but I was just having the time of my life. There was a certain freedom here I never felt anywhere else." But Tara didn't drink, avoided drugs, and went to church on Sunday. Only her best friends knew that on the odd night she stayed home, she'd curl up with hot tea and watch *Patty Duke Show* reruns.

THE SOUTH BEACH business was brutally competitive. The multi-million-dollar Club Z lasted a year before becoming Club 1235. A year later, it became Decos. Club Ovo at the Warsaw Ballroom failed after a year. Its replacement, the China Club, lasted nine months, followed by the Rhythm Club for only one. "It might have held the record for briefest run," says Canales.

The successes included Gary Farmer's The Strand, and Willy Moser and David Colby's Century Restaurant, at First and Collins, a favorite with European fashionistas. The hard-core gay club Torpedo did a booming business as the Beach attracted more gay tourists, residents, and circuit partiers.

Gary James and Mickey Rourke asked one of Torpedo's partners, Lee Schrager, to join them in a restaurant, ESP, short for Española, its location. James and Rourke did not know that Schrager was so low on cash that in 1989 he had reported an Andy Warhol lithograph of Grace Kelly stolen from his apartment. He told investigators that someone broke in and got it out of the building without being spotted. In 1990, while ESP was under way, he reported two fine art prints stolen, Helen Frankenthaler's *Walking Rain* and *Standing II* by Sean Scully. He collected $16,000 for insurance. When Schrager reported yet another robbery in 1991, the insurance adjuster noticed the "stolen" Warhol on his wall. It turned out he had kept that print and sold the other two through Sotheby's in New York for $15,000. Schrager offered to reimburse the insurance company and drop the burglary claims, but it was too late. He was charged with grand theft and insurance fraud and pleaded no contest to two counts of grand theft. The judge sentenced him to two years' probation and 200 hours of community service. He had to pay $6,323 restitution to the insurance company and reimburse the state $4,750 for investigative costs. But most important to Schrager, if he complied with his probation, he would not have a criminal record.

Andrew Delaplaine, an aspiring playwright, decided he could make a go at the Warsaw Ballroom, which had seen three clubs fail in two years. "I felt what we needed was a Studio 54 for the Beach," he says, "and I wasn't thinking celebs then, I was thinking of the concept of a basically gay club that attracted the hippest part of the straight world. Clubs were either straight or gay at that time. Nothing pulled together the right mix."

The rules favored club developers. Miami Beach was pleased with the explosion in nightlife and wasn't cracking down on club excesses. Inventive clubgoers used alleys for parking without fear of tickets or towing. If there were no complaints, a club could operate until nine or ten in the morning without any problem.

Delaplaine—who had run the popular restaurant-club Scratch—opened the new Warsaw Ballroom in 1989. But after a few months his landlord, Zuri Haydon, asked him for an $80,000 payment in addition to rent. Delaplaine walked away. Two club developers, George Nuñez and his cousin Leo, represented by Harold Rosen, had offered Haydon a more lucrative deal to take over the lease. Recalls Canales, "After a couple of weeks their general manager asked me to help them out since the club was as empty as Lincoln Road was at night."

Canales built "performance platforms," and on opening night each platform was lit with spotlights when a vignette began. In one, a 400-pound stripper dressed as Marlene Dietrich in *Blue Angel* was chained to a chair while "the smallest man in the world" sat on her lap feeding her grapes. Another was a well-endowed male acrobat who did a stylized nude ballet before performing fellatio on himself. He competed with two naked female dancers, each with a strapped-on dildo, simulating anal sex on a local male porn star. Lady Hennessy Brown, who had worked with a long ribbon and bells at Club Nu, built a remarkably versatile act around a champagne bottle.

"In between," recalls Canales, "I had drag queens dressed as early twentieth-century Bolshoi ballerinas dance on point across the floor.

Trapeze circus acts performed above the crowds. There was 'Danny, the Wonder Pony'—a really nice accountant from New Jersey—whose fetish was to wear a black jock strap, put a saddle on his back, and have women ride him around the club while they whipped his bare butt. A naked Bacchus was carried around by four barely clothed musclemen who threw condoms and drink tickets to the crowd, while Krishna, painted all in blue, was showered with rose petals on another platform and the DJs' dance music filled the entire club. Obviously everything we got away with back then would be impossible to do nowadays." There were male fashion shows in which the models wore only condoms. "I saw things done at Warsaw I didn't know you could do to the human body," says Merle Weiss, a nightlife fixture.

Warsaw became the center of the buff-boy universe. It was packed with a thousand mostly gym-pumped boys inhaling amyl nitrate and dozens of club girls led by Tara Solomon. It was also a magnet for celebs, who in a pre–cell phone camera/YouTube era had no fear that their hard partying might be publicly exposed.

"I remember Gianni Versace looking down from the balcony while Donatella danced with Elton John around 1,500 shirtless guys and Sly Stallone leaned against the bar," said Maxwell Blandford, who managed the club starting in 1992.

It would take Miami Beach Code Enforcement nearly two years to respond to anonymous complaints about the lewd acts at Warsaw. They finally cited the club for some of Lady Hennessy's performances; and a lesbian act, "Slash and Trash," which usually ended with the girls having sex. The code wrote special rules for Warsaw, including expanded G-strings. But the rules made little dent in the heavy partying.[*]

Canales convinced Ugo Colombo, a wealthy young Italian developer who bought Miami property at bargain basement prices, to invest in his first solo venture on the Beach: Sempers. It was in Colombo's Wal-

---

[*] The police, citing a series of undercover drug arrests, moved to close Warsaw the following year as a public nuisance because of the open drug traffic. Harold Rosen worked out a deal that allowed the club to remain open so long as it doubled its internal security force, promised criminal background checks on all workers, banned clubgoers caught dealing drugs, and stepped up employee training to spot drug dealers.

dorf Hotel. Colombo knew nothing about the club business but he had deep pockets, and he promised to let Canales run Sempers as he wished and gave him 15 percent equity.

A self-described playboy, Colombo was a renowned speedboat racer who had won the American Power Boat Association's Class 1 championship. Colombo's throttle man in the races, Armando "Manny" Fernandez, was indicted in 1993 for smuggling 3 tons of cocaine into the United States from 1986 to 1990, and was charged with tax evasion and money laundering. The government seized Fernandez's Coral Gables luxury car dealership, The Collection, which during the cocaine cowboy days had more cash transactions than any car dealership in the world. Colombo bought it from the government. Fernandez's cooperation led to nine other arrests, and he was sentenced to eighteen years.

Sempers was "completely the opposite of Warsaw and Ovo," Canales told me. "It was a lounge. I decided to ask Barbara Hulanicki to work on the design. I wanted British folly in an over-the-top Italian villa, a cross between London's posh Annabels and a New Orleans cathouse."

Canales pulled out all the tricks for Sempers. The club's telephone number was unlisted, making it a must-have. "Essentially, I was inviting my friends, and they brought theirs, and it created a perfect energy. Eventually you get to know everyone in the room and over time the place had become your comfortable hangout." He remembered everyone's name, tidbits about their lives, their likes and dislikes, everything from birthdays to their favorite drinks. He built a clientele of cutting-edge locals and hip travelers from New York, Paris, and Barcelona.

The 250-seat lounge did not get going until 12:30 or 1 a.m. "By four a.m.," recalls Canales, "the staff couldn't get through the crowd and people were five deep at the bar." The club did an enormous liquor business. "Alcohol goes with cocaine," he says. "You do too much coke, you need alcohol to bring you down. And it's the other way around. And the coke was so pure you would put a little on your finger and then on your gums, and you would be frozen numb. Coke was the great lubricator of Miami Beach nightlife."

One night, a Brazilian kid named Romero Britto from Kendall showed up. He had just landed a commission by Absolut Vodka to design a label for a commemorative bottle. "He was so low-key," remembers Tara, "and he said it like it was just another job. No big deal." Britto's career, like Keith Haring's, was launched by the commission.

ONE OF THE original kings of nightlife, Studio 54 co-owner Ian Schrager, decided to open a hotel in South Beach. David Geffen, who was often in town with an entourage, suggested they buy the Eden Roc. "I wasn't sure if that was the right deal," Schrager told me, "but I had no doubt that Miami Beach was going to be the first city outside of New York where I would open my next hotel. You had to be blind not to feel that the place was taking off."

NIGHTCLUBS WEREN'T THE only sparks kicking the Beach into a higher gear. Mark Soyka opened the 1,000-square-foot News Café in a Goldman-owned building at Eighth and Ocean. As much as any single place, it helped turn Ocean Drive into an outdoor café promenade.

"One of the things that was missing, or at least that I missed from New York," says Soyka, "was a great casual hangout for all the literature and magazine hounds who liked to sit, relax, and read for a while with a cup of coffee or a glass of wine. There are hundreds of bistros like that in European cities, but for South Beach, it was new."

News Café offered a diverse selection of poetry, drama, bestsellers, classics, international magazines and newspapers and sold beach sundries from folding chairs to suntan lotions. "We were, after all, across the street from the beach, and there was no other store on Ocean Drive, other than a few in the hotels, who were stocking any of that." The café was open twenty-four hours. Local writers Thomas Harris, Brian Antoni, and John Rothschild and two poets, Laura Mullen and Robert Gregory, made it their canteen.

A few months later, Mitch Kaplan—whom the *Miami Herald* described as having "the appearance of a rock 'n' roll promoter but the voice and mien of a librarian"—launched a Lincoln Road outlet of Books & Books. "I thought the Beach was ready for a literary bookstore.

There were people moving in from New York and Europe and there was no outlet for them."

He considered his store similar to other independent gems like New York's Books & Co, San Francisco's City Lights, and Denver's Tattered Cover. There were no displays touting the summer's hottest book, no bestseller racks, no board games or coffee mugs—just books. As he had in Coral Gables, he held a once-a-month poetry night. Anyone could get up and read.

It didn't take Kaplan long to realize that his Beach store was going to be different from the one in upscale Coral Gables. In the first few weeks, a man kept coming in and masturbating on James Joyce's *Finnegans Wake*. When Soyka heard about it, he laughed. "Welcome to South Beach."

When the local modeling agencies, Michelle Pommier in South Miami and Irene Marie in Fort Lauderdale, moved to South Beach, it cemented the town's image as "model central," something that Tony Goldman believes was crucial in rebranding South Beach. Pommier had started her agency in the mid-1970s after she gave up her own modeling career. In 1983, she discovered thirteen-year-old Christy Turlington, and two years later she found the male model for Calvin Klein's South Beach Obsession ads.

Irene Marie was a South Florida native and ex-fashion model who had opened her agency in 1983. "I had been booking my clients into hotels in Fort Lauderdale, and sometimes Boca," says Irene. "Then some began asking to stay in South Beach." Irene had last visited when she'd gone to the dog track that was demolished to make way for South Pointe Tower.

One of her French clients told her the town was taking off. The same year she signed thirteen-year-old Niki Taylor, she bought the run-down Sun Ray Apartments at 728 Ocean. In 1989, after a year of renovations, her agency moved in. Ocean Drive soon lured satellite offices of six top agencies.

"Maybe it was the water or something," says Irene, "but there were more long-legged, slender, pretty girls in a half-mile stretch than I had ever seen." For the first five years, her income jumped 30 to 40 percent annually and her stable of models zoomed from 250 to 900.

The German companies arrived first, often booking a couple of dozen models a day from the two agencies. The Germans had been doing midwinter beach shots in the Canary Islands, but when they realized they could do it cheaper in South Beach, they moved en masse to Florida. "For a single casting call by a German catalog, 450 hopeful models lined up on Ocean Drive," recalls Marie. Then came the British, Italians, and French. Winnebagos, where the models did quick changes between photo sessions, lined Ocean Drive. Ten photo labs opened and a small industry in makeup artists, lighting technicians, hairdressers, and stylists took hold. Six production companies opened to help book the models, get city permits, find locations, and arrange for the props. Warm-weather Los Angeles tried competing, but the flights were longer, it was much more expensive, and South Beach could look like any beach in the world.

"We've had up to 20 teams of still photographers on Ocean Drive at one time, during the height of the season," said Robert Reboso, Miami Beach's administrative assistant. The city issued 1,750 location permits in 1989, up 200 percent from the year before. The city estimated that a thirty-day shoot added $300,000 to the local economy.

The *Miami Herald* captured the moment with a photo of a new model, Claudia Schiffer, rollerblading along Ocean Drive in a tiny bikini.

The following year, *Playboy* reported that 1,500 models lived in 120 blocks. The Metro-Dade Film Office boasted that local still photography budgets topped $5 million and there were more than 5,600 models and 9,000 crew members. Combined with moviemaking, modeling had become South Florida's fifth-largest industry, almost all of it done in the Art Deco neighborhood.

All the good changes in South Beach were a little too late for Gerry Sanchez. In April 1988, he was forced to sell two hotels—the Breakwater and the Edison—to Unified Investors Group, an investment consortium based in Margate, Florida. Sanchez had bought the seventy-room Breakwater for $1.2 million in June 1986 and sold it to Unified for $1.8 million. The Edison cost him $1.1 million and he sold it for $3.3 million. Soon, with court oversight, Sanchez had divested the Waldorf Towers, Betsy Ross, and Whitehall Hotels on Ocean Drive and a group of hotels and shops on Española for $11 million. He retained only the Amsterdam Palace. The sales were bittersweet for the New Yorker who had arrived with such brash promises. Still, he could not bring himself to accept responsibility for having mismanaged his hotels and budgets. He blamed it all on the October 1987 stock market crash. "I couldn't keep myself going after that."

IN 1988, BOBBY Weinstein was released from a federal penitentiary after serving three years for drug trafficking. Instead of his old haunts on the mainland, he moved to Miami Beach after a friend in his former silver and gold trading company told him that it was the place to be. His parole required him to get a job and he landed one selling jukeboxes, pinball, and cigarette machines. "I walked along Ocean Drive and I thought, 'Wow! This is the spot.'" As he resettled, one thing struck Weinstein: "There was not one person I had known from the old days. Not one Colombian, not one flight attendant, not one money handler. I went to the Forge one night and the crowd was old people. I saw someone ask to take a breadbasket home. It was like I had landed in a different world."

CHAPTER 21

Island Outpost

ALEX DAOUD WAS reelected to an unprecedented third term as mayor in 1989. He had raised more money than any candidate ever in a Beach election and had swamped his opponent. "I ran for immortality, to make history." But there was a marked change from his previous campaigns. Daoud steered clear of Lenny Pelullo, whom he had once touted as a visionary. After he demolished the Senator and left an asphalt parking lot in its place, Pelullo was now political Kryptonite, not to mention his avalanche of mounting debts, lawsuits, SEC probes, allegations of organized crime connections, and an indictment in a kickback scheme over a bank loan.

"Pelullo promised me $20,000 for my campaign but only delivered $12,000," Daoud disclosed for the first time to me. "He handed me the money in cash in a *Miami Herald* newspaper in his office on Ocean Drive." The donation was illegal, but no one ever knew about it.

By 1990, the Royale Group's city tax bill was more than $300,000 and the IRS was demanding half a million in federal withholding taxes. Royale's many creditors again tried to force the company's liquidation, this time filing for an involuntary chapter 7 bankruptcy. Pelullo convinced the judge to convert the case to a chapter 11 and the court gave Royale until May 15, 1990, to submit a plan to save the hotels.

While struggling for survival, the Royale Group bought two national trucking companies, P-I-E and Transcon. In order to avoid Interstate Commerce Commission (ICC) scrutiny because of his pending indictment, Pelullo hid the purchase through a corporate shell game. In early April, a month before he was supposed to deliver his reworked business plans for the South Beach hotels to the bankruptcy judge, he bought Transcon with Growth Financial Corporation, a newly formed, privately held corporation, and P-I-E with another company, Olympia Holding Group. The business address for both was 1250 Ocean Drive, Pelullo's Carlyle Hotel. Olympia's president was a Royale executive, and directors for the trucking companies included two other Royale executives and a lawyer and investor who had worked with Pelullo on another deal. "He hoped that the new merger, when disclosed to the bankruptcy court, would so complicate the proceedings that he would buy himself another year to raise money," says a person closely involved in the deal.

After the *Miami Herald* ran a front-page story about Pelullo's new purchases, the ICC killed the deals. When Pelullo missed the court's deadline for the hotel reorganization plan, the judge gave him another sixty days to post $1.1 million to demonstrate Royale had the funds to reorganize itself. He missed that, too. The judge gave him a final thirty-day extension. When Pelullo could not come up with the money, U.S. District Judge Sidney Weaver ordered a foreclosure sale of the hotels. Royale's combined debt topped $35 million.

The properties were the Carlyle, Cavalier, Cardozo, Leslie, and the Victor, plus two Deco-style commercial buildings, the Flambeau and the Splendor, as well as the site of the demolished Senator. The package was sold on the county courthouse steps in downtown Miami on Monday morning, November 19. About fifty people showed up as the court officer yelled over the noise of a construction crew and jets landing at Miami International.

Royale owed FCA Bank $28 million. It bid $9.95 million for the property. Other potential bidders, including Tony Goldman, Craig Robins, and Mel Schlesser, who had hoped for a fire sale closer to $6 million, conceded defeat. The winning bid meant that FCA now had $37 million invested in the South Beach properties.

Every developer in town had his eyes on those properties.

Craig Robins wanted the Pelullo properties but not at the price the bank paid. Dacra had bought twenty-five properties in its first year of business. His first development was the Crest building at 1200 Washington. Then he tackled the problematic fifty-room Webster. A 1935 Henry Hohauser landmark, the potential hotel had been plundered and used as a crack den. But Robins saw its promise, and its location at 12th and Collins was in the heart of the district, just a block off the beach.

The redesign converted 20,000 square feet into office space and two luxury apartments. It was completed after seventeen months, for $1.3 million, in September 1990. Craig and his stepbrother, Scott, moved into the apartments; they leased the spaces to two modeling agencies, an advertising and graphics design firm, a photo lab, and a production company. Preservationists applauded the redo. "The Webster was one of the worst buildings imaginable," says Nancy Liebman. "And to see how it came from the dregs to become this magnificent restoration was heartening to all activists. It showed that if someone was creative with these buildings, they could succeed and make money as well."

"This was a turning point for quality rehabilitation on south Collins Avenue," recalls Denis Russ, executive director of the Miami Beach Development Corporation.

Craig had learned a lot from his father and from Tony Goldman. His father had taught him "my business philosophy, how to look at things abstractly, and to ensure the downside was not too big, the upside large enough, and the probabilities justified the risk. Tony had these incredible qualities of community leadership and he buys properties and holds them through long periods of transition. He taught me patience."

Shortly after moving into the Webster, Craig met Chris Blackwell, who would have just as great an impact on his early career. Blackwell was the founder of Island Records, which had discovered Bob Marley and U2. Island became the world's largest independent label before Blackwell sold it to Polygram in 1989 for $300 million. He heard about South Beach from his friend Ron Wood, and when he visited he decided it was the ideal place to launch his first hotel venture, Island Outpost. "South Beach had a character. . . . I looked at it with European eyes rather than with American prejudices that were writing it off. I thought, 'Boy, this is unbelievable,' so I bought whatever I could." Blackwell's first purchase was an empty lot next to Craig's Webster.

Says Craig, "I never met anyone in the world who could summon creativity like Chris Blackwell. He knew how to work with artists, nurture their expression, transform it into a quantifiable product, and make it happen."

Next, Blackwell bought the three-story Marlin Hotel at 12th and Collins. The 1939 Marlin was a prime example of Streamline Moderne; its architect, L. Murray Dixon, had designed the Victor, Senator, Tides, and Raleigh, among others. But after years as a residence hotel it had become a crack house.

"He was inspired by what we had done at the Webster," recalls Craig, "but it was Chris's vision." They hired Les Beilenson as the architect. "The Marlin had been really destroyed," Beilenson says. "A previous owner had started to gut it."

Blackwell wanted to turn the decrepit hotel into a colorful Caribbean fantasy. He knew Barbara Hulanicki from her swinging London days and hired her for the interiors. Dacra oversaw the entire renovation.

"When Chris asked me to make over the hotel as a hip Jamaican dive," Hulanicki told me, "at first I wasn't sure what that meant since I had never been to Jamaica." But when she toured the building, she thought the "architectural bones were fantastic" and "he gave me a great freedom to do it right."

Chris approached the Marlin as if the property were a really promising, talented band. "We approached every single component of that project as a synergistic asset, not just to the Marlin, but to the rest of South Beach."

In the Jamaican restaurant, Hulanicki painted enormous antique picture frames in primary colors. She created an open, flowing lobby sporting an ocean theme. Where support columns remained in a walkway, she added faux columns for continuity. She designed iron chairs that looked like jellyfish, suede loveseats that resembled waves, and seashell sconces. The rooms were designed by Barbara Huddy, a Jamaican hotel executive whose family had built the luxury Half Moon and Round Hill resorts. Rich island colors of orange, sunflower yellow, and ocean blue dominated the rooms, with Jamaican art and handcrafted tables.

The redesign took the hotel from fifty rooms to fourteen condo suites priced from $100,000 to $200,000. There was a state-of-the-art recording studio and Zen-like roof garden. Elite Models, then one of the most successful international agencies, opened its Miami Beach office in the converted commercial space.

"When the Marlin opened," recalls Hulanicki, "Chris used all his music industry contacts, everyone in Europe, and all the stars were here instantly; Bono, Jagger, Madonna, Prince, Grace Jones [another Blackwell artist]. We had 250 on the roof garden the first night. Bowie and U2 recorded in the studio in the first couple of months." Craig Robins, who had turned twenty-eight the night the Marlin opened, felt as though he were "in the center of the universe."

Sadly, Barbara Capitman wasn't there to see the changes. She had died in March 1990, at sixty-nine, from congestive heart failure. Lenny Horowitz had died the year before, at forty-three, from AIDS. (When the penniless Horowitz had disclosed he had AIDS two years earlier, Tony Goldman gave him a free apartment and arranged for the Miami Design Preservation League to pay some medical bills. Saul Gross often took him out in a wheelchair to tour the latest renovations.)

In June 1991, Blackwell bought five other hotel properties. He spent $3.1 million for Ocean Drive's Tides Hotel and the Molinar, directly behind the Tides on Collins. Controlled by a Pelullo family trust, they were sold to Blackwell by the court-appointed bankruptcy trustee. A couple of weeks later, Blackwell closed on the hundred-room, beachfront Netherland Hotel for $3 million and then the Kent and Palmer House. The ten-story Tides and the seven-story Netherland were two of the largest Art Deco hotels on Ocean Drive, and Blackwell, again with Craig Robins, committed $6 million to renovate them. Even other developers were impressed. "Blackwell knocked the pants off any critic who said that South Beach developers were just slapping a coat of fresh paint on the walls and calling it a renovation," says Mel Schlesser. "The Marlin put the district on steroids," says Saul Gross.

CHAPTER 22

"It's Not Like Disney World"

T HE BEACH'S REVIVAL may have taken place during Daoud's terms, but in his record six years in office he had not proposed any master plan for urban redesign. The city approached each project individually instead of considering the overall impact on the neighborhood.

"Nobody really wanted to say it because Daoud was popular, but he was only a 'feel good' mayor, not an effective one," says the attorney (who was then the Miami Beach Development Corporation chief) Neisen Kasdin. "People liked Daoud because he was the most accessible mayor ever; from condo meetings to cocktail parties to synagogue services, he went to everything. He patrolled with the Guardian Angels, attended nightclub openings, hung out with Hollywood movie idols, and accompanied wealthy socialites to special events. But he had no substance."

During his last year in office, 1990, a series of newspaper stories broke that implicated Daoud in possible misdeeds. David Paul, the head of CenTrust Bank, who in 1985 had loaned $13.6 million to save South Pointe Tower, was under federal investigation for the bank's $1.7 billion failure that year, then the fourth-biggest banking collapse in U.S. history. As part of its probe, the FBI had discovered $35,000 in checks made out to Daoud. A few weeks after the checks arrived, Daoud had made an unusual appearance at a Metro-Dade commission to support an oversized teak boat dock that David Paul wanted to build at his La Gorce Island home for his 94-foot, $7 million yacht. County commis-

240

sioners approved the dock over neighbors' objections, but the city commission ultimately rejected it. Paul threatened to foreclose on South Pointe Tower, and Daoud had to plead with him to change his mind.

Another report said that Daoud received $8,000 in cash in 1988 from a wealthy philanthropist after he gave her the city's medal of honor. He never reported that money or the $3,000 check from another Miami Beach philanthropist after he got her a permit to expand her driveway onto city property. Then there was Daoud's role in pressuring the city attorney to hire Bonnie Levin, a second-year law student who was one of Daoud's many extramarital lovers. She was his most serious relationship; he had even considered leaving his wife. Other articles described almost a quarter million dollars' worth of free or discounted renovations to Daoud's home by contractors who did millions of dollars in city business, and his use of the police to obtain free or discounted handguns from dealers competing for a city contract.

Daoud adamantly denied any wrongdoing, but in light of the revelations he decided not to run for a fourth term as mayor, and political handicappers no longer talked about him on a short list of candidates for Congress.

After the stories broke, the mayor no longer bounded out of his office, back-slapping every visitor. He left commission meetings early and stopped calling reporters whose attention he once craved. When the Forge suffered $7 million in fire damage and reopened with a grand gala, celebrating Al's passing of the baton to Shareef, Daoud called to congratulate the younger Malnik but skipped the celebrations.

On October 29, 1991, federal prosecutors handed down a forty-one-count indictment against Daoud that shocked everyone with its specificity. There was an overall racketeering charge, three counts of extortion, nineteen charges of corruption, twelve counts of money laundering, and six charges of filing false tax returns. Daoud was one of the few not shocked because he had received secret information about the grand jury proceedings from one of the jurors. When federal prosecutors learned of the leak they prepared an indictment against the juror, but that juror died before any charges could be issued.

Daoud was the latest Dade County official to make headlines for criminal charges. Thirty-seven federal indictments of state and local officials in South Florida were handed down during 1991. The previous year, the mayors of Sweetwater and Hialeah were convicted and sentenced for corruption and extortion.

"In South Florida we have a severe public corruption problem, but we are getting a handle on it," stated U.S. Attorney Dexter Lehtinen in announcing the Daoud indictment. "Previously the attitude has been that if you don't turn up the rock, the ants won't come crawling out. But here we are going to turn up the rock and gas them."

On the day of the indictment, Daoud appeared in Washington, D.C., at a press conference and made an impassioned plea for Mohammed al-Fassi, Al Malnik's Saudi friend. Daoud announced that he was representing al-Fassi and related a bizarre tale about Iraq's Saddam Hussein, the Saudi royal family, and an alleged international kidnapping. According to Daoud, al-Fassi was being held prisoner in Riyadh for having met with Hussein and speaking out on pro-Iraq radio programs broadcast from Baghdad while the American-led coalition freed Kuwait.

"Talk about your match made in heaven: a phony freeloading 'sheik' and a massively indicted, money-grubbing politician. All that's missing is a laugh track," wrote Carl Hiaasen in his *Miami Herald* column. He referred to al-Fassi as "our favorite deadbeat" and noted that "Alex has a buzzard's eye for the ultra-wealthy."

When asked at the news conference about the federal indictment, Daoud had no comment. "My trip up here is strictly for handling and helping this effort for Mohammed." He surrendered the following day at Miami's FBI office. At the court hearing, he pled not guilty and posted $500,000 bail. He held a press conference on the courthouse steps and blasted the charges as false and meritless. Daoud told me he hadn't been able to bring himself to read the indictment until FBI agents drove him to booking. He was stunned that people he considered close friends had provided evidence against him. "Some of them had gotten immunity to sell me down the river," he says, the anger still evident. His third wife, Terri Noe, felt totally betrayed by him, even though their lifestyle had been far grander than his $10,000-a-year salary and part-time legal work could have reasonably provided. He warned her that if he was found guilty, the government could seize everything they owned. "If my wife [Terri] could have driven a stake through my heart, she would have done it," he says. "No one could have imagined the horrific fights we had as the trial approached."

On November 1, Governor Lawton Chiles suspended Daoud as mayor. Commissioner Seymour Gelber replaced him. Daoud hired top legal gun Roy Black, then defending William Kennedy Smith, Senator Ted Kennedy's nephew, in his rape trial.

"I couldn't believe any of this was happening to me," Daoud says. He briefly thought about copping a plea. Black thought he could get him two years in a comfortable federal prison camp and avoid any forfeiture. But Daoud decided to fight the charges. "I had made history as the mayor of Miami Beach, and now I intended to make history by fighting the federal government. This was like being back in the ring at the Fifth Street Gym and I was going to knock them out."

A month after Daoud's indictment, the SEC filed a civil action against CenTrust's David Paul for helping Charles Keating, Jr., the convicted savings and loan titan, to improperly report $24.6 million in profits on securities transactions. "That at least made part of one day a good one for me," said Daoud, still steaming that Paul had cooperated in the case against him once the prosecutors had uncovered the unexplained checks.

IN A STRANGE way, Daoud's legal problems may have helped the Beach's growing reputation. Tourists weren't flocking to South Beach because Daoud was mayor. They saw the area as cutting edge, possibly still a little dangerous, and very different from their hometowns. Part of Miami's brand, especially since the cocaine cowboys, had been as a Wild West outpost where few rules applied. A corrupt mayor fit the town's renegade image. The indictment was a non-event for developers like Robins, Blackwell, and Goldman. Daoud had never been a great ally and they preferred that the city administration be clean.

In April 1992, Dacra, Jerry and Craig Robins, and Chris Blackwell beat forty-two other sealed bidders with a $10.5 million all-cash offer to buy the Cavalier, Cardozo, Carlyle, Leslie, Victor, Flambeau, and the Senator parking lot site. The Cavalier, Cardozo, and Leslie were operating as hotels; the Carlyle had a lobby restaurant and several businesses on its upper floors; the Victor was closed. Royale's original lender had lost almost $30 million and had been seized by the FDIC. The Resolution Trust Corporation, which had been created by the U.S. government to sell off the assets of more than 1,000 similarly failed savings and loans, handled the Royale Group auction.

"Those were among the most architecturally significant buildings in the district," says Saul Gross, "and as it turned out, the Robins family and Chris got the buy of the century. It was a great deal, but you had to have the cash to do it, and they had it."

"We never intended to hold all the Royale properties since it was too much at once for any single group," says Craig. "So we acquired them with the idea of bringing in like-minded developers interested in preserving the historical character of the buildings, but in a style that differed from what we and Island had already done on South Beach."

The Cardozo and Cavalier were soon for sale. Gloria Estefan and her husband, Emilio, bought the Cardozo for $5 million a few months after it emerged from bankruptcy. In March, they bought the Shore Park for $2.2 million.

In June, Robins and Blackwell sold the Carlyle to Renzo Rosso, the founder of the Italian fashion label Diesel, for $3 million. Between the sales to the Estefans and Rosso, Robins and Blackwell recovered 80 percent of their purchase price for the Royale properties. Meanwhile, the Netherland renovation was under way. The plans called for keeping the Art Deco shell, gutting the interior, and adding three floors to the existing seven. Retail shops would be on the street level and an upscale restaurant off the lobby; there would be offices on the third and fourth floors and twelve ocean-view luxury condos on the top.

Craig and Scott Robins used to ride their skateboards along Washington Avenue. Now they walked the streets as inspectors of the work under way on their own projects. "It was our heritage," says Craig. "We grew up on Miami Beach and now we had the chance to see the beauty of the area start to blossom as the years of neglect were swept away."

Craig had also started investing in South Pointe, where redevelopment dramatically lagged behind the Art Deco zone. The city commission had taken over the RDA's responsibilities, including the right to condemn properties, and that still kept away most investors. Many decaying buildings desperately needed renovation; vacant parcels were used for illegal garbage dumping. But Penrod's was nevertheless doing a booming business, and South Pointe Tower was completely filled. As he had in South Beach, Robins saw in South Pointe the possibility of small-scale developments that maintained the area's low-rise scale while methodically improving the neighborhood.

"We are talking about the part of Miami Beach directly adjacent to the historic district," he told me, "with the same ocean access and views. It didn't have the same quantity of wonderful architecture, but still it was hard to imagine that it would not eventually appreciate as the rest of South Beach improved." Prices there were less than half as much as similar parcels north of Fifth Street.

South Pointe had some Art Deco gems such as the Century and Nemo Hotels, but others like the Corsair had fallen to the wrecking ball. "As in the Art Deco District, it was the collection of buildings that was important," says Nancy Liebman. A major problem was that the city's zoning code placed no height restrictions along the waterfront and developer economics encouraged high-rises. South Pointe—with nearly 30 acres of bayside and ocean property—had more undeveloped waterfront property than anywhere else in the county. Neighborhood activists feared more large projects like South Pointe Tower would wall off the ocean and bay from the rest of the neighborhood.

A new crop of city commissioners, including Neisen Kasdin, swept into office in 1991—the so-called Reform Commission in the wake of the bribery and influence-peddling scandal that brought down Alex Daoud. Many of them promised to reevaluate the development problems that plagued South Pointe. Neisen had served for four years as chairman of the Miami Beach Development Corporation. "My very first campaign event was in the backyard of Jerry Robins's Star Island house in January 1991," he says. "It was a fund-raiser only for business-people from South Beach, 80 percent of whom had never participated in a Beach election. None of the other candidates knew who they were. It was very much a South Beach insurgency." Kasdin, in particular, had a reputation as a reformer and straight arrow. His introduction to Miami Beach politics arrived at his new City Hall office in a gift-wrapped box the week he was elected city commissioner. Inside, wrapped in a soiled bag, was a walking cane. An unsigned card read: "Congratulations. You'll need this." It was not the first or last act of intimidation Kasdin would receive.

"It angered a lot of people when I made it into office," Kasdin told me. "I had been used to battling special interests. They were never happy with what I did—downzoning their properties, not hiring their favorite person."

"The original group of us who were first to South Beach and had started developing it," recalls Saul Gross, "realized as the Beach grew that we had no South Beach commissioner. Neisen understood on a gut level what was happening in our neighborhood." Gross, Craig Robins, Mel Schlesser, and Tony Goldman made political contributions of $5,000 each and agreed to spread the money out over several races. "We recognized that we had been sitting on the sidelines." After Kasdin's election, Gross served on the Design Review Board, Craig Robins went to the Planning Board, Schlesser was appointed to the Zoning Board, and Tony Goldman was on the Visitors and Convention Association. "Within a year or two," recalls Gross, "we were all chairmen. We were superqualified compared to the political hacks appointed by Daoud and Abe Resnick."

Craig had learned from his father and Tony Goldman that the city had to be a partner in any effective changes. He lobbied city officials to ease some of the restrictive South Pointe zoning laws, such as permitting new construction only on 100-foot-wide lots. There were more than forty acres of vacant land and many were contiguous tracts. "Kasdin understood the issue better than anyone else."

"It was finally sinking in to the rest of the commission that the restrictions on small-scale development in South Pointe were counterproductive," Kasdin told me. "The Art Deco District had started coming back with small-scale development and rehabilitation, and the city failed to recognize that South Pointe was the same market. The forces driving change north of Fifth Street had to be given free rein south of Fifth Street. The city's zoning was intended to create larger projects, but you couldn't combine the small parcels because you couldn't get ten different owners to agree on a single development, price, and plan."

Kasdin consulted with Elizabeth Plater-Zyberk, an urban planner who had co-founded the nationally recognized architectural firm Arquitectonica with her husband, Andrés Duany. They drafted new zoning regulations that encouraged renovations and small projects instead of skyscrapers.

Some developers who ventured into South Pointe shared a vision for reasonably sized, low- to mid-rise complexes. German investors converted the Beach Colony Hotel into a sixteen-unit town house project, the first new project in the area since South Pointe Tower.

A transplanted New Yorker, Charles Vita, purchased the Nemo for $975,000, and built retail space on the ground floor and loft-style apartments on the upper floors. Jose Fernandez, an Art Deco District developer, bought the Knickerbocker Hotel at Third and Collins Avenue, and created thirteen apartments.

In 1988, the city offered to sell three blocks to any developer who would build affordable town houses at a maximum price of $80,000. The city used eminent domain and paid $8 million for several vacant lots, a few stand-alone homes, and two historic coral rock houses and sold the package to a South Florida developer, Groupe Pacific, for $4.43 million. As part of the sale, the city removed the affordable housing price targets and allowed the developer to sell at "market rates." Groupe Pacific spent seven years building a gated community of pastel-colored Mediterranean town houses called "The Courts." The eventual selling prices were between $220,000 and $650,000.

While the new developments were under way, Robins urged the city to abandon its broad condemnation powers. Miami Beach had spent more than $6 million in land acquisition and relocation costs and had only $1.65 million left in its original fund—money Robins argued could be better spent improving the area. "South Pointe still didn't have a grocery store," he says. "It had the possibility for major change, but there was a lot to do to convert it into a real neighborhood where a broad cross section of people wanted to live. It was like the Art Deco District, but a decade behind."

CHAPTER 23

"I Was Dying a Little Every Day"

I N. MAY 1992, CenTrust's David Paul was indicted on one hundred counts of racketeering, securities fraud, and tax evasion. "Again, it made my day," Alex Daoud told me.

Daoud's eighty-two-year-old mother had died in April. "If I had been mayor," he says, "hundreds of people would have paid tribute to her. But only a handful came; everybody else had run away from me. I'll never forgive those who didn't have the decency to attend her funeral."

The buildup to his trial had been the most difficult time of his life. He was low on money and had assembled a committee of prominent friends, led by Muhammad Ali, to raise a defense fund. "Guys like [Roy] Black don't come cheap," he says.

Daoud thought of the trial as just another election, a popularity contest. He kept reminding himself that he had run for office six times and never lost. If the jury liked him, they would acquit him. Philip Michael Thomas, co-star of *Miami Vice*, showed up during the first week. "Nothing but good thoughts, babe," said the TV star, as he threw his arms around Daoud.

The trial lasted eleven weeks, and dozens of witnesses took the stand. Tom Daly, the prominent developer, testified that Daoud had pressured him over some of his South Pointe properties and had asked him for a legal retainer but Daly told the mayor he didn't need a lawyer. Instead—and he insisted, without any quid pro quo—he directed a contractor to renovate Daoud's Miami Beach home. Robert Stuart Caplan, an interior designer, testified that Daoud received more than

$30,000 worth of furniture, appliances, fixtures, and professional services from Daly.

Daoud thought Daly's testimony was a treacherous betrayal. "I thought Tom Daly was my friend," he told me, "and he protects himself, gets immunity, and sells me down the river. I thought he was a stand-up guy." Daoud remembered the day he had pulled every favor he could to get county emergency crews to Daly's house when a friend's son disappeared in the rough surf. "Daly told me, 'You will always be part of my family, I can't thank you enough.'" Now, Daoud complained to Black that Daly was "a bully who likes to get drunk but when push came to shove he made a deal with the devil to save himself."

Willy Martinez, a flashy boxing promoter and local celeb, was a convicted drug dealer turned federal informant. In 1986, Daoud had given him a key to the city and proclaimed "Willy Martinez Day." On the stand, he testified that Daoud asked for $10,000 to renovate his house. Martinez said he instructed an employee to deliver a check to Daoud and that the mayor made him write "legal fees" on the bottom of the check. The money bought favors when Martinez got city permission to stage big-name fights in the Beach.

Daoud insisted to Black that his friends were distorting the truth, making fleeting business relationships appear sinister and illegal. After Martinez's testimony, he and Daoud were in the courthouse men's room together. "I wanted to take his head and smash it into the sink," Daoud told me, "but Roy suddenly realized we were in there together and came in and said, 'Get out!'"

But the biggest blow was the damaging testimony of the prosecution's star witness, Bonnie Levin. She connected Daoud to many of the crimes in the indictment and drew a picture of a man without ethics who was consumed by enormous greed. She calmly provided incriminating details about his cozy relationships with developers, contractors, bankers, and drug dealers who she said paid handsomely for his mayoral influence. When Daoud had sought another $10,000 from Willy Martinez in 1988, Levin said that Martinez didn't return Alex's calls, which infuriated him.

She testified that Daoud rarely did any work for the monthly payments from his prominent friends. Once, when David Paul gave Daoud some insurance contracts to work on, she said Daoud complained. " 'I can't believe they're sending me these documents to look over.' "

Daoud knew Levin's testimony was "devastating" and felt that her "betrayal was total. She had come to my mother's wake and told me she would help me, and her sister had called to say she would help. She told Roy Black she would be there for me. Her testimony was the coup de grâce."

Key players in the town's comeback secretly funneled thousands of dollars in cash and services to Daoud while grabbing millions in taxpayer-financed contracts and other city benefits. Other witnesses testified about the subtle pressure they felt to contribute to Daoud's re-election campaigns while they did city business. Even during Daoud's highly praised rescue of South Pointe Tower he had accepted $25,000 in "legal fees" from the developer's attorneys.

Roy Black argued that Daoud legitimately earned all the legal fees, and that there was nothing wrong with the discounts and freebies he got from unions and city contractors. Black presented a rhetorical question to the jury: "That happens to be a great American tradition, isn't it, getting something for less? People don't like to pay retail if they can get it for wholesale." He contended that there was no direct evidence that the money or favors had bought Daoud's vote or caused him to do anything illegal.

In the case of Willy Martinez, Black contended that Daoud earned the fee by lobbying Donald Trump to grant Martinez the closed-circuit television rights to a Trump-sponsored fight in Atlantic City.

Some court observers thought that while the government had forever tarnished Daoud's golden boy image, it had failed to present a convincing case that the payoffs were done to gain improper influence or city business.

WHILE THE TRIAL was under way, at 6 a.m. on Saturday, August 22, the National Hurricane Center in Coral Gables upgraded Tropical Storm Andrew to hurricane status. It was headed straight for South Florida, the region's first major hurricane in twenty-seven years. Red and black hurricane warning flags were raised Sunday morning. Almost 60,000 boat owners scrambled to get their vessels to safe harbor, and gas stations and supermarkets were jammed with long lines of people. Building supply stores sold plywood in their parking lots to keep up with the demand. Pregnant women within three weeks of their delivery date were urged to check into a hospital because a hurricane's low barometric pressure often caused premature births.

On Sunday, the National Hurricane Center announced that if Andrew stayed on track, its storm surge would be ten feet. Residents of Miami Beach, Key Biscayne, and other coastline communities were under mandatory evacuation and 2 million left. Those who refused were asked for the names of their next of kin.

Miami Beach's hurricane command post was in a windowless fourth-floor room in City Hall. Daoud spent the night there, hoping the storm might kill him. He thought it would be "utterly perfect: before my trial ended, before my verdict was rendered, nature would simply step in and finish me off. I would avoid ever being convicted of a felony and go to my grave as an innocent man."

The winds intensified by midnight to 175 mph with gusts over 200 mph. When Andrew made a last-minute jog to the south, the eye came ashore just south of Miami and directly east of Homestead Air Force base at 4:55 a.m. on Monday.

When the skies cleared, Homestead and Florida City looked as though they had been bombed. Sixty-five people were killed, more than 4,000 were injured, and 180,000 left homeless. The final tab for damages was $45 billion.

On South Beach, streets were strewn with broken glass. There was no electricity, no running water. Ocean Drive was covered in sand. In South Pointe, the winds stripped the roof off Browns Hotel. By Thursday, despite a 7 p.m. curfew and police roadblocks around the city, people reappeared on the streets and in the cafés. Electricity was restored and the state tourism board ran full-page ads in several national newspapers proclaiming "Florida: We're Still Open."

Labor Day Weekend was coming up. At Warsaw, club kids wore tank tops printed with "Hurricane Andrew: The 18 Billion Dollar Blow Job," and they joked that Andrew had been "the first gay hurricane: vicious, unpredictable, judgmental, and fashion-conscious to the extreme, sparing the chic while lashing out at the hinterlands."

Hurricane Andrew did not delay Daoud's judgment day. On Wednesday, September 23, he leapt out of his courtroom chair when a partial verdict acquitted him on nine counts. The judge sent the jury back to continue deliberating on the remaining charges. Two days later, they reached verdicts on two additional charges but were hopelessly deadlocked on the other twenty-six counts (split 10–2 in favor of acquittal on all). Prosecutors asked the judge to declare a hung jury on all outstanding counts. Daoud's co-counsel, David Garvin, made a calculated gamble and insisted the court accept the two latest verdicts before sending the jurors home. Judge Peter Fay agreed.

When the jury's foreman handed the verdict sheets to Judge Fay, Daoud stood up and shut his eyes tightly, as if in prayer. The clerk read off the two counts: As to count 1, a RICO charge that was among the most serious in the indictment, not guilty. Daoud visibly heaved a sigh of relief. As to count 17, charging Daoud with accepting a $10,000 bribe from Willy Martinez, guilty. Daoud slumped into his chair.

"When I heard guilty," Daoud told me, "the word exploded in my head. Martinez had lied on the stand. How ironic, I thought. The jury had found me guilty on one of the few charges on which I was innocent."

He faced a maximum of ten years imprisonment and a $250,000 fine. The prosecutors immediately announced that he would be retired on the deadlocked twenty-four corruption and money charges, plus a separate trial was still pending on six tax evasion charges. The judge ordered Daoud back to court in forty days to prepare for retrial. Black led his stunned client into an eleventh-floor conference room. He told Daoud to relax and left to get some ice water.

"I had been in such an extreme depression," Daoud explains. His mother's death had been on his mind. Terri Noe, his third wife, had left him weeks earlier, taking their three-year-old son. Since his indictment he'd put on 50 pounds. He was broke. He had sold his prized Corvette and knew it was only a matter of time until he would have to sell his half-million-dollar waterfront home to pay his legal bills.

"I felt like shit. I had no friends, no hope. I was dying a little every day."

Daoud thought back to the night almost exactly twelve years earlier when, at thirty-seven, he'd been elected a brand-new Miami Beach commissioner, as a crusader populist. Now he had become part of the system he'd once railed against, his avenging zeal replaced with the deadening knowledge that he had sold himself and his ideals to a corrupt machine. He admitted later, "I was so lost."

Roy Black had not returned. Daoud looked through the double doors to a large outdoor balcony. There was only a six-inch concrete parapet. He opened the doors and, as if in slow motion, stepped onto the edge.

"I looked out at Miami's skyline. It was sparkling. I thought it was ironic that it was such a beautiful day to end my life and that no one will care. It just won't matter."

As he was about to jump, he noticed a young mother and her small child enjoying a picnic in the plaza below. For a second, he wondered if he might hit them. "I was going to scream as I jumped, yell for them to get out of the way." A sudden gust of wind loosened the photo of his young son in his breast pocket. He glanced down at Alexander's face.

"The next thing I knew, I heard someone shouting, 'Hey, what the hell are you doing!'"

It was the court bailiff. "He startled me, and I actually lost my balance, but instead of going forward and ending it all, I fell backwards. I was so fucking fat I couldn't even make my body fall in the right direction."

Daoud left the courthouse in tears. That night he sat alone in darkness in his living room. His splendid house had been purchased and improved in part with illegal payoffs. "I used to love that place," he says. "But that night I hated it. It felt like a tomb.

"Sitting there feeling sorry for myself, I thought back to when I had polio as a kid and my mother was at the hospital, looking at me through this little glass window. That image was burned into my heart, into my soul."

His mind wandered to his sister, Patsy. She was seven years older and had always been a source of strength. But she had battled her own demons and had killed herself with an overdose of pills and alcohol in 1978, when she was thirty-nine. She left no note. He thought of his older brother, Jody, who had carried the responsibilities of eldest son in a traditional family. Jody had been a partner in the family's auction business when he became addicted to prescription amphetamines for weight loss. Alex had cared for his brother. He took Jody to doctors who specialized in weaning patients off drug addictions, but everything failed. Once, he even cajoled his brother to enter rehab. "But each time he returned to an addict's horrible life."

Three months after Patsy killed herself, Jody died of a heart attack at the age of forty-seven.

"What would they have thought of me," Alex wondered, "if they had lived to see me become mayor and then a convicted felon?"

He retrieved a 9mm pistol from the bedroom closet. "This is the way to end it," he thought, "no more mistakes."

He poured a large tumbler of vodka and composed a letter to his three-year-old son. Daoud wrote how much he loved him. "My desire to be dead was greater than my desire to see my own son grow up. I had wanted all the normal things any father does, but those dreams were lost in my own nightmare." He sealed it and printed neatly on the front: "For my son, Alexander. To be opened on his twelfth birthday."

He walked through each room of the house, reminiscing about family times. Most of the furniture had been sold to pay his bills. Finally, he went to his bedroom, sat on the bed, and grabbed the pistol. He pulled back the slide and chambered a bullet, put the barrel into his mouth, and pulled back the hammer. He pressed his tongue against the barrel so it would not jump as it fired.

Suddenly, there was an insistent banging on the front door. A man's voice screamed: "Alex! Alex! Are you all right? Alex, I know you're in there, open up!" It was a friend, Charley Modica.

The phone began ringing.

"All I had to do was give it one tiny tug," says Daoud, "one little squeeze on the trigger and it was all over. And there were all these interruptions. I thought at least I would have the peace and tranquillity to kill myself. I tried blocking out the distractions."

The pounding increased. "Open up, goddamn it, I know you're there. I'm gonna bust this door in otherwise!"

It was only seconds. But for Daoud it seemed an eternity. Then he made his decision. Not everyone had abandoned him. He thought of

Charlie Seraydar's words a decade earlier about the elderly man in the alleyway—"Suicide is one of the worst sins of South Beach." He put down the gun and fought back tears as he went down to open the door.

"It happened so fast I didn't even know it then," says Daoud. "But that night I had decided to take back control of my life."

WHILE PREPARING FOR his retrial in 1992, Daoud thought of fleeing the country. But after talking to Roy Black, he decided to plead guilty and cooperate with the prosecutors in exchange for a reduced sentence. The Feds wanted him to wear a wire and had targeted three prominent Miami Beach figures they thought might be corrupt: ex-mayor Harold Rosen; Russell Galbut, one of the Beach's largest condo-conversion developers and a member of the city's Zoning Board for a decade; and Capital Bank's chairman, Abel Holtz. All three were Daoud's friends. Galbut was his law partner. And Daoud had given his son the middle name Abel. Daoud knew from Black that anything could be negotiated, so he told the prosecutors that he would only wear a wire with Holtz. They pressured him, especially on Rosen. "It was a defining moment in my life," he says now. "I could have thrown Rosen under the bus. But I decided not to, and in doing that, I salvaged a bit of my own self-respect." The Feds warned that if he did not wear a wire on Rosen, he would serve Rosen's time as well. But Daoud held firm and the Feds relented.

Holtz was the first person to bribe Daoud, who had been honest for his first four years as a commissioner. Then, while running for his third term in 1983, Holtz asked Daoud to help his son, Danny, get a Zoning Board appointment. "You like my home, don't you, Alex? Someday you'll have one just like it. I'll help you buy it." He offered Daoud a payoff for any help. Daoud, tired of his $6,000-a-year commissioner's salary, decided to cross the line. The day after the election, he met Holtz in his bank office, where he received an envelope bulging with cash. "There'll be plenty more where that came from," Holtz assured him.

Daoud justified the bribe. No one appreciated his hard work when he was an idealist fighting for the elderly and the homeless. His public service had taken a toll on his family. What did people care for the sacrifices he had made? He deserved more.

Why turn only on Holtz? "He had not come to my mother's funeral," Daoud explained. "There were those who went to my mother's funeral and those who did not—she was so much a part of my life, no one knew how important it was for them to pay respect to her." Al Malnik, "a stand-up beautiful guy," had been the first to call Daoud when he learned of his mother's passing and had sent flowers. "He was not afraid of being there. Malnik was fearless."

Abel Holtz was also on Daoud's so-called shit list because he had vouched for Willy Martinez. That's why Daoud had felt so comfortable hitting Martinez up for money without really knowing him very well. "Holtz had betrayed me, and now I was going to return the favor."

Daoud arranged to meet Holtz at the Forge, their favorite spot. The FBI agents who had wired him did not know that Daoud had also brought along his pistol in case anything went awry. Seated in a corner booth, Daoud warned Holtz that the Feds might be investigating him. The banker laughed. "The Feds have been trying to get me for a long time. I'm too smart to get caught."

In September 1992, in addition to the jury's conviction for the Martinez money, Daoud pled guilty to bribery, money laundering, tax fraud, and jury tampering. (The Feds had learned that members of Daoud's Miami Beach church had financially helped one juror, and possibly others, during the trial.) U.S. District Judge King rejected a plea agreement that called for more than five years in prison and gave Daoud three years and five months plus a $75,000 fine.

Abel Holtz was indicted on racketeering, extortion, and corruption charges. He hired a large defense team headed by Gregory Craig, who would later lead Bill Clinton's impeachment team and is now Barack Obama's White House counsel. Holtz pled guilty to a single charge of obstructing Daoud's grand jury investigation by deceiving jurors about payments he made to the mayor. Under a plea bargain, Holtz, sixty-one, was supposed to be sentenced to a year in prison. But several dozen community stalwarts pleaded for him to be spared jail time and the judge gave him a slap on the wrist: forty-five days in prison, four and a half months of house arrest, and 3,000 hours of community service. "I always found that remarkable," says Daoud, "that the man most steeped in corruption was the one who got the lightest sentence."

In 1990, the county commissioners had named a stretch of Northeast Second Avenue in Miami Abel Holtz Boulevard. That same year, Miami changed Leomar Boulevard back to SW 132nd Avenue after Leonel Martinez went down for drug-smuggling charges. But despite Holtz's guilty plea, the city decided to keep his name on the boulevard. "He had also wanted a street named after him in Miami Beach," says Daoud, "so I had arranged to have the street running in front of South Pointe Tower named Abel Holtz Way."

When Steve Muss heard about it all, he blew his stack. A couple of years earlier, Muss had had Miami Beach's Convention Center named after him as a reward for getting a special hotel tax approved that funded a $78 million renovation. Six thousand five hundred thirty-seven registered voters signed a petition demanding his name be removed; they considered it political cronyism by Daoud and the commissioners, who had received large political donations from Muss. Muss finally asked the city to remove his name. It was sandblasted off the facade and twenty-seven interior locations, although hundreds of electrical boxes still have Muss's name stamped inside. "De-naming it was the worst thing that ever happened to me," Muss says. "It was like a death. It doesn't feel good to have your name taken off something like that. It taught me you should never name anything for people alive." Muss stopped the Abel Holtz Way renaming dead in its tracks.

David Paul, the CenTrust president, was convicted in 1993 of sixty-eight counts of banking fraud—largely for $3.2 million in funds he lavished on his La Gorce Island compound. The following year he pleaded guilty to twenty-nine securities law violations, mostly for CenTrust's financial dealings with other scandal-plagued institutions, including junk bond powerhouse Drexel Burnham Lambert and the rogue Bank of Credit and Commerce International (BCCI). Paul's sentence of eleven years was in the wake of the get-tough standards enacted after the savings and loan crisis. Prosecutors seized everything: his multiple homes, yacht, cars, and his multi-million-dollar art collection. In the incestuous world of Miami Beach, it wasn't long before Paul's wife, Sandy, was dating Steve Muss. Her first husband, Jay Kogan, had tried to hire a hit man to kill her. He got probation. She filed for divorce. Prosecutors, worried that Sandy was trying to hide assets, tried but failed to block her marriage to Muss, who had divorced his own wife.

Daoud's cooperation meant he'd serve only eighteen months. "That prison time was a lot harder for me than anyone knows," he told me years later. "I had the whole world and I lost it."

CHAPTER 24

"All About the Flash"

I N JANUARY 1992, *New York* magazine ran a cover story titled "SoHo in the Sun," which declared that the revived Beach was the "hippest 30 blocks in the country."

The fastest-growing segment of Beach business was the nightclub industry. "South Beach had replaced Ibiza as club central," says promoter Michael Capponi. Mark Fleischmann, who had bought Studio 54 from Ian Schrager and Steve Rubell, opened Tatou at the old Woody's. Rande Gerber, a former model, started the Whiskey Bar ("the most attitude at the velvet rope, and for no reason," quipped Louis Canales). Even Abe Resnick got into the act. He rented out a closed Jewish temple at Sixth and Collins as Stars, a 7,000-square-foot disco. And another synagogue he owned, under the shadow of the Beach's Holocaust Memorial, was turned into a wild nightclub: Van Dome. It replaced the temple's *mehitzah* with a see-through aquarium between the men's and women's restrooms. "They were empty," Resnick told a colleague when asked if he felt odd about former houses of worship becoming nightclubs. "It's better they get used for something."

The town was more celebrity-packed than ever. Madonna, just off her Blond Ambition tour, was considering a home on the Beach. Sylvester Stallone had real estate agents searching for a large waterfront estate. Until he visited in 1991, Gianni Versace had dismissed the Beach as tawdry. "He first came in the early eighties and he hated it," Louis Canales told me. "In '91, he stopped here again after flying back from Cuba. The Versace store in Bal Harbour had just been renovated. He stayed for the party. Every cutting-edge editor, fashion photographer, stylist, and model was there. It blew him away."

Versace had inquired about buying a place on the Beach, but nothing seemed grand enough until Saul Gross showed him the Amsterdam Palace. When the appraisal came in below the contract price, Versace's financial adviser wanted to cancel the deal. "But he didn't care about the appraisal," remembers Gross. "He loved the building and he was going to buy it and pay the seller whatever he was asking." Versace decided to evict the tenants, turn it into a Venetian palazzo, and return it to its original name: Casa Casuarina.

Louis Canales was going through a tough time. His wife, Jan, had died of cancer in October 1991. Louis was gay but had married her out of a sense of duty after she became pregnant when they were teenagers. They had a special bond and love that he would never find again, and he went into a clinical depression after her death.

He had spent his $300,000 in savings on Jan's cancer treatments. Louis dropped 40 pounds. In South Beach, weight loss on a gay man often meant a drug addiction or AIDS, and rumors about Canales spread fast. Some assumed he was a crack addict; others that Louis had given Jan AIDS. "The only reason it didn't drive me crazy or to suicide was that I kept reminding myself that gossip, even untrue, puts you further up the food chain of a place like South Beach. Patrick McMullen [the celebrity photographer] tried to cheer me up. 'Louis, you really have made it now, you even have the sympathy crowd.'"

Louis would come home to find dozens of phone messages offering condolences, as well as offers of work. He did not return the calls. "Then the phone stopped ringing. People edited themselves out of my life."

Club owners who had once courted Louis and paid him extravagantly now dismissed him. "And those who employed me," he recalls, not with bitterness but resignation, "would abuse me since they knew I was so destitute." They bounced checks. One owner, with whom he had worked on two major club openings, had owed Jan $4,000 for personal promotion work. When he hired Canales, he slapped him on the back. "I guess I don't have to pay the money now."

A friend gave him Elisabeth Kübler-Ross's seminal book *On Death and Dying*. "It was an epiphany. It gave me the tools to start to pull myself up from this abyss."

By April 1992, Tara Solomon had a local radio show and had just launched her must-read "Queen of the Night" column in *The Miami Herald*. And she developed a wildly successful Tuesday-night party at Barocco Beach called the Martini Club.

"I wanted an eclectic, Holly Golightly feel," she says. On a trip to New York she had discovered the Dueling Bankheads (as in Tallulah): two men in identical chic suits, brunette hair falling over one eye, smeared red lipstick, and a handbag slung over a wrist, who did a camp song-and-comedy routine. She brought the Kibble Family, an entire family in drag, to Miami, and featured Tom Jones and Tammy Faye impersonators.

Michael Capponi ran two short-lived clubs, Boomerang and the Cave, with Gary James. Unbeknownst to them, one of Boomerang's bartenders was running a drug ring. "None of us knew that our phones were tapped," Capponi recalls. "It turned out [the bartender] was already being investigated by the time she started working for us. The DEA raided the club one night around 3 a.m. Twenty armed agents put everyone against the wall, turned on the lights, and found 150 drug violations. They closed us down."

James recalls that "Capponi was always in debt and I would give him money. Then someone told me they saw his Cherokee in a lousy area and he was buying drugs. I confronted him. 'Is there something you need to tell me?' 'No.'"

But Capponi was doing lots of drugs. "Coke was everywhere," he remembers. "And I was always an extremist. I had smoked pot since I was twelve. If someone did one X tab, I did five. I lived with a box of cash in my closet and decided to be an addict."

Gary James had opened The Spot, a bar and club that the *Miami New Times* quickly named the "best rowdy celebrity hangout." Mickey Rourke came constantly when he was in town and brought The Cure, REM, Lenny Kravitz, and his boxing friends. James, who owned the restaurant with his mother, did little to disabuse anyone of the impression that Mickey was a partner. "It was good for business, that we were so tight," says James. And nobody doubted they were very close. On Gary's tattooed left wrist was a shamrock with his initials in Gaelic script and the number 6. The 6 indicated his position in the lineup of Mickey Rourke's fourteen friends who had joined him at a Los Angeles male-bonding ceremony and had gotten the same tattoos. "This means we are brothers," Rourke told them. "We would do anything for each other."

Ever since Rourke had made *The Pope of Greenwich Village*, he had been fascinated with the Mafia. Mickey had flown James to New York, where they had dinner with Gotti mob captains at an Upper East Side restaurant, Da Noi. When John Gotti went on trial in the spring of 1992, Rourke sat in the first row with the Gotti family, to support him. He told reporters that he and Gotti were friends, that they sometimes talked about movie projects. Rourke waved at Gotti and hugged and kissed his associates. One newspaper called him the "George Raft of his generation."

Michael "Mikey Scars" DiLeonardo of the Gambino family became Rourke's shadow. At the time, DiLeonardo was running loan-sharking for the Gambinos from a Staten Island café. (He later became a mob turncoat and went into witness protection after testifying that John Gotti, Jr., had ordered a hit on the Guardian Angels' founder, Curtis Sliwa.)

Gary James thought that the mob dinners in New York came with no strings attached. Then one day, Mikey Scars walked into Gary's office above The Spot. "He was this tough guy who was always talking shit and showing everyone how rough he was," says James.

"We want to see your books."

"What books?" Gary was startled.

"We want those fucking books."

James told Mikey Scars to get out. According to James, the mobster told him that if he didn't get the books in a few days, he would torch the club.

James did not know if Mickey was aware of what DiLeonardo was up to. "Mickey was into his own stuff then. He had just held a press conference that he was returning to boxing. It was a risky move." Gary telephoned his brother-in-law. "My sister was married to a heavyweight Colombian. I went to see him, and he turned out to be like Gotti's fuck-ing boss. I never heard from them again." (Gary's brother-in-law is now a wanted fugitive, believed by federal prosecutors to be hiding in Venezuela.)

That incident caused a rupture in the James-Rourke friendship. At one point, Mickey told a *USA Today* reporter that he'd like to sandblast off Gary's friendship tattoo. It took two years before Rourke, accompanied by Boy George, walked into another Gary James joint, Lua. He went straight up to Gary. " 'I'm sorry,' he said. 'I didn't know what Mikey Scars was up to. You are my brother, okay? Peace.' "

DURING THIS TIME, a new promoter, thirty-three-year-old Tommy "Pooch" Pucci arrived from Brooklyn. He seemed more hood than hipster, but no one in South Beach knew that he had two felony convictions—one for cocaine possession and one for credit card fraud—and had left behind failed business ventures, a tangle of lawsuits, and a string of gambling debts.

Pooch suffered his first South Florida arrest in the alley behind The Spot soon after arriving in 1992. "This beautiful Latin girl comes up to me and says, 'You wanna do a bump, Tommy?' I went into the alley and seconds later I got arrested for the residue of coke on my nostrils. Do you believe it?" He was also found to be in possession of ecstasy. The charges were later dropped.

Pooch decided to hitch his future to South Beach's "growing action" and he launched Tommy Pooch Productions. He also opened two Pucci's Pizzas on South Beach and two in downtown Miami and Kendall. There were rumors that he was a front for northeastern mobsters. He told a reporter that he grew up in Bensonhurst, "where five Mafia families were active, and, yeah, when I was a kid I was impressed with people like that. I mean, guys would say, 'There goes so-and-so.' And you would recognize the name." But he insisted that he was not involved with organized crime.

Michael Capponi helped Pooch break into the local scene, cutting him in on promotion deals. Later, as Capponi's heroin addiction was destroying his career, he claimed to Gary James that Pooch had supplied him with heroin. Capponi now says it was Pooch's way of removing him as a competitor in the club promo business. (The two are friends today and Pooch adamantly dismisses the heroin allegation as a "flat-out lie.")

Once James returned from Europe, he found that Pooch had taken over his Tuesday-night parties at Cassis Bistro. "Tommy had stolen the dinner party, costumes and all," remembers James. "I had met him right after he arrived. It didn't take very long to realize that Tommy was a real street hustler. He was determined to make it here. He told me that he didn't know how the Beach worked yet, but that once he figured it out he was going to climb right up the food chain. 'I will take this town over.' "

IN A TOWN where someone was only as good as their last headline, an outlandish and flashy thirty-five-year-old self-described "party animal," Thomas Kramer arrived. The German boasted he was flush with cash from a fortune made trading commodities in Munich and Frankfurt. In fact, he was married to Catherine Burda, an heiress to one of Germany's oldest-line families. His father-in-law had loaned him $145 million to invest in American businesses and real estate.

Kramer had been vacationing in St. Barts in 1992 when he "got bored, came down to South Beach, and discovered a little bit of Europe in America." In South Pointe, he saw opportunity no one else did. Developers had avoided the area largely because they anticipated expensive litigation to push through zoning changes and costly environmental cleanup operations on sites of a small oil refinery, a gasoline storage facility, a dog track, dry cleaning operations, and a meat factory. Oblivious to its history and in love with its natural scenic location, Kramer made local headlines when he spent $35 million in cash over a couple of months, buying fourteen oceanfront acres and the Ocean Haven and Leonard Hotels, at nearly double the going rate. He offered top prices for Resolution Trust Corporation properties: he paid $304 a foot for a 4,000-square-foot building that was worth, according to Saul Gross, about a third of that. A month later he added a scattering of small apartment and commercial buildings and twenty condos in South Pointe Tower. (He bought the penthouse from Mel Schlesser, who got it for $300,000 in 1989—Kramer paid $795,000 cash.) City officials and other developers watched in awe as he swiftly became the neighborhood's largest landowner, with 29 percent of South Pointe and 85 percent of the property that lined the ocean or Biscayne Bay.

In buying the property along the marina, Kramer reaped an unexpected benefit. In 1982, when the city pulled the plug on the original South Shore RDA, the marina contractor had sued the city for breach of contract. A court awarded a multi-million-dollar judgment requiring the city to repair the seawall, pay for an environmental cleanup, build parking lots and marina storage, and allow any future developer to build to the maximum legal zoning.

"Kramer was playing with other people's money," says Jorge Perez, then the largest South Florida developer of affordable housing. "If it's not your money, it's easy to ignore what is the right price in the marketplace. And in Miami, it is all about the flash. Kramer was the perfect showman. In New York, they would have thrown him out in six months. Here, he became a celebrity and power figure."

Kramer took title to most of the properties through offshore shell companies. Three of his largest parcels were registered to a Panamanian corporation, Sandpoint Financial Ltd. Kramer boasted that he would turn South Pointe into a quarter-billion-dollar European-style development inspired by Portofino, the beautiful village on the Italian Riviera where he had one of his six homes. His development would include several thousand luxury condos, retail shops, restaurants, and a five-star, thirty-five-room hotel. Faux mountains would ring the neighborhood and there would be cobblestone streets. After the unfulfilled boasts of Lenny Pelullo and Gerry Sanchez, and the giant flop of the RDA's Venice-in-America plan, there were many skeptics. "He certainly talked a good game, and had made a bold statement in buying so much property," says Craig Robins. "Now I thought we'd wait to see if he was for real or not." Robins acknowledged that by buying all of South Pointe's best land in one fell swoop, Kramer had eliminated him and other South Florida developers as competitors. "It was as if someone had come in and bought Ocean Drive, at double its value, right before Tony Goldman had arrived."

"I was wary from the first moment Kramer appeared," says Nancy

Liebman. "Something didn't seem right." Prices in South Pointe went up in part because by buying so many properties at generous prices, Kramer created the illusion that the market was stronger than it was.

In late 1992, he hired two real estate brokers to "unload" some of his "excess" properties. "The prices are skyrocketing," Kramer claimed. "I'm going to try to participate in some of the price increases in South Beach." He wouldn't say which parcels were for sale. "It depends on price," he said. "In some areas prices have quadrupled. Hopefully, I'll sell in those areas."

He bought socialite Jan Cowles's Indian Creek estate, demolished it, submitted plans to replace it with an elaborate mansion, and then decided at the last moment to leave the lot empty. Instead, he purchased a waterfront estate on Star Island. He was a regular on the party circuit, trailed by an entourage of European friends and hangers-on. "He would come in and drop $5,000 like it was water," recalls Gary James.

Kramer decided that he wanted to open a nightclub. He spent $3 million to convert the former Leonard Hotel at 54 Collins into "Hell." The Leonard had been a downtown jewel similar to the Amsterdam Palace. He hired Norman Gosney, the noted production designer, and told him that if he read Edgar Allan Poe's "Masque of the Red Death" he would understand what Kramer wanted in his club. Hell was dark, with Victorian red-flocked wallpaper, velvet couches, and draperies that ended in puddles of fabric on the floor. Plastic icicles hung from the courtyard balconies. And then there were the Goth touches, like razors embedded in the clear acrylic toilet seats. A fountain spewed blood red liquid, and there was a sequenced-slide projection of a devil licking his own face with a tongue a foot long. A naked woman with a pool of chocolate sauce in her navel reclined near the staircase, while someone dressed as a nun adorned with devil's horns dipped strawberries into the chocolate and offered them to guests. Different rooms were decorated to represent the Seven Deadly Sins. Sloth was a dark mustard color, and filled with plastic furniture and 1950s food ads. Envy had a glass booth with a bed on which a well-endowed eighteen-year-old girl browsed porn magazines. There was a "flesh ride" equipped with a bumper car that bumped into life-sized nude posters. In the "Portrait Gallery of Hell" were Elvis, Halston, Roy Cohn, Bing Crosby, and the lady from Wendy's "Where's the beef?" commercials. The "Madonna Suite" was equipped with a bedroom filled with whips, chains, and S&M masks. Outside the club, a replica Viking ship topped with human skulls was next to a 10-foot portrait of Satan throwing curios over Miami Beach.

Hell opened on October 24, 1992. Kramer's publicist invited everyone from the B-52s' Fred Schneider to Norman Mailer, who did not attend. Billy Idol and Deee-Lite, a house/dance group, were the musical acts. The police estimated 9,000 people turned up.

Drag queens simulated sex on a pool table; three female bodybuilders performed pseudo-lesbian hijinks; and an S&M sex room proved to be the real deal. "It wasn't camp, it wasn't kitsch, and it certainly wasn't cutting edge," says Louis Canales, who was hired as a doorman for the first night.

The tall, blond, baby-faced Kramer, dressed in black leather, barked orders at his doormen in his heavy German accent. At one point Richard Goff of *Out* was turned away because he wore a T-shirt advocating more research dollars for AIDS. Kramer said loudly to Canales, "These people are too ugly to come into this club, don't let them in." He told someone that he didn't want "fags like Versace" in his club. "I apologized to those folks standing up front by the ropes," says Canales, "picked it up, let myself out, and kept on walking—it was the first and only time I have walked out in the middle of a job."

"I have nothing against faggots," Kramer told me, "but I wanted a club with beautiful women and men like me. There would have been nothing worse than to have it seem like it was gay. There were already those clubs, so they weren't going to use mine."

As fast as Kramer had generated some hope that his investments might revitalize South Pointe, he seemed to lose it all in one night of playing the devil and shouting and sponsoring obscenities. "It was very hard for city officials and other developers to imagine that he was really serious about his business," recalls Saul Gross.

Kramer tried to salvage his reputation. Less than two weeks later, he sponsored a spectacular $500,000 party near South Pointe Park. Three hundred guests got a firsthand look at the high-rolling German and were treated to an eleven-course gourmet dinner in a lavishly decorated

tent. Most of the Beach's power brokers attended. There Kramer unveiled his vision of a "new frontier, a cosmopolitan center in the heart
of the Americas." He produced architectural drawings for an enormous
shopping center, several restaurants, and a skyscraper hotel to be called
Heaven. "I used to refuse invitations to leave old stinky Europe and
travel here," he told the Beach's elite. "Miami had a reputation for retirement homes and inadequate restaurants and hotels. But despite the
bashing by the media, it is a place in one of the best shapes I've ever
seen, a hot spot for models and the international crowd." He got a
standing ovation.

To further ingratiate himself, Kramer handed out donations with
great fanfare. He capped off the gala with a gift of $100,000 for city
landscaping at Fifth Street, another $100,000 for a South Pointe Ele-
mentary day care program, $50,000 to the Miami Beach Police Athletic
League for Christmas presents to needy children, and $10,000 to the
local Health Crisis Network. Miami Beach police chief Phillip Huber
and Mayor Seymour Gelber—"This city is greater because you are here
with us"—accepted their checks. He pledged another $200,000 for
South Beach Elementary. And because Kramer didn't like the beige
color of South Pointe's largest public housing project, Rebecca Towers,
he donated $70,000 to repaint the two bayfront high-rises peach.
Kramer also paid $50,000 for the highest membership level of the Bea-
con Council, the county's economic development organization. That
donation made him an instant member of the board of directors, along
with the CEOs of American Airlines, the *Miami Herald*/Knight Ridder,
the philanthropic Knight Foundation, and the Ocean Reef Club.

The evening ended with a thirty-minute Grucci fireworks display
that almost everyone agreed was grander than the city's Fourth of July.

As usual, a great party in Miami Beach worked wonders. "It was so
typical of the Beach; they were suddenly won over by him," says Nancy
Liebman. "We hadn't seen Mr. Hyde yet."

CHAPTER 25

"No Guns. No Politics"

I N 1993, JERRY Powers and Jason Binn launched *Ocean Drive* magazine. Powers's concept: "Two rules. No guns. No politics. Just a good, quick read."* The target audience was hip tourists and residents. A fashion model would grace every cover. "We *are* discriminating against the lower-income people," Powers told a local business reporter before the launch. "If they want to read the publication that's great, but we're going after the people who can spend $300 per day."

The financial plan was simple: most copies would be given away free, and the revenue would come from advertising. Annual subscriptions were $28. Fifty thousand copies would be distributed monthly at hotels, clubs, popular restaurants, and select outlets like Books & Books and the News Café. "And he stole one of my old tricks," says Gary James. "When they finally published, they had models hand them out on Rollerblades."

The forty-six-year-old Powers was as un–South Beach as possible,

---

* From 2004 to 2006, I wrote a column for *Ocean Drive*, with my wife, Trisha Posner, called "Cultural Chatter." Trisha subsequently had her own byline, "Health Watch," about developments in health and fitness. In September 2007, we appeared, along with other neighbors, in an eight-minute video shown to the Miami Beach Planning Board that urged the city to close a zoning loophole allowing small hotels to build huge entertainment complexes that created problems for residents. In her introduction, Trisha said, "I'm a journalist and columnist for *Ocean Drive* magazine." Jerry Powers, afraid that his entertainment advertisers might be offended, canceled her column. The resulting controversy was covered in the *Miami Herald*, the *Miami SunPost*, *Huffington Post*, and the *New York Post*. Jerry Powers refused to be interviewed for this book and encouraged his friends not to cooperate. Jason Binn never answered my interview request.

with his short, pudgy frame and thinning hair, but he was an excellent salesman and promoter, and the smiling, baby-faced Binn devoted his life to meeting people on the A-list. To many observers, they seemed an odd couple, but they were a match made in promotional heaven.

Binn's father, Moreton, had changed the family name from Binnstock and was known as the "Baron of Barter," having made a fortune in Atwood Richards, a Manhattan company that specialized in corporate barter.

"He was always starstruck," says a writer who has known Binn since 1991. He had impressed his college friends by getting a picture of himself with any visiting celebrity. "He got some type of thrill by hanging out with them. He was a male groupie, he just didn't put out."

Soon after he arrived in Miami in 1992, everyone knew the short kid with the cell phone and a Canon camera. "He was like glue," says Gary James. "You finally let him hang around because you couldn't be bothered dealing with him." Nightlife columnist Tom Austin thought Binn's celebrity crawling was tawdry, even by South Beach standards. Austin dubbed him the Beach's "beloved doppelganger in the fame game" and "my favorite celeb vibrator."

Tara Solomon thought Binn made his way so well because he always said yes to any request, got by with little sleep, and didn't gossip. "That made people feel safe around him," she says.

South Beach is so small that someone like Binn could become his own celebrity wrangler. He drove singer Lenny Kravitz around on errands. One day, Binn saw Michael Caine on Lincoln Road. He complained to Binn that he had waited for three hours at the DMV trying to get a driver's license. While they spoke, Binn called a friend and made an appointment for the same day. (Caine was impressed that Binn didn't look at his cell phone while dialing the number. "He's like a great piano player, you know, they never look at the keys.") Sylvester Stallone met Binn while filming *The Specialist*. He was "taken with [Binn's] vitality and ambition. . . . He's also smoothed over a few things, disagreements with local papers and what not."

Models were Binn's favorite currency. Initially, he thought he might have to pay them to show up at parties, but he quickly discovered they were only too happy to be part of his entourage. "These girls are our future," he told a local reporter. When Aerosmith recorded an album in Miami, lead singer Steve Tyler found himself playing with naked models on a yacht, courtesy of Binn. "They were all tens!" Tyler later told a reporter. "You call Jason up, and before you know it, you're on the beach with six naked models, smoking a Havana!"

The higher Binn's own profile, the better the chance for *Ocean Drive* to be successful. He would use one celeb to get to others. Russell Simmons, Def Jam's co-founder, was in a Beach movie theater when his cell phone rang—it was Binn, whom he had met in New York, telling him to rush to a nearby restaurant because Arnold Schwarzenegger and Maria Shriver were there and wanted to have dinner with him. When Simmons arrived, Binn was alone, and the Schwarzeneggers were with a large group across the restaurant. Binn grabbed Simmons and walked over. "Turns out he didn't even know them!" remembered Simmons. "He didn't know Arnold, Maria, none of them. But the next thing you know he's over at their table, taking pictures. . . . You can't help but like him. He wears you the fuck out."

Jerry Powers took a very different path to *Ocean Drive*. Jerry Michael Pulwer was born in Germany to Holocaust survivors and grew up in New Jersey. He dropped out of college and was in the crowd at Woodstock—telling friends that it was a life-changing experience. He changed his name to Powers, sold ads for a local rock station, played as a DJ, and did promo for bands.

In 1970, he met Sandi, who would become his wife, at Fun Fair, an amusement park in Miami. They moved in together the next day. Their only daughter, Jacquelynn, who would become *Ocean Drive*'s chief writer, was born two years later. She told friends she raised herself because both parents were largely absent. Powers later admitted to a reporter that he long battled cocaine, barbiturates, amphetamines, "and whatever else was around," and that his problems continued until Sandi convinced him to enter rehab in 1984. (Sandi later had her own battles with drugs.)

In 1973, the year after Jacquelynn's birth, police nicked Powers for drunkenness and cocaine possession. The charges were dismissed. In 1978, he was arrested on a felony for using a forged prescription to get drugs. It was reduced to a misdemeanor and transferred to county

court, where he was acquitted. Four years later he was arrested again for
drug possession, but those charges were also dropped.

Drugs didn't stop him from working. He published the *Daily Planet*,
an alternative newspaper that was a cross between *MAD* magazine and
Screw, devoted to harassing the establishment. He closed the *Daily
Planet* the day after Nixon resigned. (When he was asked if it felt odd
going from counterculture political coverage to fashion and gossip in
Ocean Drive, Powers said, "You have to go with what you see in the
streets.") With a free circulation of 1,500 and not many ads, he had to
hustle to pay his bills. (Court files reveal he was busted at least twenty
times in the 1970s and 1980s, mostly for writing bad checks.)* Police
twice deemed his *Daily Planet* as "obscene"—but both cases were dismissed.

He turned a corner in 1986 when he convinced the iconic Pop artist
Peter Max to hire him as his business manager. Max had been in a
fifteen-year seclusion after a bitter divorce and thought Powers could
kick-start his career. Powers told him that if he was marketed correctly
he could ride a wave of sixties nostalgia and try merchandising everything from T-shirts to coffee mugs as expressions of counterculture
kitsch. Max agreed.

Powers and his family moved to eastern Long Island, near Max's
summer home—where Powers met the Binns. When he returned to
Miami in 1991, he played up his role as Max's business manager. He
lived in a spacious home on Sunset Island, dined at the finest restaurants, and drove a new Jaguar. He had a pretty blond wife and a
nineteen-year-old daughter who had just returned from a summer in
Israel. It didn't take an operator like Powers long to meet other people
who had created new lives for themselves in South Beach. Jacquelynn be-

---

* Metro-Dade police files list five aliases for Powers, all slight variations of his name.
At various times he gave cops different dates of birth and two different Social Security numbers. At least four arrest warrants were issued for him in the 1970s and
1980s. Police and court records are sketchy about the resolution of the various cases,
most of which were felonies. But it appears all but one was eventually dismissed after
Powers paid restitution. He apparently never did any prison time. Powers was sued in
civil court—for everything from breach of contract to unpaid bills—more than a
dozen times between 1977 and 1984.

came chums with Michael Capponi, who was pulling in $10,000 a week as a promoter and renting a luxury apartment in South Pointe Tower.

When Powers described his idea for a new magazine to Thomas Kramer, Kramer thought it was great so long as it emphasized sex, "which sells all the time." He invested $100,000. As a private company, Powers and Binn weren't obligated to identify any investors, but Binn took a page from his father's bartering business and told Jerry that ad dollars should buy good press coverage, and investors should get positive press. It was, after all, one of the reasons why anyone put money into the venture.

The pair decided that one way *Ocean Drive* could stand out from competitors was to co-opt the magazine's name for high-profile events. Binn persuaded Irene Marie and Michelle Pommier to provide models for a charity volleyball game, and then he and Powers got Nike and Coppertone to pay all the costs. The magazine would cover the game and provide publicity for everyone involved. Binn called it "Volley-palooza." (Now in its sixteenth year, the game attracts about 20,000 tourists annually to the Beach.)

When the duo sold ads for their premier issue, they didn't even have a prototype. "I remember very clearly when this kid walked in, introduced himself, and said he was doing a magazine about South Beach," recalls Shareef Malnik. The readership Binn targeted seemed precisely the clientele Shareef wanted as he remade the Forge. He took a full-page color ad: a large painting of a female nude hanging against a brick wall, surrounded by ornate bronze sconces. The ad rate was $2,000, but Shareef got it for half price. Discounted ads, decided Powers and Binn, would make it easier to fill the first issue. Within two weeks, they had sold 40 pages for $25,000.

The inaugural issue in January 1993 instantly defined the magazine. The famed fashion photographer Francesco Scavullo shot Claudia Schiffer for the cover, her breasts barely hidden under a clingy black dress. The premier issue had 80 pages, 40 of them ads. By mid-year the magazine ran to 300 pages, with nearly two thirds ads. And big advertisers got the soft editorial coverage they expected. Clothing designer Betsey Johnson, a flagship advertiser, was given a glowing profile, as was another prominent advertiser, Russell Galbut, managing director of the condo colossus Crescent Heights. Absolut Vodka, one of *Ocean Drive's* first national accounts, got two profiles about artists who worked on the company's ad campaign. Those articles shared the pages with frothy pieces about the latest restaurant or hottest club.

A few weeks after the first issue hit the stands, the U.S. Attorney's office in New York indicted Powers for not filing income tax returns for 1988 and 1989, years in which the government charged he earned $560,000. Behind the scenes, Powers struck a clandestine deal with prosecutors: If they agreed to no jail time on the tax charges and complete immunity for anything else, he would deliver Peter Max for tax fraud. Prosecutor Robert Cramer approved the deal.

On January 20, 1993, Powers pled guilty to two misdemeanor counts. His sentencing was delayed while he cooperated with the Feds. It took three years before Peter Max was indicted on eleven counts of conspiracy and tax fraud. Max's attorney publicly accused Powers of having been the instigator of all the wrongdoing. Even if true, it was too late. Powers delivered the goods on Max, and all he had to do was to reimburse the government for his taxes, plus interest and penalties.

Despite the indictment, Powers found time to write a profile about Thomas Kramer for the second issue, but without disclosing that Kramer was an investor. The article glossed over questions about Kramer's finances and did not address his erratic personal behavior. Instead, Kramer lashed out at his critics.

When a *Miami New Times* columnist dissed *Ocean Drive's* reporting as "blowjob journalism," Powers and Binn were not upset. "We're not competing with *The New York Times*," Powers told Kramer.

"If South Beach's soul was shallow, *Ocean Drive* captured it perfectly," says Louis Canales.

Dona Zemo mailed a copy each month to Lenny Pelullo in federal prison. "He was so grateful," she told me. "It made him wistful for his old stomping grounds."

Binn told the *Florida Business Journal* that by December the magazine was profitable. Evidently, one of the reasons they were in the black so fast was that they hadn't paid all their start-up bills. *Ocean Drive* was sued by St. Ives Press for $18,500 in printing fees for the premier issue. Powers finally agreed to pay the printer $12,000 in installments; when he missed the first payment, the judge entered an order that the magazine immediately pay $14,500. Two former workers had also sued a couple of months after the launch, both claiming they were owed money. Cynthia Zarco, who had left for the *Miami Herald*, sued the magazine for withholding more than $3,000 in back pay and charged that they had stolen the title of her column "UpLate." It was settled out of court.

Zarco also complained that Powers and Binn had exploited trade advertising arrangements for their own benefit by getting most products and services free. Sandi Powers became well known at high-end boutiques and cosmetic surgeons' offices for demanding free goods and services.

Jerry was incredulous that there was anything wrong with the practice. "What the fuck would be the purpose of owning a magazine if you had to pay for anything you covered?"

"It's just jealousy," Binn assured him. "South Beach is an institution, and now so are we."

CHAPTER 26

King of Clubs

THE CELEBS WHO vacationed in South Beach never saw the mainland's stark, inner-city poverty, which one county official compared to that of the Third World. No one ever drove them through Liberty City, where a disturbing new trend was to hurl concrete blocks through windshields and snatch purses and jewels from the startled motorists.

In 1993, a German tourist, Barbara Meller-Jensen, drove from the airport to Miami Beach in a rented car. When she was bumped from behind, she got out to investigate. In front of her husband and children, thieves robbed her and then ran over her.

Dade County's crime rate remained the highest in the state and mainland Miami was still among the nation's poorest cities. The refugee influx continued, as did white flight.

In the cocaine wars, federal prosecutors had been victorious a couple of years earlier when they arrested two of South Florida's biggest coke dons, Sal Magluta and his partner Augusto "Willy" Falcon. But by 1993, as *Ocean Drive* concentrated on the glitter in the Beach, witnesses in major drug trials were being murdered in Miami with alarming frequency. And in the summer of '93, a most-wanted trafficker, Mario Gonzalez, was arrested at a motel near Miami International after a gunfight with a SWAT team in which hundreds of rounds sent local residents fleeing in terror. The drug business had evolved, not disappeared. Deposits made by traffickers carrying duffel bags of cash were replaced with bank wire transfers into real estate investments and start-up businesses. Harold Ackerman, a fifty-one-year-old vegetable importer who lived in North Miami Beach, was an observant Jew who looked more like an accountant than a drug dealer. He was arrested in 1992 for running a vast South Florida supply network—DEA agents found 22 tons of coke hidden in "frozen broccoli" shipments and concrete fenceposts. And although the Feds seized 50 tons of cocaine in South Florida that year, an increase of 80 percent since 1980, the wholesale street price still dropped, a sign of how much was still flooding the region.

"There was little doubt my clients knew that Miami still had a rough and tumble reputation," says one real estate broker. "For the most part, that meant that wherever they bought had to provide security. Living here was different than having a second home in the Hamptons. You had to have enough money to have fun in Miami, but also to feel safe. The violent edge added an aura of excitement for some of my clients, that they were buying a home in a place that was just a little out of control."

Gianni Versace was the only one of the early-nineties celebrities drawn to town who was determined not to live behind a secure gate. He was the first celeb to buy in the Art Deco District, but his plan for his multi-million-dollar renovation of Casa Casuarina was not well received within the preservation community. It rekindled lingering questions about development on the Beach and how best to preserve the historic district's integrity. The problem was with Versace's desire for a large garden and a swimming pool. Architect J. Wallace Tutt III had originally designed an open courtyard with towering date and royal palms, lemon trees, and silver buttonwoods surrounded by a two-story stucco facade. There was no space for a pool, but Versace bought the adjacent Revere Hotel for $3.7 million and asked to demolish it and build his pool there.

The request for a permit to demolish a building on Ocean Drive set off alarms at the Preservation League. Hard-liners, led by Matti Bower, were determined to save every building in the district at all costs. Not only did the Revere maintain a harmonious scale along the street, but all of Ocean Drive should be sacrosanct. There was also an element of elitism: granting a demolition permit for a mansion when Miami Beach still lacked adequate affordable housing irked Bower and her supporters almost as much as the demolition request itself.

Architects Richard Hoberman and Bernard Zyscovich, who was the league chairman, led a faction that was willing to cede the Revere in ex-change for a tougher law to protect similar buildings in the future, akin to what happened after the demolition of the Senator five years earlier. Nancy Liebman had not been as active in the league since her election as a city commissioner, but she sided with the moderates who felt that the Revere was not worth the fight and so much political capital. "You can't fight on every one," she told me. "You have to pick your battles, and this was not worth it. I had to remind some of my former col-leagues that the goal of preservation was not to just keep every stone in place. The district is not a museum, it is a living and changing thing. It isn't just about saving buildings, it's about saving an environment and an atmosphere."

Like many buildings in the Art Deco District, the drab, boarded-up, three-story Revere was not a landmark. Built in 1950, it had replaced a wonderful 1922 home that was demolished before anyone thought of protecting such buildings. The league's 1978 survey covered buildings built before 1950, and that cutoff date was incorporated into the dis-trict's legislation. The city attorney determined the ordinance did not cover the hotel.

The fight over the Revere threatened to wrench the league apart. It was still struggling to define its role in a changing city some three years after Barbara Capitman's death. In a contentious all-night hearing, a majority of the league's board members won a bitter vote to file a law-suit to stop the demolition. Emotions were so raw that Bower and Lieb-man stopped talking to each other and Zyscovich resigned in protest.

Versace turned on his charm. In exchange for the league's withdraw-ing its suit, he offered to use his influence to help amend the ordinance to automatically cover structures built in 1950. After weeks of bitter de-bate, the board grudgingly agreed.

By the time the Revere preservationists mustered noisy opposition, the developers had carried the day. Of the 259 hotels, apartments, and commercial buildings on Ocean Drive, Collins Avenue, and Washing-ton Avenue included in the National Register listing, 10 percent had been demolished since the historic district was established. Another 11 percent had been altered beyond hope of restoring them to their original appearance.

On Thursday afternoon, September 9, 1993, a few preservationists gathered in front of the pale pink Revere as the wrecking ball swung across the lot. A disgruntled league board member told a reporter, "The demolition derby is on full blast, and it's being brought to you by the preservationists and the Miami Beach government."

Versace used all of his new space. When it was finished, the mansion ran to 20,000 square feet. In the mansion itself, only the shell of the Amsterdam remained in its original form. The arcaded addition housed a gym, guest suites, and a Moroccan bath overlooking a swimming pool paved with glass mosaic tiles in a Versace design. Contractors created four master suites, eight guest rooms, two staff apartments, and common areas that visitors alternately described as "splendorous" or "vulgar." Stained glass in jewel tones of ruby, turquoise, and topaz filled the windows. The consensus among architecture critics was that the redesign was inspired. The preservationists hated it. One offended league member said there was no suitable use for the building except as a Versace showroom.

MIAMI BEACH NIGHTLIFE, which had driven the Beach's revival in the mid-1980s, seemed stale a decade later. The Spot's heyday had passed. Michael Capponi was battling his heroin addiction. The Turchins had left the business. Tara Solomon was off writing a hit column for the *Herald*. South Beach's new Shore Club, billed as the largest gay club/resort in the United States, shut its doors after a month. The only temporary jolt came when Prince opened Glam Slam, replacing the gay club Paragon. And while the club did a brisk business, it hemorrhaged money.

Two Brooklyn boys arrived in South Beach in the summer of 1994. Any hip South Beach clubgoer wouldn't have given the New York guidos in their gym sweats and wife-beater T-shirts a second look. But within a few years, one of them would create the most popular club in Beach history and in the process push the town's brand into overdrive.

Short, chubby Michael Caruso, twenty-four years old, was known in the New York club world as "Lord Michael." He'd begun his career at Wave Street, a nasty Staten Island club. He was the trailblazer behind ecstasy-fueled rave parties at Manhattan's Limelight disco and dealt coke, ecstasy, and angel dust on the side. His supplier was the Port Richmond Crew, the Lucchese crime family's Staten Island franchise, and with their backing he moved up to ripping off club-kid dealers working at Limelight. Caruso's friend was twenty-three-year-old Christian Paciello. At six-foot-one and 220 pounds, with his baby face and Caesar haircut, Paciello looked like a young bodybuilder. He was an accomplished car thief, burglar, and fearless fighter who protected Lord Michael's drug trade. (Chris had changed his surname from Ludwigsen to his mother's maiden name because he wanted it to sound more like a wise guy. He resented his father's German heritage since it meant that he could never be a made member of the mob.)

Paciello's street name was "Binger," because of his tendency to binge on crimes. During a brawl in New York, Paciello had split open another man's head with an ax handle. No charges were filed as it was deemed self-defense. He had three assault arrests for street brawls and one for criminal mischief. Paciello freelanced for different mob families, and in 1992, he moved up to a $360,000 smash-and-grab on a Staten Island Chemical Bank and was linked to a gang that hijacked a New Jersey cargo truck carrying $2 million in marijuana. The following year he had been the driver for a botched home invasion of a wealthy Staten Island family, the Shemtovs, in which the wife was killed.

Fearing the husband might be able to finger them and that he would be charged for felony-murder, Paciello fled to Miami Beach. Caruso joined him; he heard that South Beach was a hot place to open a new club. Paciello knew nothing about running a club but he had saved $140,000 from his New York heists. (He later told the Florida State Liquor Authority that the money was a loan from a Staten Island gym owner, Robert Currie. Currie adamantly denied it.)

When they arrived, Paciello called on a friend from the old neighborhood, Carlo Vaccarezza, John Gotti's limo driver. Vaccarezza had moved from New York a year earlier after federal prosecutors investigated whether his Upper East Side restaurant, Da Noi—where Mickey Rourke and Gary James used to have dinners with Gambino crime captains—was a money-laundering front. In South Beach, Vaccarezza ran Mickey's Place, a bar at 1203 Washington that Rourke had just opened. (Federal prosecutors suspected that the Gambinos thanked Rourke for his public support of Gotti by giving him a share in Mickey's.)

"Carlo wanted Chris Paciello to buy his place," says Louis Canales. "He had had enough of South Beach, he wanted out." He told Paciello and Caruso that South Beach nightlife was easy to conquer for someone with street smarts. Vaccarezza pointed out another Brooklyn boy, Tommy Pooch, who had taken over promoting the Forge's famous Wednesday party night. With Pooch hustling hard and Shareef seemlessly replacing his father as the ultimate host, the Forge had staged a remarkable comeback. Pooch earned a reputation for throwing a great bash, providing party favors to V.I.P.s, and keeping his mouth shut.

"Wait until you meet Pooch," Vaccarezza told them. "You'll understand why if he can make it here, you two should have no problem." Paciello bought 90 percent of Mickey's share and Caruso bought the remaining 10 percent by selling his Harley and using money left over from his Limelight drug sales. The duo decided to call their new club "Risk." Mickey Rourke's sister-in-law became their accountant. While construction was under way, Jackie "The Nose" D'Amico, a Gambino crime captain, and his soldier, Johnny Rizzo, visited Paciello to check on the club's progress.

Paciello and Caruso wanted to hire Gilbert Stafford III, South Beach's most renowned club doorman. Stafford, a tall, rail-thin black man with close-cropped white hair and long elegant fingers, had run the door at Tattoo and then Area in New York. Andy Warhol had once called Stafford the "grande dame of the velvet rope."

Stafford had arrived in South Beach only a year before Paciello. A friend had brought him a copy of the premier issue of *Ocean Drive*. "I flipped through it and everybody looked liked such assholes and dweebs that I thought to myself, 'I could be a king there.' "

Lord Michael visited Stafford at The Spot. "We've heard you're the best doorman on the Beach. We're opening a new club and would like to hire you."

Stafford liked both Caruso and Paciello instantly but it did not take him long to realize that Paciello called the shots. And while Paciello was "the kindest employer I'd ever worked for," he also had "a hair-trigger temper that could turn explosively violent."

When another club, Groove Jet, scheduled its opening for the same night as Risk's, Paciello could not tolerate it. After a call to Code Enforcement did not slow down Groove Jet's preparations, the two partners tried torching their rival. But the Miami Beach Fire Department put out the flames in minutes.

On opening night, Risk looked more like a Brooklyn disco than a typical South Beach club. Several dozen mobsters or wannabes flew in from New York, including Tommy Reynolds, who had killed the woman during the attack on the Shemtov family. Dominic Dionisio was there, and Enrico Locasio, who federal prosecutors believed worked for Colombo captain William "Wild Bill" Cutolo, and who was Paciello's principal connection to the New York crime family.

"That first night was very mobster chic," recalls Stafford. "Only later did I find out they really were gangsters."

The club was all smoke machines, zebra-print rugs, and lots of neon. One difference from other clubs was that Risk had a shower in the rear—a telltale sign that it was an ecstasy club. A side effect of the drug is a dangerous rise in body temperature; no club wants to call 911 if that happens. A cold shower lowers the temp. Another curtained-off side room in Risk called "the opium room" became the hangout for skinny models who took the moniker "heroin chic" literally.

Paciello and Caruso hosted special nights. Lord Michael brought down hip-hop DJs from New York and with a successful local promoter, John Hood, introduced Fat Black Pussycat, which attracted a large black dance audience every Monday. They also hired Jody McDonald, a gay promoter best known for his anything-goes Sunday tea dances called "Risk Your Anus," held every weekend.

Shareef Malnik and Gary James took an immediate liking to Paciello and worked to soften his guido caricature. Louis Canales advised him, "Always wear black. You melt into the background in a club and you do not compete with your guests for attention. Do not wear jewelry beyond a watch." No more "dese" and "dose"; no more guzzling champagne from the bottle. The cutoff jeans and the wife-beater T-shirts were replaced with a smart collection of clothes. He lost his Caesar haircut.

Malnik and James did not know about Paciello's criminal record. They never saw the Paciello who, on December 9, stole a neighbor's four-door BMW because he had totaled his own a few weeks earlier. On December 23, he drove the stolen car into his condominium garage. When the doorman recognized it, he called detectives. Paciello was arrested later that night and the police impounded the car. The next night, he snuck into the tow lot, stole the BMW again, and torched it. The police found it as a smoldering wreck. The car's owner refused to press charges, but it landed Paciello on the local police radar.

Paciello financed a friend's purchase of $10,000 of ecstasy in return for a cut of the profits. But when he gave Vinnie Rizzuoto, Jr., who had been indicted for a gangland slaying and was on the FBI's most-wanted list, safe haven for two weeks, Caruso was so upset that he told Paciello he was going temporarily to New York. He got back his old job at Limelight. In late January 1995, word got back to Paciello that Caruso was talking freely about their Miami escapades. Paciello flew to New York, drove to Caruso's Staten Island apartment, and pistol-whipped his former partner. "You treacherous motherfucker," Paciello screamed at him, pressing the barrel of the pistol into his forehead. "You're lucky I don't kill you."

A neighbor who heard Caruso's screams called the police. Paciello was gone by the time they arrived. Caruso was hospitalized with broken bones. He refused to identify his attacker to the police, did not talk about Paciello to others, and never saw him again.

Paciello replaced Caruso with his parents, George and Marguerite, and his brothers, Keith and George Junior. But even with the family helping out, Paciello barely managed to stay ahead of the bills. He talked to Shareef and others about closing Risk and launching a much more upscale spot.

"No matter what we did, we never managed to get a fashionable crowd," says Stafford. "It just never clicked with anyone but the causeway crowd. As clubs went, Risk was eminently forgettable."

Six months after the opening of Risk, on April 21, 1995, someone spotted smoke coming from under the rear door. By the time the fire trucks arrived, the windowless club was gutted. Miami Beach fire investigator A. J. Anderson concluded the fire started on a cushion in the VIP lounge after the club had closed. He suspected arson but could not prove it, so he classified the blaze as "accidental." The twenty-four-year-old Paciello collected $250,000 from the insurance company and set out to start a new club: Liquid.

Paciello had selected his next partner: Ingrid Casares, a thirty-year-old Cuban American princess. She had a great Rolodex of celebrity friends and acquaintances, and when Paciello asked her if she would be the "face" for his new club, she said yes immediately. "I certainly had been to plenty of clubs, so I figured I already had a leg up on some people."

INGRID WAS BORN in 1964 in Miami. The Casares family was the prototypical Cuban American success story: they worked hard, moved from Miami's Little Havana to tony Coral Gables, became ardent Republicans, and sent their three daughters to the exclusive Our Lady of Lourdes Academy. The father, Raul, was a prominent anti-Castro activist and businessman whose company, RC Aluminum, installed doors, windows, shutters, and railings in luxury high-rises. Thanks to the cocaine-fed skyscraper boom and coding changes requiring hurricane-resistant glass, Raul became one of South Florida's wealthiest Cuban immigrants. Politicians relied not only on his contributions but on his ability to deliver blocs of Cuban votes. RC Aluminum nabbed multi-million-dollar deals from the city and developers and his business boomed.

Ingrid was fifteen when the Dadeland Mall shooting shook up the region. Ever rebellious, she got into cocaine, partied late, and didn't show up at her own ruffled dress *quince*, a rite of passage for fifteen-year-old Cuban girls. She was athletic, impish, and butch.

"I was the leader in a lot of ways," she told me, "and I hung out with all the popular kids and the best athletes and the prettiest cheerleaders. It was the whole Cuban, decadent, A-crowd list. But I always knew I was different. I was much more liberal than my friends. For me, that life I saw in high school was too restrictive. I knew it wasn't for me."

Her mother attended many of Ingrid's classes during her senior year to ensure her daughter graduated. And her father gave a generous donation to the school.

At her parents' insistence, Ingrid went to college, and finally earned a communications degree from the University of Maryland. In between traveling to Europe, she played at work: she was a booking agent for Wilhelmina Models and opened a tanning salon. In 1991, she settled back into Miami. By then, she was openly bisexual. She was also using several grams of coke daily.

In a town where few Cuban women, especially those from Casares's privileged background, were open about their sexuality, she became an "it" girl with celebrity lesbians. Singer K.D. Lang, comedian Sandra Bernhard, and *Interview* editor in chief Ingrid Sischy were friends. "A butch Audrey Hepburn," one complimented her.

June 6, 1991, was Bernhard's thirty-sixth birthday. At Warsaw, Louis Canales did a themed night in her honor called "WOW" (World of Women). "I brought in three hundred drop-dead lipstick girls [feminine gay women who pass for straight]. They went insane. Half the women were topless, but then, of course, the air-conditioning wasn't that great." Another night, Bernhard performed at the Kravis Center and after the show went for a late dinner with twelve friends. Madonna left with Ingrid, making Bernhard so furious that the three did not talk for years.

There was instant gossip that Madonna and Ingrid were more than platonic friends. A few months after the birthday party, Steven Meisel shot the photos for Madonna's infamous book, *Sex*, which included Ingrid cuddling with the naked pop star and French-kissing her. In one entry Madonna describes them lying naked on a sundeck, and concludes: "I'm going to have to go now because I think I have to finger fuck Ingrid or she's going to freak."

Sarah Pettit, the former editor of *Out*, thought that by becoming Madonna's companion, Ingrid was the object of much jealousy. But none of the gay controversy mattered in South Beach. Says Gary James, "That was for New York lesbians. In South Beach, all that mattered was that Ingrid had nabbed Madonna, and that gave her incredible power in a town where celebrities ruled."*

All Chris Paciello worried about was who Ingrid could bring to Liquid. To ensure that Ingrid had some motivation to make the club work,

---

* Madonna gave her first child, born in 1996, the same name as Ingrid's sister, Lourdes.

her father agreed to invest. It was a chance for Ingrid to carve out something on her own; even she realized that she "needed a substantial profession to prove I was more than just a drug-addled sycophant."

Ingrid and Paciello hit it off instantly. Ingrid introduced Paciello to Demi Moore, Donatella Versace, Jack Nicholson, and Russell Simmons. Once Chris had Ingrid's stamp of approval, he was on Jason Binn's radar and met even more of the A-crowd. Ian Schrager opened the Delano Hotel at 17th and Collins in June 1995. Paciello and Ingrid joined Madonna, Shareef, and Craig Robins at the exclusive pre-opening party. The 1947 Delano was once a family-friendly hotel where Schrager had stayed as a boy. Working with Philippe Starck, he spent $30 million on renovations. Disliking the pastel Deco colors, Starck hung 30-foot translucent white curtains at the entrance and painted the rooms white.

Schrager decreed that only guests or those with restaurant reservations could enter. Applying a club's exclusionary door policy to a hotel had the intended effect of keeping out the causeway crowd and made the demand to get in even greater.

Paciello was infatuated with his new acquaintances. He bought a Range Rover. Shareef Malnik had one. Craig Robins assembled one of the town's best art collections, so Paciello studied modern art. He learned to play polo. Versace became his favorite designer, and a black suit his uniform. Shareef took him to Miami's premier philanthropic event, the "Make-A-Wish Foundation Ball." It was the first time he had worn a tuxedo.

Chris Paciello wanted a sober partner for Liquid's opening, so in September he and Madonna insisted that Ingrid check into rehab. Initially resistant, she finally agreed.

Liquid opened on Thanksgiving weekend 1995, just seven months after Risk burned down. Ten thousand invitations went out. Spotlights lit up the sky. Madonna was accompanied by her brother, Christopher Ciccione, who had done the deluxe design. There were the regular South Beach celebs—Naomi Campbell, Barry Diller, Kate Moss. Some of Chris's friends from New York showed up, as well as Alphonse Persico, acting boss of the Colombo family, and Christopher Wolf, Jack Basile, and Christopher Mormando, indicted for a mob stock fraud scheme; also Paciello's old muscle partners, Dionisio and Locasio.

"The South Beach equivalent of Truman Capote's Black-and-White Ball," noted Tom Austin in *New Times*. "It's the Studio 54 of the '90s," Liza Minnelli told *Entertainment Tonight*.

A twenty-four-year-old Staten Island wannabe gangster was unwittingly discovering what Al Malnik had found out twenty-five years earlier with the Forge—the hint of danger, the possible mob connection, had a seductive draw in Miami Beach. But Paciello also was good-looking, dating top model Niki Taylor, and rumored to be one of Madonna's lovers.

Two weeks after the opening, Paciello was pulled over for driving under the influence. He gave the cops a false Social Security number and name, but they knew who he was. A month later, he was arrested for assault. The following year, he confronted a group of tourists he thought had been rude to the club's doorman and pummeled one of them. When a former Mr. Universe, Mike Quinn, called basketball player Michael Christian "a nigger," Paciello beat him senseless. The ER attendant sent Paciello a picture of the disfigured bodybuilder and he hung it in his office. Another time he found a manager rummaging in his office and beat him unconscious. The police arrested him for battery, but the charges were dropped after Paciello rehired the man at double the salary. "I witnessed that beating in the alley," recalls Gilbert Stafford. "It was vicious." Stafford had had enough. He knew that Paciello's brother George had a bank robbery conviction and carried a gun. Even though Chris had thrown a benefit to raise $20,000 for his AIDS treatment, Stafford quit.

One night in the VIP room of Bar None, Paciello spied Matt Martinez; the former football player was then dating Univision television star Sofia Vergara, who was also seeing Paciello. Martinez told her Paciello was cheating on her. He and Paciello exchanged words, then Paciello punched Martinez in the face, splitting his nose and knocking out two teeth. The club's bouncers broke up the fight and kicked Martinez out for "starting it."

"Isn't that fucking great?" says Michael Capponi. "In South Beach, if you're the king of nightlife, you're king of the city. He was untouchable."

CHAPTER 27

Playing the Race Card

MIAMI BEACH CITY officials paid little attention to the tabloid headlines. In 1995, they were fulfilling the terms of a settlement with civil rights activists to end a boycott of the Beach by black tourists and businesses. The boycott had begun in 1990 when county and city officials, under pressure from conservative anti-Castro leaders, rescinded a routine proclamation welcoming Nelson Mandela after the South African had praised Castro, Yasser Arafat, and Muammar Gadhafi for their longtime support. The mayor of Miami and others who were initially boycotted apologized, but Alex Daoud made it worse. He cited $29,000 in unpaid bills at the Convention Center at which Mandela had spoken, and claimed that he and other commissioners had been told not to attend the talk. "Don't come and ask me for any apology because I'm not apologizing," he told a reporter. "An apology is owed to the city of Miami Beach."

Other than city officials, a few hotel owners, and tourism promoters, no one on the Beach was even aware a boycott was in place. It was just as difficult to get a hotel or restaurant reservation, or to find a parking spot, but the chamber of commerce estimated the boycott cost the community $55 million annually in lost revenues.

As part of its settlement, Miami Beach created Miami Partners For Progress, and agreed to spend up to $10 million to help a black developer create a convention-style hotel in the heart of the Art Deco District. Using its eminent domain powers, it purchased the run-down seven-story rooming house Royal Palm on Collins Avenue for $5.5 million. Then it established a process for the submission of competitive bids and design packages.

In July 1994, the city commission had accepted a proposal from four local black entrepreneurs: Peter Calin, an American Express vice president; Argus Construction owner Eugene Ford; Texaco tax attorney Jerry Bailey; and real estate investor Marvin Holloway. The four men, operating as HCF, were asked to team with Sheraton Hotels to build a 256-room hotel on the site. Eight months later, Sheraton backed out of the deal. HCF presented the city a new package in July 1995: by December 20, the city commission terminated HCF's development rights when it was unable to secure any financing.

The timing could not have been better for another newcomer, who would leave his own strong imprint on the Beach. R. Donahue Peebles was the founder of the nation's largest African American–owned real estate development company, the $4 billion Peebles Corporation, based in Washington. Peebles arrived for the Christmas and New Year's holidays with his wife, Katrina, and one-year-old son. In a few days they rented a three-bedroom condo with an ocean view at the new La Tour in mid-Beach. On December 31, Peebles read, in an article in the *Miami Herald,* that the Shorecrest, a decaying residential hotel on a prime stretch of the Art Deco District on Collins between 15th and 16th Streets, was for sale. Next to the Shorecrest was the Royal Palm. The article mentioned that the city was looking for a new black developer to take it over, now that HCF had lost its rights to the project.

It was the first time Peebles had ever heard of a project reserved for a specific race. "So I said to myself, 'How many African American developers are in this country? Not many. How many have the capacity to do a project of this size? Even fewer. And how many are reading the *Miami Herald* right now? Maybe just me.'"

A real estate project in Miami Beach would be just the antidote for Peebles, who had come to the Beach "to get a breather" from the controversy surrounding him and Mayor Marion Barry back in Washington, D.C.

A decade earlier, Barry had appointed the twenty-four-year-old Peebles to the Board of Equalization and Review, making Peebles the youngest ever chairman of a tax review board that *The Washington Post* dubbed "one of the more obscure but powerful roles in the D.C. government."

Peebles resigned after three years and started his own tax assessment appeals business, representing property owners before his old board. In his first year, he saved a dozen clients more than $56 million in tax assessments. With those earnings, he launched his first major D.C. real estate project, a $9 million office building on Martin Luther King Avenue in the heart of the blighted Anacostia neighborhood. When Barry announced that the city would lease most of the building's 75,000 square feet at above-market rates, it drew criticism from Raymond Lambert, who directed the city agency that awarded leases. But the controversy was buried when the FBI arrested Marion Barry on January 18, 1990, for smoking crack with one of his girlfriends in a downtown hotel. Later evidence revealed that the mayor had taken girls to Peebles's flat. Peebles, who says he didn't know about Barry's crack use, was "shocked by the mayor's recklessness." He was convicted, released in 1992, and elected mayor again in 1994.

In August 1995, Peebles's close relationship with Barry burned him. The D.C. city council rejected Barry's no-bid $48 million plan to lease two office buildings from Peebles. *The Washington Post* said that the deal "has the makings of a boondoggle, perhaps worse. . . . Just like old times, the special interests are back."

But no one in Miami Beach knew of Peebles's Washington problems and few likely would have cared. The smooth-talking, light-skinned Peebles, with his wide smile and beautiful blond wife, was tailor-made for the Beach. Peebles boasted he was one of the biggest black real estate developers in Washington, and that he and his wife had interests in historic restoration and politics.

By the time Peebles had arrived in December 1995, seven new minority-led bidders had emerged for the Royal Palm. Quickly analyzing the competition, Peebles thought the team to beat was Hyatt, whose partner was a prominent black entrepreneur, Eugene Jackson, founder of Atlanta's Christian-based Unity Broadcasting Network.

Peebles followed the steps he learned in D.C.—find out who the key politicians and businesspeople are and how the local system greases itself. Arthur Courshon, the lawyer and banker who headed the city's selection committee, was a member of a loosely aligned group of old-line power brokers that included Steve Muss, Jerry Robins, and Norman Braman, as well as the chiefs of Carnival Cruise Lines, Knight Ridder, and Burdines department stores. "You can't deal with the city on a project worth millions of dollars unless you have a very good understanding of who matters and who doesn't," Peebles told me, "otherwise you just waste your time. It was not hard to figure out that I had stepped into a town where the Anglo-Jewish community was trying to hold on to its power and the Cuban community was trying to take it away. If you were black, you had no relevance.

"I just knew that I was a very different developer than other Miami developers. I was the ultimate outsider when I arrived. I didn't socialize with any of these guys and I was not a member of their club. I was playing on their home field, and the refs were all lined against me."

He knew that he would not only have to arrange the right network to support any bid; he also wanted "an ace in the hole," to use as a hammer if negotiations turned hard, as he expected. His ace in the hole was the Shorecrest Hotel.

Peebles knew that in order to build any large project, it was essential first to collect the land. In Washington, where there were few empty lots, developers were accustomed to buying four or five contiguous parcels. On January 2, 1996, Peebles, and his Miami Beach–based real estate broker Kevin Tomlinson, visited the Shorecrest and Royal Palm. Both parcels were so slender that it was almost impossible to build an impressive hotel unless you owned both. "That day I knew I needed the Shorecrest," Pebbles says.

"It wasn't a slam-dunk," says Tomlinson. "The block was really rundown and it was like a welfare hotel. There were chickens running through the lobby. Don saw it as an indispensable part of what the city would eventually need, but no other developer had the vision because the hotel had been for sale forever."

The Shorecrest land was owned by absentee developers, the Cardona family, in New Jersey, and the hotel was owned by the leaseholder, Cyrus Mehre. Because the city had spent $5.5 million to buy the Royal Palm, it had $4.5 million left of the money it had set aside to settle the black boycott. That was not enough to buy the Shorecrest. The Cardonas and Mehre felt that since their lot was the same size as that of the Royal Palm, they should get the same price. Peebles learned that his

Hyatt competition had lowballed the Shorecrest owners. When Mehre complained, city officials said they might just condemn the property and pay fair market value. "That gave me my window of opportunity," Peebles told me.

Peebles convinced Mehre that if he gave Peebles an exclusive option, Peebles would win the city bid. He offered Mehre $4 million and the Cardonas $1.1 million. They accepted. He put down a $250,000 deposit with Mehre, and $100,000 with the Cardonas; but both were fully refundable if he failed to win the project.

Peebles and his wife, Katrina, had only until April 1 to put together a Request for Proposal (RFP) bid. Peebles chose Arquitectonica, Miami's award-winning architecture firm. One of his biggest concerns was Courshon. A year before Peebles arrived, Curshon had been instrumental in the deal the city made using $70 million in incentives—including tax breaks and low-interest loans—to seduce the Loews Corporation to build a new Deco-style 830-room hotel at 16th and Collins, just north of the Royal Palm. The $165 million Loews was the first major hotel built on the Beach in thirty years and second only in size to the Fontainebleau. Peebles cited the deal as a benchmark for what he wanted with the Royal Palm.

"The city gave Loews more than $70 million, which worked out to $75,000 per room," he told me. "Meanwhile, they were offering only $25,000 a room for the Royal Palm. I was no longer in Washington. Now I was in a town where people hoped I would just quietly accept that it was okay for them to do business oppressing the African American community while white developers got more. It's that kind of thinking that explains why there was a black boycott in the first place."

Peebles thought the Hyatt team was formidable. The minority partner, Eugene Jackson, had arranged all the financing. Craig Robins had joined as his renovation partner.

Peebles met with the publisher and top editors at the *Miami Herald*, as well as the chairman of the Miami-Dade County Commission, and the heads of the Kiwanis Club and the Miami Design Preservation League. He had lunch or dinner with each city commissioner, the mayor, and the city manager, and aggressively pursued local banks, like Ocean and Capital, which were financing Beach projects. (Ocean had financed La Tour, where he lived.) "To hedge my bets, I even met with the Hyatt team." He knew that if they won, they would have to deal with him sooner or later over the Shorecrest. He met with Craig Robins. It did not go well. Peebles is always sharply dressed in a business suit and wingtips and was put off by Robins's casual attire. Robins further irritated Peebles when he reminded him he was a newcomer and suggested he become a minority owner on the Hyatt team.

About a week later, Don and Katrina were at the Forge, where Craig was having dinner with Nick Pritzker, head of the Hyatt chain. Peebles walked over and told them that he thought they should work together. He reminded them he owned the Shorecrest, and that since his own forte was not hotel management, he would welcome Hyatt's expertise.

"I think Pritzker wanted to do it," says Peebles, "but Robins talked him out of it. I believe this was mainly out of competitiveness; he was letting his emotions cloud his judgment. I could see that Robins was going to be a problem, especially because he had political relationships on the Beach. However, after speaking with them both that night, I was confident that neither of them had what it took to beat me, not even teamed together."

Craig says he was not blocking the deal from competitiveness or jealousy. He originally thought a Jackson-Peebles joint effort would be best for the city. "But we had done a background check on him," Craig told me, "and his reputation was so negative based on his relationships and dealings in Washington that no one on the Jackson team wanted to associate with him."

Having tried the conciliatory approach, Peebles decided to "play tough." He hired Michael Milberg, the Miami Beach Budget Advisory Committee chair and the Royal Palm's former general manager, as a lobbyist. A campaign manager and good friend of Neisen Kasdin, Milberg knew where all the political bodies were buried.

Milberg told Peebles that Craig and Scott Robins had not been getting along. Peebles went after Scott, who he thought was Craig's complete opposite: "more businesslike, more professional, not at all arrogant, very level-headed. He was also a broader thinker and not so self-absorbed. And Scott also had something to prove—that he was a smart guy in business."

Scott Robins joined the Peebles team, as did Clarence Avant, then chairman of Motown. Peebles promised Avant a Motown Café in the finished hotel.

On Monday, April 1, a few weeks after his thirty-sixth birthday, Peebles personally delivered the 18-inch-thick RFP to City Hall. There were seven final bidders, each made up of a black partner, a hotel brand to manage the property, and other partners such as contractors, investors, and bankers. The finalists included Hyatt, Ritz-Carlton, Doubletree, Wyndham, Clarion Hotels, Marriott, and Peebles's Crowne Plaza. Only Peebles and Hyatt had their financing lined up. Five of the bids included a plan to develop both the Royal Palm and the Shorecrest; even though Peebles held the exclusive option to buy it, the other bidders were asking the city to use eminent domain to get the property.

The same day, the six-year-old Barry stories landed on the desks of local reporters and the city commissioners. A widespread rumor in the Jewish community was that Peebles was friends with Louis Farrakhan, then planning the Million Man March on Washington. They were unfounded, but Peebles knew that such stories could hurt him in a town with a large Jewish voting bloc, and in which all seven city commissioners were Jews.

In early May, the five-person review panel interviewed each bidder. The panel was chaired by Courshon, and consisted of Jonathan Mariner, CFO for the Florida Marlins; Maurice Weiner, owner of the Grove Isle Hotel; Vince Scully, the architect and Yale professor; and Ed Marquez, the county's chief financial officer. They cut the seven bids to three finalists: Hyatt, Wyndham, and the Crowne Plaza. By a 3 to 2 vote, the panel recommended the Jackson/Hyatt plan, citing its design as the decisive factor.

Peebles was stunned. On his way out, Randy Hilliard, Miami Beach Transportation and Parking chairman and a political campaign strategist hired by Wyndham, grabbed him. "Don't worry. Hyatt doesn't have this. They still have to go before the city commission." The commission vote was set for June 5.

Hilliard, who was so proud of his scorched-earth tactics that he listed himself in the Key West white pages as "Prince of Darkness," hit pay dirt a couple of weeks later when he uncovered that Eugene Jackson had hundreds of liens on a dilapidated Miami housing project and that the IRS was chasing him for $3.9 million in back taxes. Meanwhile, Peebles lobbied the Miami Design Preservation League, reminding them of his project's preservation of the Royal Palm and Shorecrest facades. The league endorsed his Arquitectonica design.

In late May, the three finalists made their presentations to the city commission. Peebles finished his by unveiling a scale model of his proposed hotel. In the background, Diana Ross's "Ain't No Mountain High Enough" played.

Mayor Seymour Gelber was not impressed. He asked Peebles if he was willing to give the city the Shorecrest Hotel. Peebles was taken aback.

"Pardon me, Mr. Mayor?"

"If you are not selected, will you give us the Shorecrest Property?"

Peebles said no.

The reserved, retired judge who had replaced Daoud seldom lost his cool, but now Gelber's voice rose.

"I remember he was yelling," says Peebles. "I was very calm and kept my tone low, and the calmer I was, the angrier the mayor got."

Peebles said that if his team was not selected, then he would build a hotel of his own on the Shorecrest site. "Then you will have two black hotels in South Beach."*

Gelber stormed out. Vice Mayor Kasdin apologized.

On June 5, the city commission held its public hearing on the Royal Palm venture. The chambers were packed with spectators and reporters.

"I knew I was going to win," says Peebles, who had carefully calculated which commissioners were with him. He had worked hard to lock four votes, just enough to prevail. Before the meeting started, Courshon told Peebles that he had blundered by buying the Shorecrest. "You shouldn't have done that," he said. "People thought you were arrogant. That was your mistake."

Eugene Jackson arrived in a purple suit. The conservative Peebles

---

* There was already a black-owned hotel in South Beach, the forty-two-room Chelsea at Ninth and Washington. Vernon Garraway had bought it in 1989. But the project at the heart of settling the black boycott was for a giant-sized convention-style hotel. Peebles did not even know about Garraway until later.

told his wife, "I am not going to be beaten by a guy in a purple suit. I don't care if this is South Beach or not."

After half an hour of public comments, Courshon explained that instead of the traditional procedure, where a majority vote prevailed, each commissioner had to rank the applicants first, second, or third. The lowest total would win. If the winning team failed to put together its financing and design package, the second-ranked bidder would be chosen. The final tally was Peebles's Crowne Plaza 13; Jackson's Hyatt 14; and Warren's Wyndham 15.

Peebles's win would turn into a decade-long bare-knuckles fight with his former business partners, city bureaucrats, and politicians. The hotel, scheduled to open in two years, actually took six, mired in recriminations over the property's condition and the ever-changing financing. Peebles would blame everyone but himself for the delay and the cost overruns.

He also used his political savvy in the upcoming battles to help elect and unseat commissioners in increasingly vicious campaigns. And business litigation became Peebles's trademark, although he says he was not in court any more than any other South Florida developer, and that the "litigious" label stuck to him only because "the rules are different for me."

Craig Robins told me, "Peebles turned out to be better at manipulating the politics than his competitor and delivered a marginal product to the city. His work illustrates how to exploit a public-private partnership, offering smoke and mirrors with little substance. His legacy in Miami is not particularly meaningful."

"I know I have no friends here," counters Peebles. "What I am is a hard-nosed businessman, and I don't take any bullshit from people just to get along. I fight for what I want. Miami is just not comfortable with blacks. I don't acquiesce. I am married to a white wife, I make a lot of money, and my problem is that I don't know my place."

CHAPTER 28

"An Infamous Personality"

T HE ROYAL PALM was an exception to the traditional "Miami Beach real estate developer pitched against residents" saga that played out with escalating frequency in the 1990s. But by the mid-nineties South Pointe had become the new focus for knock-down, drag-out battles between real estate developers wanting to build as much as possible on their parcels and residents who were increasingly organized and vocal in battling to keep some sense of proportion to their low-rise waterfront neighborhood.

South Pointe's Thomas Kramer had briefly seemed a serious developer a few years earlier when he had spent $300,000 sponsoring a weeklong charrette (a collaborative design session) at Joe's Stone Crab. Kramer issued an invitation to the designer elite to find a unique use for the 35 acres of South Pointe he had accumulated. Several hundred people attended, including eminent architects and design teams from as far away as Japan.

One of Kramer's problems was that he had little patience and no attention span. "Next Mood Change in 5 Minutes" announced the sign over his office entrance. He dissed Tony Goldman and other developers for having been "afraid of the risks in South Pointe." Whatever goodwill he earned for hosting an urban planning conference he destroyed by embarking on quixotic quests that reinforced his image as unpredictable and outrageous. He abandoned his early vision to turn South Pointe into a $233 million replica of Portofino, and announced that instead he'd build the world's only gay hotel. He told *Interview*, "My first plan is for a two- or three-hundred-room, totally gay hotel, designed by gays, run by gays, managed by gays. I tell you, it would be the nicest place in the United States. I'm 100 percent sure." By 1994, he had abandoned that idea and announced a partnership with Las Vegas's Steve Wynn to build a 2,000-room hotel with casino gambling. He contributed $1.5 million and Wynn pitched in $1.2 million for a state proposition that would have legalized eleven mega hotel-casinos in Florida, one of them designated specifically for South Pointe. Kramer's vision for a tropical Monaco was rejected by the voters.

Another time, he fired his chief contractor and sixty other people, hired a new team, then promptly left Miami. "I get treated like shit by everybody," he told a reporter on his way to the airport. When he returned, he said he had been skiing at St. Moritz. He proposed half a dozen residential skyscrapers encircling South Pointe, at a cost of half a billion dollars. He assured nervous residents that he would not build "ugly, ugly, any-city buildings."

Kramer hired and fired more than two hundred people over a couple of years. He'd praise a new hire as the person he'd always been looking for, and in a couple of months, when he was bored, that person would be out his revolving door.

Craig Robins questioned whether Kramer had the credentials to raise the enormous sums needed for his projects. "He had the land," says Craig, "but banks and investors did not give you several hundred million just because you have a nice set of architect's plans. You have to have credibility as an experienced and trusted developer and that reputation isn't built overnight. You don't earn it just because you have a lot of cash to buy a lot of property."

Kramer seemed to do his best to sabotage what credibility he managed to gain. Miami Beach cops broke up a fistfight at Les Bains between him and another customer who accused him of hurling anti-Semitic insults. Another time, police were called after he threw a glass of champagne in a panhandler's face. At Cassis Bistro, Kramer paid a girl to dance naked on his table while he and friends sprayed her with champagne. Restaurants were reluctant to bar Kramer because he spent thousands a night. He boasted of his orgies and that his bedroom included whips, chains, and a mirrored ceiling, and he proudly showed newspaper clips from London tabloids about how he was ostracized by the German Embassy after making an audacious pass at Princess Di.

Then there was the report in a German magazine that he had raped his wife—Kramer said that he and his wife were both "very amazed" by that charge. In 1992, a model told local police she fought Kramer off after he tried to pin her against a wall. No charges were filed. The following year, an employee, Marjorie Pulice, sued him for sexual harassment (the case was settled out of court). In 1995, the pregnant wife of a long-time friend complained to Swiss police that Kramer raped her in a Zurich nightclub restroom. He was arrested, freed on bail, and acquitted. Later that year, a twenty-two-year-old nanny told Miami Beach police that Kramer had assaulted her at his mansion. But within a week she dropped the charges and flew home to Scotland. Privately, prosecutors thought Kramer had paid her to leave the country. Kramer's wife, Catherine, who had eloped against her father's adamant opposition, divorced him in 1995 and got custody of their three-year-old daughter, Joya. (Kramer would go on to a 1998 arrest and acquittal for sexual battery in Miami Beach. The following year, London police arrested him for his second rape charge, a complaint filed by one of his secretaries, the wife of a former CEO. Kramer's defense was consensual sex. The charges were dismissed when the victim refused to testify. In 2007, he was sued by a Miami Beach woman who charged he fondled her at a restaurant. It was settled. And he was arrested in New York for "endangering the welfare of a child, abusive sexual contact and forcible touching of a minor" of a fourteen-year-old boy in the bathroom of the Rainbow Room. Kramer told me he had grabbed the boy—who was at a bar mitzvah— by the genitals because the kid and his friends had been horsing around and bumped into Kramer who was standing at the next urinal. "If you don't stop this, I will rip this off," Kramer told him as he grabbed the kid's crotch. "And then the little motherfucker ran off to his mommy to say I molested him.")

"Kramer was like watching a train wreck in slow motion," says Neisen Kasdin. "He had launched his investment presence with such high expectations. And then his private life pretty much unraveled and instead of a visionary, he chose to become an infamous personality."

By the time Peebles was causing consternation at City Hall, many politicians had concluded that Kramer was a vain, self-obsessed man with little interest beyond talking about his own grandiose visions. But they had no choice but to deal with him because of the sheer size of his South Pointe holdings.

"I was the only one who had the vision to buy this property that no one else wanted," Kramer told me. "There were no real visionaries here, no one with the balls to do what I did. But I didn't mind the risks, because I knew without taking them there could be no great payoff."

Questions continued to be raised about the source of the $145 million he used to scoop up such prime property. His most consistent answer was a variation on brilliant commodity and currency trading in which he bragged he could make $500,000 before breakfast. "Once I was skiing in Gstaad," he told *Forbes*. "I was on the top of the mountain, and suddenly I knew I must short gold, so I grabbed a phone and called my broker, and shorted $25 million worth of gold. I made between $5 and $6 million. Another time I had a dream about a burning field. I knew I should buy wheat and corn futures. That time I made millions more. That is how it is with me."

In a town accustomed to not asking questions about large amounts of cash, Kramer skated along with far less inquiry than might have greeted him elsewhere. And if everyone enjoyed gossiping about his money, many also had their hand out, from architects to bodyguards to nightclub owners to politicians, who lined up for contributions.

Kramer's next South Pointe proposal was for two sixty-story residential towers, each sporting one of his initials, and in 1995 he scared preservationists when he announced he was bringing in Donald Trump as a partner. Trump told the *Miami Herald* that Kramer was "very much misunderstood. His heart is in the right place." Moreover, Trump said, "If I'm going to do a building, it's going to be so dynamite, it's going to blow out the world." Trump wanted a 1,200-unit, 100-story tower, called Trump Tower Miami. But the two large egos parted ways as quickly as they had come together.

Without Trump, Kramer launched his first major construction project: a forty-four story, multi-tiered orange and blue condo called Portofino Tower, adjacent to South Pointe Tower. His partner was developer

Tom Daly, who had testified against Alex Daoud and who had just completed Mystic Pointe, six residential towers in Aventura, farther north. Behind the scenes there were rumblings. Kramer had begun taking mortgages on some of his properties and had fallen behind on payments to vendors. And Daly had had a nasty breakup with his Mystic Pointe partner, ran into problems on a high-end development called Ocean One in Sunny Isles, and also overspent on a series of expensive single-family homes.

"Kramer had put up $20 million," Daly told me, "but it was running over budget because he wanted to make everything 'grand and elegant' and kept changing his mind about what that meant. We got to the fourth floor before we ran out of money. Kramer and I couldn't get financing." Daly declared bankruptcy and suggested they bring in a new partner to finish Portofino Tower. He recommended Jorge Perez.

Perez was the largest builder of affordable housing projects in Florida. Raised in Argentina and Colombia by Cuban exile parents, he followed his Colombian girlfriend to America. When they broke up, he trekked through Europe. "I fell in love with cities, with the architecture of Paris and London. It set a fire in me," he says now. He spent a semester at Berkeley, where he joined the radical Students for a Democratic Society, and finally got a master's degree in urban planning at the University of Michigan.

He married his classmate, Debbie, on graduation day. The Perezes moved to Florida and the graduate school dean helped Jorge land a job in Miami's Planning Department.

Three years later, while he was scouting development sites for his first project, he met New York developer Steve Ross. Late that year they founded the Related Group of Florida, an offshoot of Ross's Related Group of New York. Within five years the firm had completed more than 100 residential complexes with 25,000 apartments. Perez counted some of the state's most powerful politicians as friends, especially in Cuban-run Miami. "Let me tell you about political power," he says. "It's not just about making donations or getting along with someone. When I have 25,000 housing units, I can control which candidates get easy access to those buildings for campaigns and which ones won't. When it's time to collect absentee ballots, things can be made easy or not. Having that much affordable housing gave me a political clout that I otherwise would not have had."

During the Clinton administration, Perez gave generously to Democratic candidates and causes. He turned down the ambassadorship to Colombia. One night he stayed over at the White House and he and the president discussed American Cuban relations into the early morning hours.

When Daly recommended to Kramer that they form a partnership with the state's affordable housing king, the German was horrified. Says Daly, "He was afraid that it would scare away the high-end European buyers he was pursuing, but I convinced him that we needed the financing right away and Perez was probably the only developer whose credentials were impeccable."

"I knew this project would be a home run," says Perez. Spurred in part by the substantial reduction in government subsidies for affordable rental housing, Perez moved into luxury development just as the market for high-end real estate was in the earliest stages of what would become the greatest Florida land boom since the 1920s.

Kramer accepted Daly's advice. The two had gotten to be good friends during their short partnership. "We did a lot of party and pussy," says Kramer.

Perez drove a hard bargain. He would become the managing partner for Portofino Tower, oversee the construction and the budget, and market the apartments, in return for which he would secure up to $50 million in financing. If Perez stayed within a tight budget, he had an option to buy the entire project for $10 million, half of what Kramer had already spent between the land and partial construction.

A few months after Perez came on board, the city commission considered the complex deal with Kramer that would give him further development rights in exchange for money and some of his land around the city's marina. The city faced still pending litigation from the marina's tenant, and the original RDA master developer had charged that the city had reneged on permits and stalled on other promises to help bayfront development. The courts had ordered the city to spend up to $20 million to provide parking, build a new sea wall, and make other significant improvements. Kramer owned a 6.6-acre parcel adjacent to the marina. If the city could get that property, it could use some of it for surface parking and the rest to strike a settlement with the plaintiffs.

Kramer used that bargaining chip to press ahead with plans for six imposing condo towers. Residents, consulting architects, and the Planning Board voiced strong objections, pleading with the city commissioners to prevent Kramer from walling off the peninsula from its horizons to the ocean and Biscayne Bay.

On July 26, 1996, the commissioners heard five hours of raucous debate about the character of the mini-city Kramer planned. Kramer's representatives said the final designs would depend on the real estate market. Joe Fleming, a lawyer for some South Pointe residents, wondered whether allowing the marketplace to determine what to build was a good idea: "As Mencken once said, 'You can never underestimate the bad taste of the American public.'" Ed Resnick, the city's lead negotiator, gave the residents only weak assurance: "The design guidelines are not wonderful. They certainly aren't perfect, but the structures will not be overwhelming."

On October 5, city commissioners voted 6 to 1 to approve the Portofino Settlement. Only Vice Mayor Martin Shapiro voted against it. In addition to six skyscrapers with thousands of new apartments, Kramer could build shops, restaurants, and town houses. The guidelines did almost nothing to control the design of the towers; in a small last-minute compromise the first twelve floors of a building could not exceed 45,000 square feet. "That did not worry me at all," recalls Perez. "Consider that on South Pointe Tower, which was then the neighborhood's tallest high-rise, the first twelve floors were a third less than the city's new rules. So I knew we could still build large." The size of all of Kramer's buildings could not exceed 2.7 million square feet, slightly less than the Empire State Building. It didn't matter whether he used that in a single 100-story building, or half a dozen mid-sized towers.

Beyond the coveted development rights, the city paid Kramer $11.3 million and gave Kramer two city-owned empty parcels. It shelved objections to an office building he had built at Fifth and Washington—*Ocean Drive*'s headquarters—that was 10,000 square feet larger than the city code allowed. The final blow to residents was the city's rezoning of Kramer's so-called Alaska Parcel, a prime 3.44-acre waterfront parcel west of South Pointe Tower.* It was changed from "marine recreational" use—which permitted the construction of a maximum of 125,000 square feet of commercial space no higher than four stories—to "commercial-intensive mixed-use with unlimited height restrictions." Soon after the settlement was announced, Kramer unveiled plans for two forty-floor towers for the Alaska Parcel.

In return, Kramer gave the city his 6.6-acre bayfront tract and commited to building a public access baywalk and plazas on the east and west sides of his planned development. He also promised to set aside $5 million for neighborhood improvements. South Pointe residents, who had long felt they were second-class citizens compared to the Art Deco District, believed the deal was a sellout that would never have happened if the neighborhood had been anywhere else on the Beach.

Said Mayor Gelber, "We got [Kramer] to make some small concessions . . . it's all we could get." With his phalanx of lawyers and architects, Kramer had outmaneuvered them.

---

*When Government Cut, the man-made shipping channel between Miami Beach and Fisher Island, was created in 1905, the U.S. government had surplus land. Indian tribes had a chance to buy it at auction, and an Alaskan Inuit tribe purchased what was then dubbed the Alaska Parcel. Kramer bought it in 1993.

CHAPTER 29

The Incorruptible
Crusader

IN THE WAKE of their experience with Thomas Kramer, local residents channeled their anger at the greed and excesses of unbridled development. In the fall of 1996, a political action committee called "Save Miami Beach" circulated a petition to get a city charter amendment on the ballot that would maintain the existing buildable square footage on all waterfront parcels; any request by a developer for a size increase would have to go to a public vote. The crux of the ballot initiative was to save South Pointe's Alaska Parcel. In the four years leading up to the Portofino Settlement Agreement, the city's Design Review Board had approved 6,300 apartment and condominium projects. Only one, the Floridian on West Avenue along Biscayne Bay, came in at thirty-five stories.

"We were trying to protect the few areas that were left in Miami Beach," David Dermer told me. The son of the two-term mayor, Dermer lost his run for a commission seat in 1995.

"There was tremendous hostility developing between the city commission and the public, and reformers felt shut out. Some were disillusioned because it seemed there was no one to take up the sword.

"Kramer at that time had spread plenty of money around the city and he controlled a lot. He had *Ocean Drive* giving him good press, local businesses thought his developments were great because they were upscale and large, and he had done enough philanthropy to buy the silence of some people who should have known better. But I knew that Kramer had insulted Jews, gays, Cubans, and I thought that if we framed the issue correctly as being about him, we might win a campaign. If there had been a bigger or better developer, it would have been much tougher."

Dermer had not yet met two newcomers, Frank and Marian Del Vecchio, who were about to revolutionize South Beach's activist community and help convert Save Miami Beach from an idea into a winning ballot campaign.

FRANK DEL VECCHIO would prove to be the most important leader of the preservation and quality of life movement since Barbara Capitman. He could wear down his better-financed opponents, including politically connected developers and the entertainment industry, but he also had advantages Capitman did not. A former attorney with the Department of Housing and Urban Development (HUD), he had a matchless understanding and empathy for low-income and inner-city urban planning. Capitman had been interested in saving buildings because of their historical architecture. Del Vecchio wanted to save neighborhoods. His HUD work taught him how local political machines worked, where the corruption was buried, and how the bureaucracy could be defeated.

Del Vecchio was born in Boston's West End. His parents had immigrated from Italy and his father was a street peddler who played an accordion and sold balloons. Young Del Vecchio went to college on a Navy scholarship and was commissioned in June 1954. Four years later, he returned home.

"I arrived just in time to see my childhood neighborhood being demolished," he told me. "How could the system displace 16,000 low-income Jews and Italians? Why wasn't there anyone fighting it?"

Never believing the city's assurances about its relocation efforts, Del Vecchio's father had moved his family out a couple of years ahead of the demolition.

Frank went back to see the streets where he grew up. "The building next to ours was torn down, and the wall was ripped away on one side of my building, and I could see the wallpaper of the room I had grown up in."

Sitting on the curb was an elderly Italian woman, dressed all in black. "Are you Frank Del Vecchio?" She had mistaken Frank for his father. He asked her what was going on. She didn't know. She was near tears.

"Those left were the ones with no capacity or means to understand or fight what was happening to them. I decided at that moment I had to come back and do something."

He got a scholarship to Harvard Law School, and after getting his degree, went to work for the Boston Redevelopment Agency (BRA), the successor agency to the one that had demolished the West End. That year, 1962, he met Marian Seidner, the daughter of secular Czech Jewish immigrants who sent their spoiled daughter to Smith. Del Vecchio was smitten. "I wanted to marry her right away but she would hear none of it."

Marian became one of his crusades. When pressed, she revealed to him that she had a severe eating disorder. After several years of failed therapy, her mother decided to commit Marian to the New York Psychiatric Center, on the advice of the noted psychoanalyst Hilda Bruch.

When Marian told him she was being hospitalized, Frank was undeterred. "It didn't matter to me." She also told him that she could not have children. "No problem," he told her, "we'll adopt."

He gave her one year "to straighten up" because at the end of that time he intended to marry her. He visited Marian every weekend. At the end of the year, he attended a meeting about Marian's progress with her analyst, the chief of the psychiatric department, several nurses, and her parents. The chief psychiatrist informed the group that Marian was not ready for discharge. "If she is set free, she is very capable of turning on the gas and blowing herself up and everyone else with her," he said.

"You are a doctor and I am a lawyer," Frank said. "We gave you one year. I will take my chances with the gas."

"My parents would have let them keep me. But Frank walked over and helped me up," said Marian. "The nurses walked us outside. My analyst came running to tell me I had to get rid of Frank, that he was dangerous. I dropped my analyst and chose Frank. He was my savior."

Frank's first job was as the project developer for the BRA. His first assignment was a run-down Irish neighborhood, Charleston, slated for demolition and rebuilding. The BRA gave him an office in City Hall but he used the basement of the neighborhood library. "I brought the surveyors and planners there and kept my door open all the time." A reservist pilot on weekends, he took aerial photos to bolster his argument that the neighborhood could be reconfigured without destroying it. He earned the trust of the residents—who trusted no one from City Hall— by meeting with them in small groups in their pubs and homes, and single-handedly crafted a plan that allowed the BRA to redevelop Charleston by preserving most of it (today it is one of Boston's thriving districts).

At the time of the Charleston success, one of Martin Luther King, Jr.'s, associates, the Reverend Douglas Moore, came to see what the thirty-two-year-old lawyer in the BRA had accomplished. Moore asked Del Vecchio to come to Washington, D.C., to see if he might be interested in becoming the project developer for the capital's blighted Shaw neighborhood.

"It was shameful," recalls Del Vecchio. "It was in the center of the urban black ghetto, only four blocks from the White House."

Del Vecchio told Moore that most of the rows of brick houses could be saved and that only a small area behind the school required demolition. Moore asked him to move to D.C. and take charge of the project. Del Vecchio's BRA bosses told him he was crazy, that a white man could never be accepted in the D.C. black power establishment.

Del Vecchio knew that the power of every city bureaucracy is wrapped around zoning and development. In D.C., the black-run Washington Urban League and the United Planning Organization wanted the Shaw project and considered Del Vecchio an outsider, but he applied for the job anyway.

Of his interview with the neighborhood's business organization, at a local funeral home, Del Vecchio said, "There were thirty black men, all very serious, mean-looking guys. They did not say a word. I sat in a chair, and said, 'I guess I better tell you my story.' I told them what I thought about the neighborhood and what could be done. I gave them examples, and explained there was a federal loan program under federal renewal, and how absentee landlords could sell to the federal government who could then give it to a non-profit." He waited while they talked among themselves for half an hour.

"When I was called in, the president stood up and put out his hand and said, 'Del Vecchio, we are with you.'"

Frank was the only white applicant at the mayor's office the following day. When it was his turn to speak, he said: "I am white and an outsider. You should pick me because I have no political ambition, I will come in for three or four years only, and I know how to do it. We will have a successful project and you will all learn and implement it time and again."

He got the job. The D.C. power establishment embraced him so thoroughly that when Martin Luther King, Jr., addressed a crowd at Cardozo High School stadium, Del Vecchio introduced him.

Del Vecchio stayed in Washington until the project received its final complement of federal grants. It was an illuminating—and disillusioning—experience.

"The tragic end of Shaw is that the district government turned it over to the black power brokers who approved all the land takings without finishing the planning we had started. All the spoils and all the jobs went to favored insiders and there was no standard any longer for performance. It was the ascendancy of Marion Barry. Shaw never got done. It continued to deteriorate while millions of dollars went into people's pockets."

After moving back to Boston, Del Vecchio was put in charge of HUD's regional Equal Opportunity Division. Later, when he was HUD's regional administrator of block grants to help low- and moderate-income residents, he caused a firestorm when he wrote a report that minority groups in Boston did not receive their fair share of the federal benefits he dispensed. When Andrew Cuomo came in as the HUD secretary in 1992, Del Vecchio was one of ten regional directors, and he gave the secretary a straight talk that became legendary. "I told him, as I had previous secretaries, that what HUD was doing was often illegal and its objective largely unachievable." He laid out why different parts of HUD were a honeypot for political insiders and described the minefield Cuomo faced if he wanted to make real changes. Del Vecchio had come to believe that government agencies often used the words "renewal" and "restoration" to launch enormous projects that created jobs, profited developers and contractors, financed campaigns, and produced legacies for the politicians who started them, all at the expense of the poor.

Instead of finding himself reassigned to a Siberian posting, Del Vecchio was respected for his credibility and unparalleled knowledge of the HUD laws.

By the time he retired in 1995, his younger brother, Joe, had bought a small one-bedroom condo in South Pointe, at Third and Ocean. Frank and Marian paid him a visit. "I had visions of old ladies on the beach," says Marian. Instead, they found it charming. In South Pointe and the Art Deco District they found more Europeans than Americans. When they landed back at Logan, it was in the middle of a miserable snowstorm.

"It certainly was a lot nicer in Miami," Marian noted.

Frank was a step ahead. "Let's buy there."

They bought a one-bedroom condo in his brother's building. "I intended to read books, learn Spanish, and Marian and I would travel to Latin and South America. This was going to be a total break. No more community activism."

As they unpacked, Joe told Frank he had to go to City Hall the following week because a developer wanted to build an enormous hotel that would destroy the neighborhood. Marian just sighed.

At the hearing the following Tuesday, the chairman asked if anyone from the public had comments. Frank, dressed in his only suit, and carrying a stack of papers a foot high, took the mike. He explained how the increased traffic from the hotel violated the zoning codes and pointed out a fatal design failure that the city's staff had overlooked. The developer ran to the mike and assured the commission that local residents favored his plans.

"And then I had a Perry Mason moment," Del Vecchio recalls. He asked the developer if he had spoken to the residents in 301 Ocean, the building closest to the planned hotel. The developer said he had, but could not remember any names. Frank then produced a document signed by the condo's board of directors confirming that they had never been approached about the hotel and that a canvassing of the building's residents showed that no one had spoken to the developer.

Saul Gross was on the Design Review Board at the time. "I thought, 'Wow, who is this guy?' " Neisen Kasdin heard about the "attorney from Boston" who had moved to South Pointe. Columnist A. C. Weinstein of the *Miami SunPost* got a call from a friend: "You've got to see this new guy. He dropped a bomb on them at the DRB today."

The committee reversed course.

The next day, Harold Rosen, the attorney for most of the major nightclub and entertainment owners, who had also been at the hearing, invited Frank and Marian to lunch at Joe's Stone Crab.

"Frank, I can tell you have a great deal to offer, and I've checked you out," Rosen said. "I would like you to work with me as a consultant."

"I've always been proud of my independence," recalls Del Vecchio. "He was charming, but I passed."

Within a week, Del Vecchio had met with Mayor Gelber and was working with the police to form a special squad that would target the drug dealers in the small Ocean Beach Park bordering his condo. The park was a homeless encampment, a hangout for crack addicts. Danger signs were posted on the former children's playground. Del Vecchio couldn't believe that the city allowed the park to fester in the shadow of South Pointe Tower and the partially completed Portofino Tower. In return for the city's cooperation on cleaning up the park, Del Vecchio agreed to draft homeless legislation with quality of life controls that protected the rights of those on the streets. "Hard to believe," he recalls, "but they were more or less doing it by the seat of their pants."*

"We've got to get this Del Vecchio on board," Charles Schaab, one of the Save Miami Beach referendum organizers, told David Dermer. Dermer and Schaab were worried about getting the required 10 percent

---

* When the city proposed paving over the park in 1988 to create a parking lot, local residents sought help from Marjory Stoneman Douglas, a Coconut Grove–based environmentalist credited with saving the Everglades from development. She came to the Beach, organized opposition, and Alex Daoud in his first year as mayor capitulated to the protests, promising it would always remain a park. In 1994, a ballot measure to rename the park after Douglas failed. Del Vecchio, when he learned of her role, lobbied the city commission to vote approval of an ordinance to put a referendum issue on the ballot without a signature campaign. This time, the naming got voter approval and the park was renamed for Douglas.

of the city's 39,548 registered voters in order to qualify the referendum for a special election the following March. Recalls Dermer, "After a while we got used to Frank, but in the beginning he was like a force of nature. He just doesn't have an off button, which is fantastic when you are on the same side of an issue."

Says Del Vecchio, "Like politicians everywhere, those in Miami Beach were the instruments of developers. Those developers were poised to get upzoning from the Miami Beach City Commission. I knew it would take Save Miami Beach to take this power away from them."

By January 1997, Del Vecchio, Dermer, and several dozen volunteers had collected nearly 6,000 signatures—far more than needed to bring the proposal to a vote.

Neisen Kasdin thought Save Miami Beach was unnecessary. "The city hadn't done any upzoning since 1979," he says. "By the time Dermer began Save Miami Beach, no city in the history of Dade County had done more zoning reform than Miami Beach." But Mark Needle, a South Pointe activist, represented many when he said the charter amendment was necessary to ensure the commission's downzoning efforts weren't reversed in the future by a pro-development City Hall. Save Miami Beach supporters didn't trust local politicians to protect the shoreline from rich developers. "The amendment is a safety blanket," Needle said.

The zoning technicalities and the details of the Portofino Settlement were too dense for most residents. But they understood that Kramer was a developer and that it was the business of most developers to squeeze every penny out of every inch of space.

A special election was set for June. Opponents of the referendum formed their own PAC, Miami Beach Citizens Against Higher Taxes, and raised $1.5 million, compared to the $13,466 by its supporters. In the closing days, television and radio ads against the amendment contended its approval would bankrupt the city, cut police and fire services, and result in increased crime. Callers to 911 would only get answering machines. Every resident's taxes would increase by $1,250.

On June 3, 1997, the Portofino-backed group deployed 250 election day workers, each paid $100 for a twelve-hour shift. Caravans of cars and buses picked up voters, especially the elderly from retirement homes, and took them to the polls. At the city's thirty-two precincts, Kramer supporters wore T-shirts emblazoned with VOTE NO. They carried signs and handed out flyers. But it didn't work. Fifty-seven percent of city voters approved the zoning restriction referendum.

"It was a historic event," says Del Vecchio. The day after the election, Ed Resnick, who had run the unsuccessful campaign to defeat the amendment, filed suit in Dade Circuit Court claiming the ballot language was unclear and asked a judge to declare the election invalid. It was dismissed.

Days after the vote, the city commission pushed aside the Portofino Settlement Agreement to honor the election results. The disputed Alaska Parcel would go on the ballot in November so voters could decide whether the zoning density should be increased.

Kramer threatened a breach of contract lawsuit, but a couple of weeks later he surprised everyone by terminating the Portofino Settlement Agreement.

Twenty-two days after the referendum vote, Kramer announced he had signed a contract to sell one of his best parcels, 13 acres of oceanfront land just north of South Pointe Park that he had bought from Capital Bank five years earlier for $13.3 million. The sales price was an all-cash $54 million. The buyer was a fifty-two-year-old Manhattan developer, Ian Bruce Eichner.

Appropriately, Kramer's first sale was dogged by financial questions, this time about how Eichner had come up with the $54 million. In 1977, Eichner was an assistant district attorney who began doing small apartment renovations in Manhattan. He built some luxury residential projects and his partnership erected the seventy-two-story CitySpire, a West Side condominium; but Eichner filed for chapter 11 bankruptcy in 1991. He had a bitter battle with the city over charges that he willfully exceeded height limits and claims by the New York Department of Environmental Protection that as a result of poor design, wind constantly blew through the tower, creating a howl that violated city noise ordinances. A year before he bought the Kramer property, Eichner settled litigation with an Australian lender who had sued him over nonpayment. His office building, 1540 Broadway, was lost in a bankruptcy, and unsold units at 2372 Broadway reverted to the banks.

As for the $54 million, Eichner said it was from the sale of the Richmond, a 121-unit condominium on the Upper East Side, and New York's Park Central Hotel. The *Miami Herald* reported that Eichner had silent Hong Kong backers for the South Beach purchase.

"My friends in New York gave me the rundown on Eichner," says community activist Joe Fontana. "When I heard about his overexpansion, the bankruptcy, and the flouting of city height rules, I thought he'll make a killing in South Beach. He's tailor-made for this town."

CHAPTER 30

"He Viewed Me as an Enemy"

THE SUCCESS OF the Save Miami Beach referendum brought to the forefront the simmering dynamic between development and the town's future growth. Politics is a foreign concept to many Beach residents. Fewer than 8,000 of the city's 40,000 registered voters went to the polls in the 1995 mayoral contest. But the politicians, contractors, and developers who depended on their approval of large projects, and activists like Del Vecchio, trying to prevent unbridled development and intrusions into the residential quality of life, all appreciated that the power wielded at City Hall affected the lives of every resident. Would it all become a concrete canyon like mid-Beach, where there was little pedestrian traffic and the ocean was hidden from view by a wall of towers? Or would activists force developers to build projects that were in keeping with South Beach's low- to mid-rise character, enhancing neighborhoods while still making a profit? The mayor and six other commissioners set the tone, and Save Miami Beach made the November 1997 election one of the most important in recent years.

David Dermer was encouraged by the reform momentum to again run for the city commission. Political alliances often make for odd partnerships. Miami Beach Unity '97, a coalition of prominent Hispanic and Orthodox Jewish leaders whose members included most of those who had worked vociferously against Save Miami Beach, now endorsed him. "In campaigns, your enemies of today are your allies of tomorrow, and your allies of today are your enemies of tomorrow," said

Armando Gutierrez, a campaign powerhouse and the consultant who organized Unity '97.

"I said to David, 'These were your enemies. They were cursing you, you were cursing them, and all of a sudden now you're accepting their endorsement?'" said Joe Fontana, the Beach activist and a commission candidate himself.

A real street fight for the mayor's seat formed between fellow commissioners Neisen Kasdin and David Pearlson, a developer who owned more than 200 hotel and apartment units. Kasdin thought the election would determine the island's future and that the town was at a crossroads. "Being mayor is the position in which you can have the most influence in setting the course of the city." But he was a lightning rod for critics who charged that as a commercial transaction lawyer he had used his commission seat to favor his law practice. Pearlson distributed a long list of Kasdin's clients—fashionable restaurants and garbage companies—that depended on favorable City Hall decisions.

He was supported by the very businesses that scared preservationists and quality of life activists. Dozens of lime green KASDIN FOR MAYOR posters were plastered in the windows of the trendiest Washington Avenue nightclubs and Ocean Drive cantinas. At a candlelit fund-raiser in the ballroom of the Delano Hotel, Kasdin mingled with a twenty-something crowd of magazine models and filmmakers. Compared to the outgoing mayor—bow-tied and nearly seventy—the forty-two-year-old candidate seemed like a new generation.

While his critics said he had too many conflicts of interest, Kasdin was quick to point out that he had recused himself forty-three times out of several thousand votes on any matter on which he had had possible conflicts. It was more than any other commissioner. "That was the best stamp of my honesty," he told me. "The old way of doing Miami Beach politics was never to disclose a conflict and just vote on it anyway. I had hoped that by being so transparent, I would set a new standard. Instead, the old power players who wanted it the way it was turned the tables on me."

In July, the dominant political news was a record $323,000 fine by the Federal Election Commission (FEC) of Thomas Kramer for making $418,600 in illegal campaign contributions to political candidates in 1993 and 1994. Federal law prohibits foreign nationals from contributing to U.S. elections or from directing others to do so. It is also unlawful for anyone to make campaign contributions in someone else's name. Kramer's contributions were funneled through intermediaries or one of his seventeen businesses. Rather than risk criminal charges, he paid the fine and admitted his guilt.

The FEC action became an issue in the mayoral race. Nancy Liebman was also running, and her campaign had received $5,000 from Kramer. Commissioner Sy Eisenberg got $1,000, but Kasdin took the heat for having received $500. Kasdin returned the $500 contribution and claimed he was not aware that it was illegal to accept contributions from foreigners.

While Pearlson had been the staunchest commission supporter of the Portofino Settlement and fought hard against Save Miami Beach, it was Kasdin who drew the ire of most activists, especially over his vote in favor of the Kramer deal. His opponents suggested he supported Kramer because of the German's $500 political contribution. Seasoned political observers knew that Kasdin mastered the minutiae of every issue that came before the commission and deliberated carefully before voting. The idea that Kramer bought his vote for $500 was laughable. But for voters who only digested sound bites, the smear put Kasdin on the defensive. He had to explain that he regretted his vote for the Portofino Settlement Agreement, and that it was time for the city to make the best of a bad deal.

Craig Robins's reaction was typical: "More than anyone, Neisen had demonstrated that he was an independent thinker and willing to fight overdevelopment in the city. He could successfully balance business interests and quality of life issues but that meant that he didn't appeal to the people on the extremes of either side." But his enemies were passionate. A. C. Weinstein, who took on Kasdin frequently, told friends that he thought that Kasdin was taking payoffs. "I thought it was possible," David Dermer told me years later. A powerful attorney in town, Kent Harrison Robins, also thought Kasdin was dirty.

When asked about the charges, Kasdin says, "To this day, the most infuriating thing was that when people disagreed with me, instead of just arguing about the issues, they smeared my decades of public service with the MDPL [Miami Design Preservation League] and raised the thoroughly unfounded charge that I was in somebody's pocket. These were people who should have known better. It's scurrilous, and just because somebody puts his name to it doesn't give it any more credibility."

Says Frank Del Vecchio: "The reason for the battle against Kasdin was that he was a great strategist who knew how to manipulate the system to get what he wanted. Of everyone I had come across in Miami Beach, he was the only one who was my counterpart in knowing how the system operated and how to work it. But he was on the other side, someone I saw who espoused preservation but really tilted invariably toward development."

THE MAYOR'S RACE was abruptly interrupted on July 15 when Gianni Versace was gunned down on the front steps of Casa Casuarina.* While the manhunt for his murderer was under way—identified as a gay spree killer, Andrew Cunanan—the Beach was gripped by news and rumors: It was a mob hit on Versace. Cunanan and Versace had been lovers. The relentless international media spotlight plunged Miami Beach into a live twenty-four-hour circus. CNN offered hourly updates. Satellite trucks lined Ocean Drive.

Chris Paciello appeared on ABC's *Prime Time Live* to talk about Cunanan's visits to Liquid in the previous weeks. The bestselling crime novelist Edna Buchanan caused a small furor when she went on NBC's *Today* and linked Versace's death to the Miami Beach City Commission's desire to attract gay tourists to the area. "They're the ones that sort of put this thing in motion."

Eight days after he murdered Versace, Cunanan shot himself to death. Police found his body in a houseboat docked in mid-Beach.

---

* One ghoulish souvenir seeker at the scene of the murder used pictures of Versace fashions torn from a magazine to soak up the blood. Two Miami Beach residents, one a celebrity dentist, the other a real estate broker, each showed me a framed page they said was one of those taken that day—the broker had paid $5,000, while the dentist would not say how much he spent.

In a city where even the smallest Art Deco hotel uses a public relations firm, and every model and surfer has an agent, the biggest concern was image. The politicians asked whether Versace's death might remove some of the Beach's hip sheen, force an exodus of celebrities made nervous by his murder, or scare away tourists.

As voting day neared, the campaign turned into nasty character assassination. Kasdin hammered Pearlson about his relationship with Armando Gutierrez, a powerful political insider. The two had been partners in 1996 in a failed tire-sealant distributorship for South America. Since then, Pearlson had supported issues helping firms linked to Gutierrez.

A week before the vote, a private investigator for the Kasdin campaign showed that workers listed as Pearlson volunteers had rounded up absentee ballots, raising the possibility of vote manipulation. Kasdin took it to circuit court. The judge found no evidence of fraud, but ruled that the ballots, which were machine-counted, needed to be counted by hand, restuffed in their envelopes, and set aside.

Kasdin won by 1,000 votes. And Dermer rode to an easy victory for the city commission. Joining him were two other first-time politicians who supported controlled, slow development: an investment banker, Simon Cruz, and Jose Smith, an attorney, the Beach's first Cuban-born Hispanic commissioners.

Shortly after Kasdin was elected, Peebles came to see him and the new city manager, Sergio Rodriguez. "He sought to change the Royal Palm deal with the city," Kasdin told me. "He wanted to reduce or defer rent because he claimed that the poor structural quality of the Royal Palm Hotel required its demolition, even though he knew he had taken the deal 'as is.' In fact, I am sure demolishing the hotel would have saved him money, because it is more expensive to selectively demolish, brace, and reinforce the remaining structure, and attach it to the new building. Sergio and I told him no, the city would not renegotiate. From that moment forward, he viewed me as an enemy. Peebles's problem is that I was one of the few people who could say no to him and he couldn't live with that."

CHAPTER 31

"There's No Morality Here"

MICHAEL CAPPONI RETURNED to South Beach in 1997. He had been on a heroin binge for several years that left him hustling on the streets of New York. "Most people thought I had died," Capponi told me. A rumor had made the rounds that he had been shot to death by police during an attempted robbery in Key West.

His first night back, he showed up at Liquid for an *Ocean Drive* party. "I knew behind my back they were all saying I was still doing drugs," he recalls, "and that in six months I'd be in a coffin." The only club owner who believed him when he said he was drug-free and gave him another chance was Chris Paciello. The Paciello-Casares entertainment business was growing. Chris dispatched Capponi to Palm Beach to check on locations for another branch of Liquid, while Ingrid tried duplicating its success in Manhattan. After false starts at two West Side locations, they settled on a 20,000-square-foot space at 16 West 22nd Street. But what looked like an easy deal turned into a year-long battle when the owner refused to assign the lease to Casares because Raul Casares was listed as the sole shareholder in the State Liquor Authority filing.

After *The Village Voice* published a story about Paciello's criminal history and links to mobsters, and *New York Post* columnist Jack Newfield wrote a series of columns praising the grassroots effort to deny Paciello and Casares a liquor license, the deal was dead. The deputy mayor vowed that he would oppose a Liquid anywhere in the city. "I can't believe those fuckers said no to me," Ingrid complained. "We were the victims of bad press." In the summer of 1997, Paciello partied with a former Miss Russia at a Manhattan nightclub. A Russian photographer wouldn't leave them alone, so Paciello punched him. Soon tables were smashed and the photographer was stabbed in the chest and neck with a fork. New York cops detained Paciello for questioning, but the photographer did not press charges.

Back in South Beach, Paciello kept distancing himself from his past. He was a vocal opponent of drugs and gave money to the right local charities and community projects. He bought a $500,000 Flamingo Drive house and the city appointed him to a committee that oversaw clubs. Ingrid's father provided the money for another venture, an upscale lounge called Bar Room. Paciello hired Gerry Kelly, a Dubliner who had run his own European couture label and had managed nightclubs in Ibiza.

Paciello realized that he had grown independent of his old mob connections and he no longer liked the innuendos and suspicions raised in news reports and by competitors. They were often a hindrance as they had proved to be in New York. He didn't mind that some of his friends thought of him as a Hollywood gangster come to life—Madonna sang to him, Marilyn Monroe–style, "Happy Birthday, Dear Mobster" over the telephone.

"Look, I never regret where I came from," Paciello told Ocean Drive in 1998. "I grew up in a certain area where everybody thinks violence is normal. Now, I look back and see that I have come a long way. I was able to leave and see that it's not a normal lifestyle. To come from where I came from and to do what I did, I can actually pat myself on the back."

The exclusive Bar Room, with its strict dress code and short guest list, was Paciello's way of finally saying good-bye to his street-tough Brooklyn friends. "That whole Italian mob thing, by the end he seemed to hate it," Gilbert Stafford told me. "He gave orders to the staff that if any tough-looking Italians showed up and dropped his name, to say he was out of the country."

But Paciello had trouble avoiding his early New York contacts. Gambino captain Jackie "The Nose" D'Amico, who had put Paciello and Caruso in business at Risk, continued to receive payoffs from Paciello and was one of the few people who had access to him. Robert

Gordon, Frankie "The Baker" Romano, and Paul Torres, Lord Michael's key lieutenants for his Limelight ecstasy ring, had moved to South Beach when the police closed Limelight. Paciello hired them at Liquid, which they dubbed "Limelight South." They did not resume selling drugs, but using information picked up around the club, they ripped off drug traffickers. In 1997, the trio got a tip that a local dealer had stashed $50,000 at his beachfront apartment. Posing as delivery-men, they went to his place, tied him up, and hunted for the money. When the dealer freed himself and ran to the balcony, screaming for help, they fled empty-handed. The dealer knew them from Liquid, and instead of going to the police, he went directly to Paciello. Paciello fired them.

Paciello and Casares expanded beyond nightclubs and opened Joia, an upscale restaurant in the Century Hotel. Despite mediocre food and typically wretched South Beach service, Joia became a requisite A-list pit stop. Madonna sent a pre-release of *Ray of Light* and celebrated her forty-first birthday party there. The *National Enquirer* tried bribing the busboys for dirt. "If South Beach is the new French Riviera, then Joia is the Hôtel du Cap," wrote *Vanity Fair*.

By the early summer of 1999, Chris Paciello wanted an extra edge to crush his nightclub rivals. He found it in a Miami Beach police officer, Andrew Dohler, whom he hired as a part-time security consultant. Dohler fed Paciello confidential information about other club owners, as well as tipping him off if the police were planning a raid looking for underage drinkers or drug dealers, but Paciello had no idea that his new hire was undercover. In order to bolster Dohler's credibility with his new boss, the police department staged a bogus raid on Liquid, which Dohler warned Paciello about in advance.

Paciello felt so comfortable that he opened up to Dohler in ways he did not with his other South Beach friends.

One time he confessed, "Some of my buddies got locked up back in New York. I used to pull a few jobs with them. I hope they don't rat me out. I'm not going to go down like John Gotti, no way." Paciello knew that some of his former Bath Avenue Crew associates who had partici-pated in the Shemtov murder had been arrested by the FBI on racke-teering charges. He was nervous that one might try to cut a deal.

"You know Sammy the Bull?" Paciello told Dohler, working himself up into a full-tilt rage. "They should kill him and his whole family."

According to the Feds, not long after that conversation with Dohler, Paciello paid $10,000 to a Mafia enforcer to threaten a family member of someone Paciello suspected was snitching about him to the FBI. If the witness cooperated, the family was told, "Everybody is dead."

During the summer of 1999, Paciello took Dohler out for a day on his 50-foot yacht to meet "a very special friend." Paciello introduced the undercover cop to Alphonse "Allie Boy" Persico, the Colombo crime family don, who had recently ordered the slaying of underboss and archrival William "Wild Bill" Cutolo. Before Cutolo was killed, Paciello was reportedly paying him $10,000 a week in tribute money that Persico now wanted.

Persico talked about the "good old days" before Russian and Israeli criminals ruined the nice relationship between New York and Miami. Ludwig Fainberg, the Russian mob's point man in South Florida, had been busted a couple of years earlier. He had run an enormous criminal empire out of a strip club near Miami International Airport called Porky's and a borscht-and-blini restaurant in North Miami Beach called Babushka. Israeli gangsters specialized in trafficking ecstasy.

Shortly before Paciello, Persico, and Dohler went for their day cruise, two nineteen-year-old Hasidic men were found guilty of running a stable of Hasidic drug couriers from Brooklyn for an Israeli mobster. In a second case, Israeli gangsters were charged with using strippers from New York bars like Scores and Tens to shuttle ecstasy from Europe to Miami and other cities.

"I don't know how you fucking put up with it," Persico said to Paciello and the cop. "These Jews don't know their place anymore."

As they sailed up the Intracoastal, two fishing boats filled with federal agents lagged half a mile behind. The Feds had long suspected that Paciello and Persico were laundering mob money through Liquid. Once Paciello introduced Dohler to Persico, they struck gold.

Over the summer Rick and Noah Lazus, father and son investors from North Carolina, asked Gerry Kelly to manage their new mega-club, Level. Rick brought him a two-year non-compete contract with a $50,000 signing bonus. Kelly was interested but first wanted to resign his Bar Room job. Rick warned him that it was possible Paciello "will beat the shit out of you."

Kelly typed a resignation letter and gave two weeks notice.

"I should have done it face-to-face," he admitted to me. "So, I was chicken. So what? I'm still alive."

Kelly left for a weekend in Orlando at 7 p.m., and his assistant delivered the sealed envelope to Paciello at ten o'clock that night.

The day Paciello got the letter, he asked Dohler to stop by when the club was closed. Dohler arrived in his police uniform and was wearing a wire. Paciello wanted to talk about Gerry Kelly.

"This fucking [Kelly] he's got a bad drug problem," said Paciello on the wire. "He always has drugs on him. People at the club give him drugs. He always drives drunk. You can arrest him, pull his fucking car over. They can pull his liquor license for that, right? I really want to hurt this guy good, and I'll take care of you big-time."

As for Noah Lazus, "I'm telling you the owner of the club, we got to get his head fucking broken in. We got to get him beat up. We got to get him whacked."

"As long as it's done on the Beach," said Dohler.

"Right, but if something happens to the kid right now, the cops are going to be so far up my ass; but if Kelly is busted for drunk driving or drugs, that's normal shit. He gets beat up, I'm fucked."

"Just remove yourself."

"Yeah, but even if I'm in my office at the time, and someone else walks in and bats him over the head, who are they going to blame? They're gonna know it's me."

At another point, Paciello complained that he couldn't personally dole out the punishment he thought Kelly and Lazus deserved.

"I'm telling ya. I got to come out of fucking retirement. I've become a fucking big pussy down here, a big sucker."

After Paciello's conversation with Dohler, the Feds arranged twenty-four-hour protection for Kelly. They didn't tell Kelly, but undercover cops tailed him and parked near his apartment. One night, Paciello left his house wearing a baseball cap and carrying a bat and drove to Salvation, a gay club Kelly frequented on his off nights. Paciello parked on a side street with a clear view of the entrance. But Kelly didn't show up, and at 3 a.m. Paciello drove home.

Finally one night a Miami Beach detective showed up at Kelly's apartment and drove him to FBI headquarters, where half a dozen agents and cops waited for him in a conference room. "I nearly died," he told me. "I did not know what to expect. I said to one of the detectives, 'You look familiar.' He told me he had been following me."

They showed Kelly some of Dohler's transcripts and told him that Paciello wanted him dead.

"They wanted to know why he wanted me dead," recalls Kelly. "They weren't really sure it was merely because I had shown disloyalty by leaving. So they were looking for a reason. They had looked at my bank records. They wanted to know if I was a secret partner of his or helped him get rid of cash."

The agents were interested in how much cash Paciello's businesses took in.

"Does $5 million a year sound right to you?" one agent asked.

"Yes. And that is just from liquor. In a bad year." (Kelly did $13 million at Level in its first year.)

"They told me to keep doing the same things as I always did and not to tell anyone what was happening. That if I changed my routine, Paciello would be tipped off that something was about to break. I left with my head swimming. It had all gone to Chris's head. He thought he was a godfather."

On November 23, 1999, a federal grand jury in Brooklyn returned a sealed indictment against Paciello and eight other defendants, all connected to the Bonanno crime family, charging them with multiple counts of murder, robbery, and racketeering. Later that same evening, Bonanno captain Anthony Graziano telephoned Paciello.

"I'm glad I got hold of you; I gotta talk to you," said Graziano. "Could you do me a favor? Could you put a kid on the list?"

"Yeah, sure," replied Paciello. "Who is it? A good kid?"

"Yeah, nice kid. He's a DJ for a friend of ours."

"You should have called me when you were down here."

"Don't be a fucking wiseguy, I called you yesterday."

"Did ya?"

"I called you and someone said you were in a meeting. I said, who the fuck is this guy? The president?"

On December 1, Paciello was inspecting the construction at Liquid Lounge, his new club in West Palm Beach, when two well-built strangers came into the club. They looked like cops. Paciello quickly went out the back door and sped away in his Range Rover. The men were FBI agents and they dialed his cell phone. "I'm driving to my lawyer's office. I'll talk to you from there," he told them. Later that day, one of Florida's best hired guns, Roy Black, accompanied Paciello when he turned himself in at the U.S. Marshals office in downtown Miami.

When Paciello was processed on charges of felony murder and robbery, DEA agent Tim Foley asked him his name for the record. "Chris Paciello. I mean, Chris Ludwigsen. Paciello is my stage name."

Black told a horde of reporters on the courthouse steps that "Mr. Paciello really helped put South Beach on the map. He is a successful, well-known Miami businessman and a high-profile entertainment figure, and unfortunately anybody who becomes a success in this country becomes an easy target for such accusations."

On December 4, while Paciello sat in a windowless cell at the Miami Federal Detention Center, Liquid Lounge Palm Beach opened. "I had to go to the mayor of Palm Beach and convince him we were going to run a kosher operation," said Michael Capponi. "The mayor had said that no way was this gangster going to open a club in his town. It took a lot of very influential members of Palm Beach society to change his mind."

Soon George Paciello, Chris's older brother, arrived and announced he was taking over the club. Said Capponi: "George was furious because the opening invites had gone out with my name on them as well as Ingrid and Chris. He accused me of trying to take over his brother's business. So I quit."*

At Chris's December 15 bail hearing, a dozen limousines pulled up outside the Miami federal courthouse. Out poured Paciello's support-

---

* George Paciello was arrested the following year, charged as one of thirteen Brooklyn gang members who had robbed thirty banks for $1.3 million starting in 1992. He was convicted in 2001.

ers, including Shareef Malnik, Sam Robin, Raul Casares, and Jason Binn. Michael Capponi was on the verge of tears, consoling Chris's distraught mother, Marguerite.

In a prepared statement Ingrid Casares said, in a faltering voice, "He's innocent, and everybody who's here today knows that. . . . I stand behind Chris one hundred percent."

Paciello's prominent friends took the stand to vouch for his credentials and to offer bail. The judge ruled that Paciello could be released on a $5 million cash bond. The prosecutor said he would appeal immediately and the judge agreed that the club owner should remain behind bars pending the appeal. Paciello was flown to New York and locked up in the high-security Metropolitan Detention Center, a windowless complex tucked under the Brooklyn-Queens Expressway, not far from his old stomping grounds.

The prosecutor successfully appealed the trial judge's bail decision and bail was increased to $15 million. Raul Casares contributed $1 million and Ingrid $50,000. Mickey Rourke's mother put up the deed to her house. To help finance Paciello's legal defense, both the Bar Room and Liquid in West Palm Beach were sold, along with his yacht and Flamingo Drive home. His empire was in tatters.

Out on bail, Paciello spent the summer under twenty-four-hour guard and house arrest at his mother's simple Brooklyn home. He had replaced Roy Black with New York's Ben Brafman. He advised Paciello to plead guilty and get a reduced sentence for cooperating with the Feds. Four days before the start of his trial, Paciello dropped his adamant protestations of innocence and pled guilty to murder, robbery, and racketeering.

In court, Paciello, dressed in a simple black suit and reading from a yellow legal pad, confessed that he was the getaway driver for the Shemtov attack. His normally strong voice was so soft that the courtroom spectators leaned forward to hear him. He also admitted orchestrating the armed robbery at the Chemical Bank. "I knew these crimes were part of a larger criminal enterprise," he said.

A few weeks later, just before sentencing, Paciello was put into a federal safe house, and his mother and brothers went into protective custody. To the shock of his Brooklyn friends, the Binger had agreed to testify against Bonanno crime family boss Anthony Spero. But eventually prosecutors put the seventy-one-year-old don behind bars without calling Paciello as a witness. The next part of his deal with the Feds was to testify against his old friend, Alphonse "Allie Boy" Persico, in what promised to be the biggest Mafia trial since John Gotti's 1992 case. But again Paciello got lucky. Persico pled guilty to money laundering and loan-sharking and got thirteen years.

Most people in South Beach thought Paciello was in witness protection, but because he never took the stand, the Feds decided it was safe for him to stay in prison. He served his time in maximum-security prisons in New York, Atlanta, and New Jersey.

"Paciello could get out of jail, come back and sit behind his desk, and the same people who are talking about him now will line up to kiss his ass," said Maxwell Blandford, the club director of Warsaw, Level, and the Forge. "Even if someone is accused of murder, if that person will help them move up the ladder of celebrity, people will do anything to try and get close to him. There's no morality here. If he comes back, he'll be more famous and have more friends than ever."

"Party people will forgive anything for a good time," said Capponi. He promised that with Paciello gone, "I was going to be the next King of South Beach."

CHAPTER 32

"He's Got Some Vindictive Streak"

THE NIGHTCLUB DRAMAS grabbed the headlines, but long-running battles between developers and residents over the development of remaining properties went on out of sight for most residents. Beyond the activists, most locals weren't interested in the drawn-out and sometimes tedious battles over zoning rights over a parcel of land.

Don Peebles thought he would attract little attention with his second major development north of the historic district, a renovation of the Bath Club at 59th and Collins. The area was already filled with large, uninspired apartment complexes and, he believed, there would be few objections. He was surprised by resistance from Kasdin, but once again with his D.C. street smarts Peebles outsmarted and outmuscled the Beach politicians.

Built by Carl Fisher in 1926, the Bath Club was named after Palm Beach's Bath and Tennis Club. One hundred charter members had put up $1,500 each as a refuge from prosperous Jews who had "ruined" the Roman Pools. For decades the Bath Club denied memberships to Jews and blacks. By 1991, the club had six Jewish members. Peebles broke the color barrier in 1996. "When Katrina and I had our apartment at La Tour," he told me, "we were only a few blocks away. Laurinda Spear suggested we join and introduced us." He claims he didn't know about the club's history or that he was its first black member until he got a call from a *Herald* reporter the next day.

In 1999, Peebles learned the Bath Club was for sale for $10 million.

He knew he'd get tremendous publicity as the black owner of a restricted club and thought the asking price was a steal. He learned that the two-story building had originally been zoned for a high-rise with no height restriction. Commercial properties in Miami Beach are taxed at the best zoning use, even if they are not utilized. To reduce its tax toll during hard times, the Bath Club had downzoned the property to a four-story maximum, figuring it could always rezone up if it wanted to sell or build. Then came Save Miami Beach, and suddenly the members had an oceanfront property worth a fraction of its developable value.

Peebles realized that real profits could be made only if the property were rezoned. He decided to feel out the city commission, knowing that Save Miami Beach required a public vote only if the developer wanted the highest zoning permit. The second maximum zoning permit could be approved by a simple five-vote majority by the commission. He already had a matter pending before the commissioners: approval for a $31 million project with Scott Robins for a 120,000-square-foot office building, retail space, and parking garage at 17th and Michigan. That was a straightforward commercial improvement. But in the anti-developer fever that had swept in since Save Miami Beach, the upzoning for the Bath Club was not a sure bet. He was asking double the current density and wanted to convert the property into a five-star hotel in a neighborhood zoned for condos only.

Peebles considered some of the commissioners his "friends." Marty Shapiro had always voted for him. Susan Gottlieb "was pro-development and was related to my zoning attorney by marriage. She was [also] solid." (In almost any other city that would have been considered a conflict of interest.) Nancy Liebman had voted against Peebles on the Royal Palm, and in her reelection in 1997 he had backed her opponent. Once polls showed her winning, the two forged an uneasy truce. "As a Jew, she despised the Bath Club, so much so that she didn't even want to set foot inside it," he told me. But Peebles gave her a personal tour and sold her on his preservation plan for the clubhouse and the sweet revenge of whites having to sell their restricted club to a black developer.

Next, Peebles met with Jose Smith, a no-nonsense real estate attorney. Smith said he'd vote yes, but if Peebles altered the plan before it came before the commission, all bets were off. One of the other Cuban commissioners, Simon Cruz, gave him a "maybe." "And while I knew Dermer would vote no," Peebles says, "I wanted him to be a quiet no, so I met with him and we agreed not to disagree loudly in public."

His conversation with Mayor Kasdin was tense. The two hadn't spoken since Kasdin had refused to help Peebles redo his city deal with the Royal Palm. Peebles explained what he wanted and finished the call believing that Kasdin "was supportive." Kasdin told me he'd been "noncommittal."

Peebles made a deal with the Bath Club once he was convinced that he had enough votes to get it rezoned. As with the Royal Palm, Peebles was adept at complicated arrangements that required putting minimal money up front. He agreed to the $10 million asking price, and under the contract's terms, he refinanced the club's loan and paid its back taxes and all the brokerage fees ($5.5 million). He also offered to preserve the one-story clubhouse and promised that the members would have full access to its luxury hotel with new pools, a gym, and a spa. And Peebles agreed to keep the members-only beach intact.

The Bath Club gave him eighteen months to finish the deal and to get the zoning changed. If he didn't make the deadline, the club was free to sell to someone else.

Peebles soon unveiled plans for a $122 million resort that he likened to Fisher Island without a ferry. Everything but the clubhouse would be demolished to make way for a luxury hotel tower. He knew that if he attached the word "preservation" or "historic" to the project it would help win public support, so his lawyers applied to the Historic Preservation Board to declare the clubhouse a historic site. "We knew that would give Liebman a comfort factor not only to support and vote for us but to champion the project. Even the conservative Miami Design Preservation League supported the project, since we were going to preserve and not demolish."

To further defuse any opposition, he met with every condo board and association, patiently explaining to residents why his project would increase their property values. He won over most. Of course, the residents most opposed were those who would lose their unobstructed ocean views.

According to Peebles, he went to Kasdin in August 1999 and urged the mayor to expedite the zoning upgrade process. Kasdin was distant. Marty Shapiro had announced that he was running against Kasdin for mayor and political insiders said that Peebles had urged Shapiro to do so. "The preliminary Bath Club vote was set for September 22," says Kasdin, "and I told him there was no reason to push it up."

Peebles tells a different version. He said Kasdin asked to put off any vote until after the election for fear that Shapiro would use it to paint the mayor "pro-development." Peebles didn't want to wait, so Kasdin agreed, "reluctantly," says Peebles, to keep the September date. Before the meeting broke up, Peebles says that Kasdin asked him for a campaign contribution and that he demurred.

"I certainly did not ask for any contributions," says Kasdin. "I knew by then he was contributing to Shapiro's campaign and was no political friend of mine."

What is undisputed is that at the September 22 hearing, Kasdin tried to defer the Bath Club vote. The Bath Club didn't come up until nearly midnight, and by then one commissioner, Susan Gottlieb, had left. There was no representative from two neighborhood groups that opposed it. But Kasdin failed to muster a majority for the deferment.

In matters before the city commission, the mayor votes last. The five other commissioners all voted for Peeble's upzoning. A yes vote by Kasdin would prevent the project from becoming a campaign issue since the two commissioners most closely associated with Save Miami Beach, David Dermer and Marty Shapiro, had voted yes. Kasdin praised Peebles as a great developer, but said that in good conscience he could not approve a doubling of the building size, and voted no. Peebles may have won, but he was furious.

"I could have let it go. But I had been publicly betrayed by a political friend and ally."

Peebles called Kasdin the next day and announced their relationship was over.

When the commission met on October 20 to decide whether the Bath Club should get a historic designation, Kasdin voted for it, but took the opportunity to reiterate his opposition to the upzoning. "Upon closer inspection [it became clear] that it was too massive and would obstruct Collins Avenue. It became clear it would be bad for the city."

Peebles grabbed the microphone.

"I am beyond puzzled, Mr. Kasdin," he said, his voice rising. "I was in your office and you said you were in favor of the project." Peebles told the startled audience that the mayor had pleaded with him to defer the vote until after the election and accused Kasdin of voting no because Peebles had given money to Shapiro's campaign.

Kasdin was outraged. "Mr. Peebles, your statements are not true." He said he was "shocked" to have learned that Peebles had collected $6,000 in contributions for Shapiro's campaign. An individual contribution is capped at $500, but people can give several times through different corporations, and their families can contribute.

Dermer then said that if Peebles's allegations were true, it would be nothing short of extortion. The commission passed a resolution to refer the issue of Kasdin's possible official misconduct to the state attorney's office.

Peebles told a *Herald* reporter, "He's [Kasdin] got some vindictive streak. I wanted to expose the mayor publicly in the hope that others that had been victimized will do the same."

When the *Herald* article commented that "wherever the truth lies, Peebles has emerged as a major player in Miami Beach politics," he showed it to friends and colleagues for days. A week before the election, Kasdin sent out a direct mailer charging that Peebles had bought Shapiro's vote on the Bath Club in exchange for campaign contributions. "I could not let this pass," says Peebles. He mounted an overnight mailing to the same voters, claiming it was the mayor who had politicized his Bath Club project. Then Peebles paid for a TV ad to let voters know that the city commission had unanimously referred to the state attorney allegations of Kasdin's misconduct as mayor. The commercial ended with the ominous words: "The investigation is pending."

Kasdin beat Shapiro in a runoff and was sworn in for a second two-year term. He joined two new city commissioners: the Cuban-born activist Matti Bower and the city's first Cuban American fire chief, Luis Garcia. They, along with Simon Cruz and Jose Smith, made up the first Hispanic majority in the Beach's history.

Peebles nevertheless declared himself satisfied. "I had let the community know that I valued loyalty and that if you went back on your word, there would be serious ramifications." Craig Robins, he says, pleaded with him at the end of the campaign to leave Kasdin alone.

The normally taciturn Robins told me, "Don has a bully mentality."

"Everyone likes to take a shot at me," responds Peebles. "But in the end, the Bath Club turned out to be extremely profitable, just as I predicted. Even before I broke ground, the rezoning increased the value of the land to more than $30 million, so I'd make $20 million. When it was fully developed, I'd make $50 to $60 million."

On November 20, the new city commission had its first meeting. Peebles's Bath Club upzoning was the final item on a long agenda. During the marathon fifteen-hour meeting, the commission had some important votes before dealing with Peebles. Craig Robins was proposing to change the zoning on Allison Island, on the site of St. Francis Hospital at 63rd and Collins. Robins wanted 8.5 acres on the island changed from hospital zoning to town houses and apartments. When some neighbors objected, he scaled back the size. But Robins wasn't proposing a normal development, but an ambitious $225 million community of 235 town homes and mid-rise condominium units that he said would reconcile the rift between two schools of architectural and urban planning: New Urbanism and Modernism.

"He was like the kid who comes to class way overprepared," recalls Kasdin. "It was a very bold and visionary project." Robins won unanimous approval.

Finally, the Bath Club was up for a vote. The upzoning was again approved, but this time Kasdin surprised everyone by voting yes, arguing that he had decided not to further feed his political battle with Peebles.

"It was just Kasdin playing politics," says Peebles. "My business is real estate, not politics."*

---

* On January 20, 2000, assistant state attorney Joe Centorino, who ran the state attorney's public corruption unit, closed out the investigation against Kasdin. At the end of that year, on December 11, he also closed a complaint Kasdin had filed against Peebles for improper campaign contributions.

CHAPTER 33

An "Incidental Billionaire"

I N SEPTEMBER 2000, Mayor Kasdin announced that one of the world's leading contemporary art shows, Art Basel, was coming to Miami Beach, its first venture outside its native Switzerland.

"Art Basel is the premier art fair in the world. Art Basel Miami Beach will become one of the most important cultural events on this continent and confirms that Miami Beach is one of the most important cultural destinations in the world today," Kasdin told the press. The fair would debut over five days in December 2001, and had committed to a three-year run.

Kasdin was passionate about the city's art and culture. Earlier in his tenure he had formed Miami Beach's first cultural arts council and established a program to help pay for art in public places.[*]

Within three months of the announcement, 400 exhibitors had applied and 150 of the finest contemporary art galleries had bought spaces at the Miami Beach Convention Center—numbers the organizers thought it would take three years to reach. World-class museums, including the Guggenheim in New York, the Art Institute of Chicago, London's Tate Modern, and the Georges Pompidou Center in Paris organized patrons to visit the Miami Beach fair. "It's a great idea to go to Miami," said Simone Reuter of German national television, who had covered Art Basel for a decade. "Miami is a glamour place, more enter-

---

[*] Kasdin lobbied hard to get city commission approval for the art fair. Skeptics thought it would attract few people. It was passed by only a 4–3 vote.

taining than Basel. For Europeans, it is very interesting." Patricia Vergez, an Argentinean collector, said: "Basel is the top of the top but it is a European fair, and we are Latins. We're looking forward to Miami Beach. When we come there, we will be locals."

For Carlos Betancourt, it was a sign that "the city was finally growing up. It was no longer just a place for dumping money and partying, but it was about to get an injection of culture that was going to help move it into the twenty-first century. Art Basel presented a doorway to an entirely different Beach. I was ecstatic."

One of the happiest art collectors was Portofino Tower developer Jorge Perez. His waterfront home in Coconut Grove contained a Who's Who of Latin American artists, ranging from paintings by Diego Rivera, a 2-ton marble statue by the constructivist Evér Fonseca, and sculptures by Colombian Fernando Botero.

"With Art Basel coming here," he says, "I was going to be a child in a candy store."

Perez also expected Basel to provide a sophisticated selling point that he could exploit for future development projects. When he was building affordable housing, Art Basel would not have helped his business. But by 2000, he had become the biggest developer in South Pointe—by buying Kramer's properties—and he had taken advantage of an early interest in mainland projects, especially downtown Miami.

Backed by enormous cash from his 25,000 affordable housing units, and his unblemished record of on-time, on-budget projects, Perez had a line of banks ready to do business with him. His transition from the King of Affordable Housing to the King of Condos was complete. With an inflated stock market, buyers who were flush with cash and confidence were making South Beach's luxury home market take off. After the dot.com crash in late 2000, the Federal Reserve flooded the economy with money and lowered interest rates. The historically low mortgage rates that followed, coupled with stock investors fleeing to the "safety" of real estate, further boosted Perez's business. "I did catch the right wave," he admitted.

Perez's forty-four-story Portofino Tower had cost him $10 million— a deal that by 2000 was worth $200 million. Its 228 units had sold out at prices 20 percent above his forecast. But he was too smart to put all his eggs into the Beach. On clear days, he took bankers and other developers to the top floor and pointed out his mainland projects: the Yacht Club at Brickell, a luxury high-rise apartment just south of downtown, and his 130-unit West Brickell apartments. His $550 million CityPlace ($80 million of which was taxpayer money) had revitalized West Palm Beach's dormant downtown. Covering eleven city blocks, with hundreds of condos, eighty upscale stores, and ten restaurants, CityPlace was, he says, "a model for city living." And he had just been tapped to develop 800 rental units for the long anticipated Miami One project, a four-city-block, mixed-use development in downtown.

Just a few blocks west of Portofino was Perez's Yacht Club at Portofino, the rental property in which he had cajoled Kramer into letting him become an equal partner. The city had approved the multicolored yacht club building between Biscayne Bay and Alton Road; but not before a neighborhood group had tried scuttling it, and the Design Review Board and city commission had charged it was too bulky and closed off the neighborhood's view to the bay.

One member of the Design Review Board, Arthur Marcus, a South Beach architect, labeled it "Coral Gables on steriods. . . . It's a 34-story building in the Mediterranean style. Mediterranean style was never meant to be 34 stories high. The tip of Miami Beach deserves world-class buildings, and Portofino Tower and Portofino Yacht Club aren't world-class buildings." Perez was a notorious bottom-line developer, and he could not understand the value of paying a top-tier architect whose design would cost him more per square foot but not bring in higher sales prices. "Somebody looking for a second home with an ocean view didn't care then whether the building had been designed by Frank Gehry or by a local architect they never heard of," he told me. "They were instead concerned about their views, their space, the finishing touches like kitchens and bathrooms, and most of all the price. Plus, I thought Portofino and the Yacht Club were great-looking."

By that time, Perez had also plotted another thirty-seven-story waterfront project, the luxury Murano at Portofino, on a 4.5-acre tract at 1000 South Pointe Drive, directly across from Fisher Island. The $120 million project—with its 189 condo units and 14 "bayhomes" at the water's edge, tennis courts, a fitness center, a restaurant, and a private beach and yacht club—was his most ambitious project to date. Perez had bought the empty parcel from Kramer and began selling condos at pre-construction prices ranging from $300,000 to $1.2 million. It was the first time any new units in South Pointe were priced over $1 million. It sold out while still under construction.

Perez told a reporter that he would be happy constructing one-story buildings, but as a businessman he fought for the maximum allowable density per square foot. When he said he was using his urban planning background to create neighborhoods, not just towers, few believed him. Perez's buildings were like private compounds in an urban setting. His condo owners avoided walking the still dodgy South Pointe streets by driving in and out of enclosed garages. This stifled the pedestrian street life that had been so critical in revitalizing the Art Deco District.

Despite any shortcomings, Perez was nowhere near the lightning rod that Thomas Kramer had been. "If that had been Kramer who built those towers," said Joe Fontana, "people would have been picketing at the sites and raising hell at City Hall. But Perez was playing with the ground rules that had been set, and all people could do was gripe about the zoning that was already in place."

In November, Perez signed a letter of intent to buy another prime Kramer parcel, seven acres at Fifth Street and Alton Road. He paid $52 million for land that had cost Kramer $7 million and announced plans for two condominiums. The new two-tower Murano Grande would be thirty-six stories each, and the second, an unnamed tower, forty stories.

After voters had approved Save Miami Beach, and the referendum's proponents had successfully vilified Kramer as the symbol of developer avarice, Perez knew that he had to keep his distance from the German speculator. It wasn't only a business decision; the more Perez had gotten to know Kramer, the less he liked him. "I had come to know Kramer over a couple of years," Perez says now. "He is much more than immoral, he is amoral. He doesn't know the difference between the two. But whatever his personal life, if he was great and trustworthy at business, I could have made it just a professional relationship. But I felt he would screw me in a second if he had the chance. And he didn't care about taking great risks because he was playing with things, it wasn't his money."

It wasn't possible to push Kramer out of the picture in South Pointe. Even after his November sale to Perez, he retained 13 acres in the neighborhood, including the much contested Alaska Parcel. In 2001, Kramer was back at City Hall, where Kasdin negotiated a ninety-day option for the city to buy the 3.4-acre Alaska Parcel for $7.2 million. Since South Pointe was still a redevelopment zone, the county would have to contribute half the purchase price, meaning the city could pick it up at a bargain price and end all the controversy over its development.

"We would have made it an extension of South Pointe Park," says Kasdin. "It was such a great deal for the last available waterfront property along the shore. But Dermer and Shapiro put on their populist hats and played to the crowd. They got people riled up by saying it would be a windfall for Kramer, who had bought it for just over $3 million."

The city commission rejected the deal.

"The reason was the incredible distrust on the part of the public to any dealing with Kramer," explains Frank Del Vecchio. "The old-line politicians in Miami Beach had discredited themselves so much by their opposition to Save Miami Beach that they had lost credibility with the public when it came to making deals with developers, especially Kramer."

"So, instead of a park, all we got was litigation," says Kasdin. Kramer again challenged the four-year-old Save Miami Beach, this time saying it unfairly restricted his property rights. He also contended that even if it was valid, it didn't apply to him because the development application for the Alaska Parcel was pending before the city when the ordinance passed. Miami-Dade Circuit judge Barbara Levenson rejected his unconstitutionality argument, but she agreed that Save Miami Beach did not apply to the Alaska Parcel.

Armed with that decision, Kramer went back to the city commission and asked for a tenfold increase in zoning density. Between Perez's Murano at Portofino and Portofino Yacht Club and Bruce Eichner's $450 million Continuum, a semicircular skyline of tall buildings was forming around South Pointe. Developing the Alaska Parcel would make it worse.

Community activists were alarmed. "This piece of land should be preserved for low-density development and water-related uses," Del

Vecchio told a reporter. "The city should do everything to keep it for that purpose."

In the middle of the fight with Kramer, attention was diverted by the chaos over the Memorial Day Weekend, acknowledged by almost every Beach resident and official as among the most crowded, rowdiest, and messiest in the city's history. Beach officials had not known that non-stop publicity on New York radio stations and over the Internet had promoted the holiday as an Urban Music and Fashion weekend, the ultimate party in South Beach. Rappers, sports stars, celebrity DJs, and weekend partiers descended in droves.

Thursday night, bouncers turned away hundreds of angry visitors. Saturday, the city closed the MacArthur Causeway. People walked in the middle of the streets, forcing the police to close Washington, Collins, and Ocean Drive between Fifth and 13th Streets. Riot police were deployed on Saturday evening and angry crowds at four clubs were dispersed with pepper spray. A bouncer at Level was stabbed on Sunday morning; a partier was shot at the Shelbourne. The city ordered clubs to close two hours earlier and special permits for parties were canceled for the rest of the weekend. Several hundred people were arrested over four days. By Sunday, the Beach looked like an armed camp.

Given the Beach's poor history with blacks, some wondered whether an unexpected surge of white college kids during spring break would have caused the same uproar. Activists said it proved that the Beach was interested in tourism—European, Latin American, and gay, just not black.

Mayor Kasdin took responsibility for the city's lack of preparedness and noted that hip-hop was the second-largest segment of the recording industry. While he said he had found a lot of the crowd's behavior personally offensive, "the Beach is for everyone, and we will study ways to handle our popularity so it ends up a better place for our residents, businesses and visitors." Kasdin assured the Art Basel organizers that the chaotic weekend was an exception to the Beach's ability to handle large events.

On August 26, the Planning Board agreed to convert the Alaska Parcel, with one of the most stunning vistas in Miami Beach, into a paved parking lot to accommodate visitors to the nearby city-owned marina.

The board also consented to a 20-foot "golf cart" access road to the parking lot so that marina customers could tote gear between their cars and boats. In exchange for giving up future development rights, Kramer got the city to drop its insistence that he build his long-promised baywalk. And the city also released Kramer from all obligations to make two properties available to the city for parking. "The city was so outmatched that it looked as if it was essentially negotiating for the developers," says Del Vecchio. "This was the mother of all bad deals."

The Planning Board recommendation had to be ratified by the city commission. With Del Vecchio leading the street organizing, the board agreed to a rehearing, and at a heated four-and-a-half-hour session on September 6, it reversed itself, unanimously recommending that the commission reject any changes with Kramer and keep the "low-density waterside use zoning on the Alaska Parcel."

Five days later was 9/11. On the 12th, the biggest question in the Beach was how badly tourism would be hit. *Miami Herald* columnist Lesley Abravanel admitted: "I talked to restaurant owners and people with clubs and those who had hotels, and they were only worried about business. Everyone on the Beach talked about how terrible it was while having cocktails. Except for its effect on the tourist season, it did not have much impact on the Beach."

In October, the city commission voted against Kramer and backed out of the plan to convert the Alaska Parcel into a parking lot. Kramer sued once again.

The entire fiasco created more bad blood between Kasdin and Dermer. Kasdin had accused Save Miami Beach of hurting the city in its battle with the big developers. He pointed to Perez's acquisition of seven Kramer acres for $56 million, on which he planned to build two towers. Kasdin argued that the original 1995 Portofino Settlement Agreement had given the city an option to buy those from Kramer for $11.5 million, 20 percent of what Perez paid. But the agreement fell apart one day after the Save Miami Beach referendum passed.

Del Vecchio and other activists bristled at the suggestion that trying to draw a line on overdevelopment had caused the underlying problem.

"All I know," Kasdin told me, "is that Kramer went back to court and the city just kept spending money, and it didn't have to be like that. Despite all the efforts to stop it, South Pointe was looking more and more like the high-rise ring that everyone was trying to stop."

At the end of his two-year term, Kasdin decided he had had enough of politics and announced he was returning to his legal practice. David Dermer threw his hat into the ring and focused on overdevelopment—the issue that had propelled him into office as a commissioner. Dermer's mantra was "Stop overdevelopment," a concept that sounded good to most voters.

Dermer's competition was Commissioner Nancy Liebman, and Elaine Bloom, a seventeen-year veteran of the Florida House of Representatives. Bloom came into the Miami Beach race with the best political contacts in the city's history and raised more than twice as much money as Dermer and Liebman combined. She also got Kasdin's endorsement, largely because he thought Dermer was "a classic politician who will do and say what he can to achieve his political goals."

Kasdin charged that Dermer was nowhere to be found when he, Susan Gottlieb, and Nancy Liebman were trying to roll back development in the mid-1990s. Still, activists like Del Vecchio and A. C. Weinstein of the *SunPost* were convinced that Dermer's anti-development theme was sincere, even though he got involved fairly late.

Anonymous flyers recited Dermer's nearly two-year-old divorce settlement from his ex-wife, Elyse, complete with standard mental cruelty and vicious temper clichés. That Mrs. Dermer had withdrawn three of her complaints after she received a $125,000 settlement, $2,500 per month child support, and the use of the family SUV didn't dampen the smears. Other pamphlets said Dermer was "a phony," since after winning his commission seat in 1991 he had become intimate friends with some of South Florida's top lobbyists and political insiders, including Armando Gutierrez and "Prince of Darkness" political consultant Randy Hilliard.

Bloom told me, "I had been through nine difficult elections, but never one as negative as the one in Miami Beach." Dermer supporters started a "Vote Against Corruption" crusade and replayed charges the Republicans had used against Bloom in her previous year's razor-thin loss in her congressional race. It was a murky issue about a potential conflict of interest with a pharmaceutical company of which she was a director, a matter Bloom thought had been put to rest. It forced her on the defensive, wasting valuable campaign time explaining away old news. A. C. Weinstein, an avid Dermer supporter, slammed Bloom every week in his column. A prominent Hispanic attorney and charismatic civic activist, Victor Diaz, worked hard to round up the Cuban vote for Dermer.

In the end, no candidate got a majority. Bloom took 44 percent of the vote to Dermer's 38 percent. In the runoff a week later, the personal differences between the two seemed sharper than ever. Bloom, sixty-four, was the perfectly poised, on-message political veteran. The thirty-eight-year-old Dermer looked boyish in his rumpled suits, and used his native-son status in a populist campaign that seemed more impromptu than it was.

Five days before the vote, Art Basel fell victim to post-9/11 fallout. The art fair promoters took out full-page ads in the *Miami Herald* and *The New York Times* explaining the cancellation and promising an even bigger event for 2002. The incoming mayor would preside over the weakest holiday revenue season in nearly two decades.

On election night, Dermer won with 54 percent of the vote. Seven years later, Elaine Bloom was still bitter, saying that Cuban power players had "painted me as the candidate of the Jewish Federation. It was inevitable that the Cubans would get power, but they made me an example of the power they could wield." She believes that many Hispanic voters were registered just for that election and that the Cuban community in the retirement homes had their absentee ballots delivered by "vote brokers" working for Dermer.

Across the causeway, Miami was in the midst of a mayoral runoff election. Manny Diaz, a political novice who had been Elián Gonzalez's attorney, defeated former six-term mayor Maurice Ferre. Diaz was developer-friendly and had a vision for renovating Miami's run-down downtown that was much like Jorge Perez's. The Related Group had already started buying up empty parcels preparing to lead a revival, much like Tony Goldman and Craig Robins had done in the Art Deco District fifteen years earlier.

By the close of 2001, Jorge Perez had become the state's largest developer of high-end apartments and condominiums. Including his affordable housing complexes, he had built or managed more than 40,000 residential units worth $4 billion. Perez, who once described himself to me as an "incidental billionaire, not something I ever set out to achieve," announced that he would lead the effort to build a new home for the Miami Art Museum in downtown's Bicentennial Park, and pledged a "substantial portion" of the $175 million price tag.

Perez knew that the development possibilities in Miami far outweighed the handful left in the Beach. Few waterfront parcels had not been claimed by a developer, but Perez kept his eye on the Alaska Parcel. He had an idea for his most luxurious development ever. Patience was one of his virtues, and he waited while Kramer and the city battled over the land's fate, ready to swoop in should the opportunity present itself.

CHAPTER 34

"The Most Corrupt Government"

EVEN WITH GENTRIFICATION as extreme as the towers at South Pointe, nightlife was unassailable in South Beach since it was such a powerful tourist magnet. Public officials' reluctance to enforce the club ordinances was in large part motivated by fear of denting the town's hard-partying image. But well before the new wave of upscale buildings and soaring property values, Amnesia, one of the city's most successful clubs, was notorious for keeping neighbors up late with mega-decibel noise and rowdiness.

Angry South Pointe residents had filed dozens of complaints with the city, which had sued Amnesia in 1994, when the court determined that the music was not unreasonably loud. The club had been written up for forty-six noise violations by the normally lax, club-friendly Code Compliance department. The fines totaled $23,000, and the city cited them as a basis for revoking the club's license. Amnesia persuaded a court to rule that the city's violations were inconsistently issued and therefore unenforceable. It was at this point that Frank Del Vecchio began his assault on the club.

"The noise from Amnesia funneled up from the atrium," he told me. "We were 600 feet away, have hurricane shutters on our windows, and even when we closed those, the bass was vibrating so much that we could not sleep."

When he checked records at City Hall, he learned that such a club was never meant to be allowed in a residential neighborhood like South Pointe. "Amnesia had falsely represented itself as a supper club to a city commission that had been eager to bring businesses into South Pointe after the RDA blight."

Del Vecchio knew that public officials responded only if they thought large numbers of voters were lined up behind an issue: "Amnesia was something on which I was able to rally the neighborhood." He began making nightly calls to Code Enforcement and the police, often meeting them in front of the club to ensure they followed the city's strict but seldom enforced noise regulations. So few violations were issued that there was speculation among the residents that code officers were accepting bribes. The following year, two Beach cops were arrested on racketeering and bribery charges, accused of soliciting money from several clubs to let them stay open after hours.

"The city and the club owners had never taken the residents seriously. They viewed them as complainers and eccentrics who had no real clout and they were mostly ignored." But Del Vecchio was a sophisticated opponent who understood the rules as well as the cops, club management, and the politicians.

Early in 1997, the police arrested Amnesia's manager at 4 a.m. after he failed to turn down the volume following two warnings. Del Vecchio then sketched out for the city attorney and city manager a legal case by which the city could revoke Amnesia's license. On March 27, 1997, the city cited fifteen pending violations and suspended the club's operating license. But Amnesia got a Dade Circuit judge to temporarily lift the decree. The club's attorney was Harold Rosen.

Since leaving office in 1977, the ex-mayor had built the largest roster of entertainment clients on the Beach. Before Kasdin blocked him, Rosen had access to the mayor's office whenever he was in City Hall. "As a former public official, his contempt for residents was remarkable," says Del Vecchio.

On April 1, the judge ordered the club closed for chronic violations of the noise code. Amnesia reopened five days later and won its appeal on the grounds that the city's closing was unconstitutional.

Characteristically, Del Vecchio developed a new tack. He had noticed that every weekend fire inspectors, escorted by police officers, went into clubs without notice, counting heads and checking exit doors. If they determined a bar was overcrowded, they could prevent more people from entering, and if it exceeded its legal capacity, it could be shut down for the night. Del Vecchio suggested fire inspectors issue on-the-spot citations for overcrowding or blocked exits. The city commission passed a new ordinance in April 1997 empowering fire inspectors to ticket bar and club owners immediately for code violations. Club owners complained that the new rules—based on a guideline of one person per 11 square feet—were being used for policy, not safety. Del Vecchio helped draft a second regulation that gave the city the power to restrict a club's sound system if it got five noise write-ups. That too passed, despite strong club opposition. The following year, Del Vecchio led an effort to get the city to adopt an ordinance that gave it the power to close a club after only four written violations ("I was moving toward three strikes and you're out, but knew I had to tread slowly"). The clubs said it threatened their livelihood, but the city passed it.

Yet Amnesia proved resilient. "For them," Del Vecchio points out, "all the legal costs, the fines, it was just the cost of doing business." He had used Amnesia, much as David Dermer had used Kramer, as a symbol of what was wrong in the nightlife industry. Citing the need to preserve the quality of life in South Pointe, he compiled a list of nearly 1,000 residents. Del Vecchio gave the impression of being a large organization, but he ran his campaign with only the help of his wife, Marian, from their one-bedroom apartment, dominated by boxes of paper and a commercial copying machine.

"There is nothing quite as effective as being able to know you can pack a room when you need to," says Saul Gross. "Frank could do that, and did, time and again."

Del Vecchio met with city officials and Amnesia's owners and attorneys. The city entered into a settlement for the club to add a roof over its courts, but Amnesia ignored it. Del Vecchio proposed to Kasdin that the city condemn the air rights over the club since the noise was knocking down property values. But the city attorney deemed the case too difficult and costly to pursue.

Del Vecchio was not dissuaded. In 1998, he reread the city codes and devised yet another strategy. The original license granted to Amnesia read "restaurant (bar, lounge)." That certificate of use stipulated it must serve meals when it was open. Del Vecchio suggested enforcing the "no kitchen" provision on all the Beach's clubs with the same licenses. On April 11, 1998, complaints were served at Warsaw, Groove Jet, Lua, and Salvation; if they did not start serving food within thirty days, they would be closed. "I thought it was a joke," recalls Gary James. "But then when I heard other clubs were hit, I put two and two together. It was really all directed at Amnesia, but they were just going after some of us so Amnesia couldn't say it was selective enforcement."

Club owners like James were furious they had been dragged into the South Pointe residents' war. Eric Milon, who ran the Living Room, spoke for many owners when he said, "Without the nightlife industry, there is no South Beach. There is no business, no profits. People used to come here for the Art Deco. Now they come for the nightlife. But it seems the city is always wanting to put us out of business. They are not just implementing the law. They are making your life impossible. They are trying to kill the goose that lays the golden eggs."

At the hearing on its failure to have a kitchen, Amnesia employees testified that they regularly served food. "The staff just lied," recalls Del Vecchio.

The property owner, Larry Kaine, and the building owner, Gino Falsetto, commenced a foreclosure proceeding against Amnesia, which owed $920,000 on its lease. By August 1998, four years after the battle with the club had begun, it was gone. Del Vecchio and other activists were wary. "We were worried that another owner would carry on business as usual," he said. He was right.

The place was taken over by the Milon brothers and Roman Jones (the son of Foreigner's lead guitarist Mick Jones), who had created The Opium Group. Their financier was Mitchell Rubinson, a successful Miami businessman and investor, who had recently sold his company that was the exclusive franchisee of Burger King and Domino's Pizza for Poland. The new club was called Opium Lounge, and it boasted an exotic Bangkok-meets-Beach outdoor courtyard, Opium Garden; a VIP adjunct, Prive, targeted celebs and Eurotrash.

The Opium Group claimed it wanted a better relationship with the neighborhood. "I would meet with Jones, Milon, and their attorneys," says Del Vecchio, "and after three months they appeared to have agreed to take steps to reduce the noise." By this time, Del Vecchio had become an acoustics expert. He had convinced Nikki Beach to install a thin bronze curtain on the south side of the beach club to muffle the noise that affected the Continuum condominium tower a couple of blocks south.

But the problems continued. Although The Opium Group had put a retractable roof over its open-air garden and altered the sound system, two years after taking control it was the same headache in South Pointe as Amnesia had been.

Del Vecchio figured it was time to stop dealing with the clubs one by one and to use the commission that had been elected in 2001—which now included Saul Gross—to pass citywide reforms. His first mission was to have the city ban all outdoor entertainment in South Pointe for any new clubs, restaurants, or hotels that opened (there were constitutional questions as to whether the ban could be applied to existing clubs). The fight, which stretched out over six months of contentious hearings and debates, was much like the Save Miami Beach movement. Del Vecchio and his supporters did not raise any money, while the club owners banded together to form "Save SoBe." It was a $200,000-funded political action committee that lobbied commissioners, set up a website where celebrities like P. Diddy said, "Stop the Madness," and took out newspaper ads claiming the ordinance would kill their industry. Their fear, of course, was that if that rule passed in South Pointe, it might be extended to the rest of the Beach.

The nightclub owners used their massive mailing lists to get South Beach partiers to let city officials know they did not want more club restrictions.

In June, at a standing-room-only meeting, Del Vecchio gave a twenty-minute presentation of all the past problems, the failures to live up to current agreements, and how the area had become one of the city's most promising residential neighborhoods. He asked the commission to preserve South Pointe, especially since it had previously been treated as the Art Deco District's poor cousin.

Roman Jones played to the commissioners' financial worries: "It's a pity that in a tourist destination, where people come for the sunshine

and the tropical air, the city is saying we don't want any outdoor entertainment. We are eroding the commercial areas, and the commercial
areas are what bring in tourists."

"I had noticed the city was giving conditional use permits with too
much occupancy for many special events," says Del Vecchio. "I confronted Rosen, who was the attorney for almost every special permit.
Turns out the law the city attorney relied on was defective and Rosen
was a registered lobbyist and hadn't disclosed it. I demolished him."

"He [Del Vecchio] is an arrogant son of a bitch," Rosen responds.
"Most people at City Hall can't stand him. But he's good at what he
does. I don't know how anyone can live with him, he's just obsessed
with this political stuff. Too bad he didn't stay in Boston."

The commission voted 6–1 to ban all further outdoor entertainment in South Pointe. It also agreed to beef up enforcement on noise
complaints.

Del Vecchio launched into his next campaign, threatening to roll
back the hours that any new restaurant or club could stay open in South
Pointe from 5 a.m.—the citywide rule—to 2 a.m. Even his friends told
him it was an impossible task. He enlisted the support of another
neighborhood association, Sunset Harbour, which was the only Beach
area zoned "light-industrial," but amid the towtruck companies, car repair shops, storage warehouses, and a Florida Power & Light substation
were two large residential towers. Sunset Harbour was several years behind South Pointe in development, but Del Vecchio argued to its condo
associations that if they joined him they would head off entertainment
problems.

On May 5, 2004, the commission, voted 5–2 that any bar, restaurant,
or club that opened in the South Pointe or Sunset Harbour would have
to close at 2 a.m. instead of 5 a.m. Those already in business were
grandfathered in under the bill.

Taken together, the citizen efforts—increased code enforcement, no
outdoor entertainment, no new 5 a.m. clubs or restaurants—meant that
South Pointe's residential status had earned long-overdue recognition.

During his career, Del Vecchio had had what he called "a great deal
of exposure to direct and indirect corruption"—including protection
rackets for cops, payoffs to city inspectors and code enforcers, nepotism

with public funds, hiring favors, indirect kickbacks to building inspectors, and favors to law firms and many others. But Miami Beach was an eye-opener. He took out defamation insurance after he was threatened with lawsuits, and had his phone checked to see if it had been tapped during particularly nasty fights with wealthy developers. "I am personally fearless, but that is not enough to protect your family or assets from a developer who wants to abuse the legal system," he told me. "In Miami, there is no agency tradition, no fear of oversight by another body, and no judicial system that has real peer review standards. Instead, the dominant political constituency, Cuban, is bound by loyalty, not ethics. Even the corrupt politicians up north knew they had to deliver to the communities they served, or they would be out of office. Here, the political interests are not to serve the public good, it's just all short-term thinking to help themselves. In Miami, the ingrained politicians have more control than the old ward bosses of the Northeast because here they control the banks and own the land. There are no checks and balances."

In 2003 and 2004, Del Vecchio fought a $487 million light rail system planned to run through downtown Miami and link the mainland to South Beach. He was the chairman of the Citizens Technical Subcommittee on the BayLink Study. "It was the motherlode of special interests," he says. Although marketed as enhanced public transportation, he exposed it as the brainchild of developers who wanted light rail stops at their new downtown condo towers—it would have created work for the construction industry, and profits for builders, consultants, attorneys, architects, and the unions. When that battle was over, Del Vecchio had no doubt that "public/private partnerships in Miami Dade are totally crooked. It is the most corrupt government, at almost every planning and implantation stage, I ever encountered."

ONLY ONE OTHER person in the Beach combined both a compulsive focus on single issues with a willingness to get into repeated battles with City Hall: Don Peebles. He and Del Vecchio shared nothing in common, but both knew the ins and outs of how the system worked and were excellent advocates for their cause. Del Vecchio could sway voters; in a town where fewer than 9,000 had voted in the last mayoral election, his 1,000 hard-core followers carried clout. Peeble's political power came from his money and the ability to raise and spend it freely, as he had done in the battle against Kasdin in the 1999 mayoral race.

In 2003, Don Peebles caused another political firestorm when he again asked to modify his eight-year-old Royal Palm deal. The new city commission seemed as incapable of handling him as the previous one, and Peebles once more demonstrated that the Beach was still bush league when it confronted an outsider who knew how to play political hardball.

Peebles had missed his planned 1998 opening for the Royal Palm by five years, and he had run $15 million over budget. He now blamed the city for his problems. He had two complaints. First, he charged that his old nemesis, banker Arthur Courshon, had concealed information that would have revealed structural defects and soil contamination at the Royal Palm site. City officials never allowed him to inspect the property before finalizing the deal, he contended. (Courshon said Peebles had the opportunity but never bothered to do so.) Second, Peebles insisted that even if the inspection issue were set aside, the city had misled him with an engineering report that stated the Royal Palm needed about $725,000 in interior repairs, when in fact decades of saltwater corrosion had destroyed most of its interior. The damage was so severe that city inspectors condemned the property two years after Peebles took control.

The city's response was to point out that the contract he signed explicitly stated he took the property "as is."

Peebles conjured up another of his convoluted deals, asking for permission to sell the neighboring Shorecrest as a time-share condo; by offering 150 units at $330,000 each, he could recoup his $15 million in cost overruns. As an incentive, he offered to pay the city the $4.5 million he owed on the Shorecrest in five years instead of the twenty-five stipulated under the original deal. The city tentatively agreed, with two provisos. One, the leaders of the tourism boycott and Union Planters Bank, which provided Peebles with construction financing, had to sign off on the deal. And two, Peebles had to drop his request for an extension of the time within which he could sue the city for damages.

On May 15, 2003, Peebles responded with a scathing letter to Mayor Dermer.

"First of all, they want me to use my goodwill in the black community to validate this deal," Peebles told a reporter, "as a way to make it appear that the city has been fair and equitable during this entire process. I can't do that. I don't believe Miami Beach has ever treated me fairly. . . . I didn't bring race into the equation. They did. To me, that's disrespectful. Have they ever asked a Jewish businessman to get the blessing of the Jewish community before he closes a deal with the city?"

He complained about being called "one of the most successful black developers in the country—I've never once heard anyone refer to the Loews Hotel as the Jewish-owned convention hotel. It's that kind of thinking that explains why there was a black boycott in the first place. That kind of thinking is why we have strained race relations here."

Peebles appeared before the city commission on June 1. Not having made any lease payments on the Royal Palm since November 2000, he owed the city $1 million but claimed it was in protest over the contaminated soil. He now insisted that his entire twenty-five-year payback schedule be extended to ninety-nine years, reducing his annual payments from $490,000 to about $80,000. "It's either that or turn back the clock and give me a sound building."

Peebles presented video clips and detailed charts, and even produced several Miami ministers to offer up testimonials on behalf of his philanthropic work for Miami's black churches. He intimated that if the city did not accept his new proposal, it could result in prolonged and costly litigation. He argued that if the Beach really believed in racial justice, it would enthusiastically embrace his new deal.

With that, Saul Gross, a calm, level-headed compromiser, lost his temper. "Enough is enough!" he shouted. "What you've proposed at a cost of $40 million to the taxpayers of Miami Beach is preposterous!

"You, Mr. Peebles, like to use litigation as a tactic in your transactions. In fact, in this very transaction [the Royal Palm], you've been involved in lawsuits with your partners, you've been involved in lawsuits with your engineers, you've been involved in a lawsuit with your contractor, and in my judgment you will be involved in a lawsuit with the City of Miami Beach. After eighteen months of protracted talks, I don't need months more of negotiating to dismiss this out of hand. I think it's preposterous!"

Fellow commissioner Richard Steinberg accused Peebles of playing a "race game" by betting that the Beach was afraid of "the headlines when it files suit to collect on the rent that you have not been paying."

Commissioner Jose Smith made it clear he wasn't willing to turn what was already a sweetheart deal into a $40 million giveaway.

Yet the surprises came from Matti Bower, Simon Cruz, Luis Garcia, and Mayor Dermer. They argued that Peebles had been wronged, and somehow so had the Beach. All four faced reelection, and Peebles made little secret of his intention, once again, to pour cash into the campaigns of those who supported him.

Peebles struck fear into the commissioners and mayor because he was the only Beach developer to boast about how he used his political muscle. It's illegal to contribute more than $500 to a candidate for each election. The previous November, Gross had introduced campaign finance reform that would have limited how lobbyists and campaign consultants were paid. Peebles argued that it was a waste of time.

"When I call up the general contractor," Peebles explained to the commission, "who I am paying $65 million to build a building for me, and tell him Saul Gross is a nice guy and I would like you, your company, and your employees to each contribute $500 to his campaign, I dare them to tell me no. . . . Or I'll get on my intercom, call up my comptroller, and ask him how many limited partnerships and entities do we have? He tells me 30 or so. I tell him to cut a check from each of them and give it to Commissioner Luis Garcia's campaign."

The Royal Palm had become a hornet's nest of lawsuits. Peebles had sued Clark Construction Group, the project's general contractor, for breach of contract. Clark countersued Peebles and Arquitectonica. The contractor and subcontractors filed liens on the Royal Palm and Shorecrest properties, seeking $8.7 million for unpaid work.

The city finally caved and gave Peebles his deal.

"It was the right thing for them to do," he says.

CHAPTER 35

"It Didn't Have to Be Tacky"

OCEAN DRIVE NO longer looked like the South of France. The prime corner of Fifth and Ocean was a TGI Friday's. Johnny Rockets had opened in Irene Marie's building at Eighth and Ocean. Wet Willies, a slightly modified Hooters that serves potent drinks like Sex on the Beach, had opened on Eighth Street. David Wallach's Mango's Tropical Café served up enormous drinks and platters of inexpensive food and live entertainment that included well-endowed women and muscular men, in leopard-print spandex, dancing to blaring salsa music.

Gary James returned to town in 2005 after a four-year absence. He had been arrested by a SWAT team near Miami International Airport in September 2001, and charged with being part of one of the then-largest ecstasy production and importation conspiracies. He served five years in a maximum-security prison.

"I was surprised how many people I ran into who told me they didn't remember the last time they had been to Ocean Drive," he says.

Lincoln Road looked more like the Mall of America than the quirky street he remembered. Banana Republic had taken over a historic, converted bank, the Chase Federal. Artists' studios, funky clothing stores, and offbeat furniture stores had been replaced by Gap, French Connection, Victoria's Secret, Pottery Barn, and Starbucks. An eighteen-screen multiplex showing the latest blockbusters had supplanted the closed Colony Theatre a block away.

Craig Robins had predicted seven years earlier to the *Herald* that "the days of Lincoln Road being a charming, community street are gone." Convinced that the street would go mainstream, Robins concentrated on revitalizing the moribund Design District in mainland Miami. He blamed Lincoln Road's homogenization on the Comras family, who had become the street's major landlords and acted as the primary lease agent for most of the retailers. Joseph Comras had started his New York real estate firm in 1973,* and opened a South Florida office in 1992, which his son Michael ran. Michael eventually acquired an inventory of 125,000 square feet of ground-level retail spaces.

Lincoln Road's quirkiness did not appeal to Comras. "There were three Payless Shoe Source stores, two Eckerd pharmacies, a Woolworth's, and a lot of cheesy T-shirt shops," he says. "It was only a matter of time before the national retailers would converge. . . . I knew the retailers follow the entertainment, the restaurants and the cafés, and we had the perfect venue."

"Comras is parasitic, not a visionary," says Craig Robins. "Lincoln was always going to be a very successful commercial operation, but it didn't have to be tacky. It could have been successful and still have style. Once the city and the first retail pioneers redid it, then Comras came in, rented out to high-credit tenants, and made it boring."

"Comras will rent to anyone," agrees Saul Gross. Gross, who owns thirty storefronts on Washington Avenue, had a chance just after 9/11 to rent one of his best corner spots to Starbucks. They offered 40 percent more than the current tenant, a funky clothing shop, Pop. After discussing it with his wife, Jane Dee, he decided to stay with Pop. Starbucks rented the corner directly across the street. "I made a promise to myself at that time," says Gross, "that I'd never rent to a national chain. And I still do very well, so it's possible to make money without stripping out the character to look like any-town America."

---

* Joe Comras had lunch several times with me, my wife, and Harold Rosen. When I once suggested that Miami Beach seemed more corrupt than many other American cities, he told me that after he had bought New York's famed Ansonia apartment building in the late 1970s, he had paid a NYC democratic powerhouse $1 million "as a legal fee" to arrange the removal of a bothersome ground-floor tenant, the sexual swingers club Plato's Retreat. "It's the same all over," he said in front of the ex-mayor.

Inside the clubs, says James, "it seemed a lot less gay and felt more straight." Salvation, a gay club, had become an Office Depot. The gay hard-core Loading Zone had closed. Warsaw was Jerry's Deli. And he noticed that hotels now competed with the clubs. The Shore Club, Setai, Astor, Shelbourne, and Delano all had either rooftop pools with a DJ and a bottle menu or lounge/clubs indoors. Andres Balazs (owner of L.A.'s Château Marmont) had redone the Raleigh, and it was packed. Partiers that used to go club-hopping would now do the same for hotels.

A few months before James returned, Peter Loftin, a North Carolinian who had made a couple of hundred million in his telecom firm, bought Versace's Casa Casuarina for a record $19 million and turned it into a tiny, ultra-expensive hotel and members-only club with a $25,000 fee.

One of the biggest nightlife changes was so-called celebrity appearance fees. Jerry Powers started it when he paid celebs to show up at *Ocean Drive* parties. Powers would nab them in return for first-class flights, hotel rooms, unlimited partying, and an entourage of models. Once celebs realized they didn't have to show for free, they started demanding appearance fees in cash. "It certainly seems like South Beach has stepped up the game," said Peter Katsis, senior vice president of The Firm, the Los Angeles management company that handles Leonardo DiCaprio, Cameron Diaz, and Snoop Dogg. For one Halloween party, Shareef Malnik brought Linda Blair to the Forge, in a tie-in with Level vodka. Her fee was $10,000.

"In the past, you would have thirty Linda Blairs hanging upside down in your club—and they all flew themselves down," said Forge marketing director Maxwell Blandford. "I remember Elton John sitting at the bar at Warsaw and running a tab."

Nicole Richie and Paris Hilton received appearance fees of up to $200,000. Kate Moss charged a bargain $25,000. Real estate heir Jeff Soffer paid Prince $1 million to perform at his fortieth birthday bash.

B-list celebs could still get a club or hotel to comp their trip. When Vin Diesel wanted to celebrate his birthday in South Beach, he arranged a party at Prive through The Opium Group, who flew him in first class and put him up at a poolside bungalow at the Sagamore. Xbox defrayed some of the party costs in exchange for Diesel plugging a new video game featuring his likeness.

"I used to get a list of the names and prices," says Gerry Kelly. "You were buying yourself a name that would get into the local nightlife columns and hopefully bring in people who wanted to be around that celeb. It became the cost of doing business. Matching celebrities and clubs had become part of the business model of South Beach nightlife. We'd often get one of the liquor companies or other corporate sponsors to pick up the tab to pitch their brands. Corporations added promotional events to their ad budgets. So it would become something like a Paris Hilton/Absolut evening."

George Coronado, owner of Give Me A Beat Productions, concentrated on gay venues when the straight, mainstream club scene became stale. "I'm sorry if it hurts people's feelings," he told me, "but the corporate types and the older guys chasing young models, it scared away a cooler crowd. Lots of the newest action is across the causeway, in still raw areas, and it's like the South Beach clubs of a decade ago."

"It's not a dilemma unique to Miami," said Andre Balazs. "I don't think there is a place in the country, or perhaps the world, where this sort of marketing frenzy doesn't happen within moments of a spontaneous outburst of culture."

Some cited the corporate invasion as proof that the Beach is more high-end than ever. *US Weekly* had stationed a full-time reporter in Miami. "Once we have access, we can ask the questions we really care about, like 'Who are you dating?' " said Ken Baker, West Coast executive editor of the magazine. "There is extreme begging to make sure we don't just say Paris Hilton was in Miami, but Paris Hilton was at the Sky Vodka party at the Shore Club. But we feel that's a fair exchange. It may be a corporate event, but Paris Hilton still gets up on a stripper pole. It's still young Hollywood being young Hollywood. It's still fun. And South Beach is as fun as it gets."

Every Friday, Michael Capponi invited Gary James on his yacht for a party. "I was glad for Michael that he had gotten what he wanted," says James. "But I found it interesting that he would take me out on his yacht, flash his money, boast about how great he was doing, and he never offered me a job. He still owed me $8,000 from his heroin days. I think he was always upset that he was my number two and I used to get all the attention. He's not inhuman, it's just his fear. He has no humility, and it could be his undoing."

James started a landscaping firm, Gary of the Jungle, moved into a tiny one-bedroom in South Pointe, and began throwing a Sunday party along the Miami River. "I don't think it's possible to re-create the old magic," he says, "but there's always something available in Miami if you're creative."

A few months ago, a friend gave James a copy of *Ocean Drive* in which there was an "exclusive interview" titled "The Redemption of Chris Paciello." Paciello had been released on September 8, 2006, and had tattooed the date on his wrist. The profile was done by Jerry Powers's daughter, Jacquelynn, who reportedly had always had an unrequited crush on Paciello. The layout included half a dozen fashion photos of Paciello looking more like a model than an ex-felon. Powers wrote that she and many of her friends "find it hard to believe that Chris was in jail for crimes he had committed in 1993." But, she said, "he is back in the game . . . with a swagger in his step . . . [and] is still as handsome as ever."

Asked if he might return to Miami, Paciello cited good friends who had stuck with him even through jail—Shareef Malnik and club promoter Nicola Siervo, and his "little brother" Keith. "Most people in Miami respect me. . . . Who knows if I'll end up back there one day. . . . Miami wouldn't be the same without me—and I don't mean that as an ego statement."

A few months before the profile, Paciello had been arrested in Los Angeles on a felony assault charge for beating up a man in an alley behind a club; but the charges were dropped. He told Powers, "Stupidity once again. Me and my temper."

"Serving time changed me," says Gary James. "It was a humbling experience that made me realize it was time to redirect my life. But Chris seems ready to reclaim his old glory. I'd advise him to do it in Los Angeles, where he's a new face. No matter what he thinks, South Beach isn't kind to yesterday's stars."

CHAPTER 36

"You Deserve to Be Paid for Your Vote"

O N DECEMBER 16, 2007, Alex Daoud, about 80 pounds over-weight, his curly hair flecked with gray, paced up and down the rear hallway of Books & Books in Coral Gables. Dressed in a tight navy blue suit and sweating profusely, he was promoting his long-promised, self-published memoir, *Sins of South Beach: The True Story of Corruption, Violence and the Making of Miami Beach.* Clocking in at 493 pages, it was payback time for the disgraced former mayor.

After serving seventeen months in prison, Daoud had returned to the Beach in 1995. He worked for a car alarm company, delivered flowers, and then scraped together money by renting out a couple of converted apartments in the back of his late mother's house. There, surrounded by a chaotic jumble of old newspapers, discarded pizza boxes, vitamin bottles, cat food bags, and an exercise bike gather-ing dust in a corner, Daoud told anyone who stopped by that he was writing an exposé that would "blow the lid off Miami Beach." After a few years most people had stopped believing he'd ever produce any-thing.

The crowd was standing room only, well over a hundred people. Flanking Daoud were two female bodybuilders. They wore tiny black T-shirts and minidresses with the title of Daoud's book picked out in rhinestones across their chests. He hugged them both and told the au-dience that the brunette had a cameo on *Miami Ink* (a cable TV show about tattooing). Pointing to the two girls, he said, "These are the sins of South Beach. If I did this when I was married, I'd be re-indicted." When someone's cell phone rang, he cracked, "If that's my ex-wife, I'm not here. If it's my psychiatrist, I'll pay the bill tomorrow." He was like a bad warm-up act.

Then he started telling his tale. Anyone who had read the few interviews he'd eagerly given since he was out of prison, knew well how as mayor he had helped usher in redevelopment between his many escapades of sex, corruption, sex, vigilante justice, sex, and finally his conviction on bribery charges. But now most of his reminiscences were about finding Elsie Cohen, the badly beaten Auschwitz survivor who was mugged, rather than describing his misdeeds.

Before taking questions, he said: "When I walked as a young boy on the beach, I saw a starfish, and I started to pick it up and throw it back so it could live. And the waves were getting rougher. This old man called out to me and said, 'Who really cares?' I picked up that starfish and put it in the water, and told him, 'I care. It matters.' Thanks for throwing me back and giving me a second chance."

The questions were all softballs, but one woman asked: "What is so appealing about being a politician when you knew it was all corrupt?"

"You are a rock star when you are a politician. I had power. Young women would ask, 'What are you doing tonight?' I loved the ink, I loved the attention, and everyone came up to me and said, 'Mr. Mayor.'"

Frank and Marian Del Vecchio were sitting in the front row. Frank shook his head and said to a friend, "He's not as good as Buddy Cianci" (the mayor of Providence, Rhode Island, who had been convicted in 2001 of a racketeering conspiracy).

Daoud's book wasn't a complete history of Miami Beach, or even his tenure in office. But the omissions paled in comparison to one thing he did include: he "gave up" his old friend, Harold Rosen. Rosen, at eighty, still rode a Harley-Davidson, hung out on Lincoln Road with his contemporary, Joe Comras, and whistled at girls. According to *Sins of South Beach*, Daoud had run into Rosen in the commission chambers after a public hearing one evening, when he stopped to retrieve his attaché case. After some small talk, Rosen pointed to the large gold medallion of the city that hung behind the mayor's chair, and asked Daoud what was in it.

"A palm tree."

"No, it isn't a palm tree; it's a money tree. And that money can all be yours."

"What are you trying to say?"

"Look, Alex, you make a measly ten thousand dollars a year as mayor. That isn't enough to pay your expenses. Being mayor is a tough job, a job you deserve to be paid generously for. I know because I sat in that same chair you're sitting in and earned the same crummy ten grand a year while trying to survive financially. They call it public service. In reality, you end up unable to pay your bills while everyone's using you without any compensation. And how do the citizens repay you for all of your noble efforts? They vote you out of office after one term. Look at what's happened to the last ten mayors."

"Is that the way it's always been?" I asked, playing for time.

"This is the way it's always been, the way it is, and the way it will always be. Politics in Miami Beach is no different from politics in any other large city, just dirtier, tougher, and with more money involved—at least for a smart mayor like you. You're good. You proved it today, and you deserve to be paid for your vote. You might even get reelected—you're that good."

Daoud asked Rosen how it worked. Rosen told him that he would come to Daoud on certain issues and pay him for his vote. " 'Just like the one today, except you'll get paid for it.' " Rosen said they'd split the money, given by developers, lobbyists, investors, businessmen, lawyers, and others wanting to do business with the city.

All wealthy developers wanting my vote were referred to Rosen. I began to accept the fact that, as mayor, everyone wanted to take their pound of flesh from me, and they could, just as long as they paid the price. We began to make money, lots of money. I received $25,000 from Rosen for voting in favor of the Gold Club, a topless nightclub that opened in South Beach. Rosen introduced me to many different developers and businessmen who made us money. Out of all the developers and the movers and shakers that passed through the mayor's office, there was one who was special. Tom Daly was a very successful builder that wanted to develop a hotel in South Beach. He paid Rosen a lobbying fee of $25,000, which of course we divided.*

At his peak, Daoud averaged $20,000 monthly in legal retainers, and that didn't count the votes he sold to Rosen, which he was "becoming adept at doing."

When the Feds threatened that he would do Rosen's prison sentence unless he gave him up, Daoud held steadfast solely because Rosen had paid respect to his deceased mother by attending her funeral. Daoud was impressed that Rosen was the "only co-conspirator who had the guts to show up."

So why did Daoud throw Rosen under the train in his book?

"He should be in prison. He should have had his life ruined like mine was ruined. I am liberated now. I don't care."

The most surprising thing about Daoud's disclosure is that it caused no fallout at all. Not a single television or radio news program mentioned it. The *Miami Herald* assigned a reporter and photographer to interview Daoud and take pictures, and then killed the story. It was as if New York's mayor David Dinkins had been convicted of bribery while in office, and when he got out of jail, wrote a book in which he said that former mayor Ed Koch had been his bagman. It's hard to imagine that such accusations would not be all over *The New York Times*.

When I ask Rosen about Daoud's charges, he says, "He's a liar, but I'd rather not give him any more ink by talking about it."

Daoud's riposte: "I always said I'm willing to take a polygraph against anyone," he says, while munching on an oversized candy bar. "I'm just the unlucky one who got caught."

---

* Daly told me that Rosen had done only legal work for him; whatever Rosen did with the money was his choice, but Daly adamantly denied ever giving Rosen payoff money.

CHAPTER 37

"A Twenty-first-Century City"

O N THE THURSDAY of the 2004 Memorial Day Weekend, a line of would-be buyers started forming before 6 a.m. at Jorge Perez's Plaza on Brickell condominium towers in Miami. One thousand units went on sale at 9 a.m. The building was in the planning stages and wouldn't be finished for at least a year. Many of those waiting to buy had no intent of living in their condos. They were the modern-day binder boys who expected to flip their contract to another buyer at a profit before the building was even finished.

By the end of the day, Perez had sold all the units, ranging from $170,000 to $500,000. "That's the new Miami," one of his Related Group sales reps told the disappointed buyers who were turned away.

Perez and other major developers encouraged the speculative trend by keeping deposits low at 10 percent of the condo's price, and allowing one "owner" to flip to a new buyer before the building was completed. Also, they built their own price increases into each project so that everyone knew the pre-construction prices set on the first day of sales were the lowest the units would ever carry. There were automatic 10 percent increases when the ground was broken, again when the foundation was poured, and usually once more as the building neared completion.

For the Brickell project, Perez could have scheduled office appointments in the order the reservation checks arrived and signed the paperwork without the public zoo. But long lines of people waiting in hot weather created news interest and the obligatory article in the *Miami Herald*—"Plaza on Brickell Condos Stir up Frenzy"—that created the impression Perez wanted: good times had arrived and more was to come. It was hard to have a conversation in South Florida that wasn't about real estate. Most people could rattle off the price per square foot of new projects. Many knew friends who had just flipped condos for fast profits, making others who weren't doing it feel as though they were somehow missing the easy money.

By the time of the one-day Brickell sellout, 17,000 residential units were under construction or announced, for a fifteen-block stretch of downtown Miami, four times what had been built in the previous decade. But despite dozens of office buildings, the new American Airlines Arena, and Performing Arts Center, downtown was desolate at night and did not even have a grocery store. The seventy-four-story Metropolitan Tower landed the first major yuppie draw, a 60,000-square-foot Whole Foods; but like every other building that filled the ad pages of the *Miami Herald* and *Ocean Drive*, the Metropolitan was but an empty lot with a great website and a glossy brochure.

This was the beginning of flip funds, in which investors pooled money to buy blocks of pre-construction units, up to 30 percent of a building, for 15 percent off the asking price. The highest-profile fund, The Formula, was started by a paralegal who had convictions for theft and insurance fraud and two heirs to a Dunkin' Donuts fortune. Soon one of the partners told a reporter they were "rolling in dough."

By the end of 2004, 40,000 condos were being built in Miami-Dade; more than half had gotten approved in the last six months of the year. In a year-end retrospective, the *Herald* noted that 2004 would be remembered as the "kick off of South Florida's real estate boom." (A year later, the *Herald*'s parent company, Knight Ridder, sold the 10 acres surrounding its faded, gulag-style headquarters for $190 million to a consortium of developers calling themselves Citisquare, that announced plans to build three 64-story condos, a hotel tower, and a massive retail center on the site.)

International Sales Group, one of Miami's largest retail brokers, started flying in foreign brokers, routinely spending $100,000 for a weekend of parties and presentations. Two thirds of the company's preconstruction sales came from Latin America, and the foreign brokers got larger commissions. At Marina Blue, a fifty-eight-story tower on the Miami edge of Biscayne Bay, 70 percent of the 517 units went through foreign brokers. A week after the sales office opened at Jade Beach, a luxury 51-story, 248-unit complex in Sunny Isles, a Mexican broker brought in forty-eight deposit checks, each for $25,000. A broker in Argentina sold twenty-two units. A leading Miami Beach realtor, Jeff Morr, dubbed Venezuelan president Hugo Chavéz his "salesman of the year" because fears about his socialist policies made über-wealthy Venezuelans his biggest customers.

Turkish-born Mehmet Bayraktar proposed a $480 million complex on Watson Island that included two high-rise hotel towers, shopping and restaurant space, a museum, and a park. The centerpiece would be a fifty-slip mega-yacht marina for boats up to 465 feet long—Miami Beach's marina could moor yachts only up to 120 feet. New York developers arrived in force. One called the Midtown Group spent $34 million for Miami's Buena Vista Railyards, a 56-acre industrial wasteland, and unveiled plans for a twenty-two-block neighborhood of offices, retail shops, and upscale condo towers with 3,000 homes. In July, Leviev & Boymelgreen Developers plopped down $130 million for fourteen empty parcels in Miami and the Beach. Three months later, they spent another $20 million for a city block at 30th and Biscayne and presented plans for a forty-five-story condo.

It was a once-in-a-generation opportunity for Miami to invest in some urban planning, but there was no political leadership, and the public was seduced and distracted by soaring home values. With no direction, Miami's planning department approved the projects one by one without any understanding of what the patchwork of buildings would do to the cityscape.

Miami Beach also abrogated overall design planning. Preservationists had kept some semblance of balance in the originally low-rise Beach, but in an overheated market, developers carried the day. Jorge Perez had won the final battles for his South Pointe project. Next to the city-owned marina, and half a block from the affordable housing complex, Rebecca Towers, he finished three 37-story towers, the Murano Grande, and announced the forty-story Icon at the very entrance to the beach. Perez, who had once believed there was no reason to pay extra for a star architect, hired Philippe Starck to design the Icon interiors. Perez gave him a small equity in return for his name on the ads and all the promo. "You are where you live" was the ad line.

"I certainly was able to charge an extra amount per square foot because of his name," Perez told me. "People had begun looking at apartments like designer clothes, and while they might not be able to live in an original Frank Lloyd Wright, they could at least buy from me an apartment designed by Starck."

One of the early Icon buyers was Julio Bermudez, the cocaine cowboys' master boat smuggler. He had retired from the trade without getting arrested, and investing in real estate—all cash—was his favorite new pastime.

Most important for Perez, in 2004 the city finally reached an agreement on the seven-year-long fight over Kramer's Alaska Parcel. Kramer sold the land, plus several adjacent properties, to Perez. Perez initially negotiated with city officials and then sued under a Florida law that allowed a developer to sue a city if its actions reduced a property's value. Del Vecchio and the residents made certain the city did not drop its resident-friendly insistence that the land be used as parkland. With an anti-development mayor and commission, the outcome hung in the balance until mid-2004. Then the city caved. In exchange for Perez's dropping his lawsuit and agreeing to build only one tower, the city gave him the zoning rights for a wide, twenty-two-story building. In return, Perez gave the city two acres for parkland.

Dermer and the commissioners had decided they could not bypass the opportunity to cash in on the real estate boom. South Pointe, the small neighborhood the RDA had wanted to demolish as a blighted eyesore, soon brought in 17 percent of all city tax revenues.

"There was a plan to make the park a great opportunity, an active, beautiful, educational space for the whole community," said Frank Del Vecchio. "It would have been a super green addition to the city. It was extremely disappointing that after so much work and input, the commission glossed over this in favor of commercial use."

Commissioner Jose Smith said it "could have been worse." If Perez had won his suit, he could have built a forty-story building. For the

Alaska Parcel, Perez planned his most luxurious and expensive Beach building: Apogee. Three penthouses sold at pre-construction prices of $22 to $25 million. One was bought by Raul Casares. A broker who sold many of the units was Joe Martino, who like Bermudez had emerged from his cocaine-smuggling days without an arrest or conviction.

All the new luxury projects chased the same buyers. Real estate ads in the *Miami Herald* tripled from the year before. One third of *Ocean Drive*'s monthly 500 pages consisted of ads touting each new condo as paradise found. Sales launch parties exemplified the frenzy. Real estate developers spent from $100,000 to $500,000 for bashes for 1,000 to 2,000 guests (regulars included Pam Anderson, Ryan Seacrest, and Mickey Rourke, local reporters, real estate agents, socialites, South Beach players, and of course, models), all in the hope that the post-party buzz would create instant sales. Everglades-on-the-Bay, a Bis-cayne Boulevard condo tower, created a fog-strewn jungle complete with fauna, a Florida panther, a baby alligator, and squawking parrots. Others had Cirque du Soleil–style acrobats and mimes; waitresses as "living tables," the hors d'oeuvres laid out on their bodies; and go-go dancers clad in bodypaint. Stealing another page from the nightclub playbook, developers often got liquor companies to co-sponsor the events in return for joint branding. Onyx 2 on Miami's waterfront paid for actress Tara Reid's airfare and hotel bill in exchange for her hosting its party. Three Brickell Avenue condo projects threw a joint party that included chocolate fondue fountains and mini-massages. Guests were shuttled from site to site by stretch Hummers.

"Those real estate parties became one big joke," *Herald* nightlife columnist Lesley Abravanel told me. "Night after night, week after week, gift bags with slick brochures ended up in the garbage. All every-one cared about were free drinks, food, and maybe a celeb sighting or two."

"It was the most amazing example of conspicuous consumption," said Linda Lee, a *New York Times* editor and author who had moved to Miami in 2004 to launch *Inside/Out*, Jerry Powers's magazine about ar-chitecture, design, and style. "Sales centers had no other purpose than to get you to think, 'There is no better place I'd want to live.' And they worked. I wanted to move into every single sales center. Then they are taken apart and destroyed."

To sell their sixty-seven-story Marquis, Leviev & Boymelgreen spent $1 million to fix up the shuttered Howard Johnson's restaurant on their Biscayne parcel with marble floors, zebra wood, and flat-screen TVs playing live bay views. It was all demolished at the start of construction a few months later, but the developers considered it a project expense, one half of 1 percent of their total construction budget. Canyon Ranch, the luxury spa conglomerate, sold $600 million in condos from its $1.7 million six connected trailers that even included a mock climbing wall for the spa preview.

Perez's Apogee sales center alone cost $2 million. "When you're going to spend $4 million or $7 million for a unit at Apogee, you need to see what you're buying," said Tom Daly, who worked with Perez. "Apogee is for a certain market. Which is why when we have a dinner party here, we serve Dom Pérignon and Château Margaux. Nobody should think they have something better at home right now than what we have to offer here."

When Art Basel rolled into town for its third year during the first week of December 2005, developers and brokers had muscled their way into the event. As Perez told Tom Daly: "The buyers of great homes and art are the same." Terra International timed the debut of its sales center for its 60-story, 561-unit condo tower, 900 Biscayne Boulevard (the project was still on the drawing board), with Basel's opening night. The developer flew in the New York installation artist Jenny Holzer to unveil a new sculpture at the sales office. For Craig Robins, Basel was a perfect convergence of his interests in art and design. It allowed him to showcase the Design District (eventually, he would develop Design Miami, a concurrent show with Basel), and to sell Aqua, his New Urbanism community in Miami Beach built on the site of the old St. Francis Hospital. He hosted 3,000 people on a VIP tour through the Design District and had 15,000 visitors for his Art Basel Street party, for which the city closed off three blocks in the district.

Ian Schrager struck a deal to convert the Shore Club into a condo-hotel. It was a play off the old time-share concept, but now each unit was sold as if it were a regular condo. The new buyer could live in the apartment or rent it out nightly as a hotel room, and the developer's hotel management company ran the rentals for a percentage of the nightly room rate. Condo-hotel sales let a hotel pass most of its debt and operating costs onto unit owners while raising millions of dollars in cash up front. "It was a win-win for any developer who had land zoned for a hotel," said one broker.

Although Schrager had had financial challenges in recent years— including his San Francisco hotel, the Clift, in bankruptcy protection and a frantic scramble to refinance $355 million in debt—he claimed his portfolio was strong enough to raise the necessary cash.

Schrager planned to spend $25 million in renovations to the Shore Club in order to add kitchens and convert the 325 hotel rooms into 240 larger units, with money from the advance sales. He pegged starting prices at $400,000 for the smallest rooms and a three-level penthouse at $22 million. Schrager had plenty of competition. Paul Makarechian, a California real estate developer, and Sam Nazarian, a thirty-year-old nightclub owner and movie producer, whose father is the multi-billionaire founder of chip maker Qualcomm, bought the Ritz Plaza and hired the ubiquitous Philippe Starck after his non-compete contract with Schrager expired. The $100 million renovation would be split between regular hotel rooms and condo-hotels.

Schrager also planned three new hip hotels, in downtown Miami, Orlando, and North Beach. The last was a neighborhood that had missed out on South Pointe's gentrification, the restorations in the Art Deco zone, and the concrete canyon takeover of mid-Beach. The island's most laid-back area, it was filled with small apartment buildings and some stores and restaurants. Yet Schrager believed it was only a matter of time until the boom extended the seventy-plus blocks further north. "I think it's the Golden Age down here," Schrager told a reporter. "It's no longer this tropical resort going through these boom and bust cycles."

Four blocks north of the Shore Club, at the site of the old Holiday Inn, W Hotels planned a 19-story, $200 million oceanfront luxury outpost boasting 425 condo-hotel rooms starting at $500,000 and running to $18 million. New York's Meatpacking District Hotel Gansevoort announced an ambitious renovation of half of the block-long

Roney Palace, into 259 condos, 102 condo-hotels, and 250 straight hotel rooms.

Don Peebles got the highest price ever paid for a hotel in Miami Beach when he sold his Royal Palm in December 2004 for $128 million. Peebles pocketed a $48 million profit. The buyers were developers Robert Falor and Guy Mitchell. They announced plans to turn the Royal Palm into a condo-hotel. Falor unveiled a deal in which Nicky Hilton licensed her name to his two other hotels, the Edison and the Breakwater, establishing a new low for hoteliers trying to leverage star power into higher room rates and profits.

Real estate heir Jeff Soffer bought the Fontainebleau with Glenn Schaeffer, former head of Las Vegas's Mandalay Bay Casino, and announced plans for a stunning $1 billion renovation.

Ross Klein, a Miami Beach native and W Hotels senior vice president and chief of marketing, said, "I remember when the Warsaw Ballroom was for sale for $18,000 and it couldn't be financed because everyone thought it was too much money. I sometimes have to check out some of the landmarks to remind myself it's the same town, the changes have been so tremendous."

South Florida's real estate boom outpaced the country's. National single-family homes had jumped 15 percent in the year, a record, but Miami-Dade's prices jumped twice as high over the same period. Thirty percent of sales above $350,000 in the Miami–Miami Beach area were with interest-only loans, much more than the national average. Nearly a quarter of all the homes and condos were bought with less than 5 percent down.

That spring my wife, Trisha, and I visited Jorge Perez's Icon Brickell, adjacent to the Miami Circle and Brickell Park. By 2008, three ultramodern glass towers, ranging from fifty-two to sixty stories, would rise on that five-acre plot. A veritable small town, it would have 1,800 residences, with pre-construction prices starting at $400,000 and running to $10 million for sky lofts and bayfront lanai-style town houses. In a town where 7,000 condominiums were built throughout the 1990s, 63,000 luxury condos were on the drawing board. Perez had more than fifty other major projects under way worth some $8 billion, more than at any time in Related's history.

In 2005, Perez made the cover of *Time* as one of the twenty-five most influential Hispanics in America. The Related Group was recognized as the country's biggest Hispanic-owned business. The University of Miami named its architecture center after Perez (thanks to a generous donation). And that same year, he broke into the *Forbes* wealthiest 400 list, at #197, worth an estimated $1.8 billion. His friend Donald Trump called Perez the "Tropical Trump" and convinced him—although Perez needed little persuasion—that he was famous enough to be his own brand. Trump wrote the foreword to Perez's book *Powerhouse Principles*—about how to get rich in real estate. Enormous billboards in Sunny Isles showed Perez, Trump, and a local father and son developing team, the Dezers, who were building three luxury condo towers on the beach. In Las Vegas, Perez had become the largest developer almost overnight. "Vegas and Miami are similar," he told me. "We're at the beginning of a great trend for both."

His biggest Vegas project was the $4 billion Las Ramblas, a gargantuan condo-and-casino complex comprising eleven towers, 4,400 hotel, condo-hotel, and condo units, with restaurants, nightclubs, and a casino, on 25 acres just off the Strip. Ads for Las Ramblas showed Perez and two of the project's smaller investors, George Clooney and Whiskey Bar creator Rande Gerber.

A few weeks before I met Perez at Icon Brickell, broker Jeff Morr told the *Herald*, "I think he [Perez] is going overboard in the number of units he is bringing to market on an annual basis. He has the potential of slowing down the market because of oversupply."

"You can't believe the heat I took for that afterwards," Morr told me. "You would have thought I said he murdered someone. People wanted me to apologize as though somehow I was raining on the parade."

Perez knew that while Florida had had only four quarters of declining prices in recent years—two in 1976 and two in 1994–95, the least of any state—it had had the mother of all U.S. housing crashes, the land bust of the mid-1920s, when buyers dried up after a disturbingly similar property explosion. Was he worried about the market's extreme vertical ascent?

"Real estate is cyclical. There will be correction, and the herd will follow just like they did with stocks in 2000. But I have a lot of cash, great locations that won't lose much value in any downturn, and I can ride it out. Other developers might not be so lucky."

He looked at the tractors on the Icon Brickell site. "There's a crane on every other corner. What we are doing here will help make Miami a twenty-first-century city, one of the world's greatest cities. You'll know I'm wrong one day if you find me under a bridge."

CHAPTER 38

The Crash

THE HOUSING MANIA reshaped the local economy and pushed South Florida into the ranks of the nation's least affordable places to live. By the beginning of 2006, Miami Beach home prices had increased a whopping 250 percent over four years, the largest jump since the 1920s boom. In January, the *Miami Herald* for the first time called the four-year upturn a "housing bubble." In the first three months of the year, the number of homes and condos for sale had doubled, fed by sellers hoping to cash in on the record prices and the 67,000 new condos in the construction pipeline. But it was taking longer for condos to sell and the days of projects opening and selling out were over. Jorge Perez didn't have to see any sales figures. His pre-construction sales at the Icon Brickell were very slow. Perez privately told Daly it was an expected cooling off after such a long run of surging prices, but he didn't think the market would turn south by any significant amount or duration.

By April, South Florida's home sales had fallen by 30 percent from the start of the year. But for the most part, prices hadn't budged—they were down only 2 percent in a year. It was a standoff. Sellers wanted what other sellers had gotten at the peak. Everyone who had a place for sale knew a friend or neighbor who had sold a similar home a few months earlier for an astronomical amount.

When a reporter caught up with Perez a month later and asked him if the market was about to nose-dive, he dismissed the talk. "Things are definitely slowing," he said. "There has been a great amount of construction, some overbuilding. . . . Speculators have almost dropped out of the market and sales have slowed down. And I think those people who should never have been in the development business—because everybody became a developer in the last few years—will suffer."

David Lereah, the prestigious chief for the National Association of Realtors, visited Miami in June, and in widely covered comments said that any long-expected shakeout would be healthy for the market and that the underpinnings of South Florida property were strong. He told reporters that the market was so good that he was looking for some investments himself. A week after his talk, the Florida Association of Realtors reported a 46 percent drop in condo sales from a year earlier. But prices were up 2 percent. It was further evidence that though sellers weren't budging, buyers had stopped buying. The residential market was frozen.

The chairman of the Federal Reserve, Ben Bernanke, told Congress in August that "any downturn in the housing market so far appears to be orderly," and that he expected home prices to rise only 3 percent to 4 percent for the year, versus the double-digit gains of the past several years. In October, the Fed's vice chairman, Donald Kohn, said that a "cyclical correction was under way," and that letting some of the speculative air out of the system would stabilize prices. The headlines made average home sellers nervous. One way to boost sales caught on like a fever in Miami's Catholic community: burying a small statue of St. Joseph upside down somewhere on the sale property. Stores sold out of the four-inch plastic statues that were dubbed the "underground real estate agent." The *Miami Herald* devoted a front-page business section story to "Praying for Profits." One broker whose condo had languished for months sold ten days after putting a St. Joseph into her balcony planter. "Every time I've put a statue in a property, it's sold," she said.

Despite the slowing sales, Jorge Perez insisted on pushing ahead. Early in 2007, a year after the first warning signs, he spent nearly $1 million in legal fees and lobbying to win a tough 3–2 Miami City Commission vote for the approval of Grove Bay Residences, three 32-story towers in Coconut Grove on land zoned for only hospital use. Residents charged that the towers were completely out of scale with their low-rise community, and historical societies opposed the development because it would rise directly behind the historic Villa Vizcaya, casting a shadow over the museum and gardens. Perez countered that Miami was grow-

ing so fast that the ultimate choice would be whether people preferred
high-rises in their own communities or wanted to "open up the Everglades." When he won the vote, he said, "This is one of the most incredible sites in the City of Miami. Every residence will have unobstructed
water views."

HOUSING PRICES BEGAN collapsing in the midst of a mayor's race
in Miami Beach between two commission members, the activist Matti
Bower, now sixty-seven, and the fifty-year-old investment banker
Simon Cruz. With either, the city would elect its first Cuban mayor. (In
1997, when Cruz had beat Bower by only 100 votes to become the first
Cuban commissioner, he told the *Herald* that he would "one day become the city's first Hispanic mayor.")

The Beach was at a critical juncture. It had already committed to
$800 million worth of capital improvement projects due to be finished
by 2012 and had the highest legacy costs—retirement plans for city
workers, plus fire and police—in the state. If property prices continued
falling, real estate taxes would not match the rosy figures in city budgets. How could the capital projects be completed without compromises elsewhere? Neither candidate tackled the tough issues; they ran as
though the Beach were somehow immune to whatever happened on
the mainland. They considered the condo glut a mainland problem and
pointed out that the Beach's small commercial market was thriving.
The eight-story Lincoln Place at 16th and Washington sold for a record
$62 million in late 2006, followed by the $74 million sale of the Lincoln,
a Scott Robins–Don Peebles–Michael Comras development.

The politicians acknowledged the dark side to the housing boom:
median home prices had reached ten times the household income in
Miami Beach, meaning that home ownership was out of reach for most
residents. Homelessness and the need for affordable housing had increased, but neither candidate suggested how City Hall might prepare
for a prolonged downturn. Instead, the campaign devolved into one of
personalities. Cruz was cast by his foes as the candidate of big developer
money and nightclub interests. Michael Capponi loaned the Opium
contact list to the Cruz campaign and volunteered as an unpaid strate-

gist. *Ocean Drive* ran a fawning profile a month before the election entitled "Miami Beach's Next Mayor?" Harold Rosen was an enthusiastic
Cruz supporter.*

Endorsed by Mayor Dermer, Del Vecchio, and Cuban powerhouse
Victor Diaz, Matti Bower ran as the underdog. Cruz raised $370,409 to
Bower's $83,000. Unassuming, and therefore underestimated, the petite
Bower was every bit a match for the smoother and more ambitious
Cruz. She campaigned the old-fashioned way, walking around the city,
knocking on doors and talking to citizens, condo and neighborhood
associations, asking them about their concerns just as Alex Daoud and
Saul Gross had done.

The campaign's single issue was real estate. Mount Sinai Hospital
wanted to rezone its Miami Heart Institute property for high-rises.
Nearby mid-Beach residents vehemently opposed the change, as did
Bower. Cruz backed Mount Sinai, but came under fire because his campaign coffers were filled with the hospital's donations. When polls
showed that his support for upzoning cast him as "developer-friendly,"
he introduced a bill to the commission to issue a $95 million bond to
buy the Mount Sinai land—at a generous profit for the hospital—and
convert it into a city park. Bower then attacked him for using taxpayer
money to put profits into the pocket of one of his biggest contributors,
the same attack Dermer had used to defeat Kasdin's proposal to use
public funds to buy Kramer's Alaska Parcel and turn it into a park.

Del Vecchio pointed out that the commission needed voter approval
for such an expensive bond. Cruz backtracked and said he'd put it on
the ballot once elected.

It would not have been a Miami Beach election without dirt. Volunteers stood outside David's Cuban Café on Lincoln Road distributing
free DVDs of Cruz's glamorous blond wife in Emmanuelle-type soft
porn films. Randy "Prince of Darkness" Hilliard ran Cruz's campaign.
Since he had last run a Miami Beach campaign—including two earlier

---

* My wife appeared in a television ad for Cruz. I did not endorse either candidate
since I was then the president of SOFNA (South of Fifth Neighborhood Association),
which represented residents in South Pointe and worked in tandem with Del Vecchio
on quality of life issues.

ones for Bower—he was named an unindicted co-conspirator and
given immunity from prosecution for helping the FBI in a corruption
probe into the mayor and county attorney in Key West. His handiwork
was soon evident. In an inflammatory mailing titled "Who Will Protect
Us?," Cruz attacked Bower for voting against $10,000 for increased se-
curity at the town's revered Holocaust Museum. When Bower countered that Cruz was in the pocket of big-money contributors, his
defense was: " 'If you can't take their money, drink their liquor, mess
with their women and [then] vote against them, you should not be in
politics.' " The Bower campaign used it as a TV ad.

Bower won in a runoff. A month after the election, the city commission, to the delight of preservationists and activists, limited the height
and density of any future buildings at the Miami Heart campus to
single-family homes and a five-story apartment complex.

IN DECEMBER 2007, Art Basel reported record sales and average
price increases of 20 percent from the year before. For the real estate developers, Basel was tantalizing evidence that there was still a lot of
money to be spent.

Perez was so confident that he tried to buy the Miami Dolphins for
$1.1 billion. But as the market deteriorated, the Dolphins deal never got
off the ground. The end-of-year figures were stunning. Smaller developers who had rushed in to get city permission for two or three mid-sized
projects suddenly threw up FOR SALE signs at their parcels in downtown
Miami, with "Already Approved for Development" as an inducement.
Cameo Apartments, on N.E. Fourth Avenue, became a symbol of the
downturn. The tenants in the former fifty-six-unit building, with affordable rents, had been pushed out in 2006 after the city gave the thumbs-
up to Portico Towers, a 324-unit luxury condo. But the two untested
developers weren't able to raise money and the Cameo ended up a gutted
shell, a hideaway for junkies and the homeless. Reeking of urine and
moldy food, it had been stripped of every bit of salvageable metal, down
to the light sockets. Instead of a new building providing extra taxes to
city coffers, the Cameo and others like it collected code violations.

The Related Group's revenues slumped 53 percent. More than

71,000 residential property owners in Miami-Dade (one out of every sixteen households) were behind on property taxes, and delinquencies were growing fast. With a majority of his projects' units still under construction, Perez pulled the plug on Las Vegas's Las Ramblas and gave the green light to Icon Brickell.

By late 2008, it was 1926 all over again. In some Miami high-rises, the foreclosure rate was as high as one in four, and owners who stayed got nailed with huge assessments to make up for the lost revenue. Florida banks repossessed 620 percent more properties than in 2007 and began dumping non-performing mortgages for as low as 30 cents on the dollar. Miami topped the *Wall Street Journal*'s list of America's worst housing markets, just ahead of Orlando. Developers feared that up to 40 percent of the speculators who had waited on lines to buy pre-construction condos might walk away from their investments. Many had turned to a new cottage industry: get-your-deposit-back lawyers. The Related Group, like other developers, faced a cascade of lawsuits, mostly from buyers trying to get out of contracts. "The ambulance chasers are everywhere," Perez said. "We've gone from euphoria to panic in a year." He shook his head in dismay.

As bad as the numbers were, South Florida hadn't hit bottom. The glutted Miami market had a five-year inventory. Twenty-two thousand more condos were under construction, doubling the supply, even though projects were still being canceled. Perez pulled the plug on three planned projects in South Pointe—the Viceroy Residences and two hotels and condos—returning the deposits before the ground was broken. The partnership of Leviev & Boymelgreen, which had spent $150 million for fifteen empty parcels, completed two, and had trouble selling either. The mega-yacht complex at Watson Island was canceled. Arte City, a two-block "village" of low-rise town houses near the Beach's Convention Center, was shelved. Tony and Joey Goldman sold some of their prime Wynwood properties to lighten their debt. Bruce Eichner, the builder of South Pointe's Continuum, lost his $1 billion Cosmopolitan Resort Casino in Las Vegas to creditors. Midtown Miami's central entertainment complex with a movie theater and restaurants was postponed, and its condos dropped from average pre-construction prices of $404 per foot to $275. Still, 70 percent remained empty.

Jason Binn bought out Jerry Powers's share of *Ocean Drive* for a reputed $17 million and moved its headquarters from South Beach to midtown Miami, saying it was a "new and upcoming area."

As for the Royal Palm, Falor and Mitchell failed to sell a single condo-hotel unit after a year of sales. Peebles sued them for gross mismanagement; in February 2009, he regained control but admitted, "The Royal Palm is essentially on life support right now."

The Fontainebleau reopened in November 2008. "Flamboyance Gets a Face-Lift," was *The New York Times* style section lead. But the construction costs had pushed Jeff Soffer deeply in the red, and Dubai bailed him out by buying half the hotel for $375 million. His Fontainebleau Las Vegas filed for bankruptcy. The recession did to Opium Gardens what Frank Del Vecchio never could—they closed their doors permanently on February 16, 2009, and reopened in a 40,000-square-foot space in the Seminole Hard Rock Casino, about thirty miles out of Miami. Books & Books had survived thanks to an inexpensive outdoor café Kaplan had opened a couple of years earlier. But by 2009, he had to move to the rear of a building off the main boulevard. "It was either that or close entirely," he told me.

When the news broke in 2008 that $47 million in tax breaks were about to be disbursed to developers of some of Miami-Dade's most luxurious new condominiums, it was difficult to overstate the extent of public anger. Unemployment in South Florida was nearing a twenty-five-year high at 10 percent. Tax breaks in the county's enterprise zone were designed to attract new businesses to distressed areas. By expanding the zone's boundaries, six luxury condo projects stood to reap millions in government subsidies, including Perez's Icon Brickell, Quantum Bay's two towers, and the massive Biscayne Landing project on the Intracoastal Waterway.

Under the rules, the developers would get cash payments of $5,000 or more for each condo they built (nearly $10 million for Perez at the Icon alone). They also got sales tax rebates, after they provided receipts for construction materials. Companies could deduct an additional 30 percent of the salary of any employees who lived in the zone. And property tax deductions were boosted for five years.

The politicians defended the windfall for developers by contending that the six projects added to the tax base and would lead to more development nearby. "It was appalling," said Del Vecchio, "but given that the developers and politicians had built a symbiotic relationship to line their own pockets, it was not surprising."

In March 2009, I returned to the Icon Brickell. *The New York Times* had called it "Miami's monument to excess," with 1,646 condos, a 28,000-square-foot fitness gym, and a two-acre pool deck with a 12-foot-high limestone fireplace. One hundred 22-foot sculptured columns—inspired by the stones on Easter Island—lined the $15 million entryway and lobby. Condos started at $400,000, but most of Icon's units were unsold after nearly three years of pre-construction sales. Of five hundred units that were supposed to close in December, only thirty did so. One hundred fourteen of those who didn't were part of a class action against Perez seeking to break their contracts.

"The world has changed so rapidly," said a subdued Perez over lunch. The cheerleader for the sanctity of real estate as a safe, big-money business, the man who had joked three years earlier that he'd be found under a bridge if his bet on South Florida failed, was facing "a complete meltdown. No one could have seen this coming. The severity of this downturn is unprecedented."

He wanted to raise $1 billion for a so-called vulture fund to buy his own units when the prices became too distressed. He and a partner had already used such a fund to buy 120 units at Related's fifty-four-story tower at 50 Biscayne Boulevard at the discounted price of $30.3 million. "Today, I could have bought them for 20 percent less," he sighed.

When the subject rolled around to speculators, who held a staggering 80 percent of the units in some buildings, Perez said he had tried to exercise caution by personally approving sales of more than two condos to a single buyer. "In retrospect, I should have been a lot firmer," he added.

He had lost $1 billion in the last year and fired a quarter of his employees. *Forbes* was about to drop him off their wealthiest 400 list for 2008. "If I die and am worth $50 million as opposed to $3 billion, it is really not important. What was Carl Fisher remembered for," he asked, "for what he created or that he died bankrupt?" Yet unless the banks that had given Perez hundreds of millions in construction loans agreed to modify the terms, some projects would fail. Icon Brickell alone accounted for $700 million of his debt; but he was also burdened by enormous loans for 500 Brickell in Miami, CityPlace South Tower in West Palm Beach, Oasis in Fort Myers, Trump Towers in Sunny Isles Beach, and Trump Hollywood.

Like most developers, Perez had structured each development as its own legal entity, so that if one collapsed, it would not bring down everything. But he said that if all the lenders called in their loans with no reduced interest or extensions, "There will be nobody left standing."

JORGE PEREZ WAS in the tradition of a long line of great risk-takers attracted to the Beach. The city's history was not made by early settlers who escaped religious persecution or yearned for freedoms denied them elsewhere. Few of its pioneers saw anything but a strip of sand on the ocean in which they could earn fame and fortune.

It was born and remains a resort that lives and dies on tourism and development. The developers considered visionaries of the Art Deco District's rebirth acted not out of civic duty or a passion for preservation and urban renewal; they were seduced by tax incentives that let them earn larger profits for taking a chance on God's Waiting Room.

The Beach retained the sun-and-fun title through two world wars. The political convulsions of the 1960s passed it by. Other than during the national political conventions, no Beach resident ever took to the streets to protest the Vietnam War. John Kennedy's and Martin Luther King, Jr.'s, assassinations were national tragedies, but for most locals they paled in comparison to the interest that Gianni Versace's murder still evokes. After 9/11, the mayor did not give a speech assuring his town of the strength of America. He posed for a photo op at a local hotel to encourage tourists not to cancel their trips; to enjoy mojitos, sunbathing, and nightclubbing.

The Beach had no moonshiners, but its residents and visitors drank more per capita than any other spot in America. When cocaine swept the country and the drug kingpins lived on the mainland, the Beach had the trade's best customers—the partygoers. The Beach has never had a single meth or ecstasy lab, but both drugs have become scourges.

It never had a gay bathhouse—they were all in Miami—but it has one of the highest per capita HIV infection rates in America. Beach promoters boast that for a decade the 33139 zip code has had the most Bentleys and Ferraris in the nation, but a few miles across Biscayne Bay, Miami ranks annually as one of the poorest big cities.

The local heroes in this sybaritic theme park are not public servants, philanthropists, or social activists; the respected icons are the ones with the most toys. "Too much is never enough" may have been Morris Lapidus's tongue-in-cheek epigraph, but it could be Miami Beach's slogan. When Somerset Maugham described Monaco as "a sunny place for shady people," he could easily have been describing Miami Beach. Jerry Powers, Tommy Pooch, or Chris Paciello would have been nothing in another city, but in Miami Beach they became celebrities. Thomas Kramer would have been persona non grata almost anywhere else. In the Beach, people excuse his behavior as uncontrolled exuberance and his Star Island parties are still crammed with those who should know better.

Spotting real wealth from someone living month to month on extended credit, or a drug dealer with millions stashed in offshore accounts, becomes an exercise in futility. The twenty-something black man driving a brand-new $400,000 Rolls-Royce Shadow: hip-hop producer or drug dealer? Two twenty-five-year-old Cubans in a $450,000 Porsche Carrera GT: real estate developers or captains in a Cuban crime family? A young Anglo kid in a million-dollar Ferrari Enzo: did he hit what locals call the "sperm lottery"—and it's his father's car—or is it his own and he runs a drug pipeline into the town's nightclubs?

Real culture has always taken a backseat to entertainment. Far more people come to play than to see Barbara Capitman's Art Deco District. The Beach's cultural contributions have been Jackie Gleason and *Miami Vice*. The town's only art museum, the Bass, has had a series of provenance problems in its collection and was recently involved in a scandal over an exhibit of Imperial Vietnamese jade that some charge was fake. The New World Symphony under conductor Michael Tilson Thomas is a wonderful teaching orchestra, but it regularly performs to a half-empty auditorium. More people attended the lavish real estate launch parties in 2006 than ever saw a performance of Miami City Ballet, forcing the company to move its performances to Miami. Art Basel attracts major buyers from around the world. But last year 10,000 people paid the ticket price to see the art exhibited at the Convention Center, whereas more than 100,000 crammed the Beach for 300 parties spread out over four days.

Has politics changed from Alex Daoud's days, when envelopes of cash bought votes? Arrests in 2008 of several Miami Beach building inspectors who ran a scheme to sell permits was a reminder of how ingrained the corruption is. Widespread graft in the very agencies designed to combat poverty and to help the city prepare for the future has led to a weary resignation among many residents. That doesn't mean there aren't politicians attracted by the best ideals of public service, and who are scrupulously honest. But the system still operates largely in a backroom old-boys club manner that ensures that friends and contributors profit from public decisions.

Nightclubs and developers believe no rule cannot be broken or at least changed by greasing the right wheels at City Hall. The Beach has one of the lowest voter turnout rates in the state, and as its elderly population dies off, it's been dropping further. Among those under thirty, no other Florida city has a higher percentage of unregistered eligible voters. That apathy allows graft to go unchallenged. One of the town's last guardians against such abuses, the *Miami Herald*, has slashed its reporting staff to the bone. The never-ending stream of scandals in Miami means that local prosecutors and reporters often focus on the larger mainland stories, giving crooked politicians and bureaucrats on the Beach free rein.

Barbara Capitman and Frank Del Vecchio are rare civic heroes. A community is in trouble, though, when it depends on volunteer activism instead of political leaders for oversight of public funds and projects. Even with Capitman's and Del Vecchio's significant achievements, the developers won the final rounds.

What is next for the Beach? By early 2009, foreclosures had hit one in every sixty-seven households. And tourism had taken a big hit. The economic tsunami that began as a credit crisis on Wall Street was manifested in half-empty hotels over spring break. Falling real estate and tourism taxes mean a budget shortfall and reduced city services. With the highest unemployment rate in three decades, crime has increased. The current malaise has disabused everyone of the pre-bust mantra that the new Beach, packed with national chain brand retailers and multi-million-dollar condos, was immune to any prolonged downturn. Boom and bust are the Beach's DNA.

Carl Fisher was right when he told his wife he'd create a place like no other. Walking along the beach in the early morning, when it is almost deserted and the ocean is calm, is one of life's small pleasures. But this schizophrenic town is a maddening combination of Third World ethics and New World aesthetics and consumerism. Miami Beach is the last frontier, both utopia and dystopia.

Notes

The reporting for this book included nearly 200 interviews, over four years, totaling more than 700 hours of recorded conversations, yielding more than 9,000 pages of transcripts. Some of those who spoke to me, particularly former law enforcement officers, and employees of powerful business executives or politicians, asked for anonymity. There were fifty-two such background or off-the-record interviews.

Every conversation in this book that does not have a source note is the result of an interview conducted by the author and his wife, Trisha. The following is a list of interviews on the record:

Abravanel, Lesley (December 15, 2007; April 24, 2008)

Abrizas, Danny (January 26, 2008)

Achenbaum, Michael (December 12, 2005)

Aguirre, Louis (August 6, 2008; August 13, 2008; August 27, 2008; October 1, 2008)

Aller, Michael (March 7, 2008; September 29, 2008)

Antoni, Brian (March 25, 2008)

Balazs, Andre (September 9, 2005)

Baumann, Roger (October 26, 2007)

Belack, William (November 10, 2007)

Bell, Brian (April 2, 2008)

Betancourt, Carlos (January 20, 2008; January 23, 2008; February 7, 2008; February 29, 2008; March 15, 2008)

Bloom, Elaine (January 8, 2008)

Blumberg, Stuart (October 22, 2007)

Boesky, Marianne (November 19, 2005)

Brandt, Fredric (March 30, 2005)

Britto, Romero (June 2, 2005; August 7, 2008; October 2, 2008)

Bruk, Kevin (August 4, 2008)

Byrne, Diane M. (July 12, 2006)

Canale, Fernando (November 10, 2007)

Canales, Louis (January 15, 2008; January 24, 2008; February 1, 2008)

Capponi, Michael (January 15, 2008; July 12, 2008)

Casares, Ingrid (January 14, 2008)

Chafetz, Myles (September 12, 2007)

Cinnamon, Charlie (September 22, 2007)

Comras, Joe (October 12, 2007)

Cooney, Kenneth (October 18, 2007)

Coronado, George (September 3, 2008)

Dalman, Lea (November 12, 2008)

Daly, Tom (April 30, 2005; December 12, 2007; February 2, 2008)

Daniels, Sid (October 19, 2006)

Daoud, Alex (September 15, 2008; September 16, 2008; September 22, 2008)

Delaplaine, Andrew (January 9, 2008)

DeLuca, Donny (November 30, 2007)

Del Vecchio, Frank and Marian (July 18, 2008; July 31, 2008; August 8, 2008; August 15, 2008; September 2, 2008)

Denain, Cedrik (April 14, 2005)

Dermer, David (August 20, 2008)

De Silva, Jean Marc (January 22, 2008)

Dunlop, Beth (June 15, 2005; April 25, 2006)

Eissmann, Jonathan (March 7, 2008)

Everingham, Philip (May 4, 2006)

Facer, Nolan (April 2, 2008)

Farmer, Gary (April 5, 2009)

Farrow, Edison (December 5, 2007)

Fendelmen, Richard (August 10, 2006)

Feinberg, Joe (December 26, 2008)

Fest, Marc (August 11, 2005)

Fontana, Joe (June 12, 2007; July 22, 2007; July 26, 2007; August 4, 2007)

Foster, Lauren (August 2, 2008)

Freed, Stephanie (July 29, 2008)

Freundlich, Marilyn (August 12, 2006)

Gallo, Julio (February 12, 2005; February 12, 2008)

Gaut, Eric (February 26, 2008)

Giles, Steven (January 26, 2008)

Goldman, Joey (April 4, 2005)

Goldman, Tony (February 26, 2008)

Gonzalez, Jorge (December 17, 2007)

Gross, Jane Dee (July 28, 2008)

Gross, Saul (October 30, 2007; November 8, 2007; January 11, 2008; January 31, 2008; April 4, 2008; November 15, 2008)

Hass, Stephen (November 29, 2007)

Hammond, Mike (August 18, 2006)

Harlan, Jason (November 8, 2005)

Hennes, Gary (August 12, 2008)

Hernandez, Julio (March 23, 2008)

Herzog, Jacques (September 12, 2006)

Hill, Robin (May 25, 2006)

Hilliard, Randy (November 30, 2007; January 9, 2008; July 7, 2008)

Hulanicki, Barbara (January 10, 2008)

James, Gary (April 6, 2008; August 4, 2008; November 12, 2008; February 28, 2009)

Kaplan, Mitch (November 27, 2007)

Kasdin, Neisen (September 26, 2007; October 27, 2007; December 28, 2007; March 26, 2009; April 18, 2009)

Kelly, Gerry (February 6, 2008; March 22, 2008; August 2, 2008)

Kramer, Thomas (October 29, 2007; December 2, 2007)

Kruszewski, Frank (December 10, 2007)

Lee, Linda (July 14, 2007)

Lejeune, François (June 1, 2006)

Lewis, Alvin (February 3, 2009)

Liebman, Nancy (December 14, 2007; December 19, 2007; January 11, 2008)

Lindemann, George (November 19, 2005)

Linzalone, Anthony (August 12, 2008)

Malnik, Shareef (November 6, 2007)

Marie, Irene (August 20, 2008; September 12, 2008; November 3, 2008)

Matteson, Arnold (December 18, 2007)

Matthews, Dan (July 12, 2005)

McDonald, Matt (April 27, 2005)

Meier, Richard (May 23, 2005)

Morr, Jeff (January 8, 2008; March 2, 2008)

Muss, Steve (December 5, 2007)

Nizri, Oren (December 12, 2007)

Oakes, Bianca (August 10, 2006)

Paik, Nam June (April 4, 2005)

Peebles, Donahue R. (October 12, 2007; October 22, 2007)

Pennetti, Anthony (November 5, 2007)

Percal, Esther (January 16, 2005)

Perez, Jorge (April 30, 2005; April 2, 2006; March 17, 2007; September 19, 2007; October 10, 2007; May 27, 2009)

Pisone, Stacy (April 8, 2005)

Podhurst, Aaron (April 3, 2006)

Pommier, Michelle (June 26, 2007)

Randolph, Alan (August 12, 2008)

Riera, Gabriel (April 7, 2006)

Riley, Terrence (June 3, 2006; November 12, 2006)

Robbins, Kent Harrison (January 17, 2008; September 19, 2008)

Robin, Sam (November 25, 2007; August 20, 2008)

Robins, Craig (September 22, 2007; October 27, 2007; March 18, 2009)

Robinson, Melissa (April 12, 2005)

Robinson, Randall (November 23, 2007)

Rosen, Harold (October 5, 2007; October 12, 2007; November 28, 2007)

Rosenthal, Steve (September 18, 2008)

Roth, Alan (January 18, 2008)

Rubell, Jennifer (February 2, 2009)

Ruiz, Rene (September 29, 2007; November 5, 2007)

Russ, Denis (November 9, 2007)

Saladino, Sean (January 12, 2005)

Sanchez, Justo (July 29, 2008)

Sbrogio, Graziano (March 8, 2008)

Schlesser, Mel (February 10, 2009)

Schrager, Ian (March 12, 2005; November 12, 2006)

Schrager, Lee (February 16, 2008)

Seraydar, Charlie (September 12, 2008; October 9, 2008)

Snitzer, Fredric (November 19, 2005)

Snyder, Gregg (December 12, 2007)

Solomon, Tara (November 15, 2007; October 18, 2008)

Soyka, Mark (December 3, 2007; January 22, 2008)

Spring, Daniel (January 22, 2008)

Spring, Michael (September 30, 2006)

Stafford III, Gilbert (July 28, 2008)

Taranu, Alex (October 15, 2007)

Tomlinson, Kevin (January 25, 2009)

Tutt, Wallace (June 2, 2006)

Urban, Heather (June 20, 2005)

Wallach, David (January 14, 2008; January 15, 2008; April 23, 2008; June 23, 2008)

Watson, Steve (February 12, 2005)

Weinstein, A. C. (January 13, 2008; April 3, 2008; June 7, 2008; September 12, 2008)

Weiss, Barton G. (March 16, 2005)

Weiss, Merle and Danny (March 3, 2008; May 2, 2008)

Wolfson, Leslie (November 21, 2007)

Wolfson, Mickey (February 26, 2008)

Valazquez, Ronaldo (November 12, 2007)

Yip, Jennie (May 6, 2005)

York, Ryan (February 2, 2008)

Zemo, Dona (September 21, 2008)

Zinkin, Alan (March 2, 2008)

CHAPTER 1: "GASOLINE ON A FIRE"

2 *"They want them"*: Recounted by Ronaldo Valazquez to author, November 12, 2007.

2 *"The United States is"*: T. D. Allman, *Miami: City of the Future* (New York: Atlantic Monthly Press, 1987), 27.

3 *To avoid generous:* Maurice A. Roberts, "The U.S. and Refugees: The Refugee Act of 1980," *Issue: A Journal of Opinion*, vol. 12, no. 1/2, African Refugees and Human Rights (Spring–Summer 1982), 4–6.

3 *U.S. Customs established:* Allman, *Miami*, 10.

3 *A popular exile saying:* James Kelly, "Trouble in Paradise," *Time*, November 23, 1981.

3 *Over 1,000:* Ibid.

4 *Black neighborhoods like Overtown:* Helen Muir, *Miami USA* (New York: Henry Holt, 1953), 272; Allman, *Miami*, 22.

4 *About 24,000 had:* Judy L. Silverstein, "Memories of Mariel," *Global Security*, 2000. See also Bill Wisser, *South Beach: America's Riviera, Miami Beach, Florida* (New York: Arcade Publishing, 1995), 20; and John Lang, Joseph Galloway, Linda Lanier, and Gordon Bock, "Castro's 'Crime Bomb' Inside U.S.," *U.S. News & World Report*, January 16, 1984.

4 *The remaining 70 percent:* Edward Schumacher, "Cuban Reunion in Newark Brings a Joyous Beginning," *New York Times*, May 24, 1980, A27.

4 *In Los Angeles:* Lang, et al., "Castro's 'Crime Bomb' Inside U.S."; see also Kelly, "Trouble in Paradise."

12 Time *reported that:* James Kelly, reported by Michael Wallis, "Absolute War in Our Streets," *Time,* November 24, 1980.

12 *"No woman or man":* Kelly, "Trouble in Paradise."

13 *Even Governor Bob Graham:* Muir, *Miami USA,* 285.

CHAPTER 2: "NO SANE MAN . . ."

14 *The region was so desolate:* Gregory W. Bush, "Playground of the USA: Miami and the Promotion of Spectacle," *Pacific Historical Review,* vol. 68, no. 2 (May 1999), 153.72; Edward Riley, *The Growth of Florida* (Edison, NJ: Chartwell Books, 2007), 50.

14 *By the late 1880s:* Theodore Steinberg, *Acts of God: The Unnatural History of Natural Disaster in America* (New York: Oxford University Press, 2000), 49–50.

14 *A succession of governors:* John Rothchild, *Up for Grabs: A Trip Through Time and Space in the Sunshine State* (New York: Penguin Books, 1985), 28.

15 *Sixty percent of Florida:* Ibid., 27; see also Riley, *The Growth of Florida,* 50–53.

15 *A New York Herald journalist:* J. Bruce Cumming, Jr., "A Brief Florida Real Estate History," West Coast Chapter of the Appraisal Institute, Region X, September 6, 2006.

15 *For years Lum tried:* Ibid.; see also Riley, *The Growth of Florida.*

16 *Collins had already:* Abraham D. Lavender, *Miami Beach in 1920: The Making of a Winter Resort* (Charleston, SC: Arcadia, 2002), 11.

16 *This presented an opportunity:* Ibid., 10; see also M. Barron Stofik, *Saving South Beach* (Gainesville, FL: University of Florida Press, 2005).

16 *For Flagler, Miami:* Ann Armbruster, *The Life and Times of Miami Beach* (New York: Alfred A. Knopf, 1995), 9.

16 *With a population:* Cumming, "A Brief Florida Real Estate History."

16 *More than 250 years:* Armbruster, *The Life and Times of Miami Beach,* 15.

17 *He planted a windbreak:* Polly Redford, *Billion-Dollar Sandbar: A Biography of Miami Beach* (New York: E. P. Dutton, 1970), 39.

17 *Despite a strict quarantine:* William M. Straight, MD, "Yellow Fever at Miami: The Epidemic of 1899," Historical Museum of Southern Florida, 39–60.

17 *"Yes," he told his son:* Redford, *Billion-Dollar Sandbar,* 39–40.

CHAPTER 3: SELLING SWAMPLAND

19 *His sales zoomed:* Redford, *Billion-Dollar Sandbar,* 46–47.

20 *He bought the first:* Ibid., 50.

20 *"I watched Carl's face":* Jane Fisher, *Fabulous Hoosier: A Story of American Achievement* (New York: Robert M. McBride & Co., 1947), 10–12.

21 *Soon after, he and:* Prest-O-Lite sold for $9 million to Union Carbide, but Fisher pocketed only $6 million.

21 *By this time, Fisher had:* Redford, *Billion-Dollar Sandbar,* 73.

21 *Biscayne Bay was:* Ibid., 106.

21 *One day he stopped:* PBS, American Experience documentary, *Mr. Miami Beach*, 1998—see the show on Fisher; Jerry M. Fisher, *The Pacesetter: The Untold Story of Carl G. Fisher* (Fort Bragg, CA: Lost Coast Press, 1998), 156–57.

21 *Within a few weeks:* Fisher, *The Pacesetter*, 154–55.

21 *"Look, honey":* Armbruster, *The Life and Times of Miami Beach*, 11.

22 *Fisher had bought:* Flagler died a month before the bridge was finished. Although it would take him a few years, Fisher built the sole tribute to Flagler, an illuminated 110-foot obelisk, on Bay Island. Fisher chose the isolated spot because it was visible to anyone crossing the only causeway at that time from Miami Beach to Miami, and most important, it was part of the view from his private suite at the Flamingo Hotel. Miami Beach eventually took control of the island after Fisher and the rest of the developers crashed. It is in serious disrepair due to exposure, vandalism, and years without maintenance.

22 *The state was so pleased:* Muir, *Miami USA*, 100.

22 *But he boasted:* Michael Grunwald, *The Swamp: The Everglades, Florida, and the Politics of Paradise* (New York: Simon & Schuster, 2006), 172; Lavender, *Miami Beach in 1920*, 8.

23 THE ENTRANCE TO FAIRY LAND: Armbruster, *The Life and Times of Miami Beach*, 6; Redford, *Billion-Dollar Sandbar*, 38.

23 *Dammers offered elephant rides:* http://www.historical-museum.org/exhibits/gables/gables3.htm.

23 *By 1915, the original:* Lavender, *Miami Beach in 1920*, 13. Miami Beach was still then a peninsula, connected by a narrow strip to the mainland. When a channel was cut at that spot in 1923, the Beach gained its island status.

24 *When the Lummuses:* Redford, *Billion-Dollar Sandbar*, 94.

24 *At its peak:* Armbruster, *The Life and Times of Miami Beach*, 13.

25 *Fisher's prison crew:* Lavender, *Miami Beach in 1920*, 139.

25 *A new link to:* Fisher felt there was great promise in air travel, but it was only seventeen years since the Wright brothers took a brief flight in the first motorized plane, the *Kitty Hawk*. The *Miami Herald* ran a banner front-page headline in April announcing the first commercial flight between New York and Miami. The Aero Limited hydroplane had three paying passengers and took 14.35 hours, with a refueling stop in North Carolina. But Fisher was realistic enough to know that while air travel might attract a few affluent visitors, his dream of converting Miami Beach into a thriving paradise getaway depended on cars.

26 *Haggert's salary was:* Lavender, *Miami Beach in 1920*, 139.

26 *He even put up:* Redford, *Billion-Dollar Sandbar*, 139.

26 *"I have some of":* Ibid.

26 *"It probably cost":* Ibid., 128.

27 *He brought in English:* Muir, *Miami USA*, 126.

27 *Johnny Weissmuller:* PBS American Experience, *Mr. Miami Beach*.

27 *(He got a lucrative):* Muir, *Miami USA*, 138.

28 *(The last restrictive):* See Redford, *Billion-Dollar Sandbar*, 274.

28 *One sported the:* Archives of the Jewish Museum of Florida, Miami Beach.

29 *One hotel, a favorite:* Joann Biondi, *Miami Beach Memories* (Guilford, CT: Globe Pequot Press, 2007), 17; Armbruster, *The Life and Times of Miami Beach,* 79–80.

29 *In one instance, Fisher:* Armbruster, *The Life and Times of Miami Beach,* 77.

29 *Overtly racist signs:* Lavender, *Miami Beach in 1920,* 83; Redford, *Billion-Dollar Sandbar,* 222.

29 *"What'll I do?":* Armbruster, *The Life and Times of Miami Beach,* 77–78.

29 *"I would not have":* Lavender, *Miami Beach in 1920,* 83.

30 *Rose Weiss caused:* Gayle White, "Miami Beach Memories: The Resort That Gives Miami Flash has Grown Younger and Hipper Without Losing Its Jewish Identity," *Atlanta Journal-Constitution,* April 9, 1995, 1N.

30 *They had to cross: Gorman v. City of Miami,* U.S. District Court, 1956.

30 *The unwritten rules:* These "rules" remained in effect until 1964's Civil Rights Voting Act—Biondi, *Miami Beach Memories,* 17; Armbruster, *The Life and Times of Miami Beach,* 106–07.

30 *In 1934, Beach:* Redford, *Billion-Dollar Sandbar,* 223.

31 *Soon after their arrival:* Lavender, *Miami Beach in 1920,* 43.

31 *So he decreed:* Rothchild, *Up for Grabs,* 77.

31 *"We'll have their pictures":* PBS American Experience, *Mr. Miami Beach.*

31 *The campaign succeeded:* Armbruster, *The Life and Times of Miami Beach,* 28.

32 *The Ludens, of the cough-drop:* Rothchild, *Up for Grabs,* 39.

32 *"The gondoliers in Boca":* Michelle Oka Doner and Mitchell Wolfson, Jr., *Miami Beach—Blueprint of an Eden: Lives Seen Through the Prism of Time and Place* (Cologne, Germany: Feierabend Unique Books, 2006), 163; Rothchild, *Up for Grabs,* 42.

33 *He was in a funk:* Muir, *Miami USA,* 138–39.

33 *John Deering, a northern:* Ibid., 139.

33 *spread beyond Miami:* Cumming, "A Brief Florida Real Estate History," 10.

33 *Widespread tales:* Armbruster, *The Life and Times of Miami Beach,* 31.

33 *The sales pitch:* Rothchild, *Up for Grabs,* 74–75; Armbruster, *The Life and Times of Miami Beach,* 30.

33 *Bolles died:* Rothchild, *Up for Grabs,* 74–75.

34 *Miami was the site:* http://www.clas.ufl.edu/users/thrall/class/g3602/florida realestatehistory.pdf.

34 *Some operators flipped:* Cumming, "A Brief Florida Real Estate History," 20.

34 *One local story:* Grunwald, *The Swamp,* 177–78.

34 *Carl Fisher didn't like:* Fisher, *The Pacesetter,* 271.

34 *"Some of the property":* Ibid., 269.

34 *Acres that had cost:* Grunwald, *The Swamp,* 177.

34 *In 1923, one-acre lots:* Rothchild, *Up for Grabs,* 78.

34 *Theodore Dreiser wrote:* Armbruster, *The Life and Times of Miami Beach,* 31.

34 *The* Miami Herald's *advertisements:* Grunwald, *The Swamp,* 180.

34 *The* Herald *routinely:* Ibid.

35 The New York Times *devoted:* Ibid., 177.

35 *the "child is the":* Ibid., 180; Muir, *Miami USA,* 127, 136.

35 *In less than three:* Muir, *Miami USA,* 131, 133.

35 *Within a week:* Ibid., 133; Redford, *Billion-Dollar Sandbar*, 152.

36 *the former was:* Cumming, "A Brief Florida Real Estate History," 19.

36 *"Beachfront" property:* Grunwald, *The Swamp*, 179.

36 *In 1925, Florida:* Ibid.

36 *As his friend Will:* PBS American Experience, *Mr. Miami Beach*. Rogers made the same mistake as most non-Floridians, assuming that alligators were native to South Florida. The related but meaner-spirited saltwater crocodile is indigenous to the area, and not nearly extinct.

36 *Locals had joked:* Muir, *Miami USA*, 98.

36 *As for the Roman Pools:* Interview with Joe Fontana, July 22, 2007; Redford, *Billion-Dollar Sandbar*, 177; Fisher, *The Pacesetter*, 271.

CHAPTER 4: RUMRUNNERS AND THE BUST

38 *Coinciding with the land:* Stan Zimmerman, *A History of Smuggling in Florida: Rumrunner and Cocaine Cowboys* (Charleston, SC: History Press, 2006), 51.

38 *Two popular bars:* Buchanan, "Miami's Bootleg Boom," 14.

38 *When challenged to prove:* Ibid., 13.

38 *It was, he said:* Rothchild, *Up for Grabs*, 131.

38 *Curtiss converted 14,000:* Grunwald, *The Swamp*, 180–81.

39 *The U.S. Coast Guard:* "Florida Drug War," *The MacNeil/Lehrer Report*, June 8, 1992.

39 *Cocaine was outlawed:* Rothchild, *Up for Grabs*, 131.

39 *Local cops smashed:* Ibid.

39 *But booze joints:* Buchanan, "Miami's Bootleg Boom," 13.

40 *He muscled a quarter:* Armbruster, *The Life and Times of Miami Beach*, 68.

40 *The Deauville Hotel Casino:* David Leddick, *In the Spirit of Miami Beach* (New York: Assouline Publishing, 2006), 47.

40 *Not everyone was thrilled:* Muir, *Miami USA*, 164, 165–67.

40 *Like many other wealthy:* Redford, *Billion-Dollar Sandbar*, 121.

40 *Fisher testified at:* Fisher, *The Pacesetter*, 354–55.

40 *For everyone who bragged:* Zimmerman, *A History of Smuggling in Florida*, 59.

41 *When he got out in late:* Ibid., 57.

41 *He even threatened:* Lavender, *Miami Beach in 1920*, 146.

41 *But his acquittal:* Buchanan, "Miami's Bootleg Boom," 15.

42 The New York Times *noted:* Ibid., 17.

42 *Miami Beach, which during:* http://en.wikipedia.org/wiki/Carl_G._Fisher.

42 *Florida banks were:* Armbruster, *The Life and Times of Miami Beach*, 56.

42 *Broken families:* Ibid., 32.

43 *When a business colleague:* Redford, *Billion-Dollar Sandbar*, 140.

43 *When friends questioned:* Armbruster, *The Life and Times of Miami Beach*, 8; Redford, *Billion-Dollar Sandbar*, 161.

43 *That overstated the case:* Redford, *Billion-Dollar Sandbar*, 173.

44 *"After we get rid":* Ibid., 175.

44 *John Pennenkamp:* Grunwald, *The Swamp*, 189.

44 *Miami's mayor refused:* Ibid.; Muir, *Miami USA*, 153, 158.

44 *Most local banks failed:* Seth H. Bramson, *Miami: The Magic City* (Charleston, SC: Arcadia, 2007), 87.

44 *Three fourths of Beach:* Biondi, *Miami Beach Memories,* 11.

45 *He was drinking:* Redford, *Billion-Dollar Sandbar,* 158.

45 *When Miami Beach's first:* Lavender, *Miami Beach in 1920,* 145.

45 *The two pet elephants:* Redford, *Billion-Dollar Sandbar,* 142.

45 *But by that time:* Ibid., 190.

46 *who converted it:* Muir, *Miami USA,* 186; Armbruster, *The Life and Times of Miami Beach,* 75.

46 *For three years:* Fisher, *The Pacesetter,* 392.

46 *"I have your bill":* Ibid., 390.

46 *"I used to be able":* Ibid., 392–98.

46 *"I wish I was":* Ibid., 392.

46 *"Living with Carl Fisher":* PBS American Experience, *Mr. Miami Beach.*

CHAPTER 5: "TOO MUCH IS NEVER ENOUGH"

47 *The story, "Pleasure Dome":* "Pleasure Dome," *Time,* February 19, 1940.

47 *In 1936, for instance:* Armbruster, *The Life and Times of Miami Beach,* 87.

47 *Illegal bookie concessions:* Ibid., 58.

47 *Winchell told his listeners:* Ibid., 72.

48 *The Army requisitioned:* Leddick, *In the Spirit of Miami Beach,* 51; Armbruster, *The Life and Times of Miami Beach,* 100.

48 *The Army made a:* Muir, *Miami USA,* 211.

48 *A fortunate few:* Robert D. Billinger, Jr., "Hitler's Soldiers in the Sunshine State: German POWs in Florida," Florida History and Culture Series (Gainesville, FL: University Press of Florida, 2000), 262.

49 *"Miami Beach is never":* Armbruster, *The Life and Times of Miami Beach,* 100.

49 Look *magazine castigated:* Ibid., 102–103.

49 *It concluded:* Lavender, *Miami Beach in 1920,* 150.

50 *Only La Gorce:* Redford, *Billion-Dollar Sandbar,* 274–75.

50 *"We are a tiny Arabia":* Ibid., 274.

50 *"We don't want any":* Ibid., 224.

51 *The organization was so successful:* "It Pays to Organize," *Time,* March 12, 1951.

51 *The evidence showed:* Ibid.

51 *Said the committee:* Ibid.

51 *Kefauver was so outraged: Saturday Evening Post,* April 1951.

51 *The* Miami Herald *ran:* Muir, *Miami USA,* 221.

52 *New York's Lucky:* Armbruster, *The Life and Times of Miami Beach,* 69.

52 *Meyer Lansky, with:* Hank Messick, *Syndicate in the Sun* (New York: Macmillan, 1968), 139.

52 *A small man:* Armbruster, *The Life and Times of Miami Beach,* 167.

52 *Internal memos show:* Redford, *Billion-Dollar Sandbar,* 232.

52 *Seventy-five percent:* Muir, *Miami USA,* 234.

52 *"It's like the Ford"*: Armbruster, *The Life and Times of Miami Beach*, 154.
53 *New attractions such as:* Bramson, *Miami: The Magic City*, 117.
53 *In 1954, two:* Ibid., 111.
53 *"I had been waiting"*: Morris Lapidus, *Too Much Is Never Enough* (New York: Rizzoli, 1996), 157, 166.
53 *Novack proudly:* Armbruster, *The Life and Times of Miami Beach*, 135.
54 *"You must have something"*: Lapidus, *Too Much Is Never Enough*, 184.
54 *The two Lapidus:* Ibid., 195.
54 *In the decade:* Muir, *Miami USA*, 233.

CHAPTER 6: LOST MOJO

56 *For twenty years:* Kelly, "Trouble in Paradise," *Time*, November 23, 1981.
57 *"What you might call"*: Allan J. Mayer with Andrew Jaffe, "Gloom Over Miami," *Time*, December 16, 1996.
57 *Miami Beach hotels slashed:* Armbruster, *The Life and Times of Miami Beach*, 162.
57 *but hotel owners did not:* Interview with Joe Fontana, July 26, 2007.
57 *Headwaiters dissed:* Armbruster, *The Life and Times of Miami Beach*, 162.
58 *Fifteen bands:* Redford, *Billion-Dollar Sandbar*, 20.
58 *the Beach remained as firmly:* Interview with Nancy Liebman, January 11, 2008.
58 *Blacks were nonexistent:* Ibid.; Muir, *Miami USA*, 264.
58 *They called several:* Armbruster, *The Life and Times of Miami Beach*, 108.
58 *A colleague of Mones:* James Cook with Jane Carmichael, "Casino Gambling: Changing Character or Changing Fronts?" *Forbes*, October 27, 1980, 89.
58 *"We had many"*: Biondi, *Miami Beach Memories*, 60.
59 *At Overtown clubs:* Jordan Levin, "The Sweet Sound of Overtown," *Miami Herald*, February 1, 2009, 1, 21A.
59 *"Novack knew"*: Biondi, *Miami Beach Memories*, 160.
59 *"You either let Sammy"*: Ibid.
59 *"Of course, Sammy"*: Ibid.
59 *Five thousand new:* Redford, *Billion-Dollar Sandbar*, 255.
60 *The city prevailed:* Interview with David Dermer, August 20, 2008.
61 *Yippie leader Abbie:* Interview with Harold Rosen, October 5, 2007.
62 *"That was the difference"*: Hunter Thompson, *Fear and Loathing on the Campaign Trail 1972* (New York: Grand Central Publishing, 2006).
62 *The average citizen:* Armbruster, *The Life and Times of Miami Beach*, 177.
62 *City Hall's Citizens':* Donn Pearce, *Dying in the Sun* (New York: Charterhouse, 1974), 14.
62 Newsweek, The Times: Armbruster, *The Life and Times of Miami Beach*, 178. See also Mayer and Jaffe, "Gloom Over Miami," 62; Frank Rasky, "Florida's Naples Artfully Dodges the Rat Race," *The Globe and Mail* (Canada), January 5, 1985; Gary Turner, "New Hot Spot Raises the Bar on Lincoln Road," *Miami Herald*, February 14, 1999, 32BC; and Bernard Cornwell, "Travel: A Sunny Side of the Heat," *The Times* (London), June 6, 1987.

63 *The only supermarket:* Pearce, *Dying in the Sun*, 25.

63 *A third supplemented:* Redford, *Billion-Dollar Sandbar*, 264.

CHAPTER 7: "THE DEATH OF AN AMERICAN CITY"

65 *for the first time:* "Ebb Tide at Miami Beach," *Time*, December 19, 1977.

65 *Although the strike:* Ibid.; Robert Turnbull, "Miami Beached! Can Foreign Funds and Facelift Set It Afloat Again?" *The Globe and Mail* (Canada), July 15, 1978.

65 *The new buyer was:* Mayer and Jaffe, "Gloom Over Miami," *Newsweek.*

66 *The RDA's jurisdiction:* Michael Kranish, "Name Game Boosts City Image: Get the Pointe?" *Miami Herald*, Neighbors Miami Beach, February 5, 1984, 3.

66 *But over the objections of many:* Mary Ann Esquivel-Gibbs, "South Pointe Update," *Miami New Times*, December 11, 1991; see also Paul Goldberger, "Miami Beach May Raze Blighted Area of Elderly," *New York Times*, March 24, 1976.

67 *If the jury sided:* "Chronology of Early Development Patterns on Miami Beach Up to 1930," School of Engineering and Environmental Design, University of Miami; see also Stofik, *Saving South Beach*, 21.

67 *Only after the state's:* Roberto Fabricio and Andy Rosenblatt, *Miami Herald*, February 2, 1977, sect. 2, 1.

67 *The RDA chose a design:* Interview with Steve Muss, December 5, 2007.

68 *In 1977, the U.S. Army Corps:* "Leaders of Miami Beach Beginning to Concede City Has Problems," *New York Times*, January 25, 1977.

68 *Muss wanted even more:* Interview with Joe Fontana, July 22, 2007.

68 *Muss's project was larger:* Stofik, *Saving South Beach*, 23.

69 *Mendelson vowed to spend:* Roberto Fabricio, "S. Beach Butcher Sharpens His Ax to Fight Redevelopment Agency Push," *Miami Herald*, February 6, 1977.

69 *He told the commission:* Michael Kranish, "South Beach: Where Dreams Die," *Miami Herald*, August 29, 1982, 1M.

69 *At one city commission meeting:* Fredric Tasker, "Asked for a Hotel, Muss Offered a Community," *Miami Herald*, September 24, 1978.

70 *"This neighborhood is irreplaceable":* Jo Thomas, "Miami Beach Conflict Pits Developers Against Lovers of Art Deco," *New York Times*, February 26, 1981.

72 *He fled to Miami:* Stofik, *Saving South Beach*, 72–73.

72 *"I really don't find":* Wisser, *South Beach*, 37.

73 *The "Let's Help Florida Committee":* Stofik, *Saving South Beach*, 48–49.

74 *To the shock of developers:* Thomas, "Miami Beach Conflict Pits Developers Against Lovers of Art Deco."

75 *She was convinced that:* Allman, *Miami*, 38–39.

75 *Capitman thought the area:* Andrew Capitman, "The Art Deco District—The Bottom Line, and Economic Perspective," *Miami Beach Art Deco District Time:Future* (booklet), Community Action and Research, June 1982, 9.

76 *He enticed conservative:* Candace E. Trunzo, "Art Deco Beach Boys; Capitman and Shantzis Rejuvenate Oceanfront Hotels," *Money*, May 1982, 31.

76 *The sellers agreed:* National Association of Home Builders, historical mortgage rate information, provided June 2008 at written request.

77 *The people who opposed it:* Laurel Leff, "A Faded Resort Fights for a Place in the Sun," *Wall Street Journal,* March 5, 1982.

77 *The year after:* Ibid.

77 *It was the state's poorest:* Armbruster, *The Life and Times of Miami Beach,* 178.

77 *Many were pullmanettes:* Miami Beach Art Deco District booklet, June 1982, 9; see also Kranish, "South Beach: Where Dreams Die."

77 *more than 1,000:* Michael Kranish, "These Are People Who Emigrated Their Whole Life, and This Is How It Ends," *Miami Herald,* August 29, 1982, 4M.

77 *City inspectors called:* Kranish, "South Beach: Where Dreams Die."

77 *Nor did she have:* Kranish, "These Are People Who Emigrated."

78 *In 1979, the RDA negotiated:* Michael Kranish, "Final Offer: Offices Instead of Venice," *Miami Herald,* August 29, 1982, 8M.

79 *The commissioners decided:* Interview with Alex Daoud, September 15, 2008.

79 *Seven developers were rejected:* "Leaders of Miami Beach Beginning to Concede City has Problems," *New York Times,* January 25, 1977.

CHAPTER 8: COCAINE COWBOYS

82 *"I've been through two wars":* Kelly, "Trouble in Paradise," *Time,* November 23, 1981.

82 *Men like Junior Guthrie:* Zimmerman, *A History of Smuggling in Florida,* 91.

83 *Only one person was arrested:* PBS Frontline, *Who Profits from Drugs?* #706, February 21, 1989, produced by Charles C. Stuart and Marcia Vivancos, written by Charles C. Stuart, and reported by Charles C. Stuart, Marcia Vivancos, and Mark Hosenball.

83 *In the upper echelon:* PBS Frontline, *The Godfather of Cocaine,* February 14, 1995, produced by William Cran and Stephanie Tepper, written and directed by William Cran.

83 *"As inelegant as":* Robert Sabbag, *Snowblind: A Brief Career in the Cocaine Trade* (Indianapolis: Bobbs, Merrill, 1976), 63.

83 *A saying began circulating:* Zimmerman, *A History of Smuggling in Florida,* 94.

84 *Despite a national:* UPI, Domestic News, February 20, 1985.

84 *Another Pistolero was renowned:* Interview with DEA source, July 2007.

86 *"If you are not off this island":* Guy Gugliotta and Jeff Leen, *Kings of Cocaine: An Astonishing True Story of Murder, Money and Corruption* (New York: Harper, 1989), 46.

86 *There were always two:* Interview with Carol Toro, PBS research into Frontline, *The Drug Wars:* http://www.pbs.org/wgbh/pages/frontline/shows/drugs/interviews/toro.html.

86 *For the 250-pound Jorge:* PBS Frontline, *The Godfather of Cocaine.*

86 *He got away after:* Gugliotta and Leen, *Kings of Cocaine,* 26–27.

87 *When their wives and parents:* Art Harris, "The Drug Game: Undercover in Miami; Where Business Is Vicious and Booming," *Washington Post,* March 11, 1984, K1.

88 *By 1980, it was flooded:* Treasury Report, South Florida Economics and Cocaine Importation, 1985.

88 *Federal Reserve districts:* Author review of Federal Reserve records, Washington, D.C. 1980.

88 *Counting the money:* Melinda Beck and Elaine Shannon, "A New Attack on Drugs," *Newsweek,* July 20, 1981, 30.

88 *When they got back outside:* Rebecca Wakefield, "Awash in a Sea of Money," *Miami New Times,* October 6, 2005, 1, 28.

88 *"The money was rolling":* PBS Frontline, *The Godfather of Cocaine.*

89 *By 1980, the IRS:* Wakefield, "Awash in a Sea of Money," 28.

89 *Restricted by law:* Zimmerman, *A History of Smuggling in Florida,* 106: Interview with IRS agent, August 1, 2007.

90 *"They were charging":* Michael Levene quoted in PBS Frontline, *Who Profits from Drugs?*

90 *Real estate agents:* Beck and Shannon, "A New Attack on Drugs."

90 *Prosecutors estimated that:* Wakefield, "Awash in a Sea of Money," 28.

91 *"And every Colombian":* Interview with Joey Martino, October 1, 2007.

91 *Defense lawyers called them:* Harris, "The Drug Game: Undercover in Miami; Where Business Is Vicious and Booming"; see also Kelly, "Trouble in Paradise."

92 *About one third of all property:* Wakefield, "Awash in a Sea of Money," 1, 28.

92 *So much was pouring in:* Interview with Jose Bermudez, May 15, 2008.

93 *each had family members:* IRS agent, Mike McDonald, PBS Frontline, *War on Drugs.*

93 *During its first six months:* Wakefield, "Awash in a Sea of Money," 87–88.

93 *A lucrative specialty:* PBS Frontline, *Who Profits from Drugs?*

93 *"The more layers":* Michael Zeldin, transcript of *Who Profits from Drugs?*

CHAPTER 9: THE PLAYERS

96 *"Miami back then":* Rebecca Wakefield, "Confessions of a Trafficker: Jon Roberts Was a Big-Time Miami Coke Dealer Who Did Time in the Big House," *Miami New Times,* October 13, 2005, 1.

96 *"I simply had":* Both Roberts and Munday served prison sentences—ten and seven years—and were featured in the 2006 documentary *Cocaine Cowboys.*

97 *For the next seven:* One of Mermelstein's partners, Rafael Cardona, did the 50-kilo coke deal in the Grand Caymans that ensnared John DeLorean.

97 *Less than a decade:* PBS Frontline, *The Godfather of Cocaine.*

97 *"I made it snow":* Max Mermelstein, *The Man Who Made It Snow: By the American Mastermind Inside the Colombian Cartel* (New York: Simon & Schuster, 1990), 11.

99 *Malnik demolished:* Laura Misch, "Forged in Luxury," *Miami Herald,* Neighbors Miami Beach, August 18, 1983, 12.

99 *An 1822 Château:* Ian Glass, "A Bottle from Bin No. 100," *Los Angeles Times,* May 11, 1975, G18A.

99 *Next there was Club 41:* Interview with Stephen Hass, November 29, 2007.

99 *"I had been on":* Ibid.

100 *Aronow had landed:* Lydia Martin, "'Rush Hour 3' Director Brett Ratner Doesn't Care What Critics Think," *Miami Herald,* August 13, 2007, E6.

100 *"I remember seeing"*: David Samuels, "Liquid Smoke," *Men's Vogue*, January 2007.

101 *Mermelstein had convinced*: Interview with Jose Bermudez, May 15, 2008.

101 *Many South Florida racers*: Anthony Lednovich and Don Christensen, "Image Woes Cloud Offshore Racing," *Fort Lauderdale News/Sun-Sentinel*, December 19, 1982, A1.

101 *"Willy" Falcon and Salvador*: Will Lester, "Willy and Sal: Trial Recalls Heyday of Miami Smuggling," Associated Press, October 22, 1995, a.m. cycle.

101 *"The druggies would"*: Samuels, "Liquid Smoke."

111 *But every attempt*: Mermelstein, *The Man Who Made It Snow*, 48.

111 *Eventually, dozens of*: Edward Frost, "$1.5 Billion Airline Employee Cocaine Ring Broken," Associated Press, March 11, 1987.

111 *When Loeb told*: Terry Atlas, "Medellin Drug Cartel: Empire Beyond Belief," *Chicago Tribune*, February 14, 1988, sec. C, 6.

CHAPTER 10: THE HEIR APPARENT

117 *Instead of the classic*: Interview with Alex Daoud, October 15, 2007.

118 *In 1961, the twenty-eight-year-old*: Hank Messick, *Lansky* (New York: G. P. Putnam's Sons, 1971), 169, 199, 232, 241.

118 *The Pennsylvania Crime Commission*: Clyde H. Farnsworth, *New York Times*, April 9, 1975, A1; Pennsylvania Crime Commission, 1980: 198; James Cook, "The Invisible Empire," *Forbes*, October 13, 1980, 120.

118 *Investigators later dubbed*: Messick, *Lansky*, 266.

118 *Malnik was a director*: Select Committee on Crime, N.Y. State Senate, Bahamian Files: ICB folder and Bank of World Commerce folder; see also Clifton D. Bryant, *Deviant Behavior: Readings in the Sociology of Norm Violations* (New York: Hemisphere Publishing Corp., 1990), 409–13.

118 *Federal authorities suspected*: Interview with Assistant U.S. Attorney, Southern District, New York, July 29, 2008.

118 *Malnik was paid*: Internal Revenue Service, Intelligence Division, "Intelligence Report, Alvin I. Malnik and Bank of World Commerce," February 12, 1964.

118 *John Pullman loaned*: Malnik v. Commissioner of IRS, Docket No. 5307–76, U.S. Tax Court, T.C. Memo 1985–467; 1985 Tax Court Memo: 50 T.C.M. (CCH) 977; T.C.M. (RIA) 85467, September 4, 1985.

118 *Malnik opened up bank accounts*: Ibid.

118 *Soon, Malnik bought his first*: Ibid.; Alan A. Block, *Masters of Paradise: Organized Crime and the Internal Revenue Service in the Bahamas* (New Brunswick, NJ, and London: Transaction Publishers, 1991), 50.

119 *By this time, Malnik*: Messick, *Syndicate in the Sun*, 185.

119 *Once he spoke about*: Interview with retired FBI agent, November 11, 2007; Block, *Masters of Paradise*, 50–51; Messick, *Syndicate in the Sun*, 185.

119 *Hartford was friendly with*: Metro-Dade County Police File 10710-C, 1959.

119 *Hartford signed a contract*: Memorandum, re: Bahamas Inquiry; interview of Huntington Hartford, from Justice Department attorneys Robert D. Peloquin and David P. Bancroft, to William G. Hundley, Director of U.S. Department of

Justice Organized Crime and Racketeering Taskforce, January 18, 1966. The date of the contract between Hartford and Golub/Malnik was October 15, 1962.

119 *"somebody, high intelligence":* Messick, *Lansky,* 267.

120 *The bureau put together:* Interview with retired FBI agent, August 10, 2007.

120 *He walked in on:* Ibid., August 16, 2008.

120 *The bureau's spy game:* Ibid., November 21, 2007.

120 *Before destroying the bug:* Ibid., November 29, 2007.

120 *Malnik's work with the: Malnik v. Commissioner of IRS,* Docket No. 5307–76, U.S. Tax Court, T.C. Memo 1985–467; 1985 Tax Court Memo: 50 T.C.M (CCH) 977; T.C.M. (RIA) 85467, September 4, 1985.

120 *Malnik bought the U.S.:* "Scooby-Ooby Scopitone," *Time,* August 21, 1964.

120 *Malnik had ten other partners:* Jasmine Kripalani and Elinor J. Brecher, "Vincent Alo, Partner of Meyer Lansky," *Miami Herald,* March 13, 2001, 4B; Michael Roberts, "Video Obscura: Boulder's Joel Haertling Uncovers the Roots of MTV," *Denver Westword,* July 11, 2002; Scott R. Schmedel, "Movie Jukebox Probe: Grand Jury Looks into Everybody Linked with Scopitone; Tel-A-Sign Assails Inquiry," *Wall Street Journal,* April 26, 1966, 32.

121 *He got $38 for every:* Schmedel, "Movie Jukebox Probe."

121 *As might be expected: U.S. v. Vincent Alo,* U.S. Court of Appeals, 2nd Circuit, 439 F. 2nd 751, decided February 19, 1971.

121 *Malnik was represented:* Ibid.

121 *Alo contended that Malnik:* Ibid.

121 *But the plaintiffs failed:* In the Matter of TEL-A-SIGN, INC., Debtor, the Slater Bros. Co., Inc., No. 17016, U.S. Court of Appeals for the 7th Circuit, 415 F.2d 1334, August 15, 1969.

121 *The other Malnik partner:* Alix M. Freedman and John R. Enshwiller, "Big Liquor Wholesaler Finds Change Stalking Its Very Private World," *Wall Street Journal,* October 4, 1999, A1.

121 *In April 1965:* Schmedel, "Movie Jukebox Probe."

122 *When a* Wall Street Journal: Ibid.

122 *Morgenthau returned indictments:* Justice Department files/SEC regarding answers to the 2nd Circuit, 1971; *U.S. v. Vincent Alo,* U.S. Court of Appeals, 2nd Circuit, 439 F. 2nd 751.

122 *Later, Morgenthau admitted:* Timeline, Malnik, New York District Attorney.

122 *Alo was convicted: U.S. v. Vincent Alo,* U.S. Court of Appeals, 2nd Circuit, 439 F. 2nd 751.

123 *Malnik and Sam Cohen owned:* The first public record of Malnik and Cohen doing business together is their creation of Azure Blue Waters #2 on August 16, 1968. In 1973, they formed ALSA Development Corporation (after the first initials of each of their first names). The business address was listed as the Forge. See also Cook, with Carmichael, "Casino Gambling: Changing Character or Changing Fronts?"

123 *The duo had bought:* The Teamsters Pension fund that held the mortgage was officially called the Central States, Southeast and Southwest Areas Pension Fund. In the Matter of the Applications of Boardwalk Regency Corporation and the Jemm Company for Casino Licenses, State of New Jersey, Casino Con-

trol Commission, 10 N.J.A.R. 295, November 13, 1980, 306; Cook, with Carmichael, "Casino Gambling"; see also, Bob Sanders, "Loan Firm Gets New OK Despite Questionable Ties," *New Hampshire Business Review*, vol. 24, no. 8 (April 19, 2002), A1. As for Savador Rizzo being "an organized crime front man," see Janson, "Caesars Defends Its Tie to Lansky Figures."

123 *The property adjoined a:* Malnik had formed Sky Lake Country Club Inc. on October 10, 1966, listing Leo Rose as principal agent, himself as president, Alan Cohen as vice president, and Sylvia Sidon as a director.

124 *He did not disclose information:* In the Matter of the Applications of Boardwalk Regency Corporation, 345.

124 *The terms called for Malnik:* Janson, "Caesars Defends Its Tie to Lansky Figures." See also Cook, with Carmichael, "Casino Gambling."

124 *Malnik and the Cohens had bought: A Decade of Organized Crime: 1980 Report,* Pennsylvania Crime Commission; interview with retired Florida State Attorney General investigator, June 2, 2007.

124 *Also, Malnik negotiated:* In the Matter of the Applications of Boardwalk Regency Corporation, 347. See also Robert A. Rosenblatt and Al DeLugach, "SEC Charges Caesars World Failed to Disclose Transactions," *Los Angeles Times,* July 24, 1970, E1.

124 *And Caesars allowed:* Janson, "Caesars Defends Its Tie to Lansky Figures."

125 *As part of their:* Pennsylvania Crime Commission, 1980: 255.

125 *"It was a known fact":* Pennsylvania Crime Commission, investigative files, 1980; interview with Alvin B. Lewis; Pennsylvania Crime Commission, 1980: 252.

125 *Pennsylvania investigators discovered that:* Interview with Alvin B. Lewis, chairman of the Pennsylvania Crime Commission, January 15, 2009; see also Al DeLugach, "Caesars Palace Firm Under Investigation," *Los Angeles Times,* November 13, 1975, 3.

125 *On December 10, 1975:* In the Matter of the Applications of Boardwalk Regency Corporation, 338.

125 *"I'm going to say":* Sanders, "Loan Firm Gets New OK Despite Questionable Ties," A1.

125 *Cove Haven also sparked:* Rosenblatt and DeLugach, "SEC Charges Caesars World Failed to Disclose Transactions," E1.

125 *Caesars World's outside auditors:* Al DeLugach, "Suit Held Nothing to Worry About, Caesars World Reassures Holders," *Los Angeles Times,* December 6, 1975, C11.

126 *When Clifford Perlman was asked:* Ibid.

126 *The SEC probe took three:* Rosenblatt and DeLugach, "SEC Charges Caesars World Failed to Disclose Transactions." Al DeLugach, "Caesars Seeking Consent Accord in SEC Probe," *Los Angeles Times,* May 23, 1979, F18.

126 *In June 1977, Richard:* Brett Sokol, "Kulchur: Nostalgic for Cuba's Music and Mobsters," *Miami New Times,* September 16, 1999, 1.

126 *"Let me tell you something":* Investigative files, New Jersey Casino Control Board, sealed file dated October 15, 1981; see also Sanders, "Loan Firm Gets New OK Despite Questionable Ties."

126 *among them, the severance:* In the Matter of the Applications of Boardwalk Regency Corporation.

126 *It concluded that because:* Ibid.

127 *In 1978, a Bahamian company:* Marcia Gelbart, "Malnik Owns Some of AG Reserve's Most Valuable Land," *Palm Beach Post*, March 5, 1999, 1A.

127 *But when asked by a:* Ibid.

127 *Sheika Faisa, the mother:* William McWhirter, "Tales from an Arabian Nightmare," *People*, Bonus Part II, May 9, 1983, 90.

127 *the prince kept a small herd:* Kurt Anderson and William McWhirter, "The Sheiks Who Shake Up Florida," *Time*, July 19, 1982.

128 *Malnik became a financial:* McWhirter, "Tales from an Arabian Nightmare."

128 *By 1980, according to some:* Ibid.

128 *Prince Turki reportedly gave:* McWhirter, "Tales from an Arabian Nightmare."

128 *On January 21, Mitchelson:* Ibid.

128 *contractors and architects said:* Marc Fisher and John Wolin, "Saudi Prince's Spokesman: 'Everybody Will Get his Money,'" *Miami Herald*, June 30, 1982, 1.

129 *He sued the city for $1 trillion:* Messerschmidt, Wolin, and Browning, "The Saga of a Wealthy Arab Clan"; see also Anderson and McWhirter, "The Sheiks Who Shake Up Florida."

129 *"What is one thousand":* Fisher and Wolin, "Saudi Prince's Spokesman: 'Everybody Will Get His Money.'"

129 *In a country where Jews:* Interview with former State Department liaison officer to Saudi Arabia, March 12, 2008.

129 *The* Miami Herald *dubbed him:* Richard Wallace, "Story Unveils 'Malniks of Arabia,'" *Miami Herald*, May 1, 1983, A1.

129 *He was likely, she said:* Ibid.

129 *"Al's gonna get it yet":* Thomas Burdick and Charlene Mitchell, *Blue Thunder: How the Mafia Owned and Finally Murdered Cigarette Boat King Donald Aronow* (New York: Simon & Schuster, 1990), 154.

CHAPTER 11: NOWHERESVILLE

131 *"Mrs. Capitman called":* Jo Thomas, "Miami Beach Conflict Pits Developers Against Lovers of Art Deco," *New York Times*, February 26, 1981.

131 *"Is Art Deco":* Ibid.

132 *"I'm going to make enough":* "Art Deco Landmark Brought Down by Wrecking Ball," *Miami Herald*, April 24, 1981.

134 *But as state and local:* See, generally, Alison Bass, "Neglect of Elderly Found at South Beach Hotel," *Miami Herald*, August 12, 1982; Stofik, *Saving South Beach*, 90–91.

135 *Two thousand seniors:* Louis Trager, "Officials Threaten Prosecution," *Miami Herald*, August 22, 1982.

135 *The caption read:* "ACLF Law to Be Rewritten Again," *Miami Herald*, Neighbors Miami Beach, January 6, 1983, 3.

CHAPTER 12: COUNTERATTACK

139 *The DEA estimated:* Harris, "The Drug Game: Undercover in Miami; Where Business Is Vicious and Booming."

140 *"Miami was an agent's":* Harris, "The Drug Game . . ."

140 *"The only thing to compare":* Wakefield, "Awash in a Sea of Money," *Miami New Times,* October 6, 2005.

140 *Trafficker arrests were up:* Remarks in Miami, Florida, to Members of the South Florida Task Force and Members of Miami Citizens Against Crime, by Ronald Reagan, November 17, 1982.

140 *Almost $200 million:* Harris, "The Drug Game."

140 *That bust netted sixty-two:* David McClintick, *Swordfish: A True Story of Ambition, Savagery and Betrayal* (New York: Pantheon Books, 1993).

141 *The task force's "powder on":* Interview with FBI agent, June 13, 2007.

141 *Despite the seizures:* Zimmerman, *A History of Smuggling in Florida,* 95.

141 *In another five years:* Ibid., 96.

CHAPTER 13: "TRASH FOR CASH"

145 *In March, the* Miami Herald: "Deco Hotels Owe $36,000 in Payroll Taxes," *Miami Herald,* Neighbors Miami Beach, March 31, 1983, 4.

146 *Miami School Board member:* "People in the News," Associated Press, Domestic News, August 25, 1982, a.m. cycle.

146 *He denounced the Havana-born:* "A History of Controversy," *Miami Herald,* July 14, 1996, Arts, 11.

146 *Vincent Canby:* Review of *Scarface, New York Times,* December 9, 1983. Hip-hop stars especially have been attracted to the film. Sean "P. Diddy" Combs has seen it sixty-three times. "You watch it for the lessons," he said. For Snoop Dogg, "It's one of the most important movies of all time." The rapper Scarface, who took his name from the film, says of Pacino's character, "This cat is just like me."

147 *The show's technical adviser:* Jerry Buck, "A Tale of Two Cities: 'Hawaiian Heat' and 'Miami Vice,'" Associated Press, September 14, 1984.

147 *Art critics compared it:* Allman, *Miami,* 43.

148 *"My company didn't have":* Dory Owens, "Deco Owner's Rocky Road," *Miami Herald,* January 12, 1986, 1F.

148 *Mark Shantzis left but:* "Briefs," *New York Times,* August 31, 1983, D3.

149 *Sgarlat—who went on:* U.S. Attorney's Office, District of New Jersey, new release, September 8, 2006.

149 *Eight thousand northerners:* Hector Florin, "Land Buyer's First Dance with Pal-Mar, During Late '60s, Ended in Lawsuits," *Palm Beach Post,* July 18, 2005, 4A.

149 *Undeterred, Cavanagh developed:* Ibid.; see also Tom Matrullo, "Rotonda Investors Agree to Settlement: The Decision Ends a 25-year-old Conflict Between 50,000 Lot Buyers and the Community's Owners," *Sarasota Herald-Tribune,* August 24, 1996, 1B.

149 *The FTC repeatedly charged:* Cavanagh Communities Corporation, et al., 93 F.T.C. 559; Cavanagh Communities Corporation, et al. (Dismissal Order), 90

F.T.C. 128; Cavanagh Communities Corporation, etc., et al. (Interlocutory Order), 86 F.T.C. 1192; Cavanagh Communities Corporation, et al. (Interlocutory Order), 87 F.T.C. 143; and see, generally, Jeffrey Mills, "Land of Broken Promises," Associated Press, May 23, 1979; also *Wall Street Journal*, January 4, 1979, 3; David C. Bacon, "Land Frauds: Their Part in the Collapse of a Boom," *U.S. News & World Report*, February 23, 1976, 27.

149 *"an amazing turnaround":* Stanley Penn, "Parlays Stake in Casinos," *Wall Street Journal*, June 17, 1980, 48; see also *Wall Street Journal*, May 11, 1979, 39.

150 *State and federal banking:* State of Colorado, banking report, December 2, 1982.

150 *The SEC settled the case:* Donald Janson, "Resorts Acquiring New Casino Site," *New York Times*, August 21, 1983, sec. 11NJ, 1.

150 *In 1979, Florida's Department:* "Cavanagh Communities Diverted Funds, Florida Panel Charges," *Wall Street Journal*, September 24, 1979, 6.

150 *When he took charge:* Susan Sachs, "Banking in the Shadows," *Miami Herald*, October 9, 1986, 1A.

151 *The bank won a $500,000: National Bank of Florida v. The Royale Group, Ltd., Leonard Pelullo, et al.,* Miami-Dade Circuit Court, July 1984.

151 *Royale paid a $500,000:* Sachs, "Banking in the Shadows."

151 *"Trash for cash":* Ibid.

CHAPTER 14: "BUILDING BLOCKS"

153 *"The architecture, the location":* Allman, *Miami*, 39.

154 *And a prominent defense:* Edna Buchanan, "Police Pan Premiere of Miami Vice: Officers and Attorneys Call Show Unrealistic," *Miami Herald*, September 17, 1984, 1A.

154 *"Sure it makes the city":* Dory Owens, "Tourism Officials Want to Study Impact of TV Show," *Miami Herald*, September 18, 1984, 1B.

154 *He correctly predicted:* Steve Sonsky, "Tonight, America Tunes in to Miami," *Miami Herald*, September 16, 1984, 1L.

154 *Michael Mann thought:* Ibid.

154 *"I wanted a city":* Jeffrey Schmalz, "Miami Journal; Sun Sets on Show That Redefined a City," *New York Times*, May 18, 1989, 23.

155 *Those cocaine kingpins:* Pico Iyer, "Fighting the Cocaine Wars," *Time*, February 25, 1982; "Cocaine: The Evil Empire," *Newsweek*, February 25, 1985.

155 *But her arrest rated only:* See UPI, February 20, 1985, Domestic News, dateline: Los Angeles.

155 *Charged with a "continuing":* Gugliotta and Leen, *Kings of Cocaine*, 217.

157 *They found a tolerant:* Bonnie Weston, "Beach Vote May Revive Gay Rights," *Miami Herald*, December 8, 1991, 1C.

159 *A decade after Betancourt:* David W. Forrest, "South Beach": 'Paradise' and Reality," *Gay and Lesbian Review Worldwide*, May 1, 2002, vol. 9, no. 3, 24(3); see also Glenn Albin, "To Live and Die in South Beach," *Out*, May 1995, 72.

CHAPTER 15: "THE SULTANS OF SOUTH BEACH"

161 *The police found thirty-five derelicts:* Michael Kranish, "Abandoned Streets Suit the People of the Night," *Miami Herald*, August 29, 1982, 7M.

164 *They paid $3 million:* Debbie Sontag, "New Yorker Buys Two Deco Hotels," *Miami Herald*, Neighbors Miami Beach, July 17, 1986, 3.

164 *The Schlesser group:* Ibid., and interview with Mel Schlesser, February 10, 2009.

164 *He wasn't interested in doing:* Interview with Jane Dee Gross, July 28, 2008.

164 *Sanchez had made news:* James Grieff, "Miami Beach: Will Money and Civic Clout Support Rebirth for This Art Deco Haven?" *St. Petersburg Times*, May 24, 1987, 11.

164 *he uncovered a "Gentiles Only":* Stofik, *Saving South Beach*, 142.

165 *Often referring to himself:* Sanchez refused repeated entreaties to be interviewed for this book. Grieff, "Miami Beach."

165 *Sanchez found financing:* Lisa Gibbs, "Deco Man Gerry Sanchez Gets Taste of Own Medicine," *Miami Review*, November 13, 1992, A6.

165 *He bought six Ocean Drive:* Interview with Mel Schlesser, February 10, 2009.

165 *His teams of Polonia workers:* "Investor Buys Espanola Way," *Miami Herald*, Neighbors Miami Beach, May 18, 1986, 3.

165 *Sanchez was evidently:* Debbie Sontag, "Investor Plays Monopoly on Beach," *Miami Herald*, July 13, 1986, 1B.

166 *"He is buying up":* Ibid.

166 *And three months after:* "Deco-Rating the Beach," *Miami Herald*, August 4, 1986; "Developer Cashing In on South Beach Restorations," *Miami Herald*, July 31, 1986.

166 *Beach commissioner Stanley:* Sontag, "Investor Plays Monopoly on Beach."

172 *"I prefer to lose money":* Michael Kranish and Jay Ducassi, "The Domino Effect as Elderly Jews Move Out or Die, Latin Refugees Take Their Place," *Miami Herald*, August 29, 1992, 6M. See also Dory Owens, "New Yorker Gambles on Reviving South Beach," *Miami Herald*, September 15, 1986, 9BM.

CHAPTER 16: "A TALE OF TWO CITIES"

175 *Late that year, the New Jersey:* Michael Huber, "The Royale Connection," *Miami Herald*, April 28, 1990, 1A.

175 *The New Jersey report:* Interviews with Tony Goldman, Craig Robins, and Saul Gross. See also "Organized Crime in Boxing," State of New Jersey, Investigation Office of Attorney General, 1985; Sachs, "Banking in the Shadows." See generally Elise Ackerman, "The Hand of Fate," *Miami New Times*, February 2, 1995, 1.

175 *Pelullo dismissed the charges:* Interview with Joe Fontana, August 2, 2007.

175 *"This is the jewel":* Debbie Sontag, "The Restoration Fever Spreads," *Miami Herald*, Neighbors Miami Beach, September 11, 1986, 3.

178 *When Prince—in purple:* "Purple Prince Parties with Chic Club Z Crowd,"

Miami Herald, April 9, 1985, 1; see also Linda Thornton, "Glittery Disco Club Z Is Waking Up the Beach," *Miami Herald*, March 22, 1985, 1D.

179 *The brothers adamantly:* Irene Lacher, "Club Z's Landlords Trying to Kick Out Stylish Beach Disco," *Miami Herald*, April 14, 1985, 4B.

180 *"Miami Beach is definitely":* Craig Gilbert, "Beach Sees Bitter Brawl for Mayor Campaign's Big Issue: Is City Recovering or Still on Decline?" *Miami Herald*, November 1, 1995, 1B.

181 *"I saw South Beach":* Irene Lacher, "Owners of Warsaw Ballroom Hatch Plans for New Club Ovo," *Miami Herald*, Neighbors Miami Beach, May 1, 1985, 3.

181 *Ovo was the first:* Joel Achenbach, "Night Spots Enliven S Beach 7-Block Strip Sprouts Trendy Clubs, Raises Hopes," *Miami Herald*, July 28, 1986, 1B; see also Irene Lacher, "So What's Nu? Club's Owners Refuse to Say," *Miami Herald*, Neighbors Miami Beach, November 23, 1986, 17, and Irene Lacher, "Deco to Disco Is a Family Affair on Beach," *Miami Herald*, Neighbors Miami Beach, September 29, 1985, 18.

181 *Gloria Estefan, who had just:* Tom Austin, "Club Nu," *Miami New Times*, July 18, 1990.

181 *(An annual March event):* Humberto Guida, "WMC Grows Up," *Ocean Drive*, May 2008, 78.

182 *Tom Austin:* Austin, "Club Nu."

182 *George Tamsitt said later:* Lacher, "Owners of Warsaw Ballroom," 3.

182 *At a few clubs:* Interview with Gerry Kelly, November 5, 2007.

183 *"It just went on and on":* Austin, "Club Nu."

184 *It was such big news:* Laura Misch, "Jet Setter, Detective, Hefty Twins," *Miami Herald*, Neighbors Miami Beach, September 25, 1983, 25.

184 *"It's nice to close":* Susan Sachs, "Lawyer Cleared of Tax-Evasion Charges," *Miami Herald*, September 10, 1982, 2D.

185 *Now the critic wrote:* Marc Fisher, "The Forge," *Miami Herald*, Tropics, October 19, 1986, 10.

CHAPTER 17: "A PRETTY SPECIAL TIME"

186 *Ellie Schneiderman:* Craig Gilbert, "Will Artists Save the Mall?" *Miami Herald*, Neighbors Miami Beach, March 10, 1985, 12.

187 *In the year after Hyperspace:* Irene Lacher, "SoBe," *Miami Herald*, August 31, 1986, 1K.

188 *The Florida Bureau:* Mary Ann Esquivel, "Artist Finds New Controversy," *Miami Herald*, Neighbors Miami Beach, July 10, 1988, 18.

189 *"We don't really need":* Irene Lacher, "Businesses Form Deco 'Network,' " *Miami Herald*, Neighbors Miami Beach, June 29, 1986, 3.

189 *It announced:* Robert Becker, "Creating a Scene," *Interview*, September 1985, 78. In describing the new club scene, Joel Achenbach, then a *Miami Herald* reporter, wrote: "What is true is that our police officers drive Ferraris and keep getting indicted for drug ripoffs; that cocaine is so cheap and easily available that at some clubs you can just walk into a bathroom, tap your nose, pick up a packet from the attendant, and leave a $20 tip."

190 *Street crime, although down:* Joel Achenbach, "Night Spots Enliven S Beach 7-Block Strip Sprouts Trendy Clubs, Raises Hopes," *Miami Herald,* July 28, 1986, 1B.

190 *When Club Ovo closed:* "Closed Nightclub Owes Plenty, Records Show," *Miami Herald,* Neighbors Miami Beach, June 18, 1987, 3.

190 *The IRS was demanding:* Securities and Exchange Commission Report, April 1985, vol. 1, National Report Series D, 91:231.

CHAPTER 18: WHERE DREAMS DIE

191 *the plan's costs had:* Michael Kranish, "Final Offer: Offices Instead of Venice," *Miami Herald,* August 29, 1982, 8M.

191 *Half of the residents:* Michael Kranish, "By City Order, Nothing Flows and Nothing Flowers," *Miami Herald,* August 29, 1982, 3M.

192 *The Beach's homeless:* Kranish, "Abandoned Streets Suit the People of the Night."

192 *Collectively, South Shore:* U.S. Government Census, Annual Data, 1982, Southeast, Florida, sec. 19, unit 4, 321:98.

192 *refugees with no family:* Kranish and Ducassi, "The Domino Effect as Elderly Jews Move Out or Die, Latin Refugees Take Their Place."

192 *"I'd say 85 percent":* Ibid.

193 *A seventy-eight-year-old caretaker:* Edna Buchanan, "Caretaker, 78, Slain Trying to Protect Woman," *Miami Herald,* August 15, 1982, 6B.

193 *A Jewish man who:* Kranish and Ducassi, "The Domino Effect."

193 *Jose Rios had spent:* Ibid.

193 *At a city commission meeting:* Interview with Alex Daoud, October 15, 2008.

194 *The landlord, Howie Bushinsky:* Kranish, "South Beach: Where Dreams Die."

194 *"We cannot wait any longer":* Michael Kranish, "By City Order, Nothing Flows and Nothing Flowers," *Miami Herald,* August 29, 1982, 3M.

194 *The new developers:* Kranish, "Final Offer: Offices Instead of Venice," 8M.

194 *The city had previously:* Michael Kranish, "Major Changes in South Beach Plan—Developers to Save More Buildings," *Miami Herald,* September 16, 1982, 1C.

195 *When Muss insisted:* Michael Kranish, "South Beach's Subsidy Feud Escalates," *Miami Herald,* May 27, 1982, 2C.

195 *In a lead editorial:* Jim Hampton, editor, "The Ivory Tower: The South Beach Plan Is Dead," *Miami Herald,* September 19, 1982, 2E.

195 *A judge dismissed:* "Beach Moratorium to Get Day in Court," *Miami Herald,* November 17, 1982, 2B.

195 *Late in November:* "Business Load Spurs Resignation," *Miami Herald,* Neighbors Miami Beach, November 28, 1982, 2.

196 *Sawitz was furious:* "Restaurateur Quits Beach Tourism Panel, Cites Intimidation by City Commissioners," *Miami Herald,* December 3, 1982, 3C.

196 *On December 18, the city:* "Beach Building Ban Lifted Plan to Raze South Shore Abandoned," *Miami Herald,* December 18, 1982, 1B.

196 *"What should really happen"*: Beth Dunlop, "What Should Really Happen in South Beach," *Miami Herald*, Viewpoint, October 6, 1985, 1E.

197 *Watt gave Miami*: Michael Kranish, "U.S. Threatens to Take Back Beach Park," *Miami Herald*, Neighbors Miami Beach, November 21, 1982, p. 3.

197 *charging that the*: Paul Shannon, "City Helps Tenants Move Out of Condemned Hotel," *Miami Herald*, Neighbors Miami Beach, May 26, 1983, 6.

198 *The city used the vacant*: Michael Kranish, "Builders Set Sail on City's Marina," *Miami Herald*, Neighbors Miami Beach, September 29, 1983, 3.

198 *By December, commissioners*: "Beach Establishes Economic Council," *Miami Herald*, Neighbors Miami Beach, December 11, 1983, 11.

198 *On the northern side*: Michael Kranish, "Diamond in the Rough Dreams," *Miami Herald*, Neighbors Miami Beach, November 17, 1983, 12.

199 *"Look what it did for Marina"*: Interview with Alex Daoud, September 15, 2008.

199 *"With," the mayor said*: Michael Kranish, "Name Game Boosts City Image: Get the Pointe?" *Miami Herald*, Neighbors Miami Beach, February 5, 1984, 3.

199 *Property in the Art Deco zone*: Kranish, "Diamond in the Rough Dreams."

199 *Cheezem claimed he had gotten*: "South Pointe," PR Newswire, Wednesday, June 20, 1984.

199 *The units were priced*: Ibid.

199 *"This place was once fabulous"*: Paul Shannon, "Beach May Bulldoze Aging Pier," *Miami Herald*, July 25, 1984, 2D.

200 *"It was a wonderful old pier"*: Dunlop, "What Should Really Happen in South Beach."

200 *The Economic Development Council*: Lawrence Josephs, "What Next for South Beach?" *Miami Herald*, Neighbors Miami Beach, July 1, 1984, 3.

200 *"You are cheating us"*: Shannon, "Beach May Bulldoze Aging Pier."

200 *South Florida real estate*: Dory Owens, "Cheezem Set to Begin South Beach Revival," *Miami Herald*, March 18, 1985, 7BM.

200 *"Promising to close"*: Dunlop, "What Should Really Happen in South Beach."

201 *By the time of the last*: Alex Finkelstein, "Condo Developers Go for the Gold," *South Florida Business Journal*, vol. 5, no. 43 (July 8, 1985), sec. 1, 1.

201 *And one month after he got*: "South Pointe Project Ready to Start," *Miami Herald*, July 11, 1985, 6D.

201 *A week later, he sold*: Phil Kuntz, "Can Rodney Propps Save South Beach?" *Miami Herald*, Neighbors Miami Beach, December 19, 1985, 10.

201 *Propps and Murray*: "$3.6 million Added to Loan," *Miami Herald*, August 4, 1985, 18H.

201 *Cheezem pocketed a $5 million*: Dory Owens, "South Pointe Developer Quits, Sells Out," *Miami Herald*, July 18, 1985, 8D; see also Craig Gilbert and Juanita Greene, "Graham Seeks South Pointe as Park Site," *Miami Herald*, October 3, 1985, 1D.

201 *before the state bureaucracy*: Paul Anderson, "South Pointe Park Rejected Panel Urges Florida Not to Buy Ocean Site," *Miami Herald*, November 26, 1985, 1B.

201 *Although obtaining the permits*: Phil Kuntz, "South Beach Project Set in Stone," *Miami Herald*, December 15, 1985, 1A.

201 *Beth Dunlop, in a typically:* Dunlop, "What Should Really Happen in South Beach."

202 *He had owned sixteen:* Mark Albright, "The Rocky Road to Penrod's Palace: From Burgers to Buildings, Owner Reached for the Top," *St. Petersburg Times*, March 2, 1976, 17E.

202 *He also planned to host:* Debbie Sontag, "Fort Lauderdale Group Plans Restaurant for Pier Park," *Miami Herald*, Neighbors Miami Beach, October 6, 1985, 4.

202 *He expected to spend:* Betty Cortina, "Sizzling, Fizzling," *Miami Herald*, Neighbors Miami Beach, June 7, 1990, 18.

203 *"The firm certainly can't":* Anderson, "South Pointe Park Rejected Panel Urges Florida Not to Buy Ocean Site."

203 *A month later, 10 million:* Kuntz, "South Beach Project Set in Stone."

203 *The 400-boat marina:* "South Pointe," *Miami Herald*, Neighbors Miami Beach, July 1, 1984, 3.

203 *Work on the $3.5 million:* "Commissioners Stall Decisions on Park," *Miami Herald*, Neighbors Miami Beach, May 6, 1984, 3.

203 *in a long profile:* Kuntz, "Can Rodney Propps Save South Beach?"

204 *After Murray's takeover:* Debbie Sontag, "Apartment Sales Stall at Tower," *Miami Herald*, Neighbors Miami Beach, October 19, 1986, 7.

204 *Murray's publicly traded firm:* Dory Owens, "New Money Sought for Beach Condo," *Miami Herald*, November 11, 1986, 5B.

204 *"Dale's a wonderful guy":* Gregg Fields, "South Pointe Puzzler: Why Now?" *Miami Herald*, May 31, 1987, 1C.

205 *David Paul told friends:* Interview with Alex Daoud, September 15, 2008; see also Fields, "South Pointe Puzzler: Why Now?"

205 *Daoud called Abel Holtz:* "South Pointe Deadline Extended, Judge Gives Condo Week to Refinance," *Miami Herald*, July 28, 1987, 4B.

205 *The new owners also:* James Grieff, "Miami Beach: Will Money and Civic Clout Support Rebirth for This Art Deco Haven?" *St. Petersburg Times*, May 24, 1987, 11.

205 *There was hope in City Hall:* Interview with Alex Daoud, September 15, 2008.

205 The New York Times *ran:* Max Berley, "National Notebook: Miami Beach; New Vitality in South Beach," *New York Times*, October 25, 1987, 1.

207 *General Noriega would have:* Sydney P. Freedberg, "Aronow Murder Left Tangled Trail," *Miami Herald*, November 23, 1990, 1A.

208 *"It was total chaos":* Samuels, "Liquid Smoke."

208 *"Who is the guy?":* Burdick and Charlene, *Blue Thunder*, 45.

208 *"Is that son of a bitch":* Ibid., 47.

208 *And when someone told him:* Freedberg, "Aronow Murder Left Tangled Trail."

209 *Aronow's secretary told the police:* Burdick and Charlene, *Blue Thunder*, 176–77.

209 *Kramer's street in Hallandale:* Ibid., 209, 211.

209 *While in prison:* Arthur J. Harris, *Speed Kills* (New York: Avon Books, 1998), 119–23.

209 *Some of his partners:* "Drug Kingpin Dethroned; Kramer Trial Ends Well," *Miami Herald*, September 2, 1990, 2C.

209 *unless Aronow returned it all:* Jeff Leen, "In the Drug Business, Bringing in the Cash Is Easy, the Hard Part Is Spending It—That's Where Mel Kessler Came In," *Miami Herald*, September 2, 1990, 9.

209 *"That cocksucker stole":* Samuels, "Liquid Smoke."

210 *He almost made it to:* Christopher Marquis and Lizette Alvarez, "Bold Jailbreak Failed," *Miami Herald*, April 18, 1989, 1A.

210 *The hit man was an ex-pimp:* Jay Weaver and David Ovalle, "Death Closes a Notorious Case," *Miami Herald*, April 1, 2009, D1.

210 *After his murder:* Ibid.

CHAPTER 19: REBUILDING A CITY

211 *The most progress:* Interview with Tony Goldman, February 26, 2008.

212 *"I looked at it as a military":* Christopher Boyd, "South Beach at the Turning Point: Old Glories, Can Deco, Disco and Developers Salvage a City," *Miami Herald*, May 31, 1987, 1A.

212 *"I'm so sure this area will change":* Ibid.

212 *"This isn't the land":* Ibid.

213 *Gary Farmer, owner:* Grieff, "Miami Beach."

213 *Pelullo claimed that his other:* "Deco Hotel to Be Razed?" *Miami Herald*, Neighbors Miami Beach, April 9, 1987, 3; see also "Owners Plan to Level Deco Hotel for Parking," *Miami Herald*, May 7, 1987, 1D.

214 *Further infuriating the:* Beth Dunlop, "Senator: Save It," *Miami Herald*, August 25, 1987, 1D.

214 *Still, preservationists tried:* "Days Inn Wants In on the Beach—250 Room Ocean Drive Hotel Planned," *Miami Herald*, June 26, 1987, 1B; see also "Days Inn Plans Face City Board in Meeting Today," *Miami Herald*, Neighbors Miami Beach, October 1, 1987, 3.

215 *"The Biscaya could be":* Beth Dunlop, "Biscaya Falls Victim to Stupidity," *Miami Herald*, February 15, 1987, 2K.

215 *Liebman proposed a tougher:* "Preservationists Fight to Change Law, Save Hotel," *Miami Herald*, Neighbors Miami Beach, August 27, 1987, 3.

215 *In August, the Miami:* Stephen Smith, "Senator Hotel Gets 6-Month Reprieve," *Miami Herald*, August 7, 1987, 1.

215 *Nancy Liebman suggested:* Interview with Nancy Liebman, January 11, 2008.

216 *The government charged:* Christopher Boyd, "Art Deco Figure Indicted for Fraud Involving Loan," *Miami Herald*, June 24, 1989; see also Michael Huber, "The Royale Connection," *Miami Herald*, April 28, 1990, 1A.

216 *And Royale's former landlord:* "Loans and Lawsuits; Banking in the Shadows," *Miami Herald*, October 9, 1986, 12A.

216 *This pattern of "noncompliance":* David Satterfield, "Hotel Firm Must File Records, SEC Says," *Miami Herald*, September 11, 1987, 1C.

217 *Susan Pelullo was its president:* "Brickell Avenue Home Sold for $2.65 Million," *Miami Herald*, October 25, 1987, 19H.

217 *"The cost to the city":* Lynn Horsley, "The Struggle to Save the Senator Past, Fu-

ture Square Off in South Beach," *Miami Herald*, Neighbors Miami Beach, September 11, 1998, 16.

217 *Using the Senator's fate:* "A Battle Lost, Deco Fans Vow to Win War," *Miami Herald*, October 17, 1988, 1C.

CHAPTER 20: CLUB HEAVEN

224 *The* Miami Herald *published:* M. Alexandra Nelson, "Boxer Model's Breezy Style Turns Heads on Beach," *Miami Herald*, October 16, 1991, 1D.

224 *warned the headline:* Leonard Pitts, Jr., "Oh No! Disco the Beast Is Back! Grab the Turntable and Run for Your Lives," *Miami Herald*, June 20, 1991, 1F.

226 *"As Holly Golightly":* Anne Hull, "Meet Tara Solomon D-I-V-A of the Deco District," *Miami Herald*, November 26, 1989, 1F.

227 *He collected $16,000:* Sam Terilli, "Beach Club Owner Arrested in Art Insurance Scam," *Miami Herald*, April 11, 1992, 1B.

228 *But most important to Schrager:* "U.S. District Court Yahweh Follower's Case Dismissed," *Miami Herald*, May 6, 1982, 2B.

229 *The code wrote special rules:* Tom Austin, "Swelter," *Miami New Times*, October 9, 1991.

230 *Colombo knew nothing about:* Interview with Louis Canales, February 1, 2008.

233 *The city issued:* Peggy Landers, "On Location Magazine Photographers Find We Are Location Perfect," *Miami Herald*, May 31, 1989, 1D.

233 *Combined with moviemaking:* Records of Metro-Dade Film Office, archives, 1990.

233 *The Edison cost him:* Lisa Gibbs, "Deco Man Gerry Sanchez Gets Taste of Own Medicine," *Miami Herald*, November 13, 1992, A6.

234 *He blamed it:* Christopher Boyd, "South Beach Hotels Sold to Investors," *Miami Herald*, April 7, 1988, 7D.

CHAPTER 21: ISLAND OUTPOST

236 *After the* Miami Herald: Michael Huber, "The Royale Connection," *Miami Herald*, April 28, 1990, 1A.

236 *When Pelullo could not:* Christopher Boyd, "Deco Units for Sale: Beach Hotels to Be Auctioned Off," *Miami Herald*, November 20, 1990, 1.

236 *Other potential bidders:* Interview with Mark Soyka, December 3, 2007; see also Gregg Fields, "Royale Group's Hotels Auctioned," *Miami Herald*, November 20, 1990, 5B.

236 *The winning bid:* In 1991, a federal jury found Pelullo guilty of diverting $2.2 million that FCA had loaned for renovation on the South Beach hotels. He was also convicted of siphoning $114,000 from a Royale subsidiary. He was sentenced to twenty-four years, but the 3rd U.S. Circuit Court of Appeals reversed the convictions because of improperly admitted evidence at trial. In 1993, Pelullo was convicted in a retrial. That conviction was again overturned by the Circuit Court. A 1994 third trial ended in a hung jury. In the fourth trial in 1995, a federal jury in Philadelphia convicted him of forty-seven counts of fraud and racketeering for diverting the money from the Miami Beach hotels and he got a twenty-four-year

sentence. In 1996, he was tried on separate felony charges for looting the pension fund of a New Jersey printing company and the jury found him guilty of eleven counts of embezzlement, forty-two counts of money laundering, and one count of conspiracy. He got another seventeen and a half years. In 2002, a District Court ordered a new trial citing the government's failure to disclose exculpatory evidence. In 2005, Pelullo's legal odyssey ended when another Circuit Court reversed the new trial decision and confirmed his convictions.

237 *"South Beach had a character"*: Marilyn Cole Lownes, "Island Man: What Do Bob Marley and U2 have in Common? Chris Blackwell," *Irish America*, vol. 15, no. 1 (March 31, 1999), 38.

239 *She had died in March:* Joan Cook, "Barbara Baer Capitman, 69, Dies; Created Miami Art Deco District," *New York Times*, March 31, 1990, 12.

239 *Lenny Horowitz had died:* "Leonard Horowitz, Industrial Designer, 43," *New York Times*, May 10, 1989.

CHAPTER 22: "IT'S NOT LIKE DISNEY WORLD"

241 *Paul threatened to foreclose:* "The Dock, Mayor Daoud, and CenTrust," *Miami Herald*, April 13, 1990, 1B; see also David Lyons, "Witness: Foreclose Done in Revenge," *Miami Herald*, June 26, 1992, B2.

241 *He never reported:* "Daoud Didn't Report Cash from Socialite, Forms Say," *Miami Herald*, April 28, 1990, 1A.

241 *When federal prosecutors:* Ibid.; see also Tom Dubocq, "Grand Juror Charged with Providing Tips to Alleged Druglord," *Miami Herald*, January 28, 1994, 1B.

242 *The previous year:* Laura Parker, "Florida Corruption Probes Proliferate," *Washington Post*, August 13, 1990, A4.

242 *"Talk about your match":* Carl Hiaasen, "Daoud, Sheik: Where's the Laugh Track," *Miami Herald*, November 13, 1991, 1B.

242 *He held a press conference:* "Mayor Beach Assails Charges," *Miami Herald*, October 31, 1991, 1A.

244 *The Resolution Trust Corporation:* Beatrice E. Garcia, "South Beach Developers Win Deco Hotels," *Miami Herald*, April 10, 1992, 1C.

CHAPTER 23: "I WAS DYING A LITTLE EVERY DAY"

248 *In May 1992:* Gregg Field, "Charges Mount Against Paul," *Miami Herald*, May 14, 1992, 1A.

250 *" 'I can't believe' ":* United States v. Alex Daoud, U.S. District Court, Miami, August 5, 1992.

251 *"utterly perfect":* Daoud, *Sins of South Beach.*

251 *At Warsaw, club kids:* Austin, "Swelter," *Miami New Times*, September 2, 1992.

256 *Holtz pled guilty:* Jerry Knight, "Banker with D.C. Ties Faces Prison," *Washington Post*, October 27, 1994, B11.

257 *Muss stopped the Abel:* Interview with Alex Daoud, September 15, 2008.

257 *Her first husband, Jay Kogan:* Joan Fleischman, *Miami Herald*, June 3, 1996, 1B.

CHAPTER 24: "ALL ABOUT THE FLASH"

259 *"They were empty"*: Austin, "Swelter," *Miami New Times*, February 26, 1992.

260 *Versace decided to evict:* Interview with Sam Robin, August 20, 2008. Interview with Saul Gross, November 15, 2007.

263 *"This beautiful Latin girl"*: John Lantigua, "Deconstructing Tommy: How a Bensonhurst Boy Rose to the Summit of South Beach's Promotion Biz," *Miami New Times*, October 8, 1998; see also *State v. Thomas Puccio*, F-92-033868, October 14, 1992; *State v. Thomas Puccio*, B-07020119, April 9, 2007.

263 *"where five Mafia families"*: Lantigua, "Deconstructing Tommy."

264 *His father-in-law:* Court records, depositions, answers to interrogatories, *Verena Von Mitschke-Sollande et al. v. Thomas Kramer*, 1996, U.S. District Court, Miami; see also Matthew Haggman, "Judge: Thomas Kramer Owes $108M," *Miami Herald*, April 18, 2007, 1C.

264 *Kramer had been vacationing:* Ingrid Sischy and Peter Brant, "Between Heaven and Hell," *Interview*, February 1993.

264 *He offered top prices:* Interview with Saul Gross, April 4, 2008.

264 *(He bought the penthouse):* Christine Evans, "Doubting Thomas," *Miami Herald*, Tropics, January 3, 1993.

265 *A court awarded a multi-million:* Peter Whoriskey, "Miami Beach's Very Big Deal," *Miami Herald*, July 23, 1995, 3.

266 *"It depends on price"*: Matthew Haggman, "Judge: Thomas Kramer Owes $108M," *Miami Herald*, April 18, 2007, 1C.

266 *He spent $3 million:* Interview with Thomas Kramer, October 29, 2007.

266 *He hired Norman Gosney:* Ibid.

267 *Outside the club, a replica:* Ibid; see also Tom Austin, "Swelter," *Miami New Times*, November 4, 1992.

267 *He told someone that:* Linda Marx, "The Thomas Kramer Affair," *Miami Metro* (April 2000), 36.

268 *The evening ended:* Interview with Thomas Kramer, October 29, 2007.

CHAPTER 25: "NO GUNS. NO POLITICS"

269 *Powers told a local:* David Kidwell, "Ocean Drive to Join Jam of Beach Mags," *Miami Herald*, October 29, 1992, 7.

270 *Austin dubbed him:* Tom Austin, "Swelter," *Miami New Times*, December 1, 1993, and November 23, 1995.

270 *He was "taken with"*: Andrew Goldman, "The Hamptons Menace? Jason Binn Is Everybody's New Best Friend," *New York Observer*, May 31, 1999, 4.

270 *"These girls are our"*: Tom Austin, "Swelter," *Miami New Times*, August 11, 1998.

271 *"They were all tens!"*: Goldman, "The Hamptons Menace?"

271 *"Turns out he didn't even"*: Ibid.

271 *She told friends:* Interview with executive, *Ocean Drive*, November 12, 2007; interview with *Ocean Drive* editor, May 2, 2008.

271 *Powers later admitted:* Steven Almond, "The Powers Behind Ocean Drive," *Miami New Times*, February 23, 1995, 1.

271 *(Sandi later had her own):* Interview with former executive for *Ocean Drive*, February 12, 2009; also interview with editor, *Ocean Drive*, October 3, 2007.

272 *He closed the* Daily Planet: Michael Kaplan, "South Beach—As It Inevitably Will," *Sun-Sentinel* (Fort Lauderdale), February 12, 1996, 6.

272 *With a free circulation:* Author review of criminal records, Miami-Dade County Courthouse, April and May 2008.

272 *Max had been in a:* See, generally, Sidney Schaer, "Set of Corvettes Going to the Max," *New York Newsday*, February 20, 1990, 11; Don Van Natta, Jr., "U.S. Charges Peter Max with Hiding Art-Sale Income Tax Fraud," *Miami Herald*, June 6, 1996.

273 *When Powers described his:* Interview with Thomas Kramer, October 29, 2007.

273 *He invested $100,000:* Ibid.

273 *It was, after all:* Interview with *Ocean Drive* editor, May 2, 2008.

274 *Prosecutor Robert Cramer:* Interview with former prosecutor, U.S. Attorney's Office, Southern District New York, August 18, 2008.

274 *Powers delivered the goods:* Joan Fleischmann, "Peter Max Has Taxing Problem with an Old Pal," *Miami Herald*, June 10, 1996, 1B.

274 *"We're not competing":* Interview with Thomas Kramer, October 29, 2007.

274 *Binn told the* Florida: Michael Kaplan, *Florida Business Journal*, vol. 25, no. 14 (1994), 18.

274 *Powers finally agreed:* Almond, "The Powers Behind Ocean Drive."

275 *Sandi Powers became well known:* Interviews with three individuals: a Miami-based doctor and dentist and a Beach newspaper columnist.

275 *"It's just jealousy":* Interview with Michael Capponi, July 12, 2008.

CHAPTER 26: KING OF CLUBS

276 *But by 1993, as:* Jim DeFede, "The Further Adventures of Willy and Sal," *Miami New Times*, November 10, 1993, 1.

277 *And although the Feds:* Tim Long, "Miami: Glitzy, Violent and Muy Caliente, It's Taking the World by Storm," *Time*, September 6, 1993, 14.

278 *Another 11 percent:* University of Miami Architecture Study, South Beach, 1997.

280 *He had three assault:* Manhattan District Attorney, author review of file on Christian Ludwigsen.

280 *Paciello knew nothing:* Frank Owen, *Clubland: The Fabulous Rise and Murderous Fall of Club Culture* (New York: St. Martin's Press, 2003), 100. Michelle McPhee, *Mob Over Miami* (New York: Onyx Books, 2002), 102.

280 *In South Beach, Vaccarezza:* Interview with Louis Canales, January 24, 2008; interview with federal prosecutor, February 12, 2008; and see also Bastone, "Thug Life: Wild Man Chris Paciello Has the Juice at Liquid," *The Village Voice*, April 7, 1998.

281 *Pooch earned a reputation:* Lantigua, "Deconstructing Tommy."

281 *"Wait until you meet Pooch":* Interview with former manager of The Spot, August 2, 2008.

281 *Paciello bought 90 percent:* Owen, *Clubland*, 100.

281 *While construction was under way:* Author review of files, Manhattan District Attorney; see, generally, Owen, *Clubland*, 100; McPhee, *Mob Over Miami*, 102.

282 *After a call to Code:* McPhee, *Mob Over Miami*, 105.

282 *Dominic Dionisio was:* Interview with federal prosecutor, February 12, 2008; see also Bastone, "Thug Life."

282 *Paciello and Caruso hosted:* Hood was a heroin addict whose talent for packing a club got interrupted with six months in prison for assault and, later, four and a half years for bank robbery.

282 *They also hired Jody:* Interview with nightclub manager, South Beach, 1989–97, March 2, 2008; interview with tea dance promoter, August 1, 2008.

283 *The car's owner refused:* McPhee, *Mob Over Miami*, 109–10.

283 *Paciello financed a friend's:* Bastone, "Thug Life."

283 *"You treacherous motherfucker":* Owen, *Clubland*, 107.

283 *He refused to identify:* McPhee, *Mob Over Miami*, 112.

283 *He suspected arson:* Bastone, "Thug Life."

284 *"I certainly had been":* Interview with Ingrid Casares, January 14, 2008.

284 *The Casares family:* Ibid.

284 *RC Aluminum nabbed:* "Top Private Companies," *South Florida CEO*, July 1, 2007, vol. 11, no. 7, 60(7).

284 *And her father gave a:* Interview with Lady of Lourdes retired teacher, March 18, 2008.

285 *By then, she was openly:* Jonathan Meter, "Who's That Girl?" *New York* magazine, July 27, 1998.

285 *She was also using several:* Interview with friend of Casares, January 6, 2008; see also Owen, *Clubland*.

285 *"A butch Audrey Hepburn":* Interview with Carlos Betancourt, February 29, 2008.

285 *In one entry:* Madonna, Steven Meisel, and Glenn O'Brien, *Sex* (New York: Warner Books, 1992); also interviews with friends of Bernhard, January 12, 2008, and March 1, 2008.

285 *Sarah Pettit, the:* Casares acknowledged to *New York* magazine that she had become a famous lesbian, "but that's because I've had high-profile female affairs." "What she really was," says ex-*Out* editor Sarah Pettit, "was the worst vice that you could be as a lesbian, which is somebody who was extremely social-climby, fairly concerned with artifice, and totally unashamed about it. She became her own inventor in a way, and if she had to go before a panel of lesbian experts, they would have turned her down. You have to be doing something for the cause."

286 *It was a chance for Ingrid:* Owen, *Clubhand*, 115.

286 *It was the first time he had:* Testimony of Michael Caruso, *U.S. v. Peter Gatien*, U.S. District Court for the Eastern District of New York, Case No. 96-CR-430, 1977.

CHAPTER 27: PLAYING THE RACE CARD

288 *The boycott had begun:* David Kidwell and Tom Fiedler, "Metro's Clark Second to Offer Apology," *Miami Herald*, November 30, 1990, 1A.

288 *"Don't come and ask me":* "Miami Beach Daoud: We're Owed Apology," *Miami Herald*, January 11, 1991, 2B.

289 *The article mentioned:* Elaine de Valle, "Dreary Shorecrest's Future May Be Brighter," *Miami Herald*, Neighbors Miami Beach, December 31, 1995, 26.

289 *A real estate project:* Interview with Don Peebles, October 12, 2007.

289 *A decade earlier:* David S. Hilzenrath, "Benefits of a Tax Board's Revolving Door; Ex-Chairman's Record on Assessment Appeals Beats the Average," *Washington Post*, April 17, 1990, A1.

290 *In his first year:* Ibid.

290 *With those earnings:* Don Peebles, *The Peebles Principles* (Englewood Cliffs, NJ: John Wiley & Sons, 2007).

290 *But the controversy was buried:* Michael York, "Excerpts from Videotape of Barry's Arrest at the Vista Hotel," *Washington Post*, June 29, 1990, A22; Tracy Thompson, "Witness Ties '87 Barry Illness to Drugs," *Washington Post*, July 12, 1990, A1.

290 The Washington Post *said that:* Sharon LaFraniere, "Barry's New Inner Circle; Mayor Looks to Five in Year of Turmoil," *Washington Post*, August 30, 1989, A1; Rudolph A. Pyatt, Jr., "Barry's Push for $48 Million Deal for Ally Signals Return of Wheeling and Dealing," *Washington Post*, August 10, 1995, D11.

290 *By the time Peebles:* "New Hotel Chain Sought for Black-Owned Project," *Miami Herald*, April 18, 1995, 2B.

290 *Arthur Courshon, the lawyer:* Interview with Don Peebles, October 12, 2007.

294 *Five of the bids included:* Ibid., September 25, 2007.

294 *They were unfounded:* Ibid., October 12, 2007.

294 *Hilliard, who was so proud:* Rick Jervis and Henri Cauvin, "Liens, IRS Cloud Proposal for Black-Owned Hotel," *Miami Herald*, May 24, 1996, 6B.

295 *"You shouldn't have done that":* Peebles, *The Peebles Principles.*

CHAPTER 28: "AN INFAMOUS PERSONALITY"

297 *He dissed Tony Goldman:* Gail DeGeorge and Peggy Salz-Trautman, "The German Tycoon Making Waves in Miami Beach," *BusinessWeek*, July 25, 1994, 77.

297 *He told* Interview: Ingrid Sischy and Peter Brant, "Between Heaven and Hell," *Interview*, February 1993.

298 *He contributed $1.5 million:* Cindy Kirscher Goodman, "Invisible Man Behind Casinos," *Miami Herald*, November 3, 1994, 1A.

298 *Kramer's vision for a tropical:* Alexis Muellner, "Kramer in Talks to Build Casino on South End of Miami Beach," *Miami Daily Business Review*, February 8, 1994, 1; see also DeGeorge and Salz-Trautman, "The German Tycoon Making Waves in Miami Beach."

298 *"I get treated like shit":* Sischy and Brant, "Between Heaven and Hell."

298 *He assured nervous:* Elise Ackerman, "Going Deutsch with Tycoon Thomas,"

Miami New Times, November 23, 1995, 1; see also Joe Chudicek, "German Investor Demands $500,000 from Contractor," *Miami Review*, February 23, 1993, 1.

298 *Restaurants were reluctant:* Evans, "Doubting Thomas."

298 *He boasted of his orgies:* Trisha and I met Kramer twice in 2008. Once for an interview and lunch in which he described how he and friends had recently shot up part of the Everglades for five hours with machine guns (he says he has a license) and how he bought out a poor Cuban's trailer for $24,000 on the spot, so he and his buddies could shoot it up. Second, for a small dinner party he hosted at his waterfront villa. He showed us his "party wagon," a British ambulance converted into a moving bedroom stocked with liquor and sexual party favors. When we left early, the party was still going. Kramer had retired to the pool and was frolicking naked with several girls, also in the buff. We asked if we should let him know we were leaving. A friend said, "Not unless you intend to participate."

299 *But within a week she dropped:* Ackerman, "Going Deutsch with Tycoon Thomas," *Miami New Times*; interview with former Miami Dade prosecutor, February 2, 2008.

299 *The charges were dismissed:* Linda Marx, "The Thomas Kramer Affair," *Miami Metro*, April 2000, 34.

300 *His most consistent answer:* Evans, "Doubting Thomas."

300 *"Once I was skiing":* Berman, "The Odd Couple," 58.

300 *Moreover, Trump said:* "Trumping South Florida," *Miami Herald*, March 24, 1995, RSVP, sec. A.

301 *Kramer had begun taking:* Ted Reed and Cindy Krisher, "Trump, Kramer: South Beach Partners?" *Miami Herald*, January 24, 1995, 1C.

301 *And Daly had a nasty:* Interview with Tom Daly, February 2, 2008; interview with Jorge Perez, October 7, 2007.

303 *Ed Resnick, the city's lead negotiator:* Peter Whoriskey, "Beach Buys into Kramer's Dream," *Miami Herald*, July 27, 1995, 1A.

303 *It shelved objections:* Fran Brennan, "Beach, Developer Close to S. Pointe Deal," *Miami Herald*, January 17, 1995, 2B.

304 *It was changed from:* Connie Prater, "Beach Vote on Building Becomes a Street Fight," *Miami Herald*, May 11, 1997, 18.

304 *He also promised to set aside:* Brennan, "Beach, Developer Close to S. Pointe Deal."

304 *South Pointe residents, who had:* The Portofino Settlement Agreement was soon overshadowed for Kramer when in 1996 his ex-wife's stepfather, Siegfried Otto, sued him in Miami-Dade county court for $145 million. He claimed the money was a loan on which Kramer had reneged. Kramer countersued in Switzerland, contending the money was a gift.

304 *Said Mayor Gelber:* Martin Wisckol, "Referendum for Constructing High-Rises Is in Voters' Hands," *Miami Herald*, June 1, 1997, 6B.

CHAPTER 29: THE INCORRUPTIBLE CRUSADER

309 *Later, when he was HUD's:* Robert A. Jordan, "Report Says Boston Minority Groups Got Shortchanged on Federal Benefits," *Boston Globe*, September 18, 1995, 25.

312 *"The amendment is a safety":* Kirk Semple, "Arrested Development," *Miami New Times*, January 16, 1997, 1.

CHAPTER 30: "HE VIEWED ME AS AN ENEMY"

315 *"In campaigns, your enemies":* Ted B. Kissell, "The Strange Bedfellows of Miami Beach," *Miami Herald*, August 21, 1997, 1B.

317 *While Pearlson:* Martin Wisckol, "Development Key Issue in Miami Beach Races," *Miami Herald*, October 21, 1997, 1B.

318 *The bestselling crime novelist:* Eugene J. Patron, "South Beach Gay Community in the Spotlight After Slaying," *Miami Herald*, Neighbors Miami Beach, July 20, 1997, 24.

318 *Cunanan shot himself:* On July 7, a week before the murder, Cunanan walked into a North Beach pawnshop near his hotel wanting to sell a 22-karat gold ring stolen from his third victim. Vivian Oliva, who worked days at her brother's business, offered him $190. Asked for ID, he produced his real passport and gave his residence as the Normandy Plaza. Oliva did not recognize the name but as required by Florida law, she mailed her paperwork. The form sat on a desk at police headquarters: by the time someone noticed it, Versace was dead.

CHAPTER 31: "THERE'S NO MORALITY HERE"

320 *"I can't believe those fuckers":* Ibid.; see also Owens, *Clubland*, 288.

321 *New York cops:* Edward Helmore, "Murder, Mafia and Madonna's Miami," *Evening Standard* (London), December 17, 1999, 28.

321 *Ingrid's father provided:* Interview with Gerry Kelly, February 6, 2008.

321 *He didn't mind that some:* Interview with Lea Dalman, November 12, 2008.

322 *Paciello hired them at Liquid:* Interview with former marketing and promotion executive, March 22, 2008.

323 *"You know Sammy the Bull":* Interview with former police chief, Miami Beach, November 12, 2007.

323 *If the witness cooperated:* Interview with retired FBI agent, Miami, February 2, 2008.

323 *Before Cutolo was killed:* Interview with FBI agent, July 7, 2008; Interview with Gary James, November 12, 2008.

323 *In a second case, Israeli gangsters:* Alan Feuer, "In Miami, an Imported Mob Scene," *New York Times*, July 3, 2000, 12.

323 *"I don't know how you":* Interview with retired FBI agent, Miami, February 2, 2008.

324 *"This fucking [Kelly]":* U.S. v. Anthony Spero, et al., U 157 L. Ed. 2d 36.

324 *"I'm telling ya."*: Ibid.

325 *"I'm glad I got hold of you"*: Owens, *Clubland*, 187.

326 *"Mr. Paciello really helped"*: "Miami Beach Club Owner Charged with Conspiracy," *Miami Herald*, December 3, 1999, 4B.

326 *George Paciello was arrested*: Paul Brinkley-Rogers, "Club Boss' Brother Indicted," *Miami Herald*, August 12, 2000, 1B; see also *New York Post*, November 2, 2001, 10.

327 *The prosecutor successfully*: Paul Brinkley-Rogers and Jordan Levin, "Owner Accused of Arson to Fund Club, Jailed Impresario Loses Support of Famed Friends," *Miami Herald*, February 12, 2000, 1A.

328 *"Paciello could get out of jail"*: Owen, *Clubland*.

CHAPTER 32: "HE'S GOT SOME VINDICTIVE STREAK"

333 *Peebles told a* Herald *reporter*: Sara Olkon, "Bath Club Dispute Envelops Council," *Miami Herald*, Neighbors Miami Beach, October 24, 1999, 3BC.

333 *When the* Herald *article*: Sara Olkon, "Builder Stealing Election Spotlight," *Miami Herald*, November 7, 1999, 1B.

CHAPTER 33: AN "INCIDENTAL BILLIONAIRE"

335 *Earlier in his tenure*: Nicole White, "Kasdin Moves Forward, Has No Regrets," *Miami Herald*, Neighbors Miami Beach, November 29, 2001, 3MB.

336 *Patricia Vergez, an Argentinean*: Elisa Turner and Jane Woolridge, "Swiss Fair Gives Taste of Art Show to Come," *Miami Herald*, June 17, 2001, 1A.

337 *One member of the Design Review*: Jeff Ostrowski, "Perez Good on Portofino and Yacht Club a Success," *South Florida Business Journal*, vol. 17, no. 3 (September 6, 1996), 1A.

338 *But Perez was playing*: Rick Jervis, "Beach OKs Accord for High-Rises Plan Would Change South Pointe Look," *Miami Herald*, Neighbors Miami Beach, April 19, 1998, 3; Sonji Jacobs, "Kramer Request to Rezone Land Opposed Again," *Miami Herald*, Neighbors Miami Beach, June 21, 2001, 3MB.

339 *Since South Pointe was still*: Jervis, "Beach OKs Accord."

339 *"This piece of land"*: Jacobs, "Kramer Request to Rezone Land Opposed Again."

341 *And the city also released*: "Planning Board OKs Parking Lot in Alaska Parcel," *Miami Herald*, Neighbors Miami Beach, August 26, 2001, 3MB.

341 *The city was so outmatched*: Interview with Frank Del Vecchio, July 31, 2008; see also letter from Frank Del Vecchio to the *Miami Herald*, "Waterfront Developers Beat Planning Board," August 12, 2001, 30MB.

341 *But the agreement fell apart*: "Hot Waterfront Property Fires Hot Debate in Miami Beach," Knight Ridder/Tribune Business News, July 30, 2001.

342 *She also got Kasdin's endorsement*: Sonji Jacobs, "Beach Rivals Await Liebman Endorsement," *Miami Herald*, November 8, 2001, 1B.

343 *She believes that many Hispanic*: Interview with Elaine Bloom, January 8, 2008.

CHAPTER 34: "THE MOST CORRUPT GOVERNMENT"

345 *Amnesia persuaded a court:* Rick Jervis, "Noise Violations Against Pointe Club Dismissed," *Miami Herald*, Neighbors Miami Beach, September 5, 1996, 3.

346 *Early in 1997, the police:* Connie Prater, "Beach Seeks to Close Club Amnesia," *Miami Herald*, March 28, 1997, 2B; see also Nicole White, "Replacement Opium Is Hell," *Miami Herald*, January 27, 2003, 1.

346 *Amnesia reopened five:* John Lantigua, "Not Just a Loud Memory," *Miami Herald*, April 6, 1997, 2B.

348 *Eric Milon, who ran the Living Room:* John Lantigua, "Conflict in Clubland," *Miami New Times*, May 21, 1998.

349 *Roman Jones played to the commissioners':* Richard Brand, "Miami Beach Officials Curb New Open-Air Clubs," *Miami Herald*, June 12, 2003, 3B.

350 *It also agreed to beef up:* Ord. No. 2003–3417, sec. 1, June 11, 2003; Ord. No. 2008–3602, sec. 1, March 12, 2008, amended March 18, 2009.

354 *"When I call up the general contractor":* Brett Sokol, "Black and White and Dread All Over," *Miami New Times*, June 26, 2003, 1.

CHAPTER 35: "IT DIDN'T HAVE TO BE TACKY"

355 *Craig Robins had predicted:* Elaine Walker, "Lincoln Road Changing," *Miami Herald*, August 1, 1998, 1C.

356 *"There were three Payless Shoe":* Suzy Buckley, "I Bring Business to the Beach," *Ocean Drive*, November 2006.

357 *"It certainly seems like South Beach":* Lydia Martin, "Glamour, Glitter of South Beach Restyled by the Corporate Touch," *Miami Herald*, October 31, 2004, 1A.

357 *"In the past, you would have thirty":* Ibid.

358 *"It's not a dilemma unique":* Ibid. Also Interview with Andre Balazs, November 2006.

358 *"Once we have access":* Ibid.

359 *"Most people in Miami":* Jacquelynn Powers, "The Redemption of Chris Paciello," *Ocean Drive*, November 2008, 250.

CHAPTER 36: "YOU DESERVE TO BE PAID FOR YOUR VOTE"

360 *After a few years:* Interview with Neisen Kasdin, October 27, 2007.

362 *"A palm tree" and the quotes that follow:* Daoud, *Sins of South Beach*.

363 *The* Miami Herald *assigned:* Interview with Alex Daoud, September 16, 2008.

CHAPTER 37: "A TWENTY-FIRST-CENTURY CITY"

364 *"That's the new Miami":* Douglas Hanks III, "Plaza on Brickell Condos Stir Up Frenzy," *Miami Herald*, May 27, 2004, 4C.

364 *But long lines of people:* Ibid.

365 *Soon one of the partners:* Matthew Haggman, "Condo Slowdown Trips Up Bulk Buyers," *Miami Herald*, September 17, 2006, A1.

365 *By the end of 2004:* Christina Hoag, "Developers Employ Slick Publicity Stunts," *Miami Herald*, December 26, 2004, 1E.

365 *At Marina Blue:* Douglas Hanks III, "S. Florida Condos Hot in Latin Capitals," *Miami Herald*, April 11, 2004, 1A.

367 *If Perez had won his suit:* "Flyover Construction Would Devastate Area," *Miami Herald*, Neighbors Miami Beach, July 25, 2004, 3MB.

368 *Guests were shuttled from site:* Lydia Martin, "They Are the Perfect Symbol for Disposable Luxury," *Miami Herald*, June 10, 2005, 1A.

369 *It was all demolished:* Ibid.

369 *"When you're going to spend $4":* Ibid.; also interview with Tom Daly, February 8, 2008.

371 *National single-family homes:* Matthew Haggman, "Home Prices Continue Steep Rise," Knight Ridder/Tribune Business News, July 26, 2005.

CHAPTER 38: THE CRASH

374 *In January, the* Miami Herald: Mark Weisbrot, "Prepare for Bubbles," *Miami Herald*, January 7, 2006, A25.

374 *Perez privately told Daly:* Interview with Tom Daly, February 8, 2008.

374 *By April, South Florida's:* Matthew Haggman, "S. Florida Home Sales Fall in April," *Miami Herald*, May 26, 2006, 1C.

374 *But for the most part:* Ibid.

374 *"Things are definitely slowing":* Jacqueline Thorpe, "Housing Boom a Bust?" *National Post's Financial Post & FP Investing* (Canada), May 13, 2006, FP1.

375 *He told reporters that:* Matthew Haggman, "Housing Market in Transition," *Miami Herald*, June 14, 2006, 3C.

375 *The chairman of the Federal Reserve:* Kenneth Harney, "As Real Estate Market Softens, Players Need to Adapt," *Miami Herald*, August 6, 2006, 1.

375 *In October, the Fed's vice chairman:* Kenneth Harney, "Housing Doomsayers Ignore Positives," *Miami Herald*, October 15, 2006, 1H.

375 *The* Miami Herald *devoted:* Alexandra Alter, "Praying for Profits," *Miami Herald*, September 28, 2007, 1C.

375 *Residents charged that:* Michael Vasquez, "Condo Project Probed," *Miami Herald*, August 30, 2007, 1B.

376 *When he won the vote:* Kirk Nielsen, "Tower Power," *Miami SunPost*, vol. 22, no. 20 (May 17, 2007), 1.

376 *With either, the city:* Rick Jervais, "Miami Beach's Future Is in the Hands of Some New Faces," *Miami Herald*, Neighbors Miami Beach, November 16, 1997, 3.

377 *Randy "Prince of Darkness":* Interview with Randy Hilliard, July 7, 2008; see also Tania Valdemoro, "Scandal Shadows Election Strategist," *Miami Herald*, October 29, 2007.

378 *In December 2007, Art:* Interview with Kevin Bruk, August 4, 2008; see also Martha Brannigan, "Buoyant Market a Good Sign for Signature Art Event," *Miami Herald*, December 4, 2007, 1A.

378 *Perez was so confident:* Barry Jackson and Patrick Danner, "Are the Dolphins Worth $1 Billion?" *Miami Herald*, December 18, 2007, 1A. Perez's New York real estate mentor and partner, Steve Ross, finally bought the Dolphins. Ross had sold a third of his company to investors from Dubai at the height of the property market for $2 billion. By 2009, Ross's entire company was valued at only $1 billion.

378 *The Related Group's revenues:* Matthew Miller and Duncan Greenberg, "Housing Honchos," *Forbes*, vol. 182, no. 6 (October 6, 2008), 208.

378 *More than 71,000 residential:* Monica Hatcher, "Property Tax Defaults on the Rise," *Miami Herald*, November 18, 2007, 1A.

380 *"Flamboyance Gets a Face-Lift":* Ruth La Ferla, "Flamboyance Gets a Face-Lift," *New York Times*, November 2, 2008, A1.

380 *But the construction costs:* Douglas Hanks, "Dubai Firm Buys Half of Fontainebleau," *Miami Herald*, April 10, 2008, 1A.

382 *But he said that if:* Matthew Haggman, "Miami Condo King Jorge Perez Battles to Survive Real Estate Slump," *Miami Herald*, March 1, 2009, A1; see also Terry Pristin, "Miami's Monument to Excess," *New York Times*, March 11, 2009, A7; interview with Jorge Perez, May 28, 2009.

Bibliography

Only primary sources are referenced. The archives of the *Miami Herald* and *Miami New Times* proved indispensable, and are cited individually in the Notes. Files and citations from federal and state court cases are also cited in the Notes.

BOOKS

Allman, T. D. *Miami: City of the Future.* New York: Atlantic Monthly Press, 1987.

Antoni, Brian. *South Beach: The Novel.* New York: Black Cat, 2008.

Armbruster, Ann. *The Life and Times of Miami Beach.* New York: Alfred A. Knopf, 1995.

Biondi, Joann. *Miami Beach Memories.* Guilford, CT: Globe Pequot Press, 2007.

Block, Alan A. *Masters of Paradise: Organized Crime and the Internal Revenue Service in the Bahamas.* New Brunswick, NJ, and London: Transaction Publishers, 1991.

Bramson, Seth H. *Miami: The Magic City.* Charleston, SC: Arcadia, 2007.

Bryant, Clifton D. *Deviant Behavior: Readings in the Sociology of Norm Violations.* New York: Hemisphere Publishing Corp., 1990.

Burdick, Thomas, and Charlene Mitchell. *Blue Thunder: How the Mafia Owned and Finally Murdered Cigarette Boat King Donald Aronow.* New York: Simon & Schuster, 1990.

Bustos, Sergio, and Luisa Yanez. *Miami's Criminal Past: Uncovered.* London: History Press, 2007.

Daoud, Alex. *Sins of South Beach: The True Story of Corruption, Violence, and the Making of Miami Beach.* Pegasus, 2006.

Didion, Joan. *Miami.* New York: Simon & Schuster, 1987.

Doner, Michelle Oka, and Mitchell Wolfson, Jr. *Miami Beach—Blueprint of an Eden: Lives Seen Through the Prism of Time and Place.* Cologne, Germany: Feierabend Unique Books, 2006.

Dunlop, Beth, and Roberto Schezen. *Miami Trends and Traditions.* New York: Monacelli Press, 1996.

Fisher, Jane. *Fabulous Hoosier: A Story of American Achievement.* New York: Robert M. McBride & Co., 1947.

Fisher, Jerry M. *The Pacesetter: The Untold Story of Carl G. Fisher.* Fort Bragg, CA: Lost Coast Press, 1998.

Gaines, Steven. *Fool's Paradise: Players, Poseurs, and the Culture of Excess in South Beach.* New York: Crown, 2009.

Grunwald, Michael. *The Swamp: The Everglades, Florida, and the Politics of Paradise.* New York: Simon & Schuster, 2006.

Gugliotta, Guy, and Jeff Leen. *Kings of Cocaine: An Astonishing True Story of Murder, Money, and Corruption.* New York: Harper, 1989.

Harris, Arthur J. *Speed Kills.* New York: Avon Books, 1998.

Lapidus, Morris. *Too Much Is Never Enough.* New York: Rizzoli, 1996.

Lavender, Abraham D. *Miami Beach in 1920: The Making of a Winter Resort.* Charleston, SC: Arcadia, 2002.

Lazo, Mario. *American Policy Failures in Cuba.* New York: Twin Circle Publishing, 1968.

Leddick, David. *In the Spirit of Miami Beach.* New York: Assouline Publishing, 2006.

Levine, Robert M., and Moisés Asís. *Cuban Miami.* New Brunswick, NJ: Rutgers University Press, 2000.

McClintick, David. *Swordfish: A True Story of Ambition, Savagery, and Betrayal.* New York: Pantheon Books, 1993.

McPhee, Michelle. *Mob Over Miami.* New York: Onyx Books, 2002.

Mehling, Harold. *The Most of Everything: The Story of Miami Beach.* New York: Harcourt Brace, 1960.

Mermelstein, Max. *The Man Who Made It Snow: By the American Mastermind Inside the Colombian Cartel.* New York: Simon & Schuster, 1990.

Messick, Hank. *Syndicate in the Sun.* New York: Macmillan, 1968.

———. *Lansky.* New York: G. P. Putnam's Sons, 1971.

Muir, Helen. *Miami USA.* New York: Henry Holt, 1953.

Nash, Eric P., and Randall C. Robinson, Jr. *MiMo: Miami Modern Revealed.* San Francisco: Chronicle Books, 2004.

O'Reilly, Andrea Herrera, ed. *Remembering Cuba.* Austin, TX: University of Texas Press, 2001.

Owen, Frank. *Clubland: The Fabulous Rise and Murderous Fall of Club Culture.* New York: St. Martin's Press, 2003.

Pearce, Donn. *Dying in the Sun.* New York: Charterhouse, 1974.

Peebles, Donahue R. *The Peebles Principles.* Englewood Cliffs, NJ: John Wiley & Sons, 2007.

Pennsylvania Crime Commission. *A Decade of Organized Crime: 1980 Report* (September 1980).

Redford, Polly. *Billion-Dollar Sandbar: A Biography of Miami Beach.* New York: E. P. Dutton, 1970.

Reid, Ed. *The Grim Reapers: The Anatomy of Organized Crime in America.* Chicago: Henry Regnery Co., 1969.

Rieff, David. *Going to Miami: Exiles, Tourists, and Refugees in the New America.* Boston: Little, Brown, 1987.

Riley, Edward. *The Growth of Florida.* Edison, NJ: Chartwell Books, 2007.

Rothchild, John. *Up for Grabs: A Trip Through Time and Space in the Sunshine State.* New York: Penguin Books, 1985.

Standiford, Les. *Last Train to Paradise: Henry Flagler and the Spectacular Rise and Fall of the Railroad That Crossed an Ocean.* New York: Three Rivers Press, 2002.

Steinberg, Theodore. *Acts of God: The Unnatural History of Natural Disaster in America*. New York: Oxford University Press, 2000.

Stofik, M. Barron. *Saving South Beach*. Gainesville, FL: University of Florida Press, 2005.

Wisser, Bill. *South Beach: America's Riviera, Miami Beach, Florida*. New York: Arcade Publishing, 1995.

Zimmerman, Stan. *A History of Smuggling in Florida: Rumrunner and Cocaine Cowboys*. Charleston, SC: History Press, 2006.

PERIODICALS

Bush, Gregory W. "Playground of the USA: Miami and the Promotion of Spectacle." *Pacific Historical Review*, vol. 68, no. 2 (May 1999).

Cook, James, with Jane Carmichael. "Casino Gambling: Changing Character or Changing Fronts?" *Forbes*, October 27, 1980.

Cumming, Jr., J. Bruce. "A Brief Florida Real Estate History." West Coast Chapter of the Appraisal Institute, Region X, September 6, 2006.

Forrest, David W. "South Beach: 'Paradise' and Reality." *Gay and Lesbian Review Worldwide*, vol. 9, no. 3, May 1, 2002.

Harris, Art. "The Drug Game: Undercover in Miami; Where Business Is Vicious and Booming." *Washington Post*, March 11, 1984.

Kelly, James. "Trouble in Paradise." *Time*, November 23, 1981.

Roberts, Maurice A. "The U.S. and Refugees: The Refugee Act of 1980." *Issue: A Journal of Opinion*, vol. 12, no. 1/2, African Refugees and Human Rights (Spring–Summer 1982).

Samuels, David. "Liquid Smoke." *Men's Vogue,* January 2007.

Acknowledgments

I met Gene Miller, a two-time Pulitzer-winning journalist for the *Miami Herald*, a few months before he died of cancer in June 2005. Trisha and I had moved to Miami Beach from New York a year earlier. Miller regaled us with stories that explained why Miami had the reputation as a sunny place for shady characters. His tales about prominent businessmen who had been coke dealers, politicians who made little effort to hide their greed and corruption, the constant battle between developers and preservationists, and the morphing of Miami Beach from God's Waiting Room for the elderly to an upscale party resort in less than a generation, all planted the seeds for this book.

Trisha and I conducted more than 200 interviews and reviewed some 20,000 pages of documents, ranging from civil lawsuits to criminal case transcripts to arcane zoning hearings before city commissions. Many people assisted us in the preparation of this book, and most are cited in the Notes. But some went out of their way to answer repeated inquiries and to provide substantial, ultimately indispensable assistance. Several key sources, who still work in local government, the police, or are business executives, prefer anonymity, and I have honored those requests.

I owe special thanks to Saul Gross, Craig Robins, Jorge Perez, Irene Marie, Tara Solomon, Tom Daly, Nancy Liebman, Mark Soyka, Shareef Malnik, Frank and Marian Del Vecchio, Sam Robin, Steven Giles, Romero Britto, Manny Hernandez, Michael Aller, and Carlos Betancourt, who were unusually generous with their time. Also, special thanks to Kent Harrison Robbins, Randy Hilliard, Neisen Kasdin, Alex Daoud, and the late A. C. Weinstein: they helped me understand the byzantine and often brutal world of Miami Beach politics. Jane Dee, Dona Zemo, and David Wallach, with their superb recall, were instrumental in re-creating the feeling for the post-Mariel boatlift Beach and setting the scene for its transformation.

I am indebted to Louis Canales, Gary James, Gerry Kelly, and Michael Capponi for their insiders' perspectives of Miami Beach's nightlife. Local author Brian Antoni generously shared his invaluable Rolodex.

Bobby Weinstein, Jose Bermudez, and Joey Martino are pseudonyms for men who allowed me unrestricted and private access to their pasts. Their stories are demonstrative of hundreds of others who emerged from the cocaine wars to become successful and legitimate businessmen in today's Miami Beach.

Reporters who assisted me include Megan O'Matz of the *South Florida Sun-Sentinel*; Shelly Acoca of the *Miami Herald*, and Brendan Howley. Television host Louis Aguirre took repeated breaks from his hectic schedule to provide an insider's view as a reporter of Miami over twenty years. Lesley Abravanel, whose "Scene in the Tropics" *Herald* column covers the social life of Miami Beach, helped open doors that would have otherwise stayed closed.

Others who assisted on a variety of issues include Linda Lee, Merle and Danny Weiss, Glenn Albin, Eric Newill, Fernando Canale, Billy Belack, Kevin Tomlinson, George Coronado, Oren Nizri, Scott Hauser, Ryan York, Maxwell Blandford, Arnold Matteson, Gary Hennes, Dan Spring, Jean Marc De Silva, Christopher Petersen, Bill Cooke, Roger and Leslie Baumann, and Alan Zinkin. Stephanie Oka Freed and Justo Sanchez were generous in providing their own solid research and archives. Arianne Perez, the Operations Clerk for the Records Division of the U.S. District Court for Southern Florida, was always helpful despite my requests, which sometimes fell late on Friday afternoon. Miami Beach Police Chief Carlos Noriega and Division Commander Hernan Cardeno were generous with their time and knowledge, as was former chief Don DeLucca. David Voigt at Lexis-Nexis kindly provided me with access to the services' remarkable legal database at a manageable cost. My friend David Alexander graciously became a valuable extra proofreader.

Dawn Hugh, Archives Manager at the Historical Museum of Southern Florida, was super in guiding me to key documents about the history of the Beach, and the Museum's Susan Garcia went out of her way to help.

This project would never have gotten off the ground if I had not been fortunate in finding a publisher who believed in it. Sam Pinkus, my great agent, was smart enough to approach Simon & Schuster. Publisher David Rosenthal is a risk-taker who gave me a book contract without any preconceptions about the story or what I'd find. He gave me room to investigate and let the book develop during the reporting. Also, I hit the lottery with Ruth Fecych, my editor, who shaped my reporting into a readable story. Her unwavering focus on the book's major themes was indispensable. Ann Adelman's copyediting was conscientious and comprehensive. Assistant Editor Michelle Rorke answered endless queries efficiently and with good humor.

Senior Production Editor Mara Lurie, with her enthusiasm for the subject and her good eye for detail, made a tight deadline seem effortless.

Anyone who knows me realizes how lucky I am to have Trisha as my wife and partner. She does every interview with me, some on her own, and sifts through the boxes of often tedious documents and frayed clippings. She is my indomitable collaborator, listening to incessant complaints and self-doubt, and keeping me focused and enthusiastic through the long reporting. She has a knack for knowing what is important and helps prevent me from taking long detours into interesting but unrelated topics. Until she one day allows me to put her name on the front of a book, this thank you is my only way of saying that *Miami Babylon* is as much hers as it is mine.

Index

446

INDEX